Eloquence Is Power

Eloquence Is Power
Oratory & Performance in Early America

SANDRA M. GUSTAFSON

Published for the Omohundro Institute of Early American

History and Culture, Williamsburg, Virginia, by the University

of North Carolina Press, Chapel Hill and London

The Omohundro Institute of Early American History
and Culture is sponsored jointly by the College of William
and Mary and the Colonial Williamsburg Foundation. On
November 15, 1996, the Institute adopted the present name
in honor of a bequest from Malvern H. Omohundro, Jr.

Set in Minion and Bickham types by
Tseng Information Systems, Inc.
Manufactured in the United States of America
Library of Congress Cataloging-in-Publication Data
Gustafson, Sandra M.
Eloquence Is Power : performance and oratory in early
America / Sandra M. Gustafson.
    p.   cm.
Based on the author's thesis (Ph.D.—University of
California, Berkeley).
Includes index.
ISBN 0-8078-2575-1 (cloth : alk. paper)—
ISBN 0-8078-4888-3 (pbk. : alk. paper)
1. Oratory—United States—History—17th century.
2. Oratory—United States—History—18th century.
3. Speeches, addresses, etc., American—History and
criticism.   I. Title.
PN4055.U5 G87   2000
808.5'1'097309032—dc21   99-086591

04 03 02 01 00   5 4 3 2 1

For

Tobias Stephen Ginsburg

(b. April 29, 1999)

and

in memory of

Stephen James Gustafson

(1975–1994)

ACKNOWLEDGMENTS

This book began as a dissertation written under the direction of the late Jenny Franchot, whose intellectual vibrancy, acumen, and enthusiasm remain among my most important influences. Also at Berkeley, Mitchell Breitwieser and Lawrence Levine provided crucial support and guidance. At the University of Notre Dame, Christopher Fox has been an unflagging mentor and friend who as department chair granted the leaves that made it possible for me to produce the book that I wished to write. My colleagues Barbara Green, Julia Douthwaite, and Glenn Hendler have been good friends, valuable interlocutors, and incisive critics.

The scholars at the Omohundro Institute of Early American History and Culture provided a road map to the scholarship of early America during my two years there. Fredrika J. Teute has been a rigorous and creative editor. M. Kathryn Burdette has polished my prose and sought the perfect balance between substance and brevity in the notes. Sally Mason's warmth and good cheer have helped me through some difficult times and buoyed me in the good ones.

A number of people have inspired me with their examples and encouraged me by their interest, among them Jay Fliegelman, David D. Hall, Janice Knight, David S. Shields, and Frank Shuffelton. Adam Potkay's work intersected with mine in a particularly felicitous way, while Alfred Young shared my enthusiasm for Deborah Sampson Gannett. Writing groups and workshops at the Institute, Berkeley, Notre Dame, and in Chicago have given me valuable feedback on individual chapters. Two medievalist friends, Laura Severt King and Willis Johnson, have helped me keep my sense of humor and equilibrium.

A number of sources have contributed in a monetary way to the production of this book. My Institute postdoctoral fellowship was partially funded by the NEH. Earlier, I had fellowship support from UC–Berkeley, the Woodrow Wilson Foundation, and Phi Beta Kappa. I am grateful to all of these institutions for their financial support and for the confidence they continue to show in humanities scholarship.

Sections of Chapter 1 are adapted from "Jonathan Edwards and the Reconstruction of 'Feminine' Speech," *American Literary History,* VI (1994), 185–212. I thank Oxford University Press for permission to reprint this article in modified form.

Throughout the making of this book, John L. and Ellen Gustafson have been unfailingly supportive. Their love and confidence are invaluable. Allene Gustafson has nurtured my historical sense with her experience of nearly a century and nourished me with her affection. John A. Gustafson's wit and fine scholarship have set me a worthy example. Eric Ginsburg has taught me that the "two cultures" of science and the humanities can indeed be wed, with the help of some time spent in the wilderness.

Finally, this book is dedicated to the memory of my brother Stephen Gustafson, who died just as the book began to emerge from the dissertation, and to his nephew and namesake Tobias Stephen Ginsburg, who was born as it was nearing completion. The unexpected loss of Steve and the joy of Tobias's arrival mark every page for me.

CONTENTS

ILLUSTRATIONS

ABBREVIATIONS

AHR   *American Historical Review*
JAH   *Journal of American History*
NEQ   *New England Quarterly*
PMHB   *Pennsylvania Magazine of History and Biography*
WMQ   *William and Mary Quarterly*

INTRODUCTION

In the flourishing periods of Athens and Rome,
eloquence was POWER.
—John Quincy Adams

The Golden Age of American Oratory had already begun when John Quincy Adams described rhetorical skill as a form of power in his 1805 inaugural address as the first Boylston Chair of Rhetoric and Oratory at Harvard University. Adams observed the preeminent importance that training in oratory had for the classical civilizations of Greece and Rome and described its revived importance in the new republic, where eloquence might once again bestow power:

> Under governments purely republican, where every citizen has a deep interest in the affairs of the nation, and, in some form of public assembly or other, has the means and opportunity of delivering his opinions, and of communicating his sentiments by speech; where government itself has no arms but those of persuasion; where prejudice has not acquired an uncontroled ascendency, and faction is yet confined within the barriers of peace; the voice of eloquence will not be heard in vain.[1]

The training that Adams offered his students would set American education apart from European societies where "even when they studied RHETORIC, as a theory, they neglected ORATORY, as an art." Political eloquence had not been properly valued since the death of Cicero, Adams lamented. Even after "the midnight of the monkish ages" gave way to "the revival of letters in modern Europe," forensic and deliberative eloquence had an influence limited by the dominance of a dead language and the burden of textual precedent. Awakening from her long sleep, the muse of eloquence "found her child, Persuasion, manacled and pinioned by the letter of the law" and "beheld an image of herself, stammering in barbarous Latin, and staggering under the lumber of a thousand volumes." Only the pulpit provided "an unbounded and inexhaustible field for eloquence." With the Revo-

---

1. John Quincy Adams, *Lectures on Rhetoric and Oratory, Delivered to the Classes of Senior and Junior Sophisters in Harvard University,* I (Cambridge, Mass., 1810), 19, 30–31. Adams was selected to fill the chair at Harvard that a Boston merchant had funded in 1771 but that had been left vacant during the turbulent interim (iii–iv). Edward G. Parker traces the origins of American art and power to Revolutionary oratory in *The Golden Age of American Oratory* (Boston, 1857), 1–2.

lution, America freed itself from restrictive textual forms, and republican government fostered the reinvigoration of the lost art of political eloquence.[2]

Long before Adams spoke, oratory had emerged as the first major form of verbal art in British North America because, as he said, "eloquence was POWER." The
multiple traditions of sacred, diplomatic, and political speech that flourished in
England's colonies derived much of their significance and complexity from the
collision of European, native American, and African cultures that defined major
aspects of the colonial experience. European colonists in North America drew on
the traditions of classical and Christian rhetoric newly invigorated by the rise of
humanism and the Protestant revitalization of the colloquial sermon, accommo-
dating those traditions to their changed circumstances. The native peoples who
inhabited the continent had highly elaborated traditions of spoken eloquence
that played central roles in religious life, government, and diplomacy, and they
adapted these traditions to the new world of European colonialism. Africans in
North America, many of them slaves, came from societies where oratory served
functions of comparable significance. Forced into the heterogeneous communities
that characterized North American slavery, they adapted and combined linguistic
forms to create a powerful new set of oral genres. In the American crucible of cultures, these oratorical traditions collided, merged, and polarized to create vibrant
traditions of verbal art.[3]

Hendrick Aupaumut's career as a diplomat for the Washington administration in the 1790s represents one form of creative adaptation among oratorical traditions. A Revolutionary war veteran, Christian Indian, dedicated leader of his
Mahican community, and preserver of Mahican traditions, Aupaumut envisioned
his role as ambassador to the northwest Indian nations as an extension of ancient
Mahican traditions of diplomacy. Negotiating on behalf of the "15 sachems of the
United States," Aupaumut employed both written text and the oral forms of the
treaty council with authority.[4] An even more complex melding of traditions occurred in the spiritual career of African American missionary John Marrant. Converted by British evangelist George Whitefield about 1770, young Marrant went
"over the fence" into the wilderness of South Carolina to escape a corrupt society.
Taken captive in a Cherokee village, Marrant first displayed the Bible as a sacred
icon, drawing the attention of a Cherokee "princess." The written Word estab-

2. Adams, *Lectures on Rhetoric and Oratory,* I, 20, 21, 24, 26.

3. On African American oral genres, see for example the discussion of signifying in Henry
Louis Gates, Jr., *The Signifying Monkey: A Theory of Afro-American Literary Criticism* (New York,
1988), chaps. 1, 2; Roger D. Abrahams, *Singing the Master: The Emergence of African American
Culture in the Plantation South* (New York, 1992).

4. Hendrick Aupaumut, *A Narrative of an Embassy to the Western Indians . . . ,* in Historical
Society of Pennsylvania, *Memoirs,* II (Philadelphia, 1827), 61–131, esp. 93.

lished his power over the princess, but a Pentecostal moment of extemporaneous prayer by Marrant in fluent Cherokee converted the Cherokee "king," who saved Marrant's life and made him a powerful figure in the village.[5]

As the careers of Aupaumut and Marrant suggest, oratory proved so vital to the dynamic world of the colonies and early republic because it permitted the staging of a variety of social and cultural relations. Whether negotiating for land, political authority, or spiritual leadership, speakers enacted their competing claims to authenticity and power through the symbolic use of speech and text. From Puritan patriarchs John Winthrop and John Eliot to Great Awakening adversaries Charles Chauncy and Gilbert Tennent, to Revolutionary leaders James Otis and George Washington, Euro-Americans made the analogy between verbal forms and social structures into a primary mode of understanding cultural relationships. Unprecedented contacts between peoples from the three continents of Africa, Europe, and North America coincided with the invention of the printing press to make verbal forms into primary markers of cultural difference, as colonization and slavery brought together increasingly text-oriented Europeans with Africans and native Americans largely unfamiliar with alphabetic literacy. Hierarchies of literacy and textual knowledge already structured gender and status relations among Europeans, for whom the possession of classical and vernacular literacies demarcated social roles.[6]

Yet the meanings of literacy technologies were ambiguous and conflicted. Although descendants of Europeans often viewed the lack of textual knowledge as a cultural inadequacy, that condescension was matched by European anxieties about the written word's vulnerability to inauthenticity and manipulation. Tensions have circulated around the role of writing in speech performance at least since textual technologies became available to ancient Greek orators. Improvisation and extempore speech might be interpreted as signs of dangerous volatility,

5. *A Narrative of the Lord's Wonderful Dealings with John Marrant, a Black . . .* , in Adam Potkay and Sandra Burr, eds., *Black Atlantic Writers of the Eighteenth Century* (New York, 1995), 75–105, esp. 81.

6. There is an extensive literature on voice and text in the colonial and early republican periods. The relevant works not cited elsewhere in this introduction include Sacvan Bercovitch, *The American Jeremiad* (Madison, Wis., 1978); Mitchell Robert Breitwieser, *Cotton Mather and Benjamin Franklin: The Price of Representative Personality* (Cambridge, 1984); Robert A. Ferguson, *Law and Letters in American Culture* (Cambridge, Mass., 1984); Ferguson, "The American Enlightenment, 1750–1820," in Sacvan Bercovitch, ed., *The Cambridge History of American Literature*, I, *1590–1820* (Cambridge, 1994), 345–537; David Simpson, *The Politics of American English, 1776–1850* (New York, 1986); Cathy N. Davidson, *Revolution and the Word: The Rise of the Novel in America* (New York, 1986); Amy Schrager Lang, *Prophetic Woman: Anne Hutchinson and the Problem of Dissent in the Literature of New England* (Berkeley, Calif., 1987); Donald Weber, *Rhetoric and History in Revolutionary New England* (Oxford, 1988); Kenneth Cmiel, *Democratic Eloquence: The Fight over Popular Speech in Nineteenth-Century America* (New York, 1990).

but they were as often taken to signify authentic inspiration and true power. A four-term set of oppositions structures Western ideas and images of language: the dead letter mirrors and disrupts stable text while demonic speech mocks the living voice. These four terms can be construed as two opposed pairs. Text that is privileged for its permanence and stability is set against the ruptures effected by demonic speech. When the powers of the living voice are celebrated, they are imagined triumphing over the dead letter. In performance, this doubled dynamic of language both emerges as a set of mutually constituting symbolic categories and produces speech and text as performatives that signify through the very choice of medium.[7]

Viewing speech and text as symbolic and performative forms of language rather than as discrete and hierarchical entities opens understanding of the ways that the bodies of language figure constructions of the social body in oratorical performance. The nature of verbal symbolism shifted subtly over the colonial period. For the first century of colonization, British Americans imagined the relationship between speech and text as a relatively static and absolute distinction that could be used to figure other supposedly absolute distinctions, particularly gender and status differences and the opposition between "primitive" oral cultures and "civilized" literate societies. Social arbiters advanced the written word as protection against the attractions of the textless "savage" or "enthusiast." Beginning with the Salem witchcraft crisis and the shifts in imperial relations in the 1690s, and achieving full theorization in the revivals of the 1740s, a complex system of meaning emerged that understood the oral and textual bodies of language, not as fixed categories, but as figures for competing constructions of the social body.

In what I call the performance semiotic of speech and text, claims to authenticity and relations of power were given form and meaning through the reliance

---

7. In *The Ascetic Imperative in Culture and Criticism* (Chicago, 1987), 3–18, Geoffrey Galt Harpham explores the symbolic meanings with which Western culture invests text and speech, tracing a pervasive "ascetic linguistics" in the Christian society of the late Roman Empire. See also Appendix, below. My use of the term *performative* is an adaptation of J. L. Austin's concept of the performative utterance, developed in *How to Do Things with Words*, ed. J. O. Urmson and Marina Sbisà, 2d ed. (Cambridge, Mass., 1975). Andrew Parker and Eve Kosofsky Sedgwick discuss the relationship between performance and Austin's performativity in "Performativity and Performance," introduction to Parker and Sedgwick, eds., *Performativity and Performance* (New York, 1995), 1–18.

Modern works that explore colonial American literature as a performance-based aesthetic domain that are not mentioned elsewhere in this introduction include Jeffrey H. Richards, *Theater Enough: American Culture and the Metaphor of the World Stage, 1607–1789* (Durham, N.C., 1991); Carla Mulford, introduction to Mulford, ed., *Only for the Eye of a Friend: The Poems of Annis Boudinot Stockton* (Charlottesville, Va., 1995); Joseph Roach, *Cities of the Dead: Circum-Atlantic Performance* (New York, 1996); David S. Shields, *Civil Tongues and Polite Letters in British America* (Chapel Hill, N.C., 1997).

on or freedom from text in oral performance. Preachers and political orators signified unmediated access to truth in extemporaneous speeches, or they dramatized the stability of their spiritual or political intent by reading from a manuscript or referring to foundational documents. Verbal form manifested social tensions produced by cultural difference. The orator made these tensions visible as he or she performed social conflict through the symbolism of the written and spoken words. The aspects of identity suggested, however misleadingly, by the speaker's physical presence shaped these performances of authority. Early American orators understood the contextual nature and strategic uses of speech and writing as signs relating the individual body to the social body. Speaking from a range of cultural positions, they adapted that system of symbols to their own ends.

As a symbolic and performative approach to verbal forms, the performance semiotic provides an important corrective to the developmental trajectory from orality to literacy that still often dominates histories of language. The most familiar narrative purporting to explain the relationship between verbal form and social order is the story of the spread of writing and print. One narrative links print, Protestantism, and democratic nationalism to shape one of America's most treasured myths about itself, a myth with both popular and scholarly variants.[8] Not all histories of alphabetic literacy embrace this narrative or understand all historical change to be bound up with the spread of textual technologies. But where the body of scholarship on the history of writing and the book offers stimulating insights into the complex world of textual forms, these insights often occur at the expense of attention to the persistence, adaptation, and creativity of oral genres.[9] Scholars frequently assume a static and homogenous oral world as a canvas upon

---

8. "The West treasures few moments in its history the way it treasures the story of the democratization of print," Michael Warner observes in *The Letters of the Republic: Publication and the Public Sphere in Eighteenth-Century America* (Cambridge, Mass., 1990), 1. Warner goes on to analyze the implications of that historical moment and to critique technological determinism in the study of print culture in chap. 1.

With its emphasis on print culture as a central factor in the emergence of nation-states, Benedict Anderson's *Imagined Communities: Reflections on the Origin and Spread of Nationalism*, 2d ed. rev. (London, 1991) offers a particularly subtle variation on the developmental narrative that imagines the spread of print as the foundation of national identities.

9. Robert St. George notes, "What remains surprising in much historical work is that, in exploring the meaning of transitions from 'oral culture' to 'written culture,' the meaning and function of speech either has been taken for granted as an historical constant or else has been overlooked." He calls for the study of oral and literate forms to be approached as "an ethnographic totality"; see "'Heated' Speech and Literacy in Seventeenth-Century New England," in *Seventeenth-Century New England: A Conference Held by the Colonial Society of Massachusetts, June 18 and 19, 1982* (Boston, 1984), 276. Brian V. Street provides an incisive critique of the hierarchical coding of "oral" and "literate" societies in *Literacy in Theory and Practice* (Cambridge, 1984), chaps. 1, 2.

which the transformative effects of the written and printed word can be painted. Those who treat text as an engine of social transformation and oral forms as fixed, "primitive" modes of expression may attach different values to textually driven change, either celebrating the developments attributed to writing and print or deploring them. But they all share a teleological understanding of language in which textual forms displace oral ones. Even the most sophisticated accounts of print culture align modernity with the spread of print and its alleged displacement of oral genres. Such accounts ignore the lively tradition of eloquence in the early republican and antebellum eras that John Quincy Adams accurately predicted. Recognizing the flexible boundaries and considerable overlap between oral and textual forms, as well as the persistence of oral genres, we must attend to the symbolic and performative meanings attached to speech and writing.[10]

Eloquence Is Power shares with a handful of critical works the emphasis on speech as a practice and signifier of an emerging national identity while expanding the focus from Euro-America to include the heterogeneous and mutually influential traditions of oratory within the colonies and the early republic.[11] The

10. These works manifest a range of attitudes toward the transition from orality to literacy while sharing a basic narrative pattern: Marshall McLuhan, *The Gutenberg Galaxy: The Making of Typographic Man* (Toronto, 1962); Jack Goody and Ian Watt, "The Consequences of Literacy," in Goody, ed., *Literacy in Traditional Societies* (Cambridge, 1968), 27–84; Elizabeth L. Eisenstein, *The Printing Press as an Agent of Change: Communications and Cultural Transformations in Early-Modern Europe*, 2 vols. (Cambridge, 1979); Walter J. Ong, *The Presence of the Word: Some Prolegomena for Cultural and Religious History* (1967; Minneapolis, 1981); Ong, *Orality and Literacy: The Technologizing of the Word* (London, 1982); Jack Goody, *The Logic of Writing and the Organization of Society* (Cambridge, 1986); Goody, *The Interface between the Written and the Oral* (Cambridge, 1987).

For an analysis of oral and text-based performance from the perspective of a student of oral cultures, see Ruth Finnegan, *Oral Poetry: Its Nature, Significance, and Social Context*, rev. ed. (Bloomington, Ind., 1992), 254–260. Mikhail Bakhtin produced the most influential literary critical work on the relationship between oral and literary forms to date; see esp. "Discourse in the Novel," in Michael Holquist, ed., *The Dialogic Imagination: Four Essays*, trans. Caryl Emerson and Michael Holquist (Austin, Tex., 1981), 259–422; Bakhtin, "The Problem of Speech Genres," in Caryl Emerson and Michael Emerson, eds., *Speech Genres and Other Late Essays*, trans. Vern W. McGee (Austin, Tex., 1986), 60–102. Garrett Stewart's *Reading Voices: Literature and the Phonotext* (Berkeley, Calif., 1990) offers an insightful analysis of the silent oral performance of text, or phonemic reading, as it affects literary works. In *Writing in the New Nation: Prose, Print, and Politics in the Early United States* (New Haven, Conn., 1991), Larzer Ziff argues that the American Revolution coincided with a cultural shift from oral to printed forms of power and self-making (x–xi). His analysis replicates the distinctions between oral and literate cultures drawn by Ong in *Orality and Literacy.* Warner describes a subtler, less technologically determined variant of the shift from oral to print culture in *Letters of the Republic.* Both works take print as their telos, ignore the rise of oratory as an important genre, and neglect the complex semiotics attached to verbal form.

11. In *Voicing America: Language, Literary Form, and the Origins of the United States* (Chi-

boundaries of the culture of performance expand dramatically when we consider African American and native American performance traditions alongside those of Euro-Americans and when we pay attention to the performative force of women's public speech. Viewed in relation to native American diplomatic eloquence, for instance, the oratorical public culture of the Revolution can be seen as a form of "playing Indian," as well as playing Greek or Roman.[12] The forms of state power that white men designed in the early republic were shaped in crucial ways by their proximity and resistance to the speech of white women, native Americans, and African Americans. The performance semiotic of speech and text provides a tool for comprehending the rich and contested traditions of eighteenth-century oratory within a shared framework of analysis.

Novel styles of oral performance propelled transformations in early American literature, and American literature reveals a peculiarly self-conscious relationship to oral forms. American writers have long deployed the symbolism of verbal medium, and from the works of Benjamin Franklin and Charles Brockden Brown to the Transcendentalist writings of Ralph Waldo Emerson and Margaret Fuller, to the vernacular idioms of Mark Twain and William Faulkner, to the oratorical poetry of Walt Whitman and Allen Ginsberg, to the ethnic American fiction of Ralph Ellison and Leslie Marmon Silko[American literature takes as a central subject the social meanings of linguistic form.] Writing about the symbolism of

---

cago, 1996), Christopher Looby notes the central role that images of a nation "spoken into being" play in the literature of the early republic and calls attention to the fact that *"voice* embodied a certain legitimating charisma that print could not" (4, 5). Whereas Looby finds evidence of the persistence of voice in printed texts, Jay Fliegelman describes the culturally central work of speech performance in the Revolutionary era, when "oratory at its most naked and transcendent became a kind of manifested spirit, an instrument and embodiment of a new Anglo-American republican authority" *(Declaring Independence: Jefferson, Natural Language, and the Culture of Performance* [Stanford, Calif., 1993], 20, 35, 54).

Nancy Ruttenberg traces the emergence of the imagery and practice of voice much earlier than either Looby or Fliegelman, to the Salem witchcraft controversy and the Great Awakening. Ruttenberg insists upon the performative origins of democratic speech, locating it in the spontaneous and untheorized antiauthoritarian utterances of possessed girls and evangelical converts; see *Democratic Personality: Popular Voice and the Trials of American Authorship* (Stanford, Calif., 1998).

12. Philip J. Deloria discusses the significance of Indian performance in the construction of white national identities in *Playing Indian* (New Haven, Conn., 1998). He treats the Revolutionary period, including the role of pseudo-Indian speeches, in chap. 1.

13. Alessandro Portelli offers a magisterial discussion of the symbolism of verbal form in the American literary tradition in *The Text and the Voice: Writing, Speaking, and Democracy in American Literature* (New York, 1994). A. La Vonne Brown Ruoff and Jerry W. Ward, Jr., eds., *Redefining American Literary History* (New York, 1990), contains a number of insightful essays on the interface of oral and literate traditions. Paul Lauter, "The Literatures of America: A Comparative Discipline," 9–34, is particularly helpful. Also important for understanding the

the semiotics of speech and text in American literature, Italian critic Alessandro Portelli aptly notes, "The perception and recollection of origins in discovery and revolution, the anxieties of the democratic experiment, the multiple stratifications of race, ethnicity, gender, and class — all these elements are shaped in unstable representations, founded in concepts of authenticity and authority identified from time to time either with the textualized documents of writing or with the elusive presence of the voice."[14] The "unstable representations" that Portelli finds in American literature first crystallized as performance choices for early American orators, and American writers adapted the innovative oral performances to textual forms. In the twentieth century, modern and postmodern improvisational artists owed their understanding of verbal forms to the early orators who developed the performative symbolism of speech and text.[15]

Eighteenth-century orators used the performance semiotic to stage forms of power ranging from spiritual insight and its attendant social privileges to intercultural conflicts and allegiances, to imperial and national order. These diverse settings produced a variety of power relations. My examination of power incorporates contemporary meanings of the word as it was used in the English-speaking world of the eighteenth century, when power was understood as the ability to control others. Bernard Bailyn notes that, during this era, "Power . . . meant the dominion of some men over others, the human control of human life: ultimately

---

importance of oral and literate forms in a multicultural context are *Signifying Monkey,* where Gates analyzes figures of speech and text in African American literature; David Murray, *Forked Tongues: Speech, Writing, and Representation in North American Indian Texts* (Bloomington, Ind., 1991).

14. Portelli, *Text and the Voice,* xiii–xiv. Portelli's subsequent interpretation is similar to my own sense of a mobile system of signification: "Orality and writing are forever exchanging roles, functions, and meanings in a mutual relationship of seeking and desire rather than exclusion and polarization. Both orality and writing are capable of standing either for absence or for presence, for society and for the individual, for certainty and for doubt, for the spirit and for the body, for life and for death, according to which facet these pairs happen to present and to the connecting matter that holds them together" (xiv). Portelli observes the precocious postmodernity that this attention to the symbolism of medium lends to American literature (28).

15. In *The Culture of Spontaneity: Improvisation and the Arts in Postwar America* (Chicago, 1998), Daniel Belgrad analyzes twentieth-century American improvisational art as it manifests the aesthetic of spontaneity that elevates "honesty," "awareness," and "authenticity" over technical mastery, thus making "cultural authority more accessible to aspirants from immigrant, working-class, and minority backgrounds" (16). Although Belgrad gestures toward Romantic precursors, I would trace a lineage to the improvisational styles of orators in the eighteenth century, when performance choices developed social significance akin to those that Belgrad identifies in the twentieth-century arts.

James E. B. Breslin discusses the importance of voice, breath, and oral performance for the poetry of the mid-twentieth century in *From Modern to Contemporary: American Poetry, 1945–1965* (Chicago, 1984), chap. 2.

force, compulsion." Power for many colonial Americans also had a Pauline face, as divine agency transmuted the preacher's physical weakness or social insignificance into spiritual authority. Less familiar to colonial theorists, but clearly visible in the dynamics between orator and audience, is the modern sense of power conceived of as strategic actions undertaken within a web of unequal and unstable social relations. Michel Foucault articulates this meaning of power, identifying it as "the name that one attributes to a complex strategical situation in a particular society" where power "is exercised from innumerable points, in the interplay of nonegalitarian and mobile relations." Some of the performances of power that I explore reflect the harsher, less subtle sense of domination, whereas others embody the more malleable power relations that today are called hegemonic.[16]

Power is related to, and often flows from, claims to authenticity. Spiritual authenticity derives from the speaker's relationship to divine authority as it is or is not mediated by learning and status. Cultural authenticity demands clear origins of its practitioners; they must be originals in the sense that they originate in the community that they claim to represent. The ethic of transparency in the late eighteenth century mandated the speaker's emotional authenticity and created a spectacle of sincerity. As forms of emotional authenticity, sincerity and sensibility helped to redefine power from domination to consent. The orator's display of emotion staged a wide range of effects that focused on the negotiation of consensual social relations.[17]

Americans strategized power and authenticity in ways that are sometimes surprising. Today, voice is most often figured as a democratic medium, and speech is understood as a mode of expression available to all regardless of educational level. Immediacy and accessibility are not intrinsic to the spoken word, however, but dependent on specific institutional forms and modes of address. Elite classical rhetoric was designed to reinforce social hierarchies, and despite the populist appeal of Revolutionary orators James Otis and Patrick Henry, democratic idioms gained legitimacy only slowly in the new republic. In a world where the press was expanding and literacy rates for Euro-Americans were high, printed text retained little of the written word's historical association with elite power, and the less

16. Bernard Bailyn, *The Ideological Origins of the American Revolution* (Cambridge, Mass., 1967), 56; Michel Foucault, *The History of Sexuality*, I, *An Introduction* (New York, 1980), 93–94.

17. G. J. Barker-Benfield offers the most comprehensive discussion of English sensibility in *The Culture of Sensibility: Sex and Society in Eighteenth-Century Britain* (Chicago, 1992). Fliegelman analyzes the relationship between sensibility, oratory, and consensual authority in *Declaring Independence*, 191. In *Sincerity and Authenticity* (Cambridge, Mass., 1972), 6–12, chap. 4, Lionel Trilling distinguishes between the pre-Romantic sincerity of public transparency and the post-Romantic authenticity of the unsocialized or unconscious mind. Barker-Benfield's work suggests that pre-Romantic sincerity and sensibility shaped the later forms of authenticity, and I assume that continuity in my analysis.

privileged often found that textual appeals allowed them the social space to challenge authority. The public speech of women was governed with particular rigor in the eighteenth century, and writing provided white women with their most accessible avenue to public "voice." For native Americans and African Americans, the relation to verbal media was more complicated. Textual practices were both strategically valuable in dealing with colonists and sources of substantial psychic and cultural strain. Colonists celebrated the supposedly textless native American or African speaker as a noble savage or reviled him as an agent of Satan. Black and Indian orators such as Iroquois leader Canassatego and evangelical missionaries Samson Occom and John Marrant soon learned to rearticulate these signs of difference. They presented a "savage" speaker whose oral heritage endowed him or her with a greater authenticity than textbound white orators. At the same time, they adapted to textual technologies and sometimes found writing the more strategically appropriate medium. By the mid-eighteenth century, native Americans and African Americans manipulated verbal symbols as effectively as the colonists. The performance semiotic was both flexible and widely understood in the colonies and the early republic.[18]

The dynamic cultural landscapes of early America contained multiple traditions of oratory, for which the symbolism of verbal and physical form carry fundamental meaning. Conflict in seventeenth-century British America gave rise to varied forms of oratory, even as Englishmen used writing to create cultural and social distinctions. The novel circumstances of colonial life exposed English settlers to native eloquence while loosening the restrictions on the speech of religious dissenters such as Anne Hutchinson. The response to both situations was the same: textual discipline that devalued native American oral forms as savage speech, remade native communities in the image of Scripture, and demonized the eloquence of inspired women.

The relatively static hierarchy of forms with which colonial patriarchs responded to challenges to their authority was complicated by the emergence of a more flexible and elaborate understanding of verbal symbolism in the eighteenth

18. The persistent force of the figure of the authentic savage speaker is evident in two modern discussions of the importance of oral tradition by influential native American writers. Describing "Language and Literature from a Pueblo Indian Perspective," Leslie Marmon Silko expresses one variant of the performance semiotic of speech and text, explaining: "Where I come from, the words most highly valued are those spoken from the heart, unpremeditated and unrehearsed. Among the Pueblo people, a written speech or statement is highly suspect because the true feelings of the speaker remain hidden as she reads words that are detached from the occasion and the audience." See her essay in *Yellow Woman and a Beauty of the Spirit: Essays on Native American Life Today* (New York, 1996), 48–59, esp. 48. N. Scott Momaday similarly describes the significance of oral tradition for native communities in "The Native Voice," in Emory Elliott et al., eds., *Columbia Literary History of the United States* (New York, 1988), 5–15.

century. After the possessed girls and women of Salem demonstrated that they could mimic the textual knowledge of the clergy, the social roles maintained by such knowledge were revealed as performances. During the 1740s, a controversy over evangelicalism's extemporaneous preaching style provoked a clear articulation of the meanings attached to manuscript-based and improvised sermons, with the stability and publicity of one set against the immediacy and spiritual inwardness of the other. Inspired by the relative freedom of the improvisational style, a significant number of evangelical women claimed the right to exercise their voices more publicly. The silencing of their public speech can be traced through the shifting symbolism of language and gender in the writings and sermons of Jonathan Edwards.

The extemporaneous evangelical style opened a more extensive terrain of intercultural accommodation among British Americans, native Americans, and African Americans. Three influential figures in that landscape demonstrate the power of the "savage speaker" imagery transformed. Despite his tendency to demonize the native peoples whom he proselytized, white missionary David Brainerd came tentatively and partially to accommodate native spiritual forms. In an encounter with a nativist leader, he recognized nativist spirituality as an authentic tradition despite its lack of a scripture. More bold in the intercultural challenge that he posed, Mohegan minister Samson Occom reimagined the figure of the debased savage speaker to present himself as an Indian orator of Pentecostal power. African American missionary John Marrant elaborated Occom's figure of a potent savage speaker through his identification with and conversion of a Cherokee community.

The performance semiotic that was elaborated in sacred oratory during the Great Awakening had important parallels and adaptations in the secular traditions of political and diplomatic eloquence, particularly as classical republicanism elevated the spoken word to a position of significance in political life and thought. The transatlantic interest in native American oratory was one feature of classical republicanism, as British Americans accommodated the speech traditions of the Iroquois League in the treaty councils of the early eighteenth century. The printed Lancaster treaty of 1744 circulated widely in the colonies as an important political document and an example of native eloquence. There, Onondaga leader Canassatego challenged the accusations of savage speech that were made by colonial diplomats, offered unflattering meditations on the deceptive uses of writing, and revealed the ability of native leaders to manipulate the symbolism of speech and text to their own ends.

Oratory emerged as a major political medium in the colonies during the Revolution. James Otis and Patrick Henry adapted evangelicalism's rhetorical strategies and symbolism of verbal forms to redefine America as an autonomous political entity through figures of voice. At the same time, the dangers of popular speech and the hegemonic potential of elite oratory permeated the Boston Massacre tradition. In his speech at the trial of the British soldiers, John Adams sought to discipline radical popular voice by making it savage when he scapegoated Boston Massacre victim Crispus Attucks. Later, the Boston Massacre orators established the authority of the whig leadership through their display of physical courage in the face of hostile auditors and through their figures of memory and mediation. In these orations, the elite white male body became a figure for the nation.

The tension between textual and oral forms of authority in the new republic appears in the verbal symbolism in the framing of the Declaration of Independence, at the constitutional conventions, and in the presidency of George Washington. The institutionalization of oratorical performance in the early republic took place in its most influential arena, the Congress, where Massachusetts representative Fisher Ames became its first celebrity orator. In the same period, two figures of difference, woman warrior Deborah Sampson Gannett and Mahican veteran Hendrick Aupaumut, used their eloquence to challenge the exclusions of the new government.

I have necessarily relied on speech texts and written descriptions of speeches to reconstruct the performances of early American orators. This textually mediated approach to an evanescent and radically context-oriented art raises a variety of problems with sources that are different in degree, if not always in kind, from those that scholars examining works of literature encounter. Even at the moment of performance, the gap between what the orator intended and what different members of the audience heard, saw, and understood produced an unavoidable indeterminacy. The translation of the elusive performance into textual form creates a stable point of reference that can be misleading if taken as a full and authentic account of the oration as event. The sources of the speeches that I examine vary widely. They include published texts by John Cotton, Thomas Hooker, Jonathan Edwards, Samson Occom, John Marrant, the Boston Massacre orators, George Washington, and Deborah Sampson Gannett. In these instances, the speaker had at least some control over the words that appeared in print. Other sources include transcripts and descriptions of the speech performances that composed the Antinomian Controversy, the Northampton revivals, the Lancaster treaty of 1744, James Otis's and Patrick Henry's famous speeches, the Boston Massacre trials, records of legislative oratory, and Hendrick Aupaumut's narrative of his embassy to the western nations. Some of these records were shaped in some way by the orator, either through the control over translation that the Iroquois delegates exercised at the Lancaster treaty or through the speaker's correction of reconstructed or recorded speeches. In some cases, no such scrutiny took place. No one of these recording methods guarantees more than any of the others that the textual record captures the words actually spoken on that occasion. Sermons and speeches that were fully composed before they were delivered were commonly revised for publication. Shorthand records of sermons or courtroom proceedings are not always fully accurate. Reconstructed speeches were shaped by memory after some passage of time. Where possible, I have compared descriptions of the same event. Some speech performances were more extensively recorded than others in multiple accounts and thus lend themselves to more detailed description. The issue of authenticity foregrounded in the performance semiotic of speech and text has necessarily influenced this analysis. My project here has been, not to reconstruct "authentic" moments of oratory, but to use the written traces of oral performances to uncover a potent source of cultural meaning. Focusing on the colonial era's most influential genre, I have examined the ways that verbal forms mirror and create social order through the staging of authenticity and power in the performances that shaped the cultures of early America.

Eloquence Is Power

Prologue *Language and Power in Seventeenth-Century British America*

I. TEXTUAL POSSESSION AND ORAL RESISTANCE

The European belief in distinct literate and oral forms of culture first emerged during the early years of colonization in the Americas. In the century after Columbus arrived in the "New World," European intellectuals expanded the ancient Western system of meaning that takes the oral and textual bodies of language as symbols for distinctions among social bodies. They now began to use this system of symbols to draw cultural (and later racial) boundaries between literate Europeans and the communities of native Americans and Africans that were largely unfamiliar with alphabetic literacy. Producing Western literacy as a technology of power, many European colonialists perceived the lack of alphabetic writing as a fundamental cultural inadequacy that justified the enslavement of Africans and the domination of native American peoples.[1]

Already in 1588, when Thomas Harriot wrote *A Briefe and True Report of the New Found Land of Virginia,* the first sustained work of English ethnography, the distinctions between literate and oral societies provided a major tool for projecting English domination over native communities. According to Harriot, the

1. For an outline of a transformation in the semiotics of speech and writing from the sixteenth to the eighteenth centuries, see Michel de Certeau, *The Writing of History,* trans. Tom Conley (New York, 1988), esp. 236. Michael Harbsmeier traces the European "discovery of orality" and the emergence of a semiotic system that establishes cultural hierarchies according to the distinction of "oral" from "literate" societies to the late sixteenth century in "Writing and the Other: Travellers' Literacy, or Towards an Archaeology of Orality," in Karen Schousboe and Mogens Trolle Larsen, eds., *Literacy and Society* (Copenhagen, 1989), 197–228. On these cultural distinctions as they relate to the project of consolidating vernacular language, see Walter D. Mignolo, *The Darker Side of the Renaissance: Literacy, Territoriality, and Colonization* (Ann Arbor, Mich., 1995), 45. For a critique of the distinctions between cultures mapped along the axis of "oral" and "literate" in scholarship, see Brian V. Street, *Literacy in Theory and Practice* (Cambridge, 1984), chaps. 1, 2. On speech and text as differential rather than absolute terms in the context of native American oral traditions, see Arnold Krupat, "Post-Structuralism and Oral Literature," in Brian Swann and Arnold Krupat, eds., *Recovering the Word: Essays on Native American Literature* (Berkeley, Calif., 1987), 113–128; Joel Sherzer and Anthony C. Woodbury, eds., *Native American Discourse: Poetics and Rhetoric* (Cambridge, 1987), 9–10.

southeastern Algonquians inhabiting Roanoke Island and its vicinity regarded "bookes, writing and reading" as "rather the works of gods [than] of men." Elaborating on his evidence of the New World's ripeness for colonization that provides the explicit rationale for his report, Harriot promises his English readers that Algonquian "wit" and ingenuity made such technologies valuable tools of domination.[2] The natives would readily recognize the pragmatic advantages of English "craftes, sciences and artes" and come to accept them along with English authority, he claimed, for "by howe much they upon due consideration shall finde our manner of knowledges and craftes to exceede theirs in perfection, and speed for doing or execution, by so much the more is it probable that they shoulde . . . have the greater respect for pleasing and obeying us." The same logic suggested to Harriot that the natives would readily embrace Christianity. Just as native technical skill promised rapid assimilation of English mechanical technologies, so native spiritual beliefs reflected their readiness to adapt allegedly more advanced English religious forms, a superiority whose preeminent sign was the Bible. Harriot interrupts his surprisingly detailed account of Algonquian religious beliefs with a meditation on the insufficiency of oral tradition, observing that they could give no complete chronology of the events in their creation narrative, since they had "no letters nor other such meanes as we to keepe recordes of the particularities of times past, but onelie tradition from father to sonne." The Western hierarchy that elevates textual "history" over oral "myth" anchors his assumption that "the contentes of the Bible" would triumph over native religion because of the written Word's greater objectivity and truth.[3]

Some forty years later, in *Hakluytus Posthumus; or, Purchas His Pilgrimes* (1625), Samuel Purchas amplified the identification of literacy technologies with cultural superiority. Just as speech distinguishes men from animals, Purchas observed, so "amongst Men, some are accounted Civill, and more both Sociable and Religious,

2. Thomas Harriot, *A Briefe and True Report of the New Found Land of Virginia* (1588; New York, 1972), 27. Harriot describes a set of distinguishing marks or scars that leading men have on their backs, the main form of writing that he attributes to the Algonquians. See "The Marckes of Sundrye of the Cheif Mene of Virginia," Plate XXIII, 74. E. Brooks Holifield discusses promotional literature and its strategies of credibility in *Era of Persuasion: American Thought and Culture, 1521–1680* (Boston, 1989), chap. 2.

3. Harriot, *Briefe and True Report*, 25–26. The moment at which Harriot interrupts his account with this reflection is worth noting. He has just remarked, "They say a woman was made first, which by the woorking of one of the goddes, conceived and brought foorth children: And in such sort they say they had their beginning." Harriot responds to this reversal of a founding assumption of European patriarchy—that Adam was created before Eve—with an emphasis on the unreliability of oral tradition, echoing Christianity's symbolic linkage of female reproductive power with disruptive voice.

by the Use of letters and Writing, which others wanting are esteemed Brutish, Savage, Barbarous."[4]

In contrast to Purchas, who described the "literall advantage" from his familiar domain near London, Harriot had the traveler's authority of experience. His report wrestles with the complex and enigmatic matter of Algonquian culture and his expedition's sometimes puzzling experiences in Virginia to produce an account designed to justify Sir Walter Raleigh's colonial project. Harriot's confident assertions of native appreciation for English cultural superiority intermingle in a tangled skein of encounters that he describes in detail and that resist his efforts to interpret them clearly. In contrast with the serene transparency that Harriot attributes to Algonquian behavior at those moments when he reassures his readers of their assimilability, his narrative of the company's interactions with the Wiròans (or sachem), Wingina, suggests a complex native response to English technologies, particularly the sacred technologies focused on the Bible. Wingina and many of his people joined in English prayers and psalm singing, Harriot notes, taking their interest as a sign of imminent conversion. Yet language differences make native comprehension of the Christian content unlikely; perhaps the Algonquians were interested in the variety of English oral forms, a possibility that Harriot does not explore. Instead, he dwells upon their reaction to the Book, recording that some Virginia natives treated the Bible as a sacred object and were "glad to touch it, to embrace it, to kisse it, to hold it to their brests and heades, and stroke over all their bodie with it." Harriot interprets these actions as evidence of "their hungrie desire of that knowledge" that he promised them the book contained, yet that their illiteracy prevented them from acquiring. Figuring native uses of the Book to be forms of exclusion and denial, Harriot positions native subjectivity as inferior to that of literate Englishmen.[5] But it may be that Har-

---

4. Harriot, *Briefe and True Report*, 27; Samuel Purchas, *Hakluytus Posthumus; or, Purchas His Pilgrimes*, I (1625; Glasgow, 1905), 486. Several scholars have criticized continuities between recent theories of literacy and Purchas's belief in writing as a sign of cultural superiority. See Stephen Greenblatt, *Marvelous Possessions: The Wonder of the New World* (Chicago, 1991), 9–12. On the parallels between Purchas's analysis and the techno-determinist thought of Jack Goody, Ian Watt, and Walter Ong, see Jill Lepore, *The Name of War: King Philip's War and the Origins of American Identity* (New York, 1998), 26–28.

Harriot's and Purchas's ideological investment in literacy as a sign of cultural superiority must also be seen in the context of campaigns for widespread lay literacy in England that began with the Reformation and crescendoed in the late sixteenth century; see David Cressy, *Literacy and the Social Order: Reading and Writing in Tudor and Stuart England* (Cambridge, 1980), 13.

5. Purchas, *Hakluytus Posthumus*, 486; Harriot, *Briefe and True Report*, 27. For his detailed analysis of Harriot's *Briefe and True Report*, see Eric Cheyfitz, *The Poetics of Imperialism: Translation and Colonization from "The Tempest" to "Tarzan,"* rev. ed. (Philadelphia, 1997), esp. 206,

4 : *Language and Power*

riot's oral exposition of "the contentes of the Bible . . . with many particularities of Miracles and chiefe poyntes of religion" was more significant to the Algonquians than its written source. Algonquian spiritual leaders possessed spoken authority that mirrored Harriot's religious lectures. "The Inhabitants give great credit unto their speeche which oftentymes they finde to bee true," he notes of the shamans whom he calls "conjurers or juglers." Even as Harriot insists that the text of the Bible evokes the Algonquians' desire, his account suggests an alternative explanation focused on the parallel roles that the spoken word played in English and Algonquian spiritual life. Insisting upon the textual symbol of cultural difference, Harriot suppresses the possibilities of syncretic oral practices.[6]

Harriot records the uses to which Wingina and his people hoped to put English spiritual power, which included the healing of the devastating new diseases that the strangers brought with them, the ending of a drought, and the punishment of their enemies "by shooting invisible bullets into them." "There could at no time happen any strange sicknesse, losses, hurtes, or any other crosse unto them," Harriot observes with an unmistakable ambivalence, "but that they would impute to us the cause or meanes thereof for offending or not pleasing us." Wary of the dangerous strangers, more interested in their "invisible bullets" than in the Bible, Wingina apparently hoped to turn this new power to his own advantage. Harriot strives unsuccessfully to maintain interpretive control over the spiritual syncretism that he describes, insisting that the English "God would not subject him selfe to anie such praiers and requestes of me[n]" as Wingina and his people made. The Algonquians found such assertions disingenuous after their enemies died despite English disavowals of divine agency. Harriot's concluding "good hope" that they might be brought to "the imbracing of the trueth" reflects the persistent En-

---

210. Works like Cheyfitz's, including older scholarship such as Roy Harvey Pearce, *The Savages of America: A Study of the Indian and the Idea of Civilization* (Baltimore, 1965), help scholars to perceive the contours of European and Euro-American ideology more clearly, but they do not eliminate the need to use nonnative sources to better understand the native past. For a description of the limitations of poststructuralist perspectivism, see Jane Tompkins, " 'Indians': Textualism, Morality, and the Problem of History," *Critical Inquiry,* XIII (1986), 101–119, esp. 118. For another exchange that limns the necessity for scholarship that focuses on European images of the New World while underscoring the incompleteness of such scholarship, see Peter Hulme, *Colonial Encounters: Europe and the Native Caribbean, 1492–1797* (London, 1986); Myra Jehlen, "History before the Fact; or, Captain John Smith's Unfinished Symphony," *Critical Inquiry,* XIX (1993), 677–692; Hulme, "Making No Bones: A Response to Myra Jehlen," Jehlen, "Response to Peter Hulme," both in *Critical Inquiry,* XX (1993), 179–186, 187–191. Henry Louis Gates, Jr., discusses illiteracy as a racializing trope in African American literature in "The Trope of the Talking Book," in *The Signifying Monkey: A Theory of Afro-American Literary Criticism* (New York, 1988), 127–169.

6. Harriot, *Briefe and True Report,* 27, 54.

glish faith in the ultimate authority of Scripture that simply failed to manifest itself in the Americas despite the efforts of Christian missionaries.[7]

Many missionaries, particularly Protestants, struggled to resolve the tension that Harriot's work reveals: though they might understand the printed Bible as foundational to their endeavor, the spoken word was necessarily central to their proselytizing efforts. Their would-be converts often did not share either their understanding of the relationship between their religious speech and the Book or the more general hierarchy of verbal forms that anchored the Europeans' sense of cultural superiority. Harriot's *Briefe and True Report* exemplifies the technologically determinist "literall advantage" with unusual clarity. By his own account, he endeavored to dominate the Algonquians through the spiritual technologies of the Book; failing to accomplish that triumph as readily as he appears to have hoped, he offered native interest in Western technologies and cultural practices as evidence that they would ultimately convert to Christianity and English identity. Yet he incorporates evidence of Indian appropriations and transformations of these new technologies, casting them as forms of resistance to God even as he records English efforts to deter Algonquians from seeing them as "gods." The shift from "God" to "gods" registers that the technologies Europeans invested with a singular, divinely guaranteed meaning could be refigured in multiple terms deriving their significance from their social context.[8]

Speech, too, has its technologies, as Renaissance students of rhetoric knew well. Humanists who sought to recuperate the ancient world developed a shared understanding of "the central rôle of rhetorical skill and achievement in human affairs." With Cicero as their model, the humanists took the pursuit of eloquence as their defining project. To Europeans in the age of humanistic eloquence, oratory was the most recognizable native speech genre as well as the one most crucial for them to interpret. Such interpretation did not come easily. Speech technologies are no more universal than textual forms and are similarly shaped by their social context. In narratives such as John Smith's description of his reception by Powhatan or the account of Sir Francis Drake's voyage to the California coast, the

7. Ibid., 28, 29. For examples of native communities interpreting European textual forms within their own immediate context, see James P. Ronda, " 'We Are Well as We Are': An Indian Critique of Seventeenth-Century Christian Missions," *WMQ,* 3d Ser., XXXIV (1977), 75. For the dynamic of interest, threat, and fear among Harriot's group and Wingina, see Cheyfitz, *The Poetics of Imperialism,* 176. For cautions against accepting European accounts of native awe before literacy technologies, see Peter Wogan, "Perceptions of European Literacy in Early Contact Situations," *Ethnohistory,* XL (1994), 407–429.

8. Street defines an "ideological," or socially constructed, model of literacy in *Literacy in Theory and Practice,* chap. 4. Wampum, skin drawings, and pictographs were among the nonalphabetic systems of writing common among native communities.

formal oratory and rituals of encounter common among native American societies enact moments of simultaneous clarity and resistance. The seeming clarity of such moments derived from the resemblances they bore to European conventions for receiving and negotiating with a foreign diplomat. In *A True Relation of Such Ocurrences and Accidents of Noate as Hath Hapned in Virginia* (1608), John Smith describes his elaborate reception by Powhatan, which included "a great Oration made by three of his Nobles" offering, Smith claimed, "a publike confirmation of a perpetuall league and friendship."[9] Smith generalizes from his particular experience to characterize the manner in which the Powhatan Indians received prominent visitors in *A Map of Virginia* (1612):

> If any great commander arrive at the habitation of a Werowance, they spread a mat as the Turkes do a carpet for him to sit upon. Upon an other right opposite they sit themselves. Then doe all with a tunable voice of showting bid him welcome. After this doe 2. or more of their chiefest men make an oration, testifying their love. Which they do with such vehemency and so great passions, that they sweate till they drop, and are so out of breath they can scarce speake. So that a man would take them to be exceeding angry or starke mad.

English readers recognized such performances as modes of negotiating akin to European diplomacy, including the negotiations with the Turks that Smith participated in and refers to here. The humanistic Latin oration featured in European embassies provided the clearest parallel.[10]

---

9. Hanna H. Gray, "Renaissance Humanism: The Pursuit of Eloquence," *Journal of the History of Ideas*, XXIV (Oct.–Dec. 1963), 497–514, esp. 498. For further discussion of the humanistic revival of oratory, see Paul Oskar Kristeller, *Renaissance Thought and the Arts*, rev. ed. (Princeton, N.J., 1990), 9–10. On Renaissance rhetoric and eloquence as tools of imperial domination, see Cheyfitz, *The Poetics of Imperialism*. On the relationship between the Renaissance recovery of classical rhetoric and the Spanish exploration and colonization of the Americas, see Don Paul Abbott, *Rhetoric in the New World: Rhetorical Theory and Practice in Colonial Spanish America* (Columbia, S.C., 1996). James Axtell describes the importance of Jesuit training in classical rhetoric for their missionary success in New France in *The Invasion Within: The Contest of Cultures in Colonial North America* (New York, 1985), 87–88. The essays that editor Maurice Bloch collected in *Political Language and Oratory in Traditional Society* (New York, 1975) survey a variety of non-Western speech technologies. For examples of simultaneous clarity and resistance, see Greenblatt, *Marvelous Possessions*, esp. chap. 4. On Smith's reception by Powhatan, see John Smith, *A True Relation of Such Ocurrences and Accidents of Noate as Hath Hapned in Virginia*, in Philip L. Barbour, ed., *The Complete Works of Captain John Smith, 1580–1631*, 3 vols. (Chapel Hill, N.C., 1986), I, 65.

10. Smith, *A Map of Virginia*, in Barbour, ed., *Complete Works of Smith*, I, 167–168. In *Renaissance Diplomacy* (Boston, 1955), Garrett Mattingly observes, "Everyone insisted that the perfect ambassador had to be deeply read in literature and eloquent in the Latin tongue, for to be an ora-

Humanism could facilitate a too-ready, and thus false, recognition of native oratory. European celebrations of Indian eloquence typically portrayed native speakers as embodiments of the classical past. Smith's accounts of the Virginia colonies draw freely on the conventions of classical historiography in their use of re-created or invented speeches to propel the narrative. The title pages of both *A Map of Virginia* and *The Proceedings of the English Colonie in Virginia* (1612) advertise that the volumes include "the discourses, Orations, and relations of the Salvages." The humanistic value of this literary device manifests itself in an episode in *The Proceedings* where Smith unfolds an account of his reception at the Powhatan capital of Paumunke after relations have grown strained between the English colonists and the Powhatan people. Describing the negotiations over trade and territory that he holds with Powhatan and his brother Opechancanough, Smith structures his narrative as an exchange of speeches between himself and the native leaders. Smith (re-)created these speeches to show the cleverness and guile of Powhatan and Opechancanough in their dealings with the English colonists and to demonstrate his own superior ability as he escapes the trap they set for him. In a famous passage that Smith entitled "Powhatans discourse of peace and warre," Powhatan pleads eloquently with Smith to live peacefully with his people:

> What will it availe you, to take that perforce, you may quietly have with love, or to destroy them that provide you food? what can you get by war, when we can hide our provision and flie to the woodes, whereby you must famish by wronging us your friends; and whie are you thus jealous of our loves, seeing us unarmed, and both doe, and are willing still to feed you with that you cannot get but by our labours? think you I am so simple not to knowe, it is better to eate good meate, lie well, and sleepe quietly with my women and children, laugh and be merrie with you, have copper, hatchets, or what I want, being your friend; then bee forced to flie from al, to lie cold in the woods, feed upon acorns, roots, and such trash, and be so hunted by you, that I can neither rest, eat, nor sleepe.

"Let this therefore assure you of our loves," Powhatan concludes, asking the English to leave aside their arms when they come to trade. Exposing Powhatan's moving plea for peaceful coexistence as the machinations of a wily diplomat, Smith responds to "this subtil discourse" with a speech insisting that the natives, not the English, are responsible for the violence that has generated tensions. The

---

tor was the ambassador's office" (217). For a description of the increasingly elaborate diplomatic rituals of the Renaissance, see Mattingly, *Renaissance Diplomacy,* chap. 3. On the identification of classical rhetoric with a display of power in the Renaissance courts, see Arthur B. Ferguson, *The Articulate Citizen and the English Renaissance* (Durham, N.C., 1965), 36.

ensuing narrative exposes the trap that Powhatan has laid to take Smith captive once he and his men have accepted his bid for peace and put down their arms.[11]

In early narratives such as Smith's, English writers pair the familiarizing strategies of humanist eloquence with descriptions of the uncanny, violent performances of the native body. They often displace attention from the language differences that presented a serious obstacle to communication, focusing instead on the descriptions of the intensified physical presence of native speakers. The signs and gestures characteristic of native oratory, which to some observers promised a universal gestural language, instead took on a resistant quality identified with bodily extravagance. Smith echoed Cicero's comparison of eloquence without wisdom to the speech of a madman when he described the physical display of the Algonquian orators whose efforts left them sweating and breathless. He suggested the breakdown of meaning and potential for violence when he characterized the speakers' appearance as "exceeding angry or starke mad." Smith reveals a similar threat of violence lurking within the native speaker's performance when he exposes Powhatan's eminently reasonable appeal for physical comfort as a mask for aggression against the English. English narratives frequently share Smith's identification of "savage" speech with physical excess and violence.[12]

Perhaps the most complex early English representations of savage eloquence

11. Smith, *A Map of Virginia,* in Barbour, ed., *Complete Works of Smith,* I, 247–248. On Thucydides' reconstruction of Pericles' funeral oration, a central source for humanist uses of reconstructed speeches, see Cynthia Farrar, *The Origins of Democratic Thinking: The Invention of Politics in Classical Athens* (Cambridge, 1988), 26–30, chap. 5. See also Sabine MacCormack, "Limits of Understanding: Perceptions of Greco-Roman and Amerindian Paganism in Early Modern Europe," in Karen Ordahl Kupperman, ed., *America in European Consciousness, 1493–1750* (Chapel Hill, N.C., 1995), 79–129, esp. 79. Howard Mumford Jones discusses Smith's use of classical conventions in *O Strange New World: American Culture: The Formative Years* (London, 1965), 238–239. The tradition of inventing speeches, always a problem for historical rhetorical scholarship, becomes even more complex when cultural authority is at stake. See David Murray, *Forked Tongues: Speech, Writing, and Representation in North American Indian Texts* (Bloomington, Ind., 1991), chap. 3. For a reproduction of the title pages mentioned above, see Smith, *A Map of Virginia, The Proceedings of the English Colonie in Virginia,* both in Barbour, ed., *Complete Works of Smith,* I, 131, 199 (the quotation varies slightly in *The Proceedings*). Cheyfitz provides an incisive critique of Smith's eloquence as a technology of domination while simultaneously pointing out the problems of translation that Smith elides in *The Poetics of Imperialism,* chap. 4.

12. On the tradition of a universal gestural language derived from classical rhetoric, see Greenblatt, *Marvelous Possessions,* 93. See also J. S. Watson, trans. or ed., *Cicero on Oratory and Orators* (Carbondale, Ill., 1970), 19. The English narratives above share the qualities of excess, ephemerality, and irrecoupability that Certeau finds in the savage speech of Jean de Léry's *Histoire d'un voyage fait en la terre du Brésil* (1578). In contrast to the eroticizing paradigm of savage orality that Certeau traces in "Ethno-Graphy: Speech, or the Space of the Other: Jean de Léry," in *The Writing of History,* 209–243, English writings typically link the voice of the savage to forms of violence.

appear in an account of Sir Francis Drake's landing on what is now the California coast during his 1579 circumnavigation of the world. Compiled by an unknown writer from the notes of ship chaplain Francis Fletcher and belatedly published in 1628, the narrative occupies a peculiar position within the English literature of colonization. The author asserts that the natives "are a people of a tractable, free, and loving nature, without guile or treachery," echoing Harriot's earlier optimistic assertions of easy conquest, but he does so at a moment when English readers of exploration narratives had become skeptical of such hopeful signs.[13] During the early years of colonial endeavor, reports of a new world filled with natural bounty, immense wealth, and submissive natives clashed with reports of failed efforts at colonization. The most famous of these English disasters was the Powhatan attack that almost wiped out the Virginia colony in 1622, a result of persistent conflicts between the English settlers and the native inhabitants over food supplies and land. When the full account of Drake's voyage appeared six years after the events in Virginia, its interpretive framework for understanding New World encounters was outdated and implausible. Especially in these circumstances, Drake's departing acts of possession — renaming the region *"Albion"* and nailing a brass plate inscribed with names and dates on a post to establish English "right and title to that kingdome" — register their imaginary nature as written signs. Such textual claims proved a poor substitute for the physical occupation that the English believed was the only true form of possession. For a time, the narrative suggests, textual possession seemed the only stable form of English property in the Americas.[14]

The tension between textual possession and oral resistance to that possession structures the narrative of the encounter between Drake's company and the native Miwok community. The account registers English efforts to control the partially recognizable but nonetheless mysterious oral forms of Miwok negotiation

13. Sir Francis Drake, *The World Encompassed* (1628; Ann Arbor, Mich., 1966), 79. For another version of Drake's experiences in California, see N. M. Penzer and Richard Carnac Temple, eds., *The World Encompassed and Analogous Contemporary Documents concerning Sir Francis Drake's Circumnavigation of the World* (London, 1926), 182–187. On the publication history of the various narratives of Drake's voyage, see David B. Quinn, "Early Accounts of the Famous Voyage," in Norman J. W. Thrower, ed., *Sir Francis Drake and the Famous Voyage, 1577–1580* (Berkeley, Calif., 1984), 33–48. Greenblatt notes the exploration narrative's convention of including an "inventory of hopeful signs" encouraging colonization in *Marvelous Possessions,* 94.

14. Drake, *The World Encompassed,* 80. By the time the full account of Drake's voyage appeared in London in 1628, the unreliability of such narratives had long been a public joke. See E. Brooks Holifield, *Era of Persuasion,* chap. 2. For an account of the decade-long Second Anglo-Powhatan War that the 1622 attack began, see Helen C. Rountree, "The Powhatans and the English: A Case of Multiple Conflicting Agendas," in Rountree, ed., *Powhatan Foreign Relations, 1500–1722* (Charlottesville, N.C., 1993), 173–205. On competing forms of territorial possession, see Patricia Seed, "Taking Possession and Reading Texts: Establishing the Authority of Overseas Empires," *WMQ,* 3d Ser., XLIX (1992), 183–209.

and purports to render them transparent within the text. At the same time, the narrative records moments when Miwok practices exceeded the author's interpretive grasp, producing an unrecuperable figure of savage orality. Miwok oral forms are obliquely revealed to contain resistance to English power, and English responses to those performances reflect their own resistance to a full recognition of distinctive Miwok oral practices.

The day after the Drake company arrived in the harbor, "the people of the country shewed themselves; sending off a man with great expedition to us in a canow. Who being yet but a little from the shoare, and a great way from our ship, spake to us continually as he came rowing on." Approaching closer he finally stopped and "began more solemnely a long and tedious oration, after his manner: using in the deliverie thereof, many gestures and signes; moving his hands, turning his head and body many wayes; and after his oration ended, with great shew of reverence and submission, returned back to shoare againe." The man approached twice more in the same manner, the third time bringing "a bunch of feathers . . . a speciall cognizance (as wee afterwards observed) which they that guard their kings person, weare on their heads. With this also he brought a little basket made of rushes, and filled with an herbe which they called *Tabáh.*" The text hints at the incomprehension with which the English observed the "gestures and signes" of the orator and suggests the partial and situational sense that they were able to make of the feathers he brought them.[15]

Once they had landed, the English sailors were met by "a great assembly of men, women, and children," and together the two groups listened to an orator who delivered his speech "with strange and violent gestures, his voice being extended to the uttermost strength of nature, and his words falling so thicke one in the neck of another, that he could hardly fetch his breath againe." The common experience of listening to the speech that momentarily joined the English and the Miwoks as an audience quickly gave way to responses that dramatically marked the differences between them. While the English listened uncomprehendingly, the physical features of the performance absorbing their attention, the Indians understood and responded to the oration in a unified fashion that the author interprets as consent to an unknown assertion: "As soone as he had concluded, all the rest, with a reverend bowing of their bodies (in a dreaming manner, and long producing of the same) cryed *Oh:* thereby giving their consents, that all was very true

---

15. Drake, *The World Encompassed,* 67–68. In *Cities of the Dead: Circum-Atlantic Performance* (New York, 1996), esp. 131, Joseph Roach suggests that, for Europeans, feathers became a symbol of cultural difference from native Americans that worked as an "ethnographic provocation and hyperbolic mirror" to highlight the "predication of overarching symbolic systems on the material basis of waste" and violence. This metasymbolic function of feathers is borne out in the ensuing events of the Drake narrative.

which he had spoken, and that they had uttered their minde by his mouth unto us." Perceiving the Miwoks' cry as collective consent, the English in their incomprehension colonized the natives' voices, appropriating meaning to their unintelligible sounds and gestures. But the next moment their hopeful picture of unified native intent suddenly erupted into monstrosity as the Indians "used unnaturall violence against themselves" in the "bloudie sacrifice" of self-torture. These acts exceed the author's previously confident grasp.[16]

The interpretive resistance to this momentary violence dissolves as he describes events with increasing confidence in their transparency. Several days passed while the Miwoks and the English sailors exchanged gifts of fabric and skins, performed competing spiritual ceremonies, and fortified themselves in the event that their tentative and uneasy exchanges took a violent turn. Then an even larger assembly of Miwoks gathered, and a man that the author identifies as "the king himselfe" arrived, preceded by "two Embassadors or messengers." The "Embassadors" delivered a long proclamation and asked for a sign of Drake's peaceable intent. Once that sign was given, the king and his retinue approached dancing and singing and finally entered the English bulwark. At that point, "the king and divers others made severall orations,—or rather indeed," the author observes, "if wee had understood them, supplications, that [Drake] would take the Province and kingdome into his hand, and become their king and patron: making signes that they would resigne unto him their right and title in the whole land, and become his vassals in themselves and their posterities." The king then set something that the author identifies as a crown upon the head of Drake, who took "the scepter crowne and dignity, of the sayd countrie into his hand" in the name of Queen Elizabeth.[17]

Interpreting the complex set of welcoming rituals and speeches as expressions of the Miwoks' desire for English domination, the account hinges on a moment of imperfect communication ("if wee had understood them") that has inexplicably been rendered transparent. Circumventing the problems of translation that briefly emerge in Harriot and Smith, the narrative purports to unfold the meaning locked within the oral performances and rituals that it portrays. Surrendering meaning within the text, the inhabitants of the California coast surrender land and power to the English. Taming the elaborate displays of artistry, power, and ritual staged by the native inhabitants and textually transforming them into a unified act of submission, the author assumes a godlike ability to penetrate the meaning of their ceremonies.[18] At the same time, like Harriot he describes English resistance to

16. Drake, *The World Encompassed*, 71, 72.
17. Ibid., 73, 76, 77.
18. Greenblatt describes such a moment as a caesura, "the place of discovery where the ex-

being taken for gods. The author's interpretive power, identified with the act of writing, places himself and his fellows at the signifying center of the encounter. As the hesitance of "if wee had understood them" resolves into the asserted understanding of Miwok submission that justifies Drake's act of possession, the author self-consciously portrays a moment when the opacity of cultural difference yields to the transparency of English domination. At a moment of uncertainty in the imperial project, writing permits the abstraction that produces transparency and possession.

Even as the author performs textual possession, his elaborately detailed descriptions of the orations, proclamations, and ceremonies retain much of their strangeness. Uninterpretable oral encounters are a residue that the colonial Imaginary produces but cannot fully assimilate. The author's attempt to create an autonomous, textual domain of colonial wish-fulfillment is built on top of, but does not fully account for, the resistance and opacity visible in his reports of oral performance. In some of these ceremonial occasions the English recognized forms of authority and negotiation though they often did not understand their specific content. The elaborate addresses that the man in the canoe delivered and the speeches of the "king" and his "embassadors" reflect indigenous protocols for exchange and negotiation that the author identified as such, even as he tendentiously interpreted their content. The meaning of other ceremonies remained elusive, their excessive and unexploitable nature marking English representations of savage orality at its core. English recognitions of and resistances to the rich, complex forms of native orature could not be fully recuperated within the hierarchy of the written word.

II. RENAISSANCE THEORIES OF LANGUAGE AND THE PLACE OF THE PULPIT

The doubleness in colonialist representations of native speech reflects English humanist views of language as both immediately accessible and opaque. Humanists understood language as a living medium produced in a particular community. That language community was to be realized not in the vernacular but through the revivification of a Latin both historically and culturally remote. Crucial language skills were cultivated as part of an educational project organized around familiarization with a dead foreign language. Humanistically educated English boys were taught to understand language as speech and speech as an opacity to be rendered

---

planatory power of writing repeatedly tames the opacity of the eye's objects by rendering them transparent signs." See *Marvelous Possessions*, 88.

transparent. In the sixteenth century, humanist writers and educators increasingly defined the standards for government offices and prepared the gentry to occupy them. The sixteenth-century English courtier occupied official, political capacities as ambassador, royal counselor, secretary, provincial governor, or magistrate. In keeping with these roles, English training in gentility stressed Ciceronian humanist ideals of moral action embodied in the figure of the orator.[19]

Sir Thomas Elyot's *The Boke Named the Governour* (1531), the first English-language treatise on moral philosophy and the character of the good ruler, portrays an important role for humanist eloquence in England. For Elyot, oratorical skill derived from the study of classical orations helped to define the public authority of the governor: "The utilitie that a noble man shall have by redying these oratours, is, that, whan he shall happe to reason in counsaile, or shall speke in a great audience, or to strange ambassadours of great princes, he shall nat be constrayned to speake wordes sodayne and disordred, but shal bestowe them aptly and in their places." Well-ordered speech creates a well-ordered society. Paraphrasing Cicero, Plato, and Tacitus, Elyot argued that eloquence transformed a group of beastly men into an organized community. The eloquent orator could speak appropriately on every topic, give good counsel on matters of importance, and stir and quicken "people languisshing or dispeiringe, and . . . moderate them that be rasshe and unbridled."[20]

Written almost a century after Elyot set forth the role of eloquence in government service, Henry Peacham's *The Complete Gentleman* (1622) suggests the extent to which Elyot's ideals had been realized. By Peacham's time vernacular oratory had developed into an important genre, shaped by the absorption and adaptation of Latin models. Peacham emphasized the importance of studying English models of eloquence such as parliamentary speeches, sermons, and court

19. On the centrality of speech to the social community formed by English humanists, see Martin Elsky, *Authorizing Words: Speech, Writing, and Print in the English Renaissance* (Ithaca, N.Y., 1989), 6. On the roles of sixteenth-century English courtiers, see Ruth Kelso, *The Doctrine of the English Gentleman in the Sixteenth Century* ([Urbana, Ill., 1929]), 53. Fritz Caspari discusses the importance to English humanists of the Roman conception of the leading citizen, with its emphasis on oratory, in *Humanism and the Social Order in Tudor England* (Chicago, 1954), 15. Martin B. Becker describes the humanists' "Ciceronian commitment to rhetoric as effective participation for civil life" in *Civility and Society in Western Europe, 1300–1600* (Bloomington, Ind., 1988), 41.

20. Sir Thomas Elyot, *The Boke Named the Governour,* ed. Henry Herbert Stephen Croft, 2 vols. (New York, 1967), I, 76, 116, 117. Cheyfitz analyzes this Ciceronian trope as a Renaissance figure for colonization in *Poetics of Imperialism,* 113. For a discussion about the 1530s launching a new era of articulate citizenship in England—with Elyot as a key figure for propagating the new ideals attached to this era—see Ferguson, *The Articulate Citizen and the English Renaissance,* 136, 150.

pleadings in addition to the classics. Such study was possible through the manuscript circulation and occasional printing of parliamentary proceedings, through newsletters containing "excellent discourses," and through separates of speeches. Singling out Sir Nicholas Bacon's and Lord William Burghley's public speeches in Parliament and the Star Chamber as having won popular praise, Peacham observed that "nothing draws our attention more than good matter eloquently digested and uttered with a graceful, clear, and distinct pronunciation." The eloquent orator had become a figure of public note and popular repute in Renaissance England.[21]

The humanist elevation of oratory to prominence invested the styles of speech with a significance unprecedented in English political life. Initially the hottest rhetorical wars were fought not in Parliament—though eventually they occupied and transformed the political realm as well—but in the pulpit, where competing styles of preaching signified contested theological commitments. The conflicts between Anglican churchmen and Puritan reformers centered upon the symbolism of speech and text. Anglican authorities maintained that God's Word must be received through ritual forms and institutional structures built up over centuries. Their emphasis on historical continuity was evident in sermons that followed Catholic tradition, where preachers employed "humane" learning in God's service, quoted classical sources in the original, and created elaborate rhetorical figures. Witty metaphysical preachers such as John Donne and Launcelot Andrewes preached learned orations of considerable literary complexity. Their rich play of allusions and images, gathering strength to climax in a powerful peroration, contrasted audibly with the carefully delineated Puritan sermon structure of text-doctrine-reasons-uses-application. The Puritan preacher took as his primary rhetorical goal the creation of a sense of the divine order that required no socially restricted language skills such as knowledge of classical rhetoric or languages to understand.[22] When William Perkins first formally defined the Puritan plain style

21. Elsky discusses Roger Ascham's widely known *The Scholemaster* (1570) as a major influence on the emergence of vernacular oratory in *Authorizing Words,* 55. Harold Love discusses the manuscript circulation of individual speeches, speech collections, and parliamentary proceedings from at least Elizabeth's reign in *The Culture and Commerce of Texts: Scribal Publication in Seventeenth-Century England* (1993; Amherst, Mass., 1998), 9–22, 134–137, 214–215 (on the printing of parliamentary proceedings, see 15, 185–186). See also Henry Peacham, *The Complete Gentleman, The Truth of Our Times, and The Art of Living in London,* ed. Virgil B. Heltzel (Ithaca, N.Y., 1962), 56.

22. David Little analyzes the competing Anglican and Puritan ways of understanding the relationship to Catholic tradition in *Religion, Order, and Law: A Study in Pre-Revolutionary England* (New York, 1969), 137–138. On Anglican preaching, see W. Fraser Mitchell, *English Pulpit Oratory from Andrewes to Tillotson: A Study of Its Literary Aspects* (1932; New York, 1962); Perry

in his *Art of Prophecying*, he insisted that the sermon must convince "even ignorant persons and unbeleevers . . . that it is not so much [the minister] that speaketh, as the Spirit of God in him and by him." Puritan sermons effected a linguistic ascesis rejecting "Philosophie, or fables, or lying Legends . . . poeticall fictions, Thalmudical dreams, Schoolmens quiddities, Popish decrees, or humane constitutions or . . . the fine ringing sentences of the Fathers." The preacher was instructed to speak only in the vernacular, avoiding the temptation to demonstrate erudition by quoting passages from Latin or Greek texts. John Dod, one of the era's most popular preachers, characterized Latin quotations as "flesh in a Sermon," and his dictum was often repeated. Dod's metaphor is revealing, for it suggests the social emphasis underlying Puritan concerns with living speech communities in opposition to the antisocial threat of sensual indulgence in language, especially a dead language. That Latin had long ceased to evolve within a spontaneous speech community and survived only in texts and the elite schools that taught those texts highlighted its worldliness and suspect materiality. Reformers sought to effect a communal linguistic reform parallel to that of the humanist Latin schools but centered instead on the vernacular Bible.[23]

English Puritans understood the relationship between written and oral forms to contain a progressive dynamic that reached into the biblical past while remaining rooted in the local speech community. The transformative impulse within Puritanism had its clearest manifestation in the pulpit, for the printed Word erupted through the existing social order only when given voice by Puritan ministers. The effect of authentic inspiration characteristic of Puritan preaching required a shared scriptural reference. Preaching to audiences familiar with the

---

Miller, *The New England Mind: The Seventeenth Century* (Cambridge, Mass., 1939), 300–304, 332–333. Miller observes that, by the mid-seventeenth century, "the distinction between these two forms had become so sharply drawn, the types so exactly stereotyped, that ordinary laymen as well as Cambridge scholars would recognize the partisan sympathies of a minister by the form and technique of his pulpit utterance." On the essential difference between Puritan and Anglican sermonizing in primarily cultural, rather than theological, terms, see William Haller, *The Rise of Puritanism; or, The Way to the New Jerusalem as Set Forth in Pulpit and Press from Thomas Cartwright to John Lilburne and John Milton, 1570–1643* (New York, 1938), 140.

23. William Perkins, "The Art of Prophecying; or, A Treatise concerning the Sacred and Onely True Manner and Methode of Preaching," in Perkins, *The Works of That Famous and Worthy Minister of Christ in the Universitie of Cambridge, M. William Perkins*, II (London, 1631), 643–673, esp. 670; Perkins, as quoted in Haller, *The Rise of Puritanism*, 131. On Puritan verbal iconoclasm, see also Norman Grabo, "John Cotton's Aesthetic: A Sketch," *Early American Literature*, III (1968), 4–10. Cotton Mather quotes Dod in a description of John Cotton's pulpit oratory in *Magnalia Christi Americana; or, The Ecclesiastical History of New-England . . .*, I (Hartford, Conn., 1855), 274. Miller discusses the Puritan ministry's ambivalent response to humanist theories of oratory in *The New England Mind*, 306–307.

printed Bible, Puritan ministers developed a new idiom rich with scriptural allusions and metaphors. Puritan speech drew on the Bible and other sacred texts while simultaneously shaping the language and function of print. The Puritans themselves traced lines of influence from the printed Bible to their sermon performances, to the printed texts of sermons and other religious treatises, which in turn influenced both pulpit oratory and everyday speech. Such reciprocity of printed and preached Words sustained an ideal Puritan language that would remake literature, pulpit oratory, and conversation. Local language communities that had been purified through their voicing of Scripture would propel moral, social, and institutional transformation. Print transformed Scripture into a script for even mundane Puritan performances.[24]

Anglicans construed the semiotics of speech and text differently. Textual forms ordained by the church hierarchy or produced by individual ministers promised a stable social order protected from the volatility of more immediate spiritual experience. Anglican preachers composed their texts carefully, delivering the same sermon to several audiences in different parishes. Less talented pulpit orators made use of the stereotyped readings distributed by the central church authority. Recasting Catholic universalism in a national form, the Anglican church used the written or printed word to create a common religious experience. Standardized printed Anglican texts, including the liturgy, Scripture readings, and occasionally even sermons, permitted a geographical as well as a historical continuity, establishing a degree of uniformity within the national church.[25]

---

24. On Puritanism's progressive core, see Little, *Religion, Order, and Law,* 70; Stephen Foster, *The Long Argument: English Puritanism and the Shaping of New England Culture, 1570–1700* (Chapel Hill, N.C., 1991), 27, 289. For a discussion of John Calvin's understanding of the relationship between Scripture and sermon and of the minister's authority as a form of spiritual discipline for the congregation, see Sandra Marie Gustafson, "Performing the Word: American Oratory, 1630–1860" (Ph.D. diss., University of California at Berkeley, 1993), 93–101. David D. Hall describes the importance of the minister and the central role of the sermon in *The Faithful Shepherd: A History of the New England Ministry in the Seventeenth Century* (Chapel Hill, N.C., 1972). Scholars often lay greater emphasis on either speech or text when interpreting Puritanism. On the spoken word as the center of Puritan experience, see Christopher Hill, *Society and Puritanism in Pre-Revolutionary England* (1958; New York, 1997), chap. 2. On print's importance to both church and linguistic reform, see Larzer Ziff, *Puritanism in America: New Culture in a New World* (New York, 1973), 3–5. I share William Haller's view of the reciprocal importance of speech and print expressed in *The Rise of Puritanism,* 172, 226. On Puritan primitivism and its treatment of sacred writ as a source of dramatic identifications producing the living theater of the present, see Theodore Dwight Bozeman, *To Live Ancient Lives: The Primitivist Dimension in Puritanism* (Chapel Hill, N.C., 1988), chap. 1.

25. On Puritan contempt for the "reading ministry," see Foster, *The Long Argument,* 26, 41. Anglicans understood the printed English text in terms similar to the roles that Benedict Anderson assigns print-capitalism in the formation of nationalism: as a verbal medium below Latin but above the spoken vernaculars, as a source of linguistic fixity, and as a language of power.

Puritans identified a minister's ceremonial reading of text—whether a sermon, a Scripture passage, or the Book of Common Prayer—as a sign of spiritual deadness. The Latin "sermo" signified a conversation or mutual talk, and reformers returned to the word's ancient sense to create a more colloquial sermon style. Puritan rhetorical theorists conceived of the sermon as a semispontaneous oral performance that permitted the preacher's response to his immediate setting. They held that sermons truly expressed the will of God only when they applied Scripture to those present in the congregation, their social circumstances and historical situation. To emphasize their responsiveness to their setting and their openness to divine inspiration, Puritan preachers spoke extemporaneously, from memory, or with only an outline. Without a full text before them, they incorporated spontaneous figures and observations, an experience they attributed to the Spirit and described as preaching with "liberty." These moments of "liberty" were designed to manifest the authenticity of unmediated access to God's will. Puritan "plain" style was not an untrained style, however. From its earliest years, the movement's leaders opposed ministers they deemed ignorant and inarticulate. Behind the Puritan preacher's semi-improvised sermon were hours of thought and preparation. Theirs was an art that disguised its own artifice, producing an effect of immediacy and transparency that became the performative sign of authentic spiritual power.[26]

John Cotton's preaching career exemplified the complex spiritual and social implications of the Puritan plain style as it emerged in competition with witty Anglican preaching. Cotton was converted while he was a rising pulpit star at Cambridge University. "That which first made him famous in *Cambridge*," Cotton's biographer John Norton writes,

> was his Funeral Oration for Doctor *Some*, Master of Peter-house; so accurately performed, in respect of invention, Elegancy, Purity of Style, Ornamens of Rhetorick, Elocution, and Oratorious beauty of the whole, as that he was thenceforth looked at as another *Xenophon*, or *Musa Attica* throughout the University.[27]

See Anderson, *Imagined Communities: Reflections on the Origin and Spread of Nationalism,* 2d ed. rev. (London, 1991), 44–45.

26. See Mitchell, *English Pulpit Oratory,* 51. On the humanistic use of "sermo" to identify "natural language and the spoken vernacular," see Elsky, *Authorizing Words,* 36–39. Babette May Levy notes that Puritan ministers followed Luther in preparing carefully and delivering freely; see *Preaching in the First Half Century of New England History* (Hartford, Conn., 1945), 83. Puritans denounced unfit ministers as early as 1586, describing several as "unable to preach." See Edmund Morgan, *Visible Saints: The History of a Puritan Idea* (New York, 1963), 8.

27. John Norton, *Abel Being Dead Yet Speaketh . . . ,* in John Cotton, *The New England Way* (New York, n.d.), 13.

A later sermon only increased his reputation with "Academical Wits." Already Cotton was an important figure in the Anglican style of witty preaching that John Donne elevated to high art a few years later. A third opportunity to hear Cotton preach raised expectations among the students, for "one Oration of *Pericles* left the hearer with an Appetite for another." They flocked "to the Sermon with an *Athenian* Itch after some new thing, as to the Ornaments of Rhetorick and abstruser notions of Philosophy." But Cotton, recently converted to Puritanism by Richard Sibbes, held fast to his new convictions and produced a sermon in the plain style:

> But his Spirit now favouring of the Cross of Christ more then of Humane literature, and being taught of God to distinguish between the word of wisdom, and the wisdom of words; his speech and preaching was not with the enticing words of mans wisdom, but in the demonstration of the Spirit and of power.

Norton's metaphor of the minister as a vessel pure enough to transmit divine grace without contamination characterized the Puritan conception of pulpit performance. Anglican pulpit orators foregrounded their own language both to locate their sacred message in the context of human traditions and to manifest the ultimate inadequacy of all language to convey divine significance. Puritan sermons were at once more modest in their presentation and more ambitious in their claims to represent God. They believed that the Lord spoke through their mouths, and all their ascetic disciplines of language, mind, and body were designed to make themselves more perfect vehicles for truth. By claiming to remove verbal obstructions, Puritans brought more clearly into focus the problematic aspects of man's pretensions to efface all traces of the self and speak with God's voice.[28]

Puritan preachers were more dramatic than their Anglican counterparts in that they maintained that they spoke, not their own words, but God's Word. They impersonated prophets. Boston minister John Wilson once remarked, "Mr. Cotton preaches with such authority, demonstration, and life, that methinks, when he preaches out of any prophet or apostle, I hear not him; I hear that very prophet and apostle; yea, I hear the Lord Jesus Christ himself speaking in my heart." By claiming to hear another speaking through Cotton, Wilson measured his pastoral colleague's achievement of the self-effacing Puritan ideal. He also marked the dif-

---

28. Norton, *Abel Being Dead,* in Cotton, *The New England Way,* 13–14. For a distinction between Puritan rhetoric's transparency and Anglican rhetoric's self-deconstruction, see Stanley Fish, *Self-Consuming Artifacts: The Experience of Seventeenth-Century Literature* (Berkeley, Calif., 1972), 75. I agree with Fish that, by simplifying their language and making it adequate to their audiences' understandings, Puritan ministers sought an appropriate vehicle for communicating truth. But by focusing solely on the linguistic aspects of sermon delivery, Fish neglects the Puritan emphasis on ministerial performance and reduces the richness of their rhetorical concerns.

ference between a biblical prophet and a Puritan preacher. Denied the ancient prophet's opportunity to converse directly with God, his latter-day spokesmen offered scriptural interpretation, mimicking the voices of prophets inscribed in sacred texts rather than asserting their own inspired understanding of the divine will. As a consequence of their textually mediated relation to the Lord, ministers could verify the truth of their interpretation only in its effects on their congregation, its success in converting listeners. The Puritan conception of preaching as holy impersonation could prove troublesome to ministerial authority, for the final register of the preacher's self-effacement was the listener's heart.[29]

III. BODIES OF LANGUAGE AND THE GENDERED SOCIAL BODY

Nowhere was the performative dynamic of Puritanism more visible or more volatile than in the Massachusetts Bay Colony during the antinomian crisis of 1636–1638. These events exposed in the new colony a heightening of the ancient tension over linguistic mediation and embodiment that permeates Western culture, and that the iconoclastic and dramatic impulses within Puritanism intensified. The conflict between the laywomen and -men of the Boston church and the colony's spiritual and political leaders is often characterized as a controversy over preparationism, the predominant clerical belief that grace matured gradually with the aid of preaching and other ministerial offices. The Boston laity, confident in its ability to analyze Scripture and dispute theological points, countered with a model of conversion that imagined grace as a spontaneous transformation of the soul largely uninfluenced by clerical interventions. At the core of the controversy, the two groups disputed the forms of ministerial performance and authority. Boston matron Anne Hutchinson drew the wrath of the clergy, not so much through the large meetings she held in her home to review and discuss the week's sermons—a practice she justly defended as well established in the colony— as through the invidious distinctions she drew among the Bay Colony ministers. At her civil trial, Hutchinson announced to the General Court that, as she listened to sermons, the Lord "hath let me to distinguish between the voice of my beloved and the voice of Moses, the voice of John Baptist and the voice of antichrist, for All those voices are spoken of in scripture." Hutchinson's claim to hear scriptural voices echoed mainstream Puritan rhetorical theory. In *The Art of Prophecy-*

---

29. Puritan preachers drew Kenneth Burke's distinction between agent and agency with particular clarity; see introduction to Burke, *A Grammar of Motives* (Berkeley, Calif., 1969). For John Wilson's comment, see Mather, *Magnalia Christi Americana*, I, 275. See also John S. Coolidge, *The Pauline Renaissance in England: Puritanism and the Bible* (Oxford, 1970), chap. 4.

ing, William Perkins explained that pulpit eloquence persuaded its audience only to the extent that they heard another voice accompanying the minister's speech. "The Elect having the Spirit of God doe first discerne the voyce of Christ speaking in the Scriptures," Perkins asserted. "Moreover, that voyce, which they doe discerne, they doe approove: and that which they doe approove, they doe beleeve." [30] But Hutchinson's aural sensitivity far exceeded Perkins's understanding of gracious listening. She claimed a complex range of perceptions that allowed her to distinguish voices outside the context of Scripture itself. To her penetrating gaze and refined hearing, the Bay Colony ministers impersonated scriptural figures— the Antichrist as well as the beloved—in the continuing drama of sacred history.

Hutchinson's conflict with the Bay Colony ministers helped bring into focus a set of personal and doctrinal differences whose meaning was enacted in the pulpits of New England. When Hutchinson claimed that she could distinguish Christ's voice from Moses' in a minister's sermon, she referred not only to the theological tenets propounded but also to the preacher's language and countenance, his whole mode of performance through which those tenets were made manifest. The performative characteristics of a ministry made visible to an attentive and informed observer such as Hutchinson the finer theological points that distinguished John Cotton from the majority of the colony's clergy. Content and form were inseparable in Reformation church politics. Quoting 2 Corinthians on the letter that kills and the spirit that gives life to distinguish between Massachusetts ministers, Hutchinson reflected a fundamental tension within reformed doctrine over the relationship between sacred texts and the spoken word. [31] Hutchin-

30. On the verbal skills of the laity, who before and to a lesser extent after the Controversy were encouraged to ask questions after sermons, "prophesy" or give religious lectures at church services, offer conversion relations, review and analyze sermons in small groups, and even preach when a town lacked a minister, see Charles E. Hambrick-Stowe, *The Practice of Piety: Puritan Devotional Disciplines in Seventeenth-Century New England* (Chapel Hill, N.C., 1982), 138. Stephen Foster traces the roots of the Controversy to the lay practice of analyzing one another's spiritual estates, a practice at which Hutchinson excelled *(The Long Argument,* 163). See also "The Examination of Mrs. Anne Hutchinson at the Court at Newtown," in David D. Hall, ed., *The Antinomian Controversy, 1636–1638: A Documentary History* (Middletown, Conn., 1968), 336–337; Perkins, "Art of Prophecying," in Perkins, *Works of That Famous and Worthy Minister,* II, 649.

31. Janice Knight notes that the differences among the ministers were "as much matters of tone and sensibility as of doctrine"; see *Orthodoxies in Massachusetts: Rereading American Puritanism* (Cambridge, Mass., 1994), 32. On how conceptions of faith shaped the "manner of presentation" and the "conception of audience" in Puritan preaching and its pulpit heirs, see Teresa Toulouse, *The Art of Prophesying: New England Sermons and the Shaping of Belief* (Athens, Ga., 1987), 8. For the debate beween Hutchinson and Ipswich minister Nathaniel Ward over 2 Cor. 3:6, see Hall, ed., *The Antinomian Controversy,* 325–326. The lineaments of Hutchinson's oppositions between spirit and letter and between old and new covenants can be read in Cotton's

son's contrast between preaching the letter and preaching the spirit reproduced the terms of the English debate over pulpit performance between Anglican authorities and their Puritan critics. But Anglican textual practices no longer defined the killing letter in the New England setting, and the symbol system of speech and text shifted meanings in the socially unstable colonial context. For Hutchinson the killing power of the letter ultimately manifested itself in the gender hierarchy that supported ministerial authority over the spiritual claims of women and other laypeople.

The Puritan understanding of speech and text at stake in the Antinomian Controversy was enacted most critically in the pulpit. Cotton's sermon performances staged the primacy of Scripture. "The Text is large," he urged, insisting on the priority and comprehensiveness of the written Word. Cotton elaborated on his chosen Scripture passage more fully than other Massachusetts Bay preachers, displaying passivity before the Word through his attentive focus on resonant words and phrases within the text. As in the cabalism that became popular among Renaissance Neoplatonists and later flourished among the radical reformers of the English civil war, Cotton approached Scripture as the container of spiritual meanings in a form of mystic literalism. Unfolding textual variants, multiplying allusions, and teasing out possible meanings, he fragmented the Puritan sermon form, resisting progressive elaboration in order to dwell in possibility even as he seemed to offer "a straightforward and logical explication of a text."[32]

Cotton's pulpit performances gave physical expression to his emphasis on Scripture-as-text. His grandson Cotton Mather figured his grandfather's physical presence in textual terms, describing his "clear, fair, sanguine complexion" as a *"prosopography"* that had in it "an inexpressible sort of majesty." Like Paul's authority, Cotton's "majesty" did not appear in bodily power or beauty. Preaching in "a clear, neat, audible voice . . . easily heard in the most capacious auditory," his delivery was not "noisy and thundering." Cotton's clarity of voice and complexion gave physical and aural expression to the clear language of his sermons in a visible subordination of the self to the Word. Cotton's eulogists celebrated

---

development of this Pauline text; see John Cotton, "The Covenant of God's Free Grace" (1645), in Cotton, *The Way of Faith* (New York, n.d.), 11–12.

32. John Cotton, *A Treatise of the Covenant of Grace . . .* (London, 1671), 138. Nicholas Hudson discusses seventeenth-century cabalism in *Writing and European Thought, 1600–1830* (Cambridge, 1994), chap. 1. Toulouse emphasizes Cotton's interest "in displaying a variety of possible logical, physical, psychological, and spiritual meanings" for the text. "He is clearly suggesting the richness of God's revelation, not rigidly controlling its interpretation," she concludes. See Toulouse, *Art of Propshesying*, 32–33. For an argument that Cotton learned his sermonic techniques from Richard Sibbes, the minister whose preaching converted him, see Knight, *Orthodoxies in Massachusetts*, 148.

him for a meekness like that of Moses, the prophet with an intimate relationship to the Lord's written law. One eulogy written in 1651 employed an extended textual metaphor for his life, comparing him to "a living, breathing Bible" with "both *covenants* . . . engraven," and anticipating "a *new edition* . . . without *erratas.*" During his lifetime, his subordination to the Word structured his daily activities as well as his pulpit presence. His preferred mode of self-discipline was an Augustinian ascesis of study, for he believed that "the time not spent in study, for the most part, *sweeled away*. . . . that more benefit was obtained . . . by conversing with the *dead* (in *books*) than with the *living* (in talks)." Absorbed in the scholarly work of reading and writing, and foregrounding scriptural interpretation in the pulpit, Cotton organized his ministry around a textual semiotics.[33]

The clarity, quiet delivery, and textual orientation that characterized Cotton's public performances all distinguished him from Thomas Hooker, Cotton's only intellectual equal among his contemporaries and the Bay Colony minister who most fully articulated and enacted the preparationist alternative to Cotton's mystical scripturalism. Cotton emphasized the individual saint's authority over conversion during the 1636–1637 exchange with his preparationist opponents, whereas Hooker insisted that congregations maintain respect for their ministers and pay attention to spiritual means such as preaching and the sacraments. Acknowledging that God was not tied to any particular means of conveying grace, Hooker nevertheless insisted upon the primary role of pulpit oratory. He claimed that "the Lord hath ordained and set apart the preaching of the word, he hath sanctified it, and set it apart to call the soul." The unredeemed could not hear God's Word preached without impatience and inattentiveness, or in the worst cases heartfelt rebellion, against both message and messenger. While the unregenerate chafed against the minister's authority, converts echoed his words, testifying to their truth by the light of their own experience. Such repetition and amplification of the minister's sermon was a strong sign of redemption, even if the speaker remained uncertain of his or her spiritual estate. While Cotton maintained that those unsure of their condition were almost certainly spiritually dead regardless of whether they were deferential to their minister, Hooker held that grace might operate unconsciously and that attentiveness at ordinances was a good sign of gradual conversion that could be furthered through human effort. Hooker worked the middle

---

33. Mather, *Magnalia Christi Americana,* I, 271, 275, 280, 284. Benjamin Woodbridge compares Cotton to Moses in his elegy "Upon the Tomb of the Most Reverend Mr. John Cotton" (Mather, *Magnalia Christi Americana,* I, 284). See also Norton, *Abel Being Dead,* in Cotton, *The New England Way,* 33. Amanda Porterfield identifies Cotton's meekness and readiness to blame himself with Puritan images of female piety in *Female Piety in Puritan New England: The Emergence of Religious Humanism* (New York, 1992). "More than any other male emigré to New England," she writes, "Cotton embodied in his demeanor the Puritan ideal of femaleness" (66).

ground between confident saints and evident sinners energetically, exhorting and threatening his auditors to achieve grace in stages. While Cotton devoted himself to study and avoided the disruptions of conversation, Hooker put personal consultations at the center of his ministry, demonstrating his confidence in the minister's interpretive and diagnostic skills in his care of troubled souls.[34]

Hooker's differences with Cotton over preparation were evident in his distinctive sermon form and pulpit style. Cotton's more analytic, text-oriented sermons insisted on the preacher's ultimate persuasive impotence. Hooker granted the pulpit orator greater authority with his congregation and greater control over Scripture. His emphasis on "practical religion" informed his synthetic approach to the Bible. Basing his sermons on his own elaborate preparationist scheme, he peppered them with scriptural allusions and incorporated a strong narrative thrust that moved sequentially through the moments in the sinner's conversion process. Hooker used the Bible to address the particular needs of his congregation framed within his model of the conversion process. He employed his scriptural images in a structurally unifying fashion, scattering them through his discourse and mingling the functions of the sermon's various parts. While Cotton generally slighted the applications section of his sermons, leaving his colleague John Wilson to provide moral lessons in the form of extempore exhortations, Hooker offered extended applications in which he brought home the messages to the listener.[35]

Hooker's theological differences with Cotton also emerged in their contrasting performances. The "lively vigour" of a Hooker performance magnified the preacher's presence in a way that Cotton's restrained clarity did not. Cotton

---

34. Mather, *Magnalia Christi Americana*, I, 284. Hooker and Cotton have long been identified as representatives of two fairly distinct versions of New England Puritanism. Perry Miller explores the differences between Hooker and Cotton in "Thomas Hooker and the Democracy of Connecticut," in Miller, *Errand into the Wilderness* (Cambridge, Mass., 1964), 23–26. Their contrasting sermon styles are usefully discussed in Alfred Habegger, "Preparing the Soul for Christ: The Contrasting Sermon Forms of John Cotton and Thomas Hooker," *American Literature*, XLI (1969), 342–354. Janice Knight finds that Cotton typifies the "Spiritual Brethren" while Hooker embodies the emphases of the "Intellectual Fathers" in *Orthodoxies in Massachusetts*, 2–3. In the debates between the colony's ministers in 1636–1637, the main source of tension proved to be conflicting conceptions of faith resting ultimately on the word's original meaning of persuasion; see Gustafson, "Performing the Word," 132–140. See also Thomas Hooker, "The Soul's Vocation, Doctrine 3," in Phyllis M. Jones and Nicholas R. Jones, eds., *Salvation in New England: Selections from the Sermons of the First Preachers* (Austin, Tex., 1977), 82–83. For some of Cotton Mather's comments on Hooker, see Mather, *Magnalia Christi Americana*, I, 346.

35. See Mather, *Magnalia Christi Americana*, I, 346–347; Habegger, "Preparing the Soul for Christ," *American Literature*, XLI (1969), 345. The division of sermonic labor between Cotton, who preached Scripture, and Wilson, who offered extempore moral applications, was a major factor in the Antinomian Controversy, when Wilson was a major target of antinomian resistance. See Gustafson, "Performing the Word," 127–130.

Mather portrayed Hooker's dramatic style as an embodiment of anticipation and desire that invited holy mimicry:

> He not only had that which Quintilian calls, "A natural moveableness of soul," whereby the distinct *images* of things would come so *nimbly*, and yet so *fitly* into his mind, that he could utter them with fluent expressions, as the old orators would usually ascribe unto a *special assistance* of Heaven . . . but the rise of this fluency in him, was the *divine relish* which he had of the things to be spoken, the *sacred panting* of his holy soul after the glorious objects of the invisible world, and the true *zeal* of *religion* giving *fire* to his discourses.

Cotton's self-effacing performances focused attention away from himself and toward Scripture and the spirit within it. Hooker's dramatic improvisations displayed his knowledge of spiritual truths, including an intimate familiarity with Scripture but encompassing as well the path of conversion. Unlike the meek Cotton, Hooker was known for a fierce temper that periodically threatened to undermine his authority. He sublimated his emotions into impassioned exhortation and improvisational energy. His experiential knowledge authenticated his claims to the more extensive ministerial authority that he believed the gradual nature of spiritual regeneration required. Powerful of voice and animated in delivery, Hooker dramatized the Spirit's motions in his own soul in an effort to elicit his congregation's echoing response.[36]

In the pulpit, Hooker and Cotton distinctively employed the performance semiotic of text and speech — that is, the enactment of meaning through the literal and symbolic use of oral and written forms — to establish competing hierarchies of power and authenticity. Cotton insisted on the priority of the Bible — "The Text is large" — while ultimately reflecting a mystical sense of the inadequacy of language. He foregrounded the words of Scripture to evoke an immediate spiritual witness whose experience issued in a radical equality of the saints. Attending Cotton's sermons, Hutchinson and her associates extrapolated from his words and demeanor that authentic, powerful speech belonged to those who had the witness of the Spirit, not to those who held a university degree. Like Hutchinson, Hooker privileged living speech over the dead letter, comparing book learning unfavorably with experiential religion: "It's one thing to see a disease in the Book, or in a mans body, another thing to find and feel it in a mans self." But for Hooker, the minister's professional training provided him with superior hermeneutic tech-

---

36. Mather, *Magnalia Christi Americana*, I, 336–337. On the threat that Anne Hutchinson's aggressive persona posed to Hooker, see Porterfield, *Female Piety*, 53. Knight describes the greater presence of masculine images of the saint in Hooker's sermons in contrast to the uniformly feminized saintliness of Cotton; see *Orthodoxies in Massachusetts*, 226 n. 30.

nologies and supervisory skills that deserved respect from the laity. His animated pulpit delivery and advice to troubled souls displayed his commitment to the authority of the minister and his belief in the sermon as the most important converting ordinance.[37]

The trials of Anne Hutchinson reveal the complex and competing understandings of speech and text as performance genres among the Massachusetts colonists and point to the intricate relationship between verbal forms and social identity in the shaping of a new cultural order. Adapting the hierarchy of textual and oral forms developed in colonization narratives to project an image of docile and assimilable natives readily accepting the authority of Scripture, Puritan patriarchs sought to contain the threat that Hutchinson posed by portraying her speech as a disruption and violation of sacred text rather than its confirmation. Puritan claims to create a more authentically spiritual oral domain than their Anglican opponents only intensified their vulnerability to challenges such as Hutchinson's. She proved such a lightning rod for patriarchal wrath because as a publicly articulate woman she incarnated Puritan linguistic anxieties that Cotton and Hooker variously sought to resolve in their distinct styles of sermon performance. Hutchinson and the other antinomians raised a question central to a Puritan faith anxious about the proper relationship between spirit and matter, voice and text: could a saint believe that "the immediate revelation of [her] good estate, without any respect to the Scriptures, is as cleare to [her], as the voyce of God from Heaven to *Paul*"? John Cotton's rigorous distinction between Word and Spirit seemed to give authoritative backing to this belief. The privileging of voice over text undercut the careful Puritan balance between oral immediacy and textual stability, mocking fears of demonic deception as the anxieties of the unconverted who were strangers to the beloved's voice. In claiming her own privileged relation to the divine voice, Hutchinson refused to submit to the discipline of scriptural text and the associated linguistic and interpretive skills that bore with them the weight of social and gender hierarchies. Governor John Winthrop, who led the prosecution of Hutchinson, offered a description of her that suggests the sources of his hostility:

37. Thomas Hooker, *The Application of Redemption, by the Effectual Work of the Word. . . . The Ninth and Tenth Books* (London, 1657), 54. Hooker's role in the Antinomian Controversy was limited by the distance between Hartford and Boston, but he did chair an August 1637 synod where unorthodox lay opinions were condemned, clerical differences disputed and temporarily settled, and congregational behavior regulated. Most significant among the new regulations governing lay behavior were the restrictions on women's meetings, strict limits on lay questioning after a sermon, and a policy denying a church member the right to move between congregations for differences of opinion not considered fundamental; see Richard S. Dunn, James Savage, and Laetitia Yeandle, eds., *The Journal of John Winthrop, 1630–1649* (Cambridge, Mass., 1996), 232–235.

A woman had been the breeder and nourisher of all these distempers, one Mistris *Hutchinson,* the wife of Mr. *William Hutchinson* of *Boston* (a very honest and peaceable man of good estate) and the daughter of Mr. *Marbury,* sometimes a Preacher in *Lincolnshire,* after of *London,* a woman of a haughty and fierce carriage, of a nimble wit and active spirit, and a very voluble tongue, more bold than a man, though in understanding and judgement, inferiour to many women.[38]

Winthrop's characterization falls into two parts: descriptions of her husband and father, whose identities are stably grounded through references to their financial condition or career and their places of residence; and a portrait of Hutchinson's public behavior or "conversation," in which Winthrop lets loose a vituperative rhetorical flow that exceeds the bounds of his earlier plain prose much as Hutchinson allegedly exceeded the bounds set by her role as wife and daughter. Winthrop's antithesis squeezes Hutchinson between its pincers. Not timid as a proper woman should be, she is even bolder than a man, yet less intelligent than the best of her inferior sex.[39]

As a lawyer, Winthrop was well versed in the ambiguities of the rhetorical artifice that he employed against Hutchinson and profoundly aware of the power it conferred. For centuries, rhetoric had been linked to the classical education and legal training restricted to men, providing a tool of linguistic control that allowed those knowledgeable in the art entrance into elite public discourse. But historically, rhetoric has also been figured in feminine terms as a luxurious linguistic dress or cosmetic, an embellishment of bare meaning, a verbal ornament that de-

38. Winthrop, *A Short Story of the Rise, Reign, and Ruine of the Antinomians, Familists, and Libertines,* in Hall, ed., *The Antinomian Controversy,* 238, 262–263. For conflicting views on Hutchinson as a figure of dissent, see Patricia Caldwell, "The Antinomian Language Controversy," *Harvard Theological Review,* LXIX, nos. 3–4 (1976), 345–367; Amy Schrager Lang, *Prophetic Woman: Anne Hutchinson and the Problem of Dissent in the Literature of New England* (Berkeley, Calif., 1987). in Hall, ed., *The Antinomian Controversy,* 238. Hutchinson and her followers were branded "Antinomians" by their opponents after their defeat. They seem not to have adopted a party label, as suits their linguistic and social theory. Major discussions of the Antinomian Controversy that I have found helpful include Emery Battis, *Saints and Sectaries: Anne Hutchinson and the Antinomian Controversy in the Massachusetts Bay Colony* (Chapel Hill, N.C., 1962); William K. B. Stoever, *'A Faire and Easie Way to Heaven': Covenant Theology and Antinomianism in Early Massachusetts* (Middletown, Conn., 1978); Philip F. Gura, *A Glimpse of Sion's Glory: Puritan Radicalism in New England, 1620–1660* (Middletown, Conn., 1984), chap. 9; David S. Lovejoy, *Religious Enthusiasm in the New World: Heresy to Revolution* (Cambridge, Mass., 1985), chap. 4.

39. For an analysis of the prevalent understanding of women's nature that bears on Winthrop's curious description of Hutchinson, see Phyllis Mack, *Visionary Women: Ecstatic Prophecy in Seventeenth-Century England* (Berkeley, Calif., 1992), esp. 24, 29, 31.

stabilizes and distracts, thus potentially undermining the social hierarchy.[40] Puritan rhetorical writings are riddled with such feminizing metaphors. Anne Hutchinson represented the threat of a more literally feminine language that Winthrop used his rhetorical training to contain. Winthrop's language both at the trial and in his subsequent written account evokes both meanings associated with rhetoric, bringing them simultaneously into play only to project the effeminacy on Hutchinson while retaining the verbal power for himself. His figurally sophisticated description of Hutchinson, particularly in contrast to the plain prose he uses to characterize her father and husband, suggests the destabilizing effects he associated with her speech and seeks to contain those effects in recognizable linguistic forms identified with elite masculine eloquence.

Winthrop makes clear that Hutchinson's excess was verbal. An articulate woman ("high-flowne in spirit and speech," Thomas Welde called her), she felt comfortable addressing large groups, holding forth to "sixty or eighty" in her home. At her church trial, John Wilson, who had borne the brunt of Hutchinson's criticism, identified the source of her errors in her slighting and disrespectful behavior toward both magistrates and ministers when he blamed her for wanting "to set up *your selfe in the Roome of God above others that you might be extolled and admired and followed after, that you might be a greate Prophites . . . and Undertake to expound Scriptures, and to interpret other Mens Sayings and sermons after your minde."*

Bay Colony historian Edward Johnson's portrayal of one Hutchinsonian's boastful description of her speech captured the way spiritual and social issues complemented each other:

> Come along with me, says one of them, i'le bring you to a Woman that Preaches better Gospell then any of your black-coates that have been at the Ninneversity, a Woman of another kinde of spirit, who hath had many Revelations of things to come, and for my part, saith hee, I had rather hear such a one that speakes from the meere motion of the spirit, without any study at all, then any of your learned Scollers, although they may be fuller of Scripture . . .

---

40. Richard J. Schoeck, "Lawyers and Rhetoric in Sixteenth-Century England," in James J. Murphy, ed., *Renaissance Eloquence: Studies in the Theory and Practice of Renaissance Rhetoric* (Berkeley, Calif., 1983), 274–291. See also Patricia Parker, "On the Tongue: Cross Gendering, Effeminacy, and the Art of Words," *Style*, XXIII (Fall 1989), 445–465. She argues that, in rhetorical treatises of Renaissance humanists and in the theater those treatises influenced, the "spectre of effeminacy is one that haunts, with a remarkable commonality of instances, the whole province of the lingual" (459). She concludes with a reading of a play addressing such linguistic anxieties that was performed by Cambridge undergraduates around 1602, approximately the time that Winthrop would have been at the university.

and admit they may speake by the helpe of the spirit, yet the other goes beyond them.[41]

Johnson portrayed what he perceived to be the conflict's essence: a debate over the nature of preaching—including its relationship to textual forms—and the preacher's social status. These remarks cut to the heart of the Puritan plain style. Perkins's characterization of the Puritan sermon's artless artifice as "the hiding of human wisdom" joined to "the demonstration or showing of the Spirit" is taken apart and the two requirements set in irresolvable opposition.[42] "Ninneversity" training or the acquisition of human wisdom could not be adequately hidden, Johnson's antinomian implied. Its possession necessarily conceals the Spirit rather than demonstrates it. Even a genuinely inspired scholar will be a less effective preacher than one free from learning's impedimenta. And who would be less impeded by such obstacles, more authentic in her articulations of the divine will, than a woman formally excluded from institutions of higher education? When Deputy Governor Thomas Dudley, referring to Hutchinson's written recantation, charged that "her *Repentance is in a paper* . . . but suer *her Repentance is not in her Countenance,* none cane see it thear I thinke," he captured the pervasive image of Hutchinson as a woman who transgressed by performing oral, embodied excess in relation to scriptural texts and their gendered technologies.[43]

At her General Court trial in the Newtown meetinghouse, Hutchinson explained to the assembled magistrates and ministers "the ground of what I know to be true." Her mystical sense of the insufficiency of all human forms gave her confidence to speak despite the fact that, as she said, "the Lord knows that I could not open scripture; he must by his prophetical office open it unto me." In the midst of the competing viewpoints represented by the learned elders, Hutchinson spoke with the prophetic voice of assured truth. Her prophecy began as a narration of decisive moments when she heard the Spirit speaking to her soul, in which she interwove her life events with scriptural passages:

41. Winthrop, *A Short Story of the Rise,* in Hall, ed., *The Antinomian Controversy,* 269, 380–381; Edward Johnson, *Johnson's Wonder-Working Providence, 1628–1651,* ed. J. Franklin Jameson (New York, 1910), 127.

42. Perkins, "The Art of Prophecying," in *Works of That Famous and Worthy Minister,* II, 670.

43. *A Report of the Trial of Mrs. Ann Hutchinson before the Church in Boston . . .* (1638), in Hall, ed., *The Antinomian Controversy,* 379. John Morgan discusses Puritan ambivalence toward learning in *Godly Learning: Puritan Attitudes towards Reason, Learning, and Education, 1560–1640* (Cambridge, 1986), esp. chap. 4. This is not to say, as Patricia Caldwell does in "The Antinomian Language Controversy," *Harvard Theological Review,* LXIX (1976), 345–367, that Hutchinson occupied a universe closer to "primary orality" than the universe of the clergy. A profoundly literate woman, Hutchinson contested gendered spiritual hierarchies by endowing inspired speech with a higher, divine authority than the manmade and -controlled scriptural technologies that ministers employed to prepare their sermons.

When our teacher [Cotton] came to New-England it was a great trouble unto me, my brother Wheelwright being put by also. I was then much troubled concerning the ministry under which I lived, and then that place in the 30th of Isaiah was brought to my mind. Though the Lord give thee bread of adversity and water of affliction yet shall not thy teachers be removed into corners any more, but thine eyes shall see thy teachers. The Lord giving me this promise and they being gone there was none then left that I was able to hear, and I could not be at rest but I must come hither. Yet that place of Isaiah did much follow me, though the Lord give thee the bread of adversity and water of affliction. This place lying I say upon me then this place in Daniel was brought unto me and did shew me that though I should meet with affliction yet I am the same God that delivered Daniel out of the lion's den, I will also deliver thee.

Hutchinson structured her prophecy as personal narrative, charting the scriptural conjunction between her earthly travails and her spiritual condition. The metaphors that she employed in her prophetic speech echoed and sought to transform negative figurations of female voice that were often used to control women's public expression. Acknowledging that she was untrained in the interpretive skills that allowed preachers to "open" scriptural texts, Hutchinson described her relation to the Bible as simultaneously passive and procreative. Passages were brought to her, followed her, even, in a sexual metaphor, laid upon her, producing more texts. The Lord promised to "deliver" her. Two of Hutchinson's acknowledged beliefs later deemed heretical are relevant here: "We are united to Christ with the same union, that his humanity on earth was with the Deity" and "In union with Christ, Christ comes into the man, and he retaines the seed, and dieth, and then all manner of grace in himselfe, but all in Christ." A midwife and mother of fifteen, Hutchinson modeled justification on the potency of female reproduction, imagining it as a form of impregnation resembling the Virgin Mary's experience as the Mother of God. We should not underestimate Hutchinson's rhetorical sophistication or her awareness of the threat she posed. The pervasive language of feminized sainthood characteristic of Puritan spirituality, and realized with particular directness in the ministry of John Cotton, only intensified Hutchinson's claims to social and spiritual power based on a theological imagery of female sexuality.[44]

Responding to a disunified and uncertain court, Hutchinson's concluding words projected a thoroughly univocal and transcendent subject, emptied of selfhood and speaking with the Lord's voice. She had effected a verbal union with God, and now she ended with a prediction and a curse directed at the court, identifying herself as a Jeremiah warning the Israelites against apostasy:

44. Winthrop, *A Short Story of the Rise*, in Hall, ed., *The Antinomian Controversy*, 302, 336–338.

Therefore I desire you to look to it, for you see this scripture fulfilled this day and therefore I desire you that as you tender the Lord and the church and commonwealth to consider and look what you do. You have power over my body but the Lord Jesus hath power over my body and soul, and assure yourselves thus much, you do as much as in you lies to put the Lord Jesus Christ from you, and if you go on in this course you begin you will bring a curse upon you and your posterity, and the mouth of the Lord hath spoken it.

The elders found her words threatening precisely because she claimed to offer a singular and unmediated access to the divine truth that they by their own admission could only approximate in collective fashion through scriptural interpretation. The act of prophecy itself was by no means an uncommon Puritan exercise. John Wilson was particularly noted for his predictive powers, and Thomas Hooker, like Hutchinson, once predicted the destruction of England. But Hutchinson lacked the objectivity and authority imputed on the basis of gender and education to a Wilson or a Hooker.[45]

Hutchinson's "I" began as a restless, troubled self that when coupled with scriptural revelations achieved stability of divine authority transcending even Scripture. Starting from a position of dependence on Scripture and the preached Word, Hutchinson simultaneously narrated and enacted her achievement of prophetic authority. She spoke with the Lord's voice, freed from the limitations that Scripture text imposed. Hutchinson later admitted to believing that "her particular revelations about future events are as infallible as any part of Scripture, and that she is bound as much to beleeve them, as the Scripture, for the same holy Ghost is the author of them both." Her emancipation from the written word and its ministerial purveyors permitted a liberation that was both psychological and linguistic.[46]

Developing a rhetorical countertradition to the Puritan sermon, Hutchinson sought to retain the positive associations of women's spirituality and sexuality as figurations of authentic voice while suppressing the hostile interpretive tradition derived from the misogynist literature. Her prophetic speech structurally resembles impregnation with grace: as the Lord's mouthpiece, she gave birth to the Word. This was a more intimate relation to the Lord than the prophetic impersonations available to the ministry. Her efforts to reshape female mysticism into a culturally acceptable mode of rhetorical performance were met by the thoroughly

---

45. Ibid., 338.
46. Ibid., 303. For a French feminist-inspired reading of the trial transcript, see Lad Tobin, "A Radically Different Voice: Gender and Language in the Trials of Anne Hutchinson," *Early American Literature*, XXV (1990), 253–270.

conventional yet powerfully effective strategy of control present in accusations of sexual misconduct and even witchcraft. Responding to Hutchinson's assertions, her accusers exploited conventional Renaissance beliefs about the relationship between female speech and sexuality and the need to establish male control over both.[47] John Cotton's warning to Hutchinson at her church trial that she was in danger of falling into adultery, his preoccupation with her alleged belief in a "Comunitie of Woemen," and the enormous interpretive investment in the "monstrous births" of her advocate Mary Dyer and Hutchinson herself all reveal the Puritan patriarchy's commitment to the figure of female speech as disruptive sexuality and disordered reproduction.

In the end Hutchinson was condemned for her independence of both speech and spirit. Winthrop attacked her for quoting

> one scripture after another, but all this while there is no use of the ministry of the word nor of any clear call of God by his word, but the ground work of her revelations is the immediate revelation of the spirit and not by the ministry of the word. . . . Ey it is the most desperate enthusiasm in the world, for nothing but a word comes to her mind and then an application is made which is nothing to the purpose, and this is her revelations when it is impossible but that the word and spirit should speak the same thing.

Winthrop denounced Hutchinson for demonstrating an inadequately modest relation to Scripture and a neglect of the preached Word. Even John Cotton concluded that Hutchinson's error was an insufficient reliance on sermons, her failure to reproduce the words of the ministry. As he related in *The Way of Congregational Churches Cleared* (1648), he warned her "that her Faith was not *begotten* nor (by her relation) scarce at any time strengthened, by publick Ministery, but by private Meditations, or Revelations onely." For Cotton as for Winthrop and the other ministers, the absence of the socially accepted linguistic forms that men defined and controlled demonstrated, not the immediate access to God that Hutchinson claimed, but the deviance of her imagination, the absence of humility, the failure to efface her erring and sinful self. She became the Puritan patriarchy's figure for female speech that claims an erotic intimacy with the Lord but falls instead into the spiritually and socially disruptive forms of autonomous and proliferating femininity that they labeled demonic.[48]

47. *Report of the Trial of Mrs. Ann Hutchinson*, in Hall, ed., *The Antinomian Controversy*, 372. Jane Kamensky summarizes seventeenth-century English attitudes toward women's speech in *Governing the Tongue: The Politics of Speech in Early New England* (New York, 1997), chap. 1.

48. *The Examination of Mrs. Anne Hutchinson at the Court at Newtown* (1637), in Hall, ed., *The Antinomian Controversy*, 341–342. In *Female Piety*, Porterfield echoes Winthrop in accusing

At her church trial, Hutchinson was punished like the biblical Miriam for claiming a special relation to the Lord and ordered *"as a Leper to withdraw your selfe out of the Congregation."* The leprosy with which the Lord afflicted Miriam for prophesying in competition with Moses functioned as a sign for disordered structures of authority marked on the body's surface. The visibility of that sign distinguished it from the mysteries of reproduction contained within the depths of the body. Hutchinson and her opposers employed competing tropes of the body to figure different theological paradigms of redemption. With the preparationist victory, physical signs were invested with meaning, and Miriam-like subjection became a type of the humiliated sinner that men as well as women could occupy. In John Winthrop's 1645 speech to the General Court, he identified himself with Miriam when he declared his humble acceptance of his admonishment, for "if her father had spitt in her face, (sayth the Lord concerninge Miriam) should she not have been ashamed 7: dayes?" Rejecting the role of Miriam, Hutchinson was soon cast as the idolatress Jezebel.[49]

Hutchinson and other female dissenters passed the boundaries of what was, in some ways, a relatively broad social arena within which Puritan women's voices could be heard. Women in seventeenth-century New England exercised a greater degree of verbal authority than their English sisters, particularly in the courtroom. As long as they participated in the effort to create a godly society as defined by the colony's male leaders, women were encouraged to speak out publicly against moral infractions. But the most persistent and influential role for a female speaker was the one that Anne Hutchinson conspicuously refused to play: the role of the Miriam-like penitent. Even in this "feminized" role, the genders were distinguished through their relationship to text. Women's confessions often involved the public display of the silent penitent with her written confession, suggesting the stabilizing, disciplinary functions that text performed upon female voice. When the courts compelled men to confess, they typically offered spoken repentance, demonstrating the magistrates' greater confidence in male verbal self-discipline. Women after Hutchinson who challenged the Puritan patriarchy's structures of

---

Hutchinson of "a disregard for language and lack of self-control that diminished her authority" (102). Her interpretation of Hutchinson overlooks the differently gendered constraints on public speech and Hutchinson's radical rhetorical project. See also Hall, ed., *The Antinomian Controversy*, 413 (emphasis added). Cotton Mather foregrounded the issue of fecundity in his account of Hutchinson in the *Magnalia*. For further discussion of Mather's approach, see Lang, *Prophetic Woman*, 68. Ivy Schweitzer explores the gendered dynamics of Puritan poetics in Schweitzer, *The Work of Self-Representation: Lyric Poetry in Colonial New England* (Chapel Hill, N.C., 1991); see esp. 27, 45 on a gendering of lyric voice in the Puritan elegy.

49. *Report of the Trial of Mrs. Ann Hutchinson*, in Hall, ed., *The Antinomian Controversy*, 388. See Appendix, below, for further discussion of Miriam and Moses. For Winthrop quotation, see Dunn, Savage, and Yeandle, eds., *Journal of John Winthrop*, 586.

authority through their public speech were repeatedly subjected to New England's efforts to govern women's tongues with textual discipline.[50]

IV. NATIVE SPEECH AND THE DISCIPLINE OF TEXT

The textual prophylaxis that Puritan leaders employed to control the internal threat of multiplicity that women's oppositional speech represented was matched by their use of text to distinguish English eloquence from native speech traditions and thus to contain a threat of multiplicity from outside their speech community. Puritan descriptions of native American government based on oral suasion revealed their anxiety about the uses of eloquence in their own communities. Puritan rhetorical theory sought to define forms of eloquence that did not in and of themselves persuade the audience. Only the Spirit could truly convert a saint. Puritan writers both identified with and excoriated the figure of the eloquently manipulative Indian orator, their ambivalence registering the danger of symbolic contamination from his proximity. "If they be eloquent," Roger Williams observed of native leaders in *A Key into the Language of America* (1645), their followers "esteeme them Gods, as Herod among the *Jewes.*" Puritan writers imagined native Americans held captive within their own communities through the persuasive force of eloquence and contrasted their own sacred and secular orders drawn from holy writ to what they perceived as Indian idolatry. Williams claimed that among the Narragansetts "the Sachims, although they have an absolute Monarchie over all the people; yet they will not conclude of ought that concernes all, either Lawes, or Subsides, or warres, unto which the people are averse, and by gentle perswasion cannot be brought." Characterizing a ruler who exerts "gentle perswasions" as an absolute monarch, Williams demonstrates the inadequacy of European political concepts for understanding native cultures. The twinned conceptions of native American government as anarchic and tyrannical have their source in Western fascination with and distrust of oratorical influence, an ambivalence that has roots in the ancient world.[51]

50. See Cornelia Hughes Dayton, *Women before the Bar: Gender, Law, and Society in Connecticut, 1639–1789* (Chapel Hill, N.C., 1995), 9–10, esp. 199, 322; Kamensky, *Governing the Tongue,* 182–184. On the social uses and practices of confession and apology in New England, see Kamensky, *Governing the Tongue,* chap. 5, esp. 134–135. On the symbolism of speech, text, and silence in Quaker theology, see Richard Bauman, *Let Your Words Be Few: Symbolism of Speaking and Silence among Seventeenth-Century Quakers* (Cambridge, 1983), Kamensky describes the Puritan conflict with the Quakers as "a struggle over the cultural meanings of speech" in *Governing the Tongue,* 118. On female dissenters in New England, see Lyle Koehler, *A Search for Power: The "Weaker Sex" in Seventeenth-Century New England* (Urbana, Ill., 1980).

51. On the coincidence of the Antinomian Controversy with the Pequot War in 1637, see Ann

Williams offers a more astute analysis of Narragansett rhetorical practices in the chapter on "Discourse and Newes," where he sketches the nature and function of Indian assemblies:

> Their manner is upon any tidings to sit round double or treble or more, as their numbers be; I have seene neer a thousand in a round, where *English* could not well neere halfe so many have sitten: Every man hath his pipe of their *Tobacco,* and a deepe silence they make, attention give to him that speaketh; and many of them will deliver themselves, either in a relation of news, or in a consultation, with very emphaticall speech and great action, commonly an hour, and sometimes two houres together.

Like other European observers at such assemblies, Williams remarks on the impressive and emphatic eloquence of native speakers, their stamina in highly physical performances, and the strict order and respect that the audience granted the orator. At such scenes of collective decision making, Indian councils debated the most crucial issues for their societies, including whether to make war or peace, sell land, negotiate a treaty, or hold a ceremony to combat illness or bring rain.[52]

The translated phrases with which Williams surrounds his description of a council meeting demonstrate the Narragansetts' rich vocabulary for describing belief and doubt, understanding, knowledge, opinion, and persuasiveness. He notes that "Coanaumwem," or "You speake true," and "Wunnaumwaw ewo," or "He speaks true," were frequently heard terms of approval and flattery. Spoken truth became an increasingly pressing and conflict-ridden issue as native Americans held conferences and made treaties with Europeans whose written records did not always reflect Indian memories of the agreement.[53] The question of

---

Kibbey, *The Interpretation of Material Shapes in Puritanism: A Study of Rhetoric, Prejudice, and Violence* (Cambridge, 1986), 107. For Williams's comment, see Roger Williams, *A Key into the Language of America,* in *The Complete Writings of Roger Williams,* 7 vols. (New York, 1963), I, 83, 164. On descriptions of Indian government as both tyrannical and anarchic, see Francis Jennings, *The Invasion of America: Indians, Colonialism, and the Cant of Conquest* (New York, 1975), 59–60; Axtell, *The Invasion Within,* 136. On the breakdown of the Massachusett Indians' political order following the devastating mortality brought on by European disease, see Dane Morrison, *A Praying People: Massachusett Acculturation and the Failure of the Puritan Mission, 1600–1690* (New York, 1995) 18–19. Williams's paradox may reflect a similar situation among the Narragansetts. Brian Vickers usefully analyzes the anti-rhetorical strain in Western philosophy in *In Defence of Rhetoric* (Oxford, 1988), chap. 2. On the history of ambivalence about language as a tool for political life in the West, see Thomas Gustafson, *Representative Words: Politics, Literature, and the American Language, 1776–1865* (Cambridge, 1992), part 2.

52. Williams, *A Key into the Language of America,* in Williams, *The Complete Writings of Roger Williams,* 82–83. For a useful discussion of oratory's importance within native societies, see Axtell, *The Invasion Within,* 87–88.

53. Williams, *A Key into the Language of America,* in Williams, *The Complete Writings of*

whether the English spoke truth dominated Williams's diplomatic conference with Canounicus, the sachem of the Narragansetts, at the time of the Pequot War (1637), which Williams reported in one of the earliest recorded Indian orations from New England. "I have never suffered any wrong to be offered to the *English* since they landed; nor never will," Canounicus insisted, repeating "this word, *Wunnaumwayean, Englishman;* if the *Englishman* speake true, if hee meane truly, then shall I goe to my grave in peace, and hope that the *English* and my posteritie shall live in love and peace together." Williams responded that "he had no cause (as I hoped) to question *Englishmans, Wunnaumwauonck,* that is, faithfulnesse, he having had long experience of their friendlinesse and trustinesse." Canounicus then "tooke a sticke and broke it into ten pieces, and related ten instances (laying downe a sticke to every instance) which gave him cause thus to feare and say." Williams remarked on some of the features of native eloquence that most struck European listeners: the repetitive wording and the use of mnemonic devices that served as a form of writing, most familiarly belts of wampum but in this instance a broken stick.[54]

In his chapter on native religion, Williams describes a sacred rhetorical practice strikingly similar to the Puritan sermon: "Their wise men and old men of which number the Priests also, whom they call Taupowauog they make solemn speeches and Orations, or Lectures to them, concerning Religion, Peace, or Warre and all things." Both Europeans and native Americans identified textuality, particularly the use of Scripture, as the crucial difference between Puritan preaching and Indian sacred oratory. Like Thomas Harriot, Williams claimed that the Narragansetts shared the English view of text as a mark of technological and spiritual superiority, asserting that the European possession of "*Clothes, Bookes,* [and] *Letters*" persuaded the Indians "that the *God* that made *English* men is a greater *God*" than their own. Williams recorded an occasion when he "had (as farre as my language would reach) discoursed (upon a time) before the chiefe *Sachim* or *Prince* of the Countrey, with his *Archpriestes,* and many other in a full Assembly" on Christian doctrine. When a Connecticut Indian challenged some of Williams's assertions, the sachem Miantunnomu reportedly replied, "He hath books and writings, and one which God himselfe made, concerning mens soules, and therefore may well know more then wee that have none, but take all upon trust from our forefathers." Even Williams admitted that not all native Americans agreed with the idea that the European possession of sacred texts demonstrated superior spiritual

Roger Williams, I, 83. On the inaccuracy of European treaties regarding agreements reached in negotiations, see Jennings, *The Invasion of America,* 121, 124, 191.

54. Williams, *A Key into the Language of America,* in Williams, *The Complete Writings of Roger Williams,* I, 85.

. knowledge. Williams records one skeptical native response to Christian doctrine: "When I had discoursed about many points of God, of the creation, of the soule, of the danger of it, and the saving of it, he assented; but when I spake of the rising againe of the body, he cryed out, I shall never believe this."[55]

Williams was a devout Puritan deeply committed to the authority of Scripture. Yet his dissenting relationship to the New England Puritan hierarchy made him quite literally a marginal figure whose experiences in exile gave him insights into Narragansett society that were unusual for an Englishman.[56] Williams's relatively deep understanding of and appreciation for Narragansett society included a lively sense of the spoken word's power for them and the importance of authentic speech that Canounicus demanded. Williams warned that mastery of native languages must precede evangelism, for pidgin Narragansett would never convert native speakers: "It must be a great deale of practise, and mighty paines and hardship undergone by my selfe, or any that would proceed to such a further degree of the Language, as to be able in propriety of speech to open matters of salvation to them. In matters of Earth men will helpe to spell out each other, but in matters of Heaven (to which the soule is naturally so averse) how far are the Eares of man hedged up from listening to all improper Language?" Only persuasive speeches delivered in native tongues would adequately overcome sinful man's aversion to holy truths. Despite his familiarity with the Narragansett tongue, Williams doubted that God had called him to a converting ministry. He remained unsure about missionizing and its motives, holding that the millennium must ensue "before the Law and word of life be sent forth to the rest of the Nations of the World, who have not heard of Christ." Had Williams continued with his early missionary efforts, he might have developed a missionary style with some fidelity to native oral modes of spiritual practice.[57]

Instead, Roxbury minister John Eliot provided a radically text-oriented model for Puritan missionary activities that remained the standard into the eighteenth century. New England's earliest sustained missionary efforts began only around 1645, after the colonists had established significant territorial control and con-

55. Ibid., 23, 84, 152–153, 159–160.

56. Anne Golda Myles highlights the relationship between Williams as a dissenter from the New England Way and Williams as an astute and sympathetic student of Narragansett language and culture in " 'Called Out': Languages of Dissent in Early America" (Ph.D. diss., University of Chicago, 1993), chap. 3. Two other readings of *A Key into the Language of America* that work out related but slightly different understandings of Williams's marginal position are Gordon Brotherston, "A Controversial Guide to the Language of America, 1643," in Francis Barker et al., eds., *1642: Literature and Power in the Seventeenth Century* (Essex, 1981), 84–100; Schweitzer, *The Work of Self-Representation,* chap. 5.

57. Roger Williams, "Christenings Make Not Christians," in Williams, *The Complete Writings of Roger Williams,* VII, 40.

trol over native bodies through war and assassination.[58] Pressure from England and Eliot's commitment led to the creation of Praying Towns, which required the physical relocation of native individuals and whole communities. Preaching and religious debate were essential aspects of the missionary effort, facilitated by translators such as Montauk Indian Cockenoe-de-Long Island and Massachusett Indian Job Nesuton. Accounts of the Praying Indian church services emphasize the participatory oral activities of catechizing, psalm singing, and praying, sacred forms that might have permitted accommodation of traditional practices. But the semiotic center of the missionary project as Eliot imagined it resided in the culturally and spiritually converting powers of text. For Eliot, Indian conversions were metaphoric transcriptions, textualizations of a blank oral culture, and in his conversion accounts "the Book" is the central symbol. "My scope is to write and imprint no nother but Scripture principles in the *abrasa tabula scraped board* of these naked people," he declared.[59] Eliot planned to overcome cultural difference defined as Indian scriptlessness through the introduction of text into all aspects of native life, secular as well as sacred. Written legal codes, literacy training, and daily religious meetings where prayers were read aloud from a booklet characterized life in the Praying Towns. If Eliot's Indians were to escape idolatry, then Algonquian language, bodies, and social practices must be written over with Scripture. Moving between "utopian writing and practice," the Praying Towns had a textual origin and gave rise to Eliot's prolific textual production. Eliot relied on a cadre of native translators, writers, and printers, some of them educated at Harvard's Indian College after its establishment in 1656. His most famous text, produced in large numbers with the assistance of James Printer (Wowaus), was his 1663 Algonquian translation of the Bible, the first attempt to render Scripture in a native American tongue.[60]

---

58. James Holstun's astute analysis of "John Eliot's Empirical Millennialism" foregrounds the textual thematics and practices in Eliot's Praying Towns and his writings about them. See Holstun, *A Rational Millennium: Puritan Utopias of Seventeenth-Century England and America* (New York, 1987), chap. 3. Neal Salisbury argues that the Puritan commitment to dominating prospective converts postponed missionary efforts until the colonialists had established substantial territorial control in "Red Puritans: The 'Praying Indians' of Massachusetts Bay and John Eliot," *WMQ*, 3d Ser., XXXI (1974), 27–54. On Puritan explanations that language barriers, the rigors of settlement, and the projected temporary nature of the commonwealth experiment prevented earlier efforts, see Morrison, *A Praying People*, 38–41.

59. On Eliot's effacement of his translators, who are unnamed in his published works, see Murray, *Forked Tongues*, 7. On native American oral culture as a blank slate, see John Eliot, "The Learned Conjectures Touching the Americas," quoted in James Holstun, *A Rational Millennium*, 111; see also 138.

60. On the written legal codes of John Eliot's Praying Towns, which regulated everything from Sabbath worship and lapses into "idolatrous" powwowing to hair length and louse biting,

Eliot's textual orientation shaped his hopes for his own society as well. In *A Christian Commonwealth* (1659), Eliot envisioned a scriptural utopia that he imagined could be applied to England and New England, remaking them along lines drawn from the Bible. His ambitions to turn the communities of New England into *"abrasa tabula"* on which to write "Scripture principles" proved too radical for Puritan magistrates, who suppressed its publication. Although the colonists themselves resisted remaking their communities so radically in a biblical image, Eliot was able to test his utopia on the decimated and deracinated Algonquian communities of New England. These communities had lost the "wisdom" that had once provided them with structures of order and meaning. Towanquatick, a Wampanoag sachem from Martha's Vineyard, told of cultural knowledge that was lost when large numbers of elders died suddenly. His community had once had "wise men, which in a grave manner taught the people knowledge," Towanquatick explained, "but they are dead, and their wisdom is buried with them." In 1646 the Massachusetts government contributed to this deracination by outlawing native forms of worship. The loss of oral traditions created a cultural void that Christian Scripture helped fill in a complex and contested process of native accommodation to the written word.[61]

The English reliance on written deeds made literacy a crucial secular as well as sacred skill for natives involved in land transfers. Although native literacy rates probably remained low, some Algonquians were drawn to the technological and symbolic power of text, including James Printer and Harvard's four seventeenth-century Indian graduates, Caleb Cheeshahteaumauk, Joel Hiacoomes, John Wompowess, and Eleazar. Yet literacy did not assure assimilation. Despite the intimate ties to the Puritan community exemplified in his work on Eliot's Bible, James Printer joined Wampanoag sachem King Philip in resisting the English in 1675, his shift in allegiance exposing the ambivalence that often attended native acquisition of literacy. John Sassamon, the literate native whose murder sparked King

---

see Axtell's discussion in *The Invasion Within*, 142. Murray discusses Eliot's "textualisation of Indian speech" (7) in *The Dying Speeches of Several Indians* (1685) in *Forked Tongues*, 34–35.

For descriptions of the native translators, printers, and writers who participated in Eliot's missionary project, see Walter T. Meserve, "English Works of Seventeenth-Century Indians," *American Quarterly*, VIII (Fall 1956), 264–276; Bernd Peyer, *The Tutor'd Mind: Indian Missionary-Writers in Antebellum America* (Amherst, Mass., 1997), 35–53.

61. On the populist Fifth Monarchism of *The Christian Commonwealth* in the Interregnum debates over a scriptural polity, see Holstun, *A Rational Millennium*, 145–158. For Towanquatick's comment, see Morrison, *A Praying People*, 28, 48–49. On the outlawing of native forms of worship, see Salisbury, "Red Puritans," *WMQ*, 3d Ser., XXXI (1974), 31. On missionaries' accounts of written law and Scripture as sources of stability and order, see Morrison, *A Praying People*, 63–64. As King Philip's War revealed, "Praying Indians" often held complex affiliations, and textual knowledge could be a source of antagonism and disruption.

Philip's War, demonstrated a different kind of ambivalence in his complicated and possibly duplicitous uses of his bilingual literacy. His efforts to parlay his reading and writing skills into an influential (and perhaps self-interested) mediatory role between Philip and the English might have cost him his life. Philip, who resisted conversion to Christianity and could not read or write himself, perhaps suspected Sassamon of cheating him in land deeds and other English legal documents.[62] That suspicion might have been behind Sassamon's murder, which sparked a war that threatened the existence of the English colonies, devastated the Algonquian population of New England, and largely ended the missionary effort. All but a few copies of *The Indian Bible,* the central textual symbol of Eliot's missionary effort, were destroyed, perhaps by Algonquians hostile to Christianity, perhaps by English colonists hostile to the Praying Indians.

Even as native Americans began to acquire the technologies of alphabetic literacy, then, text persisted as a sign of cultural difference in seventeenth-century New England. The symbolic power and actual uses of the written and printed word were so fully determined by the English colonists that the Algonquians remained unable to develop alternative textual practices and meanings. The Puritan patriarchy's symbolic use of text is strikingly consistent with Thomas Harriot's from a century earlier: a source of fixed, divinely guaranteed truths that could be authentically and authoritatively voiced only by the English men who possessed the tools of interpretation. Alternative forms of speech, whether of dissenting women or of native American leaders, elicited figurations of embodied excess—including sexual volatility and physical violence—that required textual discipline. By century's end, cultural shifts began to undermine this system of verbal symbolism, bringing into clearer focus the socially constituted nature of the written and spoken words.

---

62. Jill Lepore cites Plymouth literacy rates in 1674, when 29 percent of 497 converted Indians could read the Massachusett language, 14 percent could write, and 2 percent could read English (*The Name of War,* 36–44). Lepore notes that Sassamon's literacy skills put him in an untenable position that led to his death (43).

1 Gender in Performance

I. EVANGELICAL PERFORMANCE OF SPEECH AND TEXT

Like the events of Boston in 1636–1637 and on the colonial frontier in 1675–1676, the events in Salem in 1692 revolved around a complex symbolism of speech and text. The group of girls and young women who leveled accusations of witchcraft against a large number of prominent men and women in their community exercised a social and spiritual power unprecedented in the Bay Colony for those of their age and gender. They achieved such power through their ability to manipulate the meanings that the Puritan community attached to oral and written forms.

The witchcraft crisis can be construed as a set of performances in which accusers and accused staged a parodic reversal of the social order based upon the Puritan patriarchy's textual discipline of unruly (female, native American) figures of speech. The proceedings at Salem were driven less by the magistrates than by the possessed girls and women whose early allegations of spectral torments echoed the established paradigm of the witch as a verbally transgressive woman. Some of the accused reinforced this paradigm, particularly the Indian slave Tituba. Tituba represented not only the dangers of female voice but also the forms of native American speech that the patriarchal order rigorously sought to control, particularly in the aftermath of King Philip's War. Crucial aspects of the trials were determined by Tituba's testimony. In her coerced confession early in the proceedings, she wove together English folkways and magic lore with Indian and perhaps African spiritual practices, introducing at a defining moment the figure of "savage" orality behind a Puritan facade. The possessed girls, the magistrates and ministers, and even some of the accused witches themselves collaborated to construct the deviant orality of the accused in relation to a central textual symbol: the devil's book containing their marks or signatures, a parody of the holy covenant upon which the Puritan community based itself.[1] The accusations

1. On the verbal transgressions of accused witches, see Carol F. Karlsen, *The Devil in the Shape of a Woman: Witchcraft in Colonial New England* (New York, 1987), chap. 4. On the rela-

of supernatural maleficence at Salem erupted shortly before the new governor Sir William Phips arrived carrying a royal charter to replace the old colonial charter that had been suspended in 1685. The new charter tied the colony more closely to England and required religious toleration for Quakers and other Dissenters. Like the new charter, the satanic pact overturned an old order and compromised the identity and autonomy of its signatories. The single alleged act of signing the pact had the power to dismantle even the most saintly personality, transforming godly women into agents of Satan. As more and more people across the social spectrum were accused and imprisoned, they formed an abject body that quickly threatened to destroy social distinctions of rank as well as godliness, incorporating the elite with the lowly.

The accused witches were portrayed as figures of destabilizing, demonic voice tendering a false text, but their speech during the hearings was constrained, subject to the discipline of the court. Records of the proceedings incorporate the speech of the accusing girls and women in much richer detail. In the courtroom where they enacted the spectral torments, in their bedrooms where they admitted observers, and in public places such as the church, the possessed women and girls performed vigorous verbal assaults that had as their double target the men and women that they accused of witchcraft and, more obliquely, figures of patriarchal authority. Mimicking the verbal skills of the ministry, the demoniacs provided a mirror for the colony's spiritual leaders, who heard in their speech the voices of God and Satan battling over the colony's future. At times the possessed women and girls resisted the ministers' authority directly, denying the authenticity of their sermons or challenging their use of Scripture. Elizabeth Knapp told Samuel Willard that he preached "a company of lies" and ordered him to "hold your tongue." At public worship Abigail Williams demanded of visiting minister Deodat Lawson, *"Now stand up, and Name your Text,"* commented derisively on the length of the text, and asserted that he had no doctrine that she could remember. Bashua Pope announced at the beginning of Lawson's sermon, *"Now there is*

---

tionship between witchcraft accusations and women's public speech, see Sarah Grimké, "Letters on the Equality of the Sexes and the Condition of Women" (1838), in Alice S. Rossi, ed., *The Feminist Papers: From Adams to de Beauvoir* (New York, 1973), 306.

Despite a nineteenth-century tradition identifying Tituba as African, all of the contemporary records designate her as "Indian." On Tituba's ethnicity, see Elaine G. Breslaw, *Tituba, Reluctant Witch of Salem: Devilish Indians and Puritan Fantasies* (New York, 1996), 161–167; Bernard Rosenthal, "Tituba's Story," *NEQ*, LXXI (June 1998), 190–203. Tituba's testimony included a reference to the devil's reading to her from his book. Her interrogators ignored her description, focusing instead on the signatures they believed that the book contained. For an analysis of the references to literacy technologies, including the resemblance between Tituba's description of signing the devil's pact and signing a servant's indenture, see Breslaw, *Tituba, Reluctant Witch of Salem*, 122–126, 166, 188–197.

enough of that." Interpreted as the words of Satan, these performances of possession threatened to upset the ministry's claims to scriptural authority and disrupt
the sermon form built upon it.[2]

Undermining clerical authority through their stagings of verbal power, the demoniacs held sway over magistrates and ministers through their strategic deploy-
ment of textual knowledge. They recited Greek and Latin works, displaying the
language skills essential to the ministry's hermeneutic authority, or they cited
Scripture with clerical fluency in debates with Satan.[3] The speech of the possessed
differed from that of Anne Hutchinson, who distinguished her prophecy from a
sermon by modestly denying her ability to "open" Scripture even as she asserted a
more immediate access to the divine will. Hutchinson spoke as the Lord's mouth,
exceeding Scripture itself. The demoniacs voiced Scripture, exceeding the limits
of their prescribed gender identity. Flaunting forms of literacy that defined masculine authority, they posed a verbal challenge to the textual discipline that anchored the patriarchy of Puritan New England. The ministers and magistrates deflected this challenge by attributing their words to God and Satan.

The possessed women and girls in Salem exposed the performative nature of
the textual hierarchies that structured their society. When the possessed disrupted
a sermon, their disturbances registered a broad but unspecified resistance to clerical authority.[4] That authority was similarly challenged when women and girls
spoke in the dead languages of elite literacy or quoted Scripture as fluently as a
minister, exposing the artificiality of their exclusion from forms of power predi-
cated on command over these texts. The duplicity of possession that produced
the witchcraft crisis was exposed in subsequent decades when former demoniacs
confessed the falseness of their allegations. So, too, was revealed the duplicity of

2. Samuel Willard, "A Brief Account of a Strange and Unusual Providence of God Befallen
to Elizabeth Knapp of Groton" (1882), in John Demos, ed., *Remarkable Providences, 1600–1760*
(New York, 1972), 358–371, esp. 368; Deodat Lawson, *A Brief and True Narrative of Some Remarkable Passages Relating to Sundry Persons Afflicted by Witchcraft, at Salem Village . . .* (Boston,
1692), 3.

3. On the carnivalesque speech of the demoniac marked by uncommon linguistic skill, fluency, and authority, see Jane Kamensky, *Governing the Tongue: The Politics of Speech in Early
New England* (New York, 1997), 166.

4. Breslaw argues that Tituba helped to shape a "new idiom of resistance" that obliquely conveyed "a range of discontent with social, political, and religious conditions, particularly anti-
clerical sentiment among young women and servants" (*Tituba, Reluctant Witch of Salem*, 179).
On the witchcraft crisis, female voice, and the emergence of democratic personality, see Nancy
Ruttenberg, *Democratic Personality: Popular Voice and the Trials of American Authorship* (Stanford, Calif., 1998), chap. 1. Although Ruttenberg insists on the untheorized nature of the democratic challenge posed by such assertions of voice, I argue that from the Great Awakening the
challenge of popular voice as an antiauthoritarian realm was, in fact, theorized in the terms of
the performance semiotic.

the system of knowledge that excluded the afflicted from legitimately wielding the power they could manifest only in an elaborate and deadly masquerade.

The performances of the possessed were only one indication that the Puritan symbolic system that identified elite literacy with authentic spiritual knowledge was being denaturalized and recognized as a set of signs rather than a foundational truth. In a series of innovations that revealed the emergence of an increasingly metropolis-oriented seaboard culture with a novel understanding of textual and oral meaning, the elite Brattle Street Church that formed in 1699 under the leadership of Benjamin Colman challenged central components of Puritan spiritual practice. When the Anglicized Colman introduced the Anglican practices of set prayers and Bible readings into church services, these changes undermined assumptions about the appropriate uses of speech and text in religious life that had been fundamental to the New England way since colonization. The new textual practices served two symbolic functions. They were more orderly and predictable, less vulnerable to the vicissitudes of personal expression and the disruptions of the unlearned than the improvised prayers and personal testimonies that still characterized worship at most Congregational churches. And they tied the church into an expanding transatlantic world of print at a time when the meaning of the written or printed word was shifting. Books and writing were coming to be regarded less as icons of truth than as aesthetic objects, expressions and symbols of taste and sensibility.[5] This shift in textual symbolism was most evident on the urban seaboard, where printed matter was more readily available and manuscript literature circulated in the college, the coffeehouses, and the taverns. Sermons, particularly election sermons, became more literary, even incorporating the "flesh" of Latin quotations and classical allusions. Colman made important contributions to this transformation in the semiotics of text, producing elegant literary sermons in the English latitudinarian tradition of polite sensibility and publishing poetry that advanced the power of written representation to capture the inspired spoken Word.[6]

---

5. Larzer Ziff, *Puritanism in America: New Culture in a New World* (New York, 1973), 268–269; Harry S. Stout, *The New England Soul: Preaching and Religious Culture in Colonial New England* (New York, 1986), 130–131; David D. Hall, *Worlds of Wonder, Days of Judgment: Popular Religious Belief in Early New England* (New York, 1989), 243. On the emergence of a transatlantic, manuscript-based literary culture, see David S. Shields, *Civil Tongues and Polite Letters in British America* (Chapel Hill, N.C., 1997), chap. 2. Grantland S. Rice challenges Enlightenment accounts of the expansion of a free press in the eighteenth century, finding instead a debasement of public discourse due to market-oriented shifts in uses of print (*The Transformation of Authorship in America* [Chicago, 1997]).

6. Stout describes the trend toward "new styles of speech and new vocabularies" (*The New England Soul*, 140) as New England ministers addressed royal audiences, and he argues for the persistent importance of traditional covenant theology in the sacred portions of these sermons.

Cotton Mather represented a different side of the new semiotics of textuality among the Boston clergy who increasingly felt the pull of the imperial tie. Mather had an Augustinian commitment to the written word as a technology of self-discipline that produced a stable artifact in which God's will could be traced. This belief fueled the extraordinary stream of publications through which he sought both godliness and transatlantic literary fame. In two works published in the midst of the witchcraft crisis of 1692, *The Wonders of the Invisible World* and *Ornaments for the Daughters of Zion; or, The Character and Happiness of a Vertuous Woman,* Mather sought to reconstruct Puritan patriarchal authority through two starkly opposed, competing images of womanhood built around the distinction between pious writing and satanic speech. Writing *Ornaments* with his portraits of the verbally transgressive Salem witches as implicit foils, Mather sketched a figure for the daughters of Zion to emulate. He singled out for particular praise women who "have been the *writers* of [God's] *declarative word,*" noting, "*The Woman may not Speak in the Church;* Yet our God has Employ'd many *Women* to *Write* for the *Church,* and *Inspir'd* some of them for the Writing of the *Scriptures.*" Writing and even publication were desirable practices for women, according to Mather, who celebrated the literary career of Bay Colony poet Anne Bradstreet, whose works had been published in London. He linked women's writing to the production of an ascetic self-restraint similar to his own textual practices; female speech, however, required careful government. The noble faculty of speech is often abused, Mather complained, and "*womankind* is usually charged with a [pe]culiar share in the Worlds *Abuses* of it." "While you thus maintain the, *Fear of God,*" he urged, "Let it very particularly discover it self in your keeping the purpose of the Psalmist, *I will take heed unto my Ways that I Sin not with my Tongue; I will keep my Mouth with a Bridle.*" Imagined as a medium appropriate for self-effacement, in contrast to the self-enlarging qualities of demoniac speech, textual expression marked cultural distinctions and exerted social control. Mather constructed a similarly textualized identity for New England in his history *Magnalia Christi Americana,* which he began shortly after the witchcraft crisis and first published in England in 1702.

On Colman as an advocate of gentility and a practitioner of polite sensibility, see Ziff, *Puritanism in America,* 273–278. On Colman's influential elegy *A Poem on Elijahs Translation, Occasion'd by the Death of the Reverend and Learned Mr. Samuel Willard . . .* (1707) as an example of the literature of the religious sublime preoccupied with the "tension between the written and the spoken," see Shields, *Civil Tongues and Polite Letters,* 224–226. On Colman's sermon style, see Teresa Toulouse, *The Art of Prophesying: New England Sermons and the Shaping of Belief* (Athens, Ga., 1987), chap. 2.

On the English latitudinarian sources of sensibility beginning in the 1660s, see G. J. Barker-Benfield, *The Culture of Sensibility: Sex and Society in Eighteenth-Century Britain* (Chicago, 1992), 66–67. Norman Fiering traces the cult of sensibility to Puritan strains in *Moral Philosophy at Seventeenth-Century Harvard: A Discipline in Transition* (Chapel Hill, N.C., 1981), chap. 4.

Drawing on the rare materials collected in the extraordinary library that he inherited, Mather produced a chronicle of New England that proclaimed its distinctive identity as the modern Israel. Though Mather hoped that his printed history could produce stable, autonomous, and highly visible identities for himself and New England, his hopes were disappointed when his opus sold poorly.[7]

In 1723, Northampton minister Solomon Stoddard challenged the literary orientation of his Boston colleagues and signaled a shift in the symbolic forms of performance in *The Defects of Preachers Reproved,* an attack on preachers who substituted learning and morality for the authority of divine grace. Marking the emergence of an extemporaneous colonial style of preaching that resisted metropolitan literary influences, Stoddard insisted upon the potentially corrupting effects of texts. "Men of Learning may be led aside by reading erronious Books," he warned. "Learned Education will not deliver Men from carnal Reason."[8] Stoddard focused on the towns as places where true godliness was most rare and the people "carry on some what of the Form of Godliness, but mind little but the World and the Pleasures of this Life." The cause of urban spiritual deadness? "The Scribes did not preach with Authority." As an experienced revivalist with numerous spiritual "harvests" to his credit, Stoddard knew that preaching with authority meant stressing the stages of conversion and describing the horrors of damnation to undermine the complacency of the listener. Delivery was as important as content: *"The reading of Sermons is a dull Way of Preaching,"* Stoddard asserted. Like his predecessor on the colonial frontier with whom he is often compared, Thomas Hooker, Stoddard asserted the authority of the minister's energetic physical presence, creating an effect of extemporaneous immediacy. He championed vigorous delivery, performing without notes in order that "the Looks and Gesture of the Minister" may "command Attention, and stir up Affection." "Sermons that are read are not delivered with Authority," Stoddard stressed; "they savour of the Sermons of the Scribes."[9]

Defects located competing symbolisms of speech and text in sermon performance. Stoddard's repeated references to "the scribes" and book learning signaled the varied roles that writing and print played in binding Boston ministers to En-

7. Cotton Mather, *Ornaments for the Daughters of Zion; or, The Character and Happiness of a Vertuous Woman* (Cambridge, Mass., 1692), 5, 49–50. On Bradstreet, see Mather, *Magnalia Christi Americana; or, The Ecclesiastical History of New-England . . . ,* I (Hartford, Conn., 1855), 135. On Mather's anxious relationship to the London literary marketplace, see Ziff, *Puritanism in America,* 216–217, 297. Stout describes Mather's "almost mystical faith in the power of writing" (*The New England Soul,* 137). On the significance of writing as a technology of self-discipline for Mather, see Mitchell Robert Breitwieser, *Cotton Mather and Benjamin Franklin: The Price of Representative Personality* (Cambridge, 1984), 49–50, 63–64, 73–87.

8. Solomon Stoddard, *The Defects of Preachers Reproved . . . ,* 2d ed. (Boston, 1747), 5.

9. Ibid., 16, 18.

gland, transforming their sense of place and their relationship to their congregations and fostering preaching that was to his mind theologically unsound and performatively dead. With the arrival of George Whitefield in 1739, the tension about the proper performance of the sermon erupted into open partisanship in New England and throughout the colonies. Whitefield made affective extemporaneous preaching of the sort that Stoddard advocated the sign of evangelical commitment.[10] South Carolina's Josiah Smith remarked on the "noble negligence" of Whitefield's improvisational style. "With what a flow of words, what a ready profusion of language, did he speak to us upon the great concern of our souls?" Smith asked. But Whitefield impressed his audiences most with his "action and gesture, in all their strength and decencies." Famous throughout England and the English colonies for his talents as a performer, Whitefield brought the actor's appeal to the pulpit. Exercising the full power of his astonishingly flexible and appealing voice; posing, gesturing, and acting out biblical scenes; preaching to huge crowds outdoors rather than within the narrow confines of a meetinghouse pulpit; and speaking directly to spectators in order to draw the audience into the whole performance—Whitefield presented the sacred orator as passionate, embodied, and directly engaged with his viewers. "He appeared to me, in all his discourses, very deeply affected and impressed in his own heart," Smith observed. "How did that burn and boil within him, when he spake of the things he had made, touching the King?" The spiritual narrative of Nathan Cole, a Connecticut farmer, offers another vivid description of Whitefield's power as a performer:

> When I saw Mr Whitfield come upon the Scaffold he Lookt almost angelical; a young, Slim, slender, youth before some thousands of people with a bold undaunted Countenance . . . he looked as if he was Cloathed with authority from the Great God; *and a sweet sollome solemnity sat upon his brow* And my hearing him preach, gave me a heart wound; By Gods blessing: my old Foundation was broken up, and I saw that my righteousness would not save me.[11]

10. Whitefield was influenced by *Defects,* and he recommended the work to Harvard students. Richard L. Bushman notes, "The style of the itinerants in the Great Awakening, far from being an innovation in New England, was merely the continuation of the tradition Stoddard represented." *Defects* was brought out in a second edition for the instruction of the ministry in 1747 (*The Great Awakening: Documents on the Revival of Religion, 1740–1745* [Chapel Hill, N.C., 1969], 4). On Whitefield's rhetorical innovations as a new form of mass communication that anticipated the mobilizing techniques of the American Revolution, see Harry S. Stout, "Religion, Communications, and the Ideological Origins of the American Revolution," *WMQ,* 3d Ser., XXXIV (1977), 519–541. On the innovative uses to which Whitefield put the expanding resources of print in his ministry, see Frank Lambert, *"Pedlar in Divinity": George Whitefield and the Transatlantic Revivals, 1737–1770* (Princeton N.J., 1994).

11. Josiah Smith, *The Character, Preaching, etc. of the Reverend Mr. George Whitefield . . . ,* in George Whitefield, *Seventy-five Sermons on Various Important Subjects,* I (London, 1812), 25. "In

After Whitefield's first American tour, ministers declared their dedication to the evangelical party by leaving their manuscripts in their studies and preaching extemporaneously. When a minister took up the new improvisational preaching style modeled on Whitefield, he proclaimed his theological position as clearly as John Cotton did when he delivered a plain Puritan sermon to a Cambridge audience anticipating a witty Anglican oration. Evangelists treated extemporaneity as a rhetorical sign of grace rather than as a product of illiteracy. Despite their critics' claims to the contrary, most successful evangelical preachers were literate and all were well versed in the Bible. Very few evangelists, perhaps only the quickly ostracized James Davenport, claimed to be "conducted by the Spirit" and thus able to "disregard . . . scripture." Rather than reject the written Word, the extemporaneous ideal required the speaker to inhabit Scripture fully and personally experience its meaning. Even a prepared sermon could seem extemporaneous if the preacher delivered it properly from memory, creating an authenticity effect of divine inspiration through voice, gesture, emotional display, and spontaneous interactions with the audience. The absence of a prepared text had a double consequence. It both permitted a greater intensity of emotional expression of the sort that Whitefield manifested so ably, and it subjected the preacher to the risk of failure, leaving him vulnerable to humiliation. Connecticut minister Jonathan Parsons described one such failure when New Jersey New Light Gilbert Tennent visited his church on his tour of New England. Tennent was a leader of the revival in the Middle Colonies and a colloquial preacher of great power. Nevertheless, during his first sermon he "seem'd to be very dull," even to "have had nothing, almost to say." Though he "got thro'," he did so "with no Freedom," leaving the people without "much Sense of what was deliver'd." The vulnerability to such rhetorical failure was essential to the demonstration of a spiritual power whose claims to immediacy would otherwise have strayed into antinomian terrain.[12]

---

seeing Whitefield preach, many Americans were for the first time in their lives seeing a form of theater" (Harry S. Stout, *The Divine Dramatist: George Whitefield and the Rise of Modern Evangelicalism* [Grand Rapids, Mich., 1991], 94). For additional analysis of Whitefield's preaching, see Eugene E. White, "The Preaching of George Whitefield during the Great Awakening in America," *Speech Monographs*, XV (1948), 33–43; James Downey, *The Eighteenth Century Pulpit: A Study of the Sermons of Butler, Berkeley, Secker, Sterne, Whitefield, and Wesley* (Oxford, 1969), 155–158; Ruttenberg, *Democratic Personality*, 83–119. For Nathan Cole's comments, see Michael J. Crawford, ed., "The Spiritual Travels of Nathan Cole," *WMQ*, 3d Ser., XXXIII (1976), 92–103, esp. 93.

12. Charles Chauncy, *Enthusiasm Described and Caution'd Against . . .* (Boston, 1742), 7. With his emphasis on inspired authority regardless of scriptural precedent and his elevation of laywomen and -men, James Davenport in his extreme career represented the extreme case of evangelical innovation. Harry S. Stout and Peter Onuf describe the controversy in "James Davenport and the Great Awakening in New London," *JAH*, LXX (1983–1984), 556–578. On Ten-

Many New Lights viewed reliance on a sermon text as proof that a preacher was unconverted and thus, to their minds, unable to preach the gospel as it should be preached, from personal and intensely emotional sacred experience. In a provocative and contentious sermon, "The Dangers of an Unconverted Ministry" (1740), Tennent reproached ministers who preached with notes but without feeling. Such preachers resembled the "Orthodox, Letter-learned and regular Pharisees." Tennent deliberately cultivated the emerging frontier speaking style, colloquial idiom, personal charisma, and aggressive argument that challenged both lackluster pulpit performers and the talented literary preacher whose "Art" and "Rhetorick" he identified with mere "Appearances of Piety." Only through a deeply felt understanding of the Bible's sacred truths could the pulpit orator transcend the dead letter's corrupt materiality and convey Scripture's true spirit, Tennent argued. Defending the rights of those "under the Ministry of dead Men" to seek out effective preachers, Tennent developed a series of contrasts between established ministers who opposed the revival and authentically inspired itinerant preachers.[13] The opponents of the Great Awakening were like the scribes and pharisees, who with "a little of the Learning then in Fashion, and a fair Outside" took up the ministry "as a Trade, and therefore endeavoured to make the best Market of it they could." At once disdainful of the common people and eager to win popular applause, such ministers gave their congregants premature comfort and strengthened them in "carnal Security" with sermons "cold and sapless" that "freeze between their Lips." True converts could recognize false preaching despite the minister's learning and social standing, for they had an inner sense of grace: "Let *Tertullus* ascend the Theatre, and gild the Objection with the most mellifluous Ciceronean Eloquence; it will no more perswade them, that what they have felt is but a Fancy . . . than to tell a Man . . . that sees, That it is but a Notion, he does not see: Or to tell a Man that feels Pleasure or Pain, That it's but a deluded Fancy; they are quite mistaken." The famished souls who paid to support a minister who gave them "sapless Discourses" and "a long fine String of Prayer" that he had "by Heart" should not be bound to attend his sermons. Each one had "a Right to the Gifts of all God's Ministers . . . *as they have Opportunity*," even if that meant attending a different church or gathering in a field. Tennent celebrated the New Light itinerant's interiority organized around a sense of grace readily expressed in

---

nent's unsuccessful sermon, see Jonathan Parsons, "Account of the Revival at Lyme," in Alan Heimert and Perry Miller, eds., *The Great Awakening: Documents Illustrating the Crisis and Its Consequences* (Indianapolis, [1967]), 196–197.

13. Gilbert Tennent, "The Dangers of an Unconverted Ministry" (1740), in Heimert and Miller, eds., *The Great Awakening*, 71–99, esp. 73, 97, 99. For a fine analysis of the symbolism of itinerancy in the Great Awakening, see Timothy D. Hall, *Contested Boundaries: Itinerancy and the Reshaping of the Colonial American Religious World* (Durham, N.C., 1994), esp. 6–7, 33.

"Cries, Tears, Pleadings and Groanings" and manifested in sermons that were a gracious gift and not a commodity.[14]

In 1742, Boston minister Charles Chauncy responded to Tennent and the New Lights in "Enthusiasm Described and Caution'd Against," a sermon criticizing what he believed were the excesses of the revivals. The Awakening's most articulate opponent, Chauncy identified the challenge to the social order posed by the fervent actions and modes of expression that the New Lights took as signs of grace. Chauncy had a reputation for relying so fully on Scripture and written scriptural analysis in his own pulpit oratory that he was virtually incapable of improvising. Asked to "improve" the sad news of a young boy's death for his Sabbath audience, Chauncy could only implore God "to—to—to bless to them all the boy that was this morning drowned in Frog Pond." Ralph Waldo Emerson once remarked that Chauncy "so disliked the 'sensation' preaching of his time, that he had once prayed that 'he might never be eloquent;' and, it appears, his prayer was granted."[15] Motivated by Whitefield's first American tour and the displays of sacred feeling and social disorder that it promoted, Chauncy made adherence to Scripture and rationality the twin pillars of a Christianity immune to the disruptive appeal of immediate inspiration and extemporaneous preaching.

In a theological claim that was fundamental to his social message, Chauncy translated the revivalists' characteristic emphasis on experiential faith into a rejection of the written Law. Comparing the revivalists to the misguided Corinthians, he invested Paul's warning against disorderly speech in 1 Corinthians 14:37 with a particular emphasis on respect for the written word:

> *If any man think himself to be a prophet, or spiritual, let him acknowledge that the things that I write unto you are the commandments of the Lord.* As if the apostle had said, you may imagine your selves to be *spiritual* men, to be under a divine afflatus in what you do; but 'tis all imagination, meer pretence, unless you pay a due regard to the *commandments* I have here *wrote to you;* receiving them not as the *word of man, but of* GOD.[16]

Like the ministers and magistrates at the trials of Anne Hutchinson, Chauncy singled out evangelical claims to divine inspiration and disregard for Scripture as compelling evidence that the revivalists and their converts flirted with the devil. Seeking to restrain the behavior of laypeople, who were entering into religious life

14. Tennent, "The Dangers of an Unconverted Ministry," in Heimert and Miller, eds., *The Great Awakening*, 75, 78, 84–85, 89, 95–96, 98.

15. Emerson recounted this anecdote in "Eloquence," in Emerson, *Letters and Social Aims*, rev. ed. (Boston, 1883), 124.

16. Chauncy, *Enthusiasm Described and Caution'd Against*, 2. For a discussion of Pauline attitudes toward verbal media, see Appendix, below.

more actively and with less deference for clerical authority than they had since the Antinomian Controversy, he offered signs for diagnosing "enthusiasm": a wildness of countenance, a "fluency and volubility in speaking," bodily convulsions, "freakish or furious conduct," and an "imaginary peculiar intimacy with heaven." Chauncy proposed an intensive encounter with Scripture as the best way to control enthusiasm, insisting "if you will but express a due reverence to this *book* of GOD, making it the great rule of judgment, even in respect of the SPIRIT's *influences* and *operations,* you will not be in much danger of being led into delusion." Scripture was "received from GOD, and committed to writing under his immediate, extraordinary influence and guidance." Since the Lord must be "consistent with himself," his written Word should be the measure of public truth: "He cannot be suppos'd to be the author of any *private* revelations that are contradictory to the *public standing* ones, which he has preserved in the world to this day." The consistency and publicity that Chauncy attributed to Scripture when rightly interpreted were ultimately dependent upon human reason, which was also essential to a proper hermeneutic: "You must use your reason in order to understand the *bible.* . . . Nay, if no reasoning is to be made use of," Chauncy asked, "are not all the senses that can be put on Scripture equally proper?" Scripture and reason together would combat *"enthusiasm."* Chauncy's semiotics of textual performance elevated reason over emotion, publicity over inwardness, consistency over immediacy, and social deference over authenticity.[17]

Just as Cotton Mather celebrated the self-discipline that writing made possible, particularly for women, so Chauncy maintained the necessity of sacred text as a form of social control. Among the practices that such attention to Scripture was designed to repress, Chauncy made particular mention of "the suffering, much more the encouraging WOMEN, yea, GIRLS to speak in the assemblies for religious worship." Female prophets and exhorters violated Paul's demand that "WOMEN *keep silence in the churches.*" Along with women, Chauncy singled out uneducated men and slaves as extemporaneous speakers whose supposed lack of respect for Scripture threatened the colonies with social disruption on a far larger scale than the unrest in Boston a century before or in Salem half a century earlier. Amplifying Puritan forms of textual discipline, Chauncy's sermon gives exceptionally clear expression to a system of meaning in which challenges to the existing social and political hierarchy are figured as passionate assertions of "voice" and appeals for social stability are imagined in textual terms. Like the Puritan patriarchs,

17. Chauncy, *Enthusiasm Described and Caution'd Against,* 4, 7, 17–19. Chauncy employed a common distinction between private and public persons, through which the gentry and clergy participating in literary culture "situated themselves in a transatlantic 'public' of 'reasonable men' which stood apart from the 'private persons' whose views seldom appeared in the press or other organs of public expression" (Hall, *Contested Boundaries,* 60).

Chauncy cast the differential relationship between speech and text as an absolute distinction used to figure other supposedly absolute distinctions: woman and man, the people and the elite, "primitive" oral and "civilized" literate cultures. But now Chauncy's view represented one side of a more complex system of meanings. During the Great Awakening, the new visibility and significance of extempore performance exposed the Puritan symbolism of speech and text as a strategy for demarcating privileges, not as absolute truths founded on divine authority.[18]

II. WOMEN'S SPEECH AND WOMEN'S SILENCE IN JONATHAN EDWARDS'S FIRST NORTHAMPTON REVIVAL

Jonathan Edwards's role in the Great Awakening was in important ways shaped by his engagement with the possibilities and dangers of the liminal form that most disturbed Charles Chauncy: women's sacred speech. Pious women and girls dominate his influential account of the 1734–1735 Northampton revival in *A Faithful Narrative of the Surprising Work of God* (1737). This prelude to the Great Awakening opened new representational and performative possibilities for evangelical women. Abigail Hutchinson's ecstatic spiritual visions and resignation under extreme physical suffering framed an influential type of female holiness, and young Phebe Bartlett demonstrated the emerging possibilities for infant conversion. Edwards's conversion narratives resemble Mather's witchcraft narratives in their youthful female subjects and in their concern with feminine voice. But whereas Mather positioned women's public speech on the boundary between the human and the demonic, Edwards tentatively and ambivalently identified liminal feminine expression with the voice of God. Portraying representative young women and girls as exemplary Christian converts, Edwards provisionally legitimized the type of feminine spiritual authority that made Anne Hutchinson's charismatic eloquence so compelling. But his description of Abigail Hutchinson's conversion redirected female spiritual ecstasy away from heightened articulateness and toward silence and death. Those revisions proved crucial to his own authority. Edwards's pulpit performances sought to evoke and assume the affective spiritual potential inherent in women's speech. Shaping and interpreting feminine speech,

18. Chauncy, *Enthusiasm Described and Caution'd Against,* 13. Timothy Hall summarizes the transgressive practices of the laity, which included ecstatic emotional and physical displays, parading through the streets singing hymns, and lay preaching by women, "illiterate" men and youths, and African Americans and native Americans (*Contested Boundaries,* 52–57). On the relationship between a reconceptualization of popular voice and the emergence of democratic structures of personality during the Great Awakening, see Ruttenberg, *Democratic Personality,* 83–211.

he controlled its parodic, subversive potential, its power to disrupt traditional gender hierarchies. At the same time, he claimed its affective impact as his own.

But Edwards could not fully govern the social and spiritual forces that he tentatively sanctioned. The revivals sparked by Whitefield's preaching tour temporarily broke down prohibitions against women's speaking in church, and many evangelical women testified to their faith by crying out, exhorting, and, like the demoniacs at Salem, breaking into their ministers' sermons. These prophetic women sometimes claimed that their spiritual knowledge based on dreams, visions, and voices was more authentic than the textual analysis that the college-educated ministry could provide. Such defiance was soon brought home to Jonathan Edwards. When Sarah Edwards underwent a religious crisis that included moments of ecstatic speech during Northampton's second awakening in the early 1740s, she posed a covert challenge to her husband's ministerial and personal authority. Initially recording these events in a self-justifying document that remained unpublished until 1830, Jonathan shaped Sarah's experience according to the paradigm established in his earlier narratives of holy women. Increasingly committed to the abstract and often disciplinary style that characterizes his late sermons and theological works, Edwards thoroughly revised Sarah's narrative as "An Example of Evangelical Piety" in *Some Thoughts concerning the Revival* (1742), removing all traces of her gender and recasting it in a nonnarrative form that eradicates signs of social conflict. Here and throughout his later writings, Edwards's stylistic transformation was in part a response to the threat inherent in the feminine erotic appeal that his early works helped legitimate and that his wife briefly claimed as a source of independent authority.[19]

In 1735, the dramatic suicide of Joseph Hawley, Sarah Edwards's uncle, brought Jonathan's first awakening to a conclusion depressingly short of the universal and ongoing revival for which he had hoped. Two years later, his Northampton congregation urged their young minister, now near the peak of his power in the community despite the revival's dismaying conclusion, to allow them to publish the five sermons that they had found most moving. The congregation told their minister that they were willing to do him this great honor because they hoped that "the reading these Discourses would have a Tendency in some Measure to renew the same Effect in them that was wrought in the hearing, and revive the Memory

19. On women's public speech during the Great Awakening, see Catherine A. Brekus, *Strangers and Pilgrims: Female Preaching in America, 1740–1845* (Chapel Hill, N.C., 1998), 11. Brekus discusses the claims of female exhorters to derive spiritual power from dreams, visions, and voices (54). On the textual history of the two versions of Sarah Edwards's narrative and Jonathan's revisions of the document, see Julie Ellison, "The Sociology of 'Holy Indifference': Sarah Edwards' Narrative," *American Literature*, LVI (1984), 479–495, esp. 480–481. The original manuscript of the narrative has been lost, although a short fragment quoted below does exist.

of that great Work of God, which this Town has so much Cause ever to remember." If Edwards's spoken word no longer inspired conviction, perhaps the written trace of his former eloquence would rekindle memories of a shared elevation.[20]

Included in this volume, along with the more familiar "Justification by Faith Alone," "The Justice of God in the Damnation of Sinners," and "The Excellency of Christ," was a sermon entitled "Ruth's Resolution," whose manipulation of social ties and anxieties reveals an unfamiliar side of Edwards's preaching. "Ruth's Resolution" draws on three powerful motifs that characterized the 1735 awakening: the affective bonds and competitions between women that played a vital role in stimulating the revival; the image of the convert as an alien woman brought into the Christian community provisionally through her ties to another woman and finally through marriage to that woman's kinsman, who represents Christ; and the accompanying image, at once contradictory and complementary, of the convert as Christ's mother giving birth to Christ in the redeemed soul. These images of a feminized spirituality echo and amplify a gendered language familiar to evangelical Protestants, who commonly figured the soul as Christ's mother and bride.[21]

Like the Book of Ruth itself, "Ruth's Resolution" locates both spirituality and sexuality within a conflict-ridden network of social and affective bonds between women. As was his standard practice, Edwards began by contextualizing the Scripture text, summarizing the Book of Ruth in a passage that will serve as our introduction to the sermon:

> *Naomi* was now returning out of the Land of *Moab,* into the Land of *Israel,* with her two Daughters-in-law, *Orpah* and *Ruth;* who well represent to us, two Sorts of Professors of Religion; *Orpah* that Sort, that indeed make a fair Profession, and seem to set out well, but dure but for a while, and then turn back; *Ruth* that Sort, that are sound and sincere, and therefore are stedfast and persevering in the Way that they have set out in. *Naomi* . . . represents to these her Daughters the Difficulties of their leaving their own Country to go with her.

This is the background for Edwards's text, Ruth 1:16: "And Ruth said, Intreat me not to leave thee, or to return from following after thee; for whither thou goest, I

20. Jonathan Edwards, preface to *Discourses on Various Important Subjects, Nearly concerning the Great Affair of the Soul's Eternal Salvation* (Boston, 1738), i–ii.

21. On Edwards's reasons for publishing these sermons, see ibid. On feminine spirituality and biblical imagery, see David Leverenz, *The Language of Puritan Feeling: An Exploration in Literature, Psychology, and Social History* (New Brunswick, N.J., 1980), chap. 5. On the significance of feminization for evangelical Protestants, see Amanda Porterfield, *Female Piety in Puritan New England: The Emergence of Religious Humanism* (New York, 1992). On "feminized" evangelicals and their oedipal dramas, see Philip Greven, *The Protestant Temperament: Patterns of Child-Rearing, Religious Experience, and the Self in Early America* (New York, 1977), 124–140.

will go, and where thou lodgest, I will lodge; thy People shall be my People, and thy GOD, my GOD." The biblical Ruth fulfills her commitment to Naomi, accompanying her to Israel, providing her with food, and finally marrying Naomi's kinsman Boas in a union significant in Hebrew and Christian cultures, for it eventually produced David and later Jesus.[22]

Interpreting this story of a Moabite woman's intense personal loyalty to her Hebrew mother-in-law as a type of Christian conversion, Edwards at first reverses Ruth's stated priorities, effacing the importance of affectional bonds in her decision to follow Naomi to Israel: "I would particularly observe that wherein the Virtuousness of this her Resolution consists, *viz.* That it was for the Sake of the God of *Israel,* and that she might be one of His People, that she was thus resolved to cleave to *Naomi.*" Since the Hebrew God is in fact Ruth's last declared reason for following Naomi, and indeed, since she accepts him as part of Israelite tribal culture rather than as a personally experienced power, Edwards's interpretation rather abruptly wrenches the tale's emphasis from the social to the transcendent. But this shift in focus turns out to be remarkably brief, for by the time Edwards reaches his doctrine in the following paragraph, the social context has returned with a significance surprising from a man with a reputation as the preacher of private, even mystical, religious experience: "*When those that we have formerly been conversant with, are turning to God, and joining themselves to his People, it ought to be our firm Resolution, that we will not leave them; but that their People shall be our People, and their God, our God.*"[23]

"Ruth's Resolution" oscillates between the social and the transcendent aspects of religious experience, demonstrating Edwards's early hesitancy to ascribe a final cause to conversion, his willingness to tolerate an overdetermined religious response. Such tolerance, characteristic of Edwards's early revival writings, comes under his own sharp scrutiny in later theoretical works, such as *True Virtue,* where he seeks to distinguish true from false conversion. Throughout "Ruth's Resolution," however, Edwards openly exploits affectional bonds and social shame to draw the unredeemed to Christ. Alluding to gospel passages warning that Judgment Day will separate families and friends forever, Edwards offers detailed verbal portraits of kin and social groups spiritually sundered by the still-temporal and thus mutable course of the revival. Such portraits give Edwards the occasion to urge those yet unsaved, "Let it not be the Foundation of a final Parting!" Turning to God, sinners will escape their sudden and terrifying alienation from sanc-

22. Edwards, "Ruth's Resolution," in Edwards, *Discourses on Various Important Subjects,* in *Works of President Edwards,* V, 173–191, esp. 173–174.

23. Ibid., 175–176.

tified loved ones, reestablishing emotional ties within a newly spiritualized social terrain.[24]

Most significant among the numerous events that contributed to the 1735 awakening as Edwards describes it in *A Faithful Narrative* was the conversion of an unnamed young woman who "had been one of the greatest company-keepers in the whole town." Her exemplary influence underlies Edwards's sense of the communal forces at work in the revival. This "loose-living" young woman, whose sinful spirit Edwards imputed to her excessive openness to male companionship, came to him with "an account of . . . a glorious work of God's infinite power and sovereign grace; . . . that God had given her a new heart, truly broken and sanctified." Edwards describes his fear that her improbable conversion would only harden skeptical hearts, but the effect was the opposite: "The news of it seemed to be almost like a flash of lightning, upon the hearts of young people all over the town, and upon many others. Those persons amongst us who used to be farthest from seriousness, and that I most feared would make an ill improvement of it, seemed greatly to be awakened with it; many went to talk with her, concerning what she had met with; and what appeared in her seemed to be the satisfaction of all that did so."[25]

Following the "company-keeping" young woman's conversion, the whole town became absorbed in spiritual matters, until "other discourse than of the things of religion would scarcely be tolerated in any company." Business became a secondary concern (though Edwards is careful to note that it was not neglected, as neglect would indicate enthusiasm); private meetings proliferated among people of all ages; the tavern was deserted while people "kept very much at home" for prayer and private conference or met in "throng[s]" at Edwards's house. Communal absorption in religious topics achieved its most public expression during worship services, when the auditors were "eager to drink in the words of the minister as they came from his mouth" and openly displayed intense emotion over their own or others' spiritual states. Edwards identifies the crucial role he played in promoting the revival, but he also confesses, indeed insists on, the limits of his own power. He remarks that "there is no one thing that I know of, that God has made such a means of promoting his work amongst us, as the news of others' conversion."[26]

Edwards's account of Abigail Hutchinson's spiritual experiences reveals with

24. Ibid., 184.

25. Edwards, *A Faithful Narrative of the Surprising Work of God in the Conversion of Many Hundred Souls . . .* (1737), in C. C. Goen, ed., *The Great Awakening*, vol. IV of Perry Miller et al., eds., *The Works of Jonathan Edwards* (New Haven, Conn., 1957–), 149.

26. Ibid., 150–151, 161, 176.

arresting candor the complex social dynamics at work in the revival. When Hutchinson first heard of the company-keeper's conversion, he notes, "this news wrought much upon her, and stirred up a spirit of envy in her towards this young woman, whom she thought very unworthy of being distinguished from others by such a mercy"; "but," he goes on to insist, recuperating corrupt motives for holy purposes, "withal it engaged her in a firm resolution to do her utmost to obtain the same blessing." Her spiritual technique reveals much about lay attitudes toward the relative authority of minister and Scripture. Hutchinson dedicated herself at once to a thorough search for "the principles of religion to render her capable of conversion," and rather than turn to Edwards she "accordingly immediately began at the beginning of the Bible, intending to read it through." Such independent Scripture reading occupied a weeklong trial of the soul implicitly modeled—whether by Edwards or by Hutchinson herself is unclear—on Passion Week: from Monday through Thursday she read consecutively through the Old Testament until "an extraordinary sense of her own sinfulness" came upon her, and she turned for relief to the New Testament. Three more days of spiritual exercises and Scripture reading reenacted the harrowing of hell until she "saw nothing but blackness of darkness before her." Finally she awakened on Monday with comforting Scripture passages running through her mind, convinced that she had "seen" the resurrected Christ the night before.[27]

Edwards presents Hutchinson's conversion experience as a dramatic yet thoroughly interiorized response to the Bible, both to its content and to its literal material existence. Imaginatively reenacting Christ's death and resurrection, the convert transforms the Bible-as-thing, the merely read object, into sacred performance. On the Saturday when Hutchinson's sense of her own sin was so intense that "(as she said) she saw nothing but blackness of darkness before her," her overstrained eyes failed until "she could not know the letters" in the book before her. The image suggests that the words on the page blurred together beyond recognition, the smeared print mimicking her perceived spiritual condition. Scriptural meaning, opaque from the start, grew more rather than less resistant. Edwards writes: "She seemed that day to feel in herself an enmity against the Bible, which greatly affrighted her."[28]

Mortally anxious, nearly blind, and seeking spiritual solace, Hutchinson turned her thoughts increasingly from the Bible to her minister. During her weeklong struggle to win salvation, Hutchinson fully experienced the alienating effects that Calvin predicted would attend a too-exclusive reliance on the printed Word, justifying the minister's mediate role as scriptural interpreter and spiritual guide.

27. Ibid., 192–193.
28. Ibid.

But although Hutchinson longed for Edwards's advice and comfort, in the end she was justified by faith alone independent of ministerial counsel. Too ill to attend Sabbath services, her own body as much of an obstruction to her spiritual well-being as the blurred letters of Scripture, she stayed at home in bed. That night, without ever consulting Edwards, she had the first of her "discoveries" of Christ, spiritual illuminations that intensified over three days, confirming her sense that she was one of the elect.

Edwards knew that he was negotiating the perilous territory of inspiration and enthusiasm in this narrative, and his concern to deflect the sense that Abigail Hutchinson might too much resemble the woman whose surname she shared and whose spiritual life she in important ways reproduced appears on every page. Indeed, Edwards seems intent on revising Anne Hutchinson's legacy, deflecting a model of feminine spirituality that began with a mystical experience of Christ and ended in prophetic speech into a more quiescent, even repressive, path from spiritual illumination to silence and death. From the narrative's beginning, Edwards seeks to allay suspicions that Abigail's experience might sound to hostile ears like zealotry, characterizing her as "of a rational understanding family" free from enthusiastic tendencies. Her bodily weakness, he reassures the reader, "had never been observed at all to incline her to be notional or fanciful, or to occasion anything of religious melancholy."[29]

Likewise, her religious "discoveries" were not visible to the senses. They conformed to the requirements that Edwards set forth most clearly in *A Divine and Supernatural Light* (1734), where he characterized the divine light that the awakened Hutchinson later perceived as *"a true sense of the divine Excellency of the things revealed in the Word of* GOD, *and a conviction of the truth and reality of them, thence arising."* Hutchinson's spiritual perceptions included a new religious sense, demonstrating the sensations that Edwards later analyzed as characteristic of the converted. As words representing Christianity's severest abstractions — "wisdom," "justice," "goodness," and "truth" — passed through her mind, her awakened soul "was filled with a sense of the glory of each of these divine attributes." Here Hutchinson independently realized the effect that Edwards hoped to achieve with his own sermonic language, his "rhetoric of sensation": a sense of abstractions as transcendent realities evoking clear emotional responses.[30]

As Edwards represents her, Hutchinson longed to articulate her sense of spiritual realities, to make them real for others just as Edwards sought to make real his religious vision, that they might share her experience of the divine. Immediately

29. Ibid., 191.

30. Jonathan Edwards, *A Divine and Supernatural Light* . . . (Boston, 1734), 10; Perry Miller, *Errand into the Wilderness* (Cambridge, Mass., 1964), 167–183.

after her first "view of Christ's glory and fulness," she "felt in herself a strong in-clination immediately to go forth to warn sinners; and proposed it the next day to her brother to assist her in going from house to house." Edwards notes that her brother "restrained her" from such public proselytizing. Again, when at a private religious meeting "her mind was full of a sense and view of the glory of God all the time," she began to relate her experience to her neighbors, but "as she was re-lating it, it revived such a sense of the same things that her strength failed; and they were obliged to take her and lay her upon the bed." No brother need re-strain her this time. Internalizing his proscriptions against public speech, Abigail Hutchinson manifested them through a display of physical weakness. Yet Hutch-inson's swooning and fainting register her own significance in her very public acts of self-silencing. In an important sense, her collapse was divine exhibitionism. It was also an implicit protest against the suppression of her public testimony.[31]

Hutchinson's collapse, like the experiences of Sarah Edwards and other evan-gelical women who fainted or became physically incapacitated while address-ing groups about their sense of divine things, reflects their internalization of the prohibitions against women's speaking publicly. Her display of incapacity also posed an indirect challenge to those prohibitions through a ritual performance of the self-silencing required of women. An inability to articulate transcendent experiences, the traditional mystic's impasse, fails to explain these specifically public moments of incapacity. Nor did her collapse into inarticulateness reflect the Quaker celebration of silence as attentive listening to God, for, when Quaker women remained silent, they did so by choice rather than social restriction. Ed-wards acknowledges his narrative's dependence on Hutchinson's very articulate private testimony, confessing that he offers only "a very broken and imperfect account" and insisting that "her eminency would much more appear, if her ex-periences were fully related, as she was wont to express and manifest them, while living." Like the image in a fractured mirror, Edwards's textual representation of Hutchinson points toward the absence that only her expressive presence could fill. Yet his account simultaneously reveals the degree to which social anxieties re-stricted her expressive potential, limiting her to private speech and public displays of self-silencing.[32]

---

31. Edwards, *A Faithful Narrative,* in Goen, ed., *The Great Awakening,* 194–195.

32. Ibid., 199. Edwards's remarks here recall Jacques Derrida's claim in *Of Grammatology,* trans. Gayatri Chakravorty Spivak (Baltimore, 1976), 6–18, that a writing construed as absence and analogically related to the signified's deferral in the metaphor disrupts the metaphysical hierarchies identified with speech and physical presence. Yet for Edwards, Hutchinson's death permits him to write a narrative that constructs female silence and absence as evidence of a tran-scendent spiritual force. Rather than deconstructing metaphysical hierarchies, including patri-archy, the narrative ultimately reinforces them. Edwards explains that he chose Hutchinson "be-

Given the external restraint and internal resistance that attended her attempts to speak publicly, Hutchinson's ultimate fate suggests an ironic revision of Anne Hutchinson's life and death. Contemporaries admired Anne Hutchinson's robust good health through numerous pregnancies. Called before the General Court and the Boston church for discipline, however, she complained frequently of weakness, even postponing her church trial because of ill health. Given the stresses to which she was subject, it seems likely that social, psychological, and physiological factors all contributed to her infirmity. In contrast to the robust Anne, whose physical decline followed social constraint, Abigail was weak from the first, an early type of the fragile young maiden so popular in later literature. Conversion intensified her aversion to her own body, exciting "great longings to die, that she might be with Christ." Though Abigail decided that such longings demonstrated a suspect self-assertion rather than proper submission to divine Providence, her wishes were ultimately realized when an unexplained swelling of the throat prevented her from eating. Hutchinson actually starved to death. Though Edwards attributes her death to a mysterious ailment that made eating physically impossible, the reason she starved is less clear than his medical account might suggest. Medieval saints and Victorian anorexics proffered the same explanation for refusing food: their throats were swollen shut. Hutchinson's fate calls to mind Samuel Richardson's novel, written only a decade later, in which Clarissa's suicide by starvation constitutes that young woman's only successful attempt to exert control over her body, an effort explicitly articulated as a dedication to God, whatever competing psychological motivations Richardson suggests. Though Edwards deflects suspicion that similar issues might have been at stake for Hutchinson when he compares her to "a little child," her longing "to live at my house that I might tell her her duty" suggests the adolescent's complicated and ultimately tragic blend of piety, hostility, and erotic awakening.[33]

Both the actual Hutchinson and the fictional Clarissa participate in a tradition of self-starving women. As Edwards portrays her, Hutchinson occupies a position midway between medieval holy women and modern anorexia patients: she epitomizes pious self-sacrifice and calm resignation to the divine will in the face of tremendous physical suffering. Edwards gives no hint that he suspects anything other than a purely organic disease caused her death. Offering a medical explanation for Hutchinson's fast while spiritualizing her emotional response, Edwards reclaims the medieval heritage of sanctified female self-starvation for Protestant

---

cause she is now dead, and so it may be more fit to speak freely of her than of living instances" (191). His motivations were doubtless complex, involving fears of provoking spiritual pride in his subject or stirring her peers to jealousy. But one should also note that a dead woman exerts no control over her own life story.

33. Edwards, *A Faithful Narrative*, 195–196.

America, unlike Cotton Mather, who attributed the lengthy fasts of Mercy Short and Margaret Rule to demonic torments. But beyond the immediate physical cause of death, Edwards explicitly identifies Hutchinson's eagerness to die with a mystic's longing to escape from the corrupt material world into the ecstatic realm of pure spirit: "She wanted to be where strong grace might have more liberty, and be without the clog of a weak body." For Edwards, then, Hutchinson's desiccated body obstructed mystical experience, much as the physical Bible earlier proved a barrier to understanding that only her sense of Christ could overcome. The female body and the Bible-as-book function analogously in Edwards's narrative: both prove themselves material obstacles to holy ecstasy.[34]

But the narrative will bear alternative readings that problematize Edwards's interpretation, offering insight into his own motives as he shaped Hutchinson's experiences. The aphasia accompanying Hutchinson's starvation complicates the symbolic meaning of her fatal illness. In part a result of weakness, her inability to speak was symptomatically related to her inability to ingest food and drink and the consequent failure to expel matter. Refusing nourishment, she emitted neither excrement nor words, achieving a perfect, if provisional, self-containment. Reduced at the end to communicating with gestures, Hutchinson "could say but little, and manifested her mind very much by signs. She said she had matter enough to fill up all her time with talk, if she had but strength."[35] For Edwards, Hutchinson's insatiable longing to speak, like the raging appetite that her swollen throat would not let her satisfy, demonstrated that her will remained essentially healthy and uncorrupted. Only physical limitation prevented her from realizing that will in performance. But Edwards's own characterization of Hutchinson's dilemma suggests an additional significance. The matter she could not take in was symbolically equivalent to the "matter" that would "fill all her time" if she could talk. Just as Thomas Welde and Cotton Mather identified Anne Hutchinson's verbal matter with her monstrous birth, so Jonathan Edwards's narrative of Abigail Hutchinson associates feminine speech with bodily functions, in her case eating and eliminating. For Abigail, a truncated gestural language proved less material than speech. Contrary to Edwards's interpretation, then, Hutchinson's body was not merely something to be cast aside as an obstruction to divine meaning. It proved her only arena of communication, a vehicle for acting out her own symbolic meanings.

34. Ibid., 199. On the shifting cultural meanings of women's self-starvation, see Caroline Walker Bynum, "Fast, Feast, and Flesh: The Religious Significance of Food to Medieval Women," *Representations*, XI (1985), 1–25; Rudolph Bell, *Holy Anorexia* (Chicago, 1985); Joan Jacobs Brumberg, *Fasting Girls: The History of Anorexia Nervosa* (New York, 1989), chap. 2. Brumberg discusses Mather's demonic interpretation of female fasting on 52.

35. Edwards, *A Faithful Narrative*, 198.

The connection between appetite and voice shown in Abigail's starvation gained an intensified significance for post-Reformation Christians whose religious practice focused increasingly on the sermon. Medieval women's holy fasting posed an implicit challenge to clerical authority centered on control of the holiest of foods, the host. Rejecting transubstantiation, Protestant reformers ruptured the continuity that Catholicism established between Christ, flesh, and food. In so doing, they transferred competitions for authority to the verbal realm. Speaking, not feeding, became the act most fraught with consequence for holy women, as Anne Hutchinson's experience with the Bay Colony elders powerfully demonstrates. Abigail Hutchinson's life and death suggest the most extreme consequences of internalizing Anne's lesson. Reduced at the end to the barest articulation of desire, Hutchinson was able to answer only yes or no to questions. Her last words were exclusively responsive. Weakness and inhibition prevented her from making the long deathbed spiritual exhortations common among later evangelical women.

III. THE "FEMININE" IN PERFORMANCE

Edwards's pulpit oratory drew much of its power as performance from an asceticism similar to Hutchinson's, though markedly less severe and resonant with his masculine clerical authority. The habits of denying himself food and sleep that he acquired while a tutor at Yale took their toll on his health. Though self-denial did not immediately cause his death, his fasting and insomnia weakened him, drained his vitality, and predisposed him to serious illnesses, including the fatal bout of smallpox that he contracted from an inoculation. At the same time, however, his ascetic habits registered visibly on his body, increasing his pulpit authority in crucial ways that suggest the different cultural meanings attached to similar behaviors in men and women. Food deprivation has historically been much more common among women than men. Puritan preachers, like certain monastic orders, are a limited but important exception to this rule. A holy life served a crucial rhetorical function for the Puritan minister, and ascetic self-denial offered the most popular way to demonstrate the flesh's subordination to spirit. In *Manuductio ad Ministerium,* a ministerial handbook that remained popular into the nineteenth century, Cotton Mather recommends "a Spare, Lean, Fluid sort of a Diet" primarily consisting of vegetables, grains, and cold water. Ministers could point to Moses' fast on Mount Sinai, when he received the covenant and prepared to deliver God's law to the Israelites, as justification for their own pre-Sabbath abstinence. The fasts of Elijah and Jesus in the desert offered further support for behavior that might otherwise seem too closely to resemble the suspect self-torments of the Desert Fathers. But while ministers and monks did fast, they almost never suffered from the uncontrollable fasting of the anorexic.[36]

Asceticism's consequences were writ large on Edwards's body. A sparse diet intensified the natural vertical lines of his six-foot frame and long, pale, narrow face. Weakness and repeated illness left him rather listless. But while his organic infirmity might have accentuated his physical presence, suggesting a mind absorbed in merely corporeal suffering, Edwards transformed physical debility into the rhetorical effect of holiness. Resisting gesture in his pulpit performances, he signaled a severe self-restraint that contributed to an impression of near-disembodiment. Like Abigail Hutchinson, then, Edwards displayed an emaciated frame as testament to his heightened spirituality and freedom from the contaminations of the flesh. His strategy differed slightly from Hutchinson's, however, registering a crucial, gendered distinction: where she employed a silent gestural language to avoid emitting spoken "matter," he constrained his movements to focus attention on his words. Deflecting the signs of heightened materiality that disease might indicate, Edwards reinterpreted them as demonstrations of physical transparency and revealed spirit, augmenting his spoken Word's authority.

Numerous observers, in this case Samuel Hopkins, described Edwards's manner in the pulpit as languid, serious, quiet, and rigorously untheatrical:

> His Appearance in the Desk was with a good Grace, and his delivery easy, natural and very solemn. He had not a strong, loud Voice; but appear'd with such gravity and solemnity, and spake with such distinctness, clearness, and precision; his Words were so full of Ideas, set in such a plain and striking Light, that few Speakers have been so able to command the Attention of an Audience as he.

Clarity was central to the performance of an Edwards sermon, as it had earlier defined John Cotton's pulpit eloquence. Focusing attention on his precisely articulated words, Edwards invested his oral performances with textual authority. He staged the erasure of his material self in order to create the effect of text— "distinctness, clearness, and precision"—in the oral register. Hopkins elsewhere noted that Edwards "particularly commended the well-placed pauses and great distinctness in pronunciation." Intensifying individual words and phrases, he voiced the reading experience for his listeners.[37]

From all accounts Edwards did not literally read his sermons but followed the

36. Cotton Mather, *Manuductio ad Ministerium: Directions for a Candidate of the Ministry* (1726; New York, 1938), 130–132.

37. Samuel Hopkins, *The Life and Character of the Late Reverend Mr. Jonathan Edwards . . .* (Boston, 1765), 48; Ola Elizabeth Winslow, *Jonathan Edwards, 1703–1758: A Biography* (New York, 1940), 134.

FIGURE 1. Reverend Jonathan Edwards. *By Joseph Badger. c. 1750–1755.*
Courtesy, Yale University Art Gallery, bequest of Eugene Phelps Edwards

common practice of delivering them from memory, sometimes introjecting extemporaneous remarks. Yet he held his sermon manuscript in front of him as he
preached, cradling it in the open pulpit Bible and following the lines with his finger. Perhaps this habit reflected his sense that he could write better than he could
speak.[38] But even if Edwards felt himself to be more textually than orally adept, the

38. Hopkins observed Edwards's habits of writing out his sermons and carrying his notes
into the pulpit as well as his skillful improvisations upon his written sermon and his talent for ex-

feeling masks a performance choice behind a statement of natural ability. One important determinant of his preaching style was its simultaneous proximity to and significant contrast with that of his grandfather and predecessor Solomon Stoddard, who held that sermons should be memorized so that they could be delivered with proper physical and expressive emphasis. Stoddard's evangelical successes attested to the persuasive influence that looks and gestures carried when the preacher actively performed rather than read.

Bringing sermon manuscripts or notes into the pulpit with him and following along with his finger, Edwards partially violated his grandfather's most vigorously defended rhetorical rules. He cultivated his own distinctive preaching style both as a means of asserting independent authority and as a way to arouse jaded Northampton sinners who for decades had listened to Stoddard preach unmoved. Edwards even wore a wig, a worldly affectation that Stoddard found unacceptable in laypersons, much less in ministers. Edwards's wig might have been a strategy to increase his authority over his parishioners; perhaps he sought to resemble his aged grandfather more closely and thus approximate Stoddard's influence. But Stoddard argued that wearing one was *"contrary to Gravity.* There is a Masculine Gravity that should appear in the Countenances of Men, discovering a Solemnity of Spirit. But this *Practice* is *Light,* and *Effeminat."* [39] Stoddard's criticism suggests that Edwards might deliberately have chosen to appear *"Effeminat"* in evangelical eyes. Symbolically identifying himself with the feminine soul, Christ's bride, Edwards evoked the affective power of the liminal feminine speech to which he ascribed so much significance in his first awakening. Both wig and sermon pamphlet provided obvious props, signs of artifice that it was Edwards's peculiar talent to convert into the effect of extemporaneous speech and indwelling spirit. Holding his sermon manuscript before him, Edwards publicly performed the translation of text into a textualized orality, exposing the covert manipulation of his grandfather's seemingly authentic orality. Similarly, his wig heightened the effect of (feminine) embodiment through which the (masculine) Spirit was more clearly revealed.[40]

---

tempore prayer *(Life and Character of Jonathan Edwards,* 48). On Edwards's shifts between composed and improvised performance, see Jonathan Edwards, *Sermons and Discourses, 1723–1729,* ed. Kenneth P. Minkema (New Haven, Conn., 1997), 12–13. On the interplay between written and extempore sections in Revolutionary-era evangelical sermons, see Donald Weber, *Rhetoric and History in Revolutionary New England* (Oxford, 1988). On Edwards's predilection about his writing, see Elisabeth D. Dodds, *Marriage to a Difficult Man: The "Uncommon Union" of Jonathan and Sarah Edwards* (Philadelphia, 1971), 191.

39. Solomon Stoddard, *An Answer to Some Cases of Conscience,* in Perry Miller and Thomas H. Johnson, eds., *The Puritans,* 2 vols., rev. ed. (New York, 1963), II, 456–457.

40. Judith Butler discusses the construction of gender identity in performance in Butler, *Gender Trouble: Feminism and the Subversion of Identity* (New York, 1990), 128–141. On how "the

In his response to biblical text as well as in his assumption of an "effeminate" wig, we can trace a revealing similarity between Edwards's pulpit drama and his account of Abigail Hutchinson's conversion. Reading the Bible until she was nearly blind, Hutchinson experienced sin as a physical sensation, the "blackness of darkness." The Bible's materiality provoked a hatred as intense as her revulsion against her corrupt self. Only her sense of Christ as a divine and supernatural ·light breaking through the blackness of text and sin redeemed her. Edwards reproduced Hutchinson's experience of the material Word's resistance every time he preached, for the fine, dense writing in his tiny pamphlets and the near-absence of punctuation made actual reading all but impossible. His preaching performed the interpretation and inspiration of Scripture's dead letter, constantly reenacting text's evocation. As mentioned above, Edwards's skill as a preacher depended in large part on his ability to clarify opaque Scripture passages with spoken words set in "a plain and striking Light," an effect crucially dependent on his voice's "distinctness, clearness, and precision."[41]

If creating the verbal effect of illumination was part of Edwards's rhetorical skill, equally important was his ability to stir powerful emotions in his audience. In Hopkins's account, Edwards evoked emotion because his speech displayed it:

> His Words often discover'd a great degree of inward fervor, without much Noise or external Emotion, and fell with great weight on the Minds of his Hearers. He made but little Motion of his Head or Hands in the Desk, but spake so as to discover the Motion of his own Heart, which tended in the most natural and effectual manner to move and affect others.[42]

Hopkins's description suggests that Edwards performed the conversion experience for his audience. His voice's clarity imitated the saint's new sense of divinely illuminated Scripture while his "inward fervour" revealed itself aurally rather than visually, demonstrating the abstract, immaterial quality of his emotion's object, the revealed Christ. Like Abigail Hutchinson's idealized piety, Edwards's pulpit style was "feminine" in its restrained physicality. Here the logic behind Edwards's rejection of Stoddard's more physical style grows clearer: motions of the head or hands detract from, rather than reveal, motions of the heart. The would-be saint

---

suggestion of fragility in [Edwards's] frame and femininity in his countenance merely added to his power in the pulpit," see Cedric B. Cowing, "Sex and Preaching in the Great Awakening," *American Quarterly,* XX (1968), 624–644, esp. 628–629.

41. For a reproduction of the first page of "Sinners," see Winslow, *Jonathan Edwards,* 192–193. On Edwards's "notoriously punctuationless" prose, see Helen Petter Westra, "Jonathan Edwards on 'Faithful and Successful Ministers,'" *Early American Literature,* XXIII (1988), 281–290, esp. 289 n. 1.

42. Hopkins, *Life and Character of Jonathan Edwards,* 48.

must carefully distinguish holy emotion from mere physical motion, for the devil can imitate the latter but not the former: "Natural Men may have lively *Impressions* on their *Imaginations;* and we cant determine but that the Devil, *who transforms himself into an Angel of Light,* may cause *Imaginations* of an outward Beauty, or visible Glory, and of Sounds and Speeches, and other such Things; but these are Things of a vastly inferior Nature to *Spiritual Light.*"[43]

Though he casts his observations in theological terms, Edwards here shares Cicero's central insight into the dual nature of emotional persuasion. In *De oratore* (55 B.C.E.), Cicero claimed that the body communicates feeling more directly than words, holding out the possibility for an understanding unmediated by language. But virtually at the same moment that he makes this claim for a purely communicative gestural language, Cicero warns that emotion's physical display is always a representation of emotion rather than emotion itself, a simplified and schematized performance of feeling that can mask intent as well as reveal it. In all the varieties of his work, including his narrative histories, his pulpit performances, his theological treatises, and especially *The Nature of True Virtue,* Edwards sought to unravel this communicative knot, identifying mere physical display with the satanic imitation of feeling while diagnosing sanctified emotion as that which emerges despite bodily constraint.[44]

Edwards's combination of emotional self-display and physical self-effacement proved a crucial rhetorical strategy for distancing himself not only from grandfather Stoddard but later from the controversial George Whitefield and especially from more radical New Lights like James Davenport. Davenport came to represent the Awakening's worst antinomian extravagances after 1743, when in response to spirit messages received in a dream he and his New London, Connecticut, followers spent two frenzied days burning classic Puritan tracts and all manner of material possessions—including wigs. The perceived excesses of the event hastened the Awakening's demise. Davenport's preaching style was a heightened, almost caricatured, version of Whitefield's famously theatrical manner. One hostile commentator noted that "His *Gestures* in preaching are *theatrical,* his *Voice tumultuous,* his whole Speech and Behavior discovering the *Freaks of Madness,* and *wilds of Enthusiasm*"; another complained, "His expressions in Prayer are often indecently familiar." Davenport's services were far more participatory and egalitarian than Edwards's Sabbath and lecture-day meetings, and, as the book-burning episode suggests, they were oriented toward a textually unencumbered, extemporaneous oral performance. Davenport himself discarded the traditional

---

43. Edwards, *A Divine and Supernatural Light,* 8.
44. See J. S. Watson, trans. or ed., *Cicero on Oratory and Orators* (Carbondale, Ill., 1970). For further discussion of Cicero and the tradition of classical rhetoric, see Appendix, below.

sermon form based on opening and applying a specific Scripture passage, and he encouraged lay participants of both sexes to pray, exhort, sing, testify, or cry out as the Spirit moved them.[45]

Though he allowed some public lay participation, Edwards kept a much tighter interpretive rein than Davenport on lay speech, particularly the speech of women. As argued above, Edwards constructs Abigail Hutchinson's conversion narrative as a progress from ecstatic illumination into silence, reversing Anne Hutchinson's expressive trajectory. Phebe Bartlett, his other model convert, was a barely articulate four-year-old girl speaking a childish language midway between meaningless sound and speech. Of Edwards's holy women, only his wife Sarah was both mature and alive when he transcribed and edited two versions of her narrative. Describing Sarah's ecstatic performances under the preaching of Samuel Buell during her husband's absence, the first narrative strategically reveals and ultimately contains their aesthetic, even erotic, appeal. Signs of social and psychological stress are evident in Jonathan's record of Sarah's narrative: her irritation with Jonathan for rebuking what he claimed was a tactless speech to a personal rival; her isolation within the Northampton community; her repeated efforts to "see to it that I was perfectly resigned to God, with respect to the instruments he should make use of to revive religion in this town, and be entirely willing, if it was God's pleasure, that he should make use of Mr. Buel" rather than her husband. Edwards's transcriptions of both Abigail's and Sarah's narratives begin with a rebuke by an influential male; both frankly reveal the rivalrous tensions leading up to spiritual illumination.[46]

Sarah at first performed her ecstasy through a heightened public articulateness rather than an immediate lapse into silence. Where Abigail's brother quickly squelched her proselytizing impulse, Jonathan's absence permitted Sarah a temporary and unaccustomed expressive freedom. By all accounts Sarah was a talented performer, more comfortable before the public eye than her shy husband. Contemporaries celebrated Sarah's personal beauty and conversational talents. Biographers compare her to her kinswoman, the brilliant English conversationalist, epistolary writer, and poet Lady Mary Wortley Montagu. They also remark on the painful discrepancy between her verbal and social skills and those of her awkward, distraught swain during the years when she and Jonathan were courting. Given Sarah's verbal ability and social poise, it may be significant that her narrative never demonstrates her agreement with her husband's accusation of con-

45. Harry S. Stout and Peter Onuf, "James Davenport and the Great Awakening in New London," *JAH*, LXX (1983–1984), 568–570.

46. Sarah Edwards's narrative is available only as published in Sereno E. Dwight, *The Life of President Edwards*, in *The Works of President Edwards*, I (New York, 1830), 171–186, esp. 174–175. The manuscript from which Dwight drew was subsequently lost.

FIGURE 2. Mrs. Jonathan Edwards (Sarah Pierpont). *By Joseph Badger. c. 1750–1755. Courtesy, Yale University Art Gallery, bequest of Eugene Phelps Edwards*

versational imprudence. His rebuke precipitates, not submissiveness to him, but a submissiveness to God that will allow her to transcend all interest in his opinion. Like Anne Hutchinson, she will worship God, not man in God's place.[47]

47. An unpublished fragment in Jonathan's hand reveals this dynamic even more starkly than the version that Dwight published. In the unpublished draft Sarah imagines "Mr Edwards . . . Kicking me out of the House and finally casting ⟨me off⟩," and claims that even "if he should . . . turn to be most cruel to me and should horsewhip me every day I would so rest ⟨in⟩ . . . God that It would not touch ⟨my Heart⟩ . . . or diminish my Happiness . . . I could still go on in the

Sarah's repeated testimonies to her willingness that other ministers should succeed where her husband failed read rather differently if one assumes some tension, even competition, in their marriage: "I rejoiced when I saw the honour which God put upon [Buell], and the respect paid him by the people, and the greater success attending his preaching, than had followed the preaching of Mr. Edwards immediately before he went to Leicester." Sarah does not simply transfer her allegiance to the new minister in Jonathan's absence. She claims ministerial authority for herself, reading the signs of an authentic awakening, describing her experiences, reciting psalms, even breaking into the Reverend Mr. Buell's conversations to offer her own, more immediately felt understanding of a holy life:

> About 11 o'clock, as I accidentally went into the room where Mr. Buell was conversing with some of the people, I heard him say, "O that we, who are the children of God, should be cold and lifeless in religion!" and I felt such a sense of the deep ingratitude manifested by the children of God, in such coldness and deadness, that my strength was immediately taken away, and I sunk down on the spot. Those who were near raised me, and placed me in a chair; and, from the fulness of my heart, I expressed to them, in a very earnest manner, the deep sense I had of the wonderful grace of Christ towards me, of the assurance I had of his having saved me from hell, of my happiness running parallel with eternity, of the duty of giving up all to God, and of the peace and joy inspired by an entire dependence on his mercy and grace.[48]

Sarah's collapse dramatizes Buell's description of a cold, lifeless Christian; once "raised" up, she articulates her sense of Christ's redemptive power. Buell then reads several psalms that Sarah experientially realizes, enacting a call-and-response between Buell's reading and Sarah's physical and verbal performances. Like Anne Hutchinson interpreting John Cotton's sermons, Sarah takes Buell's words as her text, providing a feminine experiential content for male language.

Sarah's quasi-sermons suggest that when she asserted her "perfect willingness, that God should employ some other instrument than Mr. Edwards, in advancing the work of grace in Northampton" she might at some level have meant herself. If in fact her performance demonstrated a repressed competitive animus toward her husband, the greater resemblance of her embodied "preaching" style to Solomon Stoddard's than to Jonathan's bears remarking. Her gender crucially complicates the comparison, however, for when a woman spoke publicly her physical display

Performance of all acts of duty to my Husband and my Happiness remain whole and undiminished." See Edwards Collection, Andover Newton Theological School, file ND2.13.3. Thanks to Kenneth P. Minkema for bringing this to my attention. (Angle brackets denote interlineations.)
    48. Dwight, *Life of President Edwards,* in *Works of President Edwards,* I, 175, 177.

threatened to expose the sublimated erotics of Puritan performance, a threat only intensified in a woman of Sarah's reputed beauty. Sarah sought to avoid Anne Hutchinson's sexual exposure even as she repeated Hutchinson's strategy of identifying herself with the Virgin Mary, the original Christian holy woman and bearer of the Word, whom Puritanism could never entirely eradicate from its cultural unconscious. Mary's clandestine presence in Sarah's narrative manifests the persistent Catholic residue latent in American Protestantism, a residue that opened up expressive potentials outside the dominant male discourse for women like Anne Hutchinson and Sarah Edwards. Rather than imagine grace as akin to impregnation, as Hutchinson had done, Edwards portrayed her experience of grace as an embodied form of transcendence. A repeated phrase suggests that Sarah at first imagined herself, like the Virgin, ecstatically uniting spirit and flesh in performance, even ascending bodily into heaven: "I seemed to be drawn upwards, soul and body, from the earth towards heaven; and it appeared to me that I must *naturally and necessarily ascend thither.*" The Virgin makes a second covert appearance when Sarah quotes the hymn that begins with the Magnificat's first line ("My soul doth magnify the Lord"). The Magnificat commemorates the moment of Annunciation when Mary learned of her impregnation by the Spirit, yet Sarah does not elaborate upon these dimensions of the allusion. Leaving the reproductive analogy implicit and subordinate to the imagery of ascension, Sarah temporarily deflects the sexual connotations that both constituted and ultimately undermined Anne Hutchinson's spiritual project.[49]

Embodying the divine Word, Mary provides Sarah with a model for female expressiveness that temporarily unites voice and gesture. Yet Sarah's sense of expressive wholeness is fleeting, a sadly brief moment in a progression toward verbal and fleshly self-discipline. The second half of her narrative introduces a metaphysical division, a sense that "my soul seemed to be gone out of me to God and Christ in heaven, and to have very little relation to my body" accompanied by a newly pressing need for verbal self-restraint. Significantly, the perceived rupture between her body and her soul follows the nightlong vision of Christ that occurs at the narrative's midpoint. The eroticism of this ecstatic union presses near the surface when she describes how divine love came "from the heart of Christ in heaven, into my heart, in a constant stream, like a stream or pencil of sweet light" and when she says: "It was a pure delight, which fed and satisfied the soul. It was pleasure, without the least sting, or any interruption." Sarah's narrative demonstrates the internal divisions that erotic language intrudes upon sacred experience. No longer united to her soul, her body becomes mere matter, alternately cold and inert or distractingly agitated. It is important to note the narrative's identification

49. Ibid., 177 (emphasis added), 178, 180.

of this self-division with writing: Sarah describes her union with Christ as like a penetration by a "pencil." This image of self-division with a writing implement suggests male proscription of her oral expression, a proscription directly linked to the sexualizing of feminine sacred experience.[50]

The remainder of the narrative recapitulates key aspects of Abigail Hutchinson's experience: a need to restrain herself from speaking and a longing to die, followed by a willingness to live and suffer for God's glory. Though Sarah continues to describe her mystical visions until the end of the narrative, a heightened self-consciousness and bodily discomfort mark the latter half of the account. The narrative itself gives no indication whether Sarah actually experienced this transformation or whether Jonathan introduced it. Regardless of authorship, after a brief interval of release into ecstatic speech Jonathan's Sarah repeats Abigail Hutchinson's movement from spiritual illumination to physical incapacity and verbal self-restraint.

Revising his description of Sarah's experience for *Some Thoughts concerning the Revival* (1742), Jonathan transposes the first version's essentially time-bound, socially situated narrative into a static analysis of the saved soul that experiences the mortal body as at best an encumbrance, at worst the site of corruption. In keeping with this translation, Sarah's specific body becomes an anonymous and sexless type. The paradoxical effect of this abstraction is to accentuate further the unnamed saint's materiality. Jonathan stresses the saint's "vapory habit of body" and its uncontrollable physical manifestations, among which he includes ecstatic speeches. In times of "high transports," he writes, the saint is "disposed to speak of those great and glorious things of God and Christ, and the eternal world, that are in view, to others that are present, in a most earnest manner, and with a loud voice, so that it is next to impossible to avoid it: these effects on the body," he continues, do not arise "from any bodily distemper or weakness, because the greatest of all have been in a good state of health." Though manifestly spiritual, these words remain "effects on the body." In a passage with no antecedent in the original narrative, Edwards relates moments when "the consideration of sin that was in only speaking one word concerning the infinitely great and holy God, has been so affecting as to overcome the strength of nature." Anticipating charges of antinomianism, Edwards obtrudes a sense of Calvinist corruption only latent in Sarah's original narrative. Appropriately enough for one redefining Anne Hutchinson's legacy, he then surreptitiously associates that corruption with women's unruly public speech.[51]

50. Ibid., 178–179. The reference is to the writing implement: according to the *Oxford English Dictionary*, 2d ed., the first recorded mention of lead pencils appeared in 1602.

51. Jonathan Edwards, *Some Thoughts concerning the Revival*, in Goen, ed., *The Great Awakening*, vol. IV of Miller et al., eds., *Works of Jonathan Edwards*, 336.

When Edwards effaces Sarah's identity and transforms what the original record of her words presented as a socially contextualized narrative into the list form of *Some Thoughts concerning the Revival,* his representational choices create an abstract effect. His shift to a more abstract style reflects his increasingly distanced and disciplinary relationship to the people of Northampton. These developments correspond to the increasingly textual focus of his later work, most evident in his treatises. In the early 1740s, Edwards began to expand his sermons into the lengthier, more argument-oriented form of the treatise. That the shift of Edwards's energies away from a textualized oral performance into actual text was tied to his tense relationship with the Northampton laity seems clear. Edwards wanted his resistant parishioners to read his defense of restricted communion in *A Humble Inquiry,* a request that they conspicuously refused him. He even wrote out the contested oral professions that he demanded from his congregation — scripted professions that no one ever performed as her or his own.[52]

Given that the tensions between Edwards and his parishioners circulated around the minister's text-oriented authority, specifically his ability to categorize and diagnose stable, textlike saintly types, the "bad books" incident of 1744 that contributed to Edwards's eventual downfall takes on new significance. Most of the young men who gawked over an illustrated midwife's manual were Edwards's converts. Literalizing the erotic content of Jonathan's pulpit oratory and Sarah's ecstatic speeches, they brought an explicitly sexualized discourse into the public domain, taunting girls for being "nasty creatures," even teasing young women in the streets about menstruation. The rebellious impulse motivating these deeds emerged with striking clarity in Edwards's parsonage, where one young man claimed that he would not "worship a wig" and echoed Anne Hutchinson's contempt for the elders as "nothing but men, molded up of a little dirt." Three years later, Elisha Hawley, son of the Joseph Hawley who slit his throat in despair during Edwards's first revival, seduced and impregnated a Northampton woman. Here again Edwards confronted an overt challenge to his ministerial authority focused on illicit sexuality.[53]

52. On Edwards's shift in style, see Ellison, "The Sociology of 'Holy Indifference': Sarah Edwards' Narrative," *American Literature,* LVI (1984), 493. See also Wilson H. Kimnach, "The Brazen Trumpet: Jonathan Edwards's Conception of the Sermon," in William J. Scheick, ed., *Critical Essays on Jonathan Edwards* (Boston, 1980), 284. Christopher Grasso discusses the politics of oral, written, and printed media in the controversy between Edwards and his congregation in Grasso, *A Speaking Aristocracy: Transforming Public Discourse in Eighteenth-Century Connecticut* (Chapel Hill, N.C., 1999), 113–117.

53. Edwards, *Some Thoughts concerning the Revival,* in Goen, ed., *The Great Awakening,* vol. IV of Miller et al., eds., *Works of Jonathan Edwards,* 162. Patricia J. Tracy discusses this episode in *Jonathan Edwards, Pastor: Religion and Society in Eighteenth-Century Northampton* (New York, 1980), 160–165.

A decade earlier, in "Ruth's Resolution," Edwards had described conversion as a marriage celebration: "The lovely Bride calls you to the Marriage Supper. She hath Authority to invite Guests to her own Wedding; and you ought to look on her Invitation and Desire, as the Call of Christ the Bridegroom. . . . *'The Marriage of the Lamb is come, and his Wife hath made her self ready. And to her was granted that she should be arrayed in fine Linnen, clean and white: for the fine Linnen is the righteousness of saints.'* "[54] On a certain level, the picture-gazers and seducers merely responded to the implicit content of this invitation. As the socially destabilizing erotic freedom that accompanied the Awakening elsewhere manifested itself in Northampton, Edwards retreated from the power of his own feminized oral affect. Seeking to contain the volatility of a feminine sexuality associated with voice, Edwards absorbed himself in the rigors of a thoroughgoing textual ascesis.

Edwards contributed to efforts to close or narrow the space of public speech that New Light women briefly occupied. In *Some Thoughts concerning the Revival*, Edwards characterized women as "private Christians" and noted that, although they could "profess . . . the faith of Christ" with propriety and "without any fear of men," they must not "instruct, rebuke, and exhort, with a like sort of boldness as becomes a minister when preaching." The following year, Edwards participated in a special church council that meted out discipline to Bathsheba Kingsley, a Westfield woman who wandered from house to house as Abigail Hutchinson had wished to do, preaching her visionary message and claiming a spiritual authority superior to the clergy. Edwards and the other ministers on the council urged Kingsley to stay within her station and remain at home, sharing her faith privately with other Christians and refraining from attacks on the clergy. The few exceptions to the restraint enjoined upon women such as Kingsley only highlight the silencing of women's voices in the increasingly masculine public domains of eighteenth-century colonial British America. In their early years, evangelical sects such as the Baptists typically allowed greater freedom to women but later grew more rigid and exclusionary.[55] Sarah Osborn led a numerous and long-lived revival primarily for women and African Americans in her home in New-

---

54. Edwards, "Ruth's Resolution," in Edwards, *Discourses on Various Important Subjects,* in *Works of President Edwards,* V, 190–191.

55. Edwards, *Some Thoughts concerning the Revival,* in Goen, ed., *The Great Awakening,* vol. IV of Miller et al., eds., *Works of Jonathan Edwards,* 289–530, esp. 427. See also Ruttenberg, *Democratic Personality,* 455 n. 142. Edwards contributed to the widespread efforts to create a more decorous, less socially disruptive evangelicalism (Hall, *Contested Boundaries,* 91–99). On the Bathsheba Kingsley episode, see Brekus, *Strangers and Pilgrims,* 23–26. On the waxing and waning of encouragement toward evangelical women, see Susan Juster, *Disorderly Women: Sexual Politics and Evangelicalism in Revolutionary New England* (Ithaca, N.Y., 1994), esp. chap. 4. On routinization and the silencing of women's public voice, see Brekus, *Strangers and Pilgrims,* 60–61, 66.

port, Rhode Island, during the 1760s. Despite her impressive successes, she faced resistance particularly to the idea of her preaching from a Scripture passage, a practice that she vigorously denied. Small numbers of Quaker women continued to itinerate throughout the colonies and to England during the eighteenth century. And after the Revolution, Ann Lee and Jemima Wilkinson led innovative but marginal spiritual movements derived from Quakerism. But throughout the eighteenth century, the most acceptable styles of spiritual performance for women were limited to two: one was the confession of sin or guilt; the other was the display of inarticulate ecstasy and self-silencing like that practiced by Abigail Hutchinson and Sarah Edwards and described by Jonathan Edwards in his influential and much-reprinted works.[56]

Edwards revived strategies for the textual discipline of women's speech that the Puritan fathers of the seventeenth century had long employed but that the witchcraft controversy undermined. The recasting of verbal symbolism in New Light circles had rendered those strategies even more suspect as the emotional expressiveness and inwardness that New Lights identified with extempore preaching made spiritual leadership seem accessible to women such as Kingsley, Hutchinson, and Sarah Edwards. Yet, as Jonathan Edwards's practice in the Kingsley case and his narrative strategies in his accounts of Hutchinson and Sarah Edwards reveal, the evangelical redefinition of spiritual power did not in the end much expand women's religious authority. As a central figure in the conservative retrenchment of New Light practices after the Davenport controversy, Edwards adopted and embellished textually oriented techniques for restricting the sacred speech of women and made them available within evangelical circles. Such an approach is familiar from Cotton Mather's use of the written word to discipline female expression as well as from the insistence upon scriptural authority that marked Old Light Charles Chauncy's response to the socially disruptive dimensions of the Awakening. Edwards's career and writings make visible the subtler symbolism of verbal control—Abigail Hutchinson's aphasia and anorexia and her relationship to the Bible as a material form; Sarah Edwards's penetration by a "pencil" of light and the subsequent sundering of her body and spirit—that reintroduced the textual hierarchies of gender into the oral domain of the evangelicals.

56. Mary Beth Norton discusses Sarah Osborn's religious leadership in *Liberty's Daughters: The Revolutionary Experience of American Women, 1750–1800* (Boston, 1980), 129–132. For a list of a small handful of evangelical women exhorters, see Hall, *Contested Boundaries,* 134. On the Quakers, Lee, and Wilkinson, see Brekus, *Strangers and Pilgrims,* chap. 2. Nineteenth-century reprints from Edwards's *A Faithful Narrative* included excerpted editions of Abigail Hutchinson's conversion narrative. By midcentury, evangelical women such as Harriet Beecher Stowe had made over Edwards's accounts of feminine inarticulateness into tales celebrating female eloquence. See Sandra Gustafson, "Jonathan Edwards and the Reconstruction of 'Feminine' Speech," *American Literary History,* VI (1994), 185–212, esp. 185–188, 208.

2 The "Savage" Speaker Transformed

I. CULTURAL HYBRIDISM IN EVANGELICAL ORATORY

The extemporaneous preaching that Solomon Stoddard defended and George Whitefield popularized led to a range of cultural adaptations and exchanges among the peoples of British North America. After 1740, the evangelical community led by Whitefield cultivated a vision of spiritual empire that awoke a new interest among white Christians in proselytizing to native Americans and African Americans. White evangelicals produced forms of worship and lay participation more oriented toward the spoken word that made those missionary efforts an unprecedented success. To a significant extent, this success resulted from the prominence and symbolic value afforded oral performance within evangelicalism. Such elevation of the spoken word allowed native American and African American converts and preachers to adapt Christianity to their own spiritual practices and traditions, creating syncretic and hybridized forms of worship and belief.

Christian convert and Presbyterian minister Samson Occom experienced the Awakening as a teenager in a Mohegan community in southern Connecticut. Occom recalled that his first sense of the revival came from "a Strange Rumor among the English, that there were Extraordinary Ministers Preaching from Place to Place." Eventually, "Some Ministers began to visit us and Preach the Word of God; and the Common People all Came frequently and exhorted us to the things of God." Occom's description captures the surprising suddenness with which, during the 1740s, itinerant ministers and lay exhorters began traveling in large numbers to missions and native communities on the frontier to preach the gospel. They radically transformed the isolated and laborious efforts of a few missionaries who, following John Eliot, organized their proselytizing efforts around literacy and holy writ. Even as they privileged extempore preaching, these itinerant ministers and exhorters violated traditional decorum and occupied a liminal space that encouraged cultural mixing.[1] British cartoonists targeted such mixing as the

---

1. Occom, "A Short Narrative of My Life" (1768) was first published in Bernd Peyer, ed., *The Elders Wrote: An Anthology of Early Prose by North American Indians, 1768–1931* (Berlin, 1982),

problematic outcome of evangelical empire, portraying Whitefield as the lover of an American Indian princess in a recasting of the match between John Rolfe and Pocahontas. The improvisational Whitefieldian style did "seduce" native Americans, though not in the way the cartoonists portrayed. Confirming Roger Williams's insights into the importance of orally oriented missionary efforts, for instance, many Narragansetts converted to Christianity in the 1740s, "embracing a religious movement that challenged the intellectual elitism of Puritanism" and that "more closely resembled their traditional religion, emphasizing visions, the spoken rather than the written word, and religious leadership based on a 'calling' rather than on formal education."[2]

Evangelical redefinitions of Christian worship lent even greater success to the first sustained white missionary interest in enslaved Africans. Whitefield was the first minister to convert blacks to Christianity in significant numbers, including such prominent evangelical writers and orators as Phillis Wheatley, John Marrant, and Jupiter Hammon. Wheatley's elegy "On the Death of the Rev. Mr. George Whitefield, 1770" singled out his sacred oratory for praise and lamentation:

We hear no more the music of thy tongue,
Thy wonted auditories cease to throng.
Thy sermons in unequall'd accents flow'd,
And ev'ry bosom with devotion glow'd;
Thou didst in strains of eloquence refin'd
Inflame the heart, and captivate the mind.[3]

African American preachers and exhorters quickly became visible and controversial figures in the evangelical movement. Particularly in the South, African-influenced forms of worship radically shaped church life. The Awakening also set in motion the process that led to the formation of what in the nineteenth century

---

12–18, esp. 13. Timothy D. Hall discusses itinerancy and cultural mixing in *Contested Boundaries: Itinerancy and the Reshaping of the Colonial American Religious World* (Durham, N.C., 1994), 1–15, 134–135.

2. Cartoons: Harry S. Stout, *The Divine Dramatist: George Whitefield and the Rise of Modern Evangelicalism* (Grand Rapids, Mich., 1991), 246. Narragansetts: Colin G. Calloway, *New Worlds for All: Indians, Europeans, and the Remaking of Early America* (Baltimore, 1997), 84.

3. Julian D. Mason, ed., *The Poems of Phillis Wheatley,* rev. ed. (Chapel Hill, N.C., 1989), 55–56. On the evangelical rhetorical strategies in Wheatley's poetry, see Phillip M. Richards, "Phillis Wheatley and Literary Americanization," *American Quarterly,* XLIV (1992), 163–191. The poet Jupiter Hammon, another disciple of Whitefield's, may for a time have been an evangelical exhorter. Hammon's prose and poetic works include three prose sermons and poetry that recalls the poetic rhythms of the folk preacher. Two of Hammon's religious poems, one of them addressed to Wheatley, can be found in Vincent Carretta, ed., *Unchained Voices: An Anthology of Black Authors in the English-Speaking World of the Eighteenth Century* (Lexington, Ky., 1996), 26–31.

became dynamic and culturally distinctive black churches. In 1833, the Reverend Richard Allen singled out the extempore preaching style as fundamental to the emergence of these churches, noting that black Christians "are beholden to the Methodists, under God, for the light of the Gospel we enjoy; for all other denominations preached so high-flown that we were not able to comprehend their doctrine. Sure am I that reading sermons will never prove so beneficial to the colored people as spiritual or extempore preaching."[4]

In the eighteenth century, evangelical preachers from a range of backgrounds staged a rich variety of intercultural performances in the pulpit and in print. The preaching careers of three men in particular—David Brainerd, Samson Occom, and John Marrant—reveal how the evangelical privileging of the spoken word could be used to challenge the social hierarchies built on textual discipline. White missionaries such as David Brainerd, a follower of Jonathan Edwards who took the New Light message to the Pennsylvania frontier, located parallels in the spiritual practices of their native proselytes. Brainerd's journal reveals how those identifications sometimes trapped the evangelist in a restricted version of his own culture, at other times permitted him to adapt creatively to his audiences, and at still other times allowed him to recognize the integrity of alternative religious traditions. Imagining that his sacred speech possessed a divine power in direct competition with the demonic verbal powers of the native powwows, or shamans, Brainerd nonetheless displayed an interest in and respect for the spiritual beliefs of an unnamed nativist reformer.

Far more directly than Brainerd's missionary preaching, Samson Occom's pulpit performances challenged static, racialized cultural oppositions. Occom was fluent in both oral and textual modes, and he staged himself as a cultural mediator. As a contributor to emergent styles of "Indian Christianity," Occom's translations were truly reciprocal: introducing Christianity to his "brother" Indians, he simultaneously introduced Indian cultural practices to Britons and colonial

---

4. On eighteenth-century awakenings as "a shared black and white phenomenon," see Mechal Sobel, *The World They Made Together: Black and White Values in Eighteenth-Century Virginia* (Princeton, N.J., 1987), 180. On the transfer of spiritual practices from Africa to America, see Sylvia R. Frey and Betty Wood, *Come Shouting to Zion: African American Protestantism in the American South and British Caribbean to 1830* (Chapel Hill, N.C., 1998), chaps. 1, 2. See also Michael A. Gomez, *Exchanging Our Country Marks: The Transformation of African Identities in the Colonial and Antebellum South* (Chapel Hill, N.C., 1998), 252–253; Albert J. Raboteau, *Slave Religion: The "Invisible Institution" in the Antebellum South* (Oxford, 1978), part 1; Sterling Stuckey, *Slave Culture: Nationalist Theory and the Foundations of Black America* (New York, 1987), chap. 1; Philip D. Morgan, *Slave Counterpoint: Black Culture in the Eighteenth-Century Chesapeake and Lowcountry* (Chapel Hill, N.C., 1998), 420–437. For Richard Allen's comments, see Allen, "Life Experience and Gospel Labors" (1833), in Milton C. Sernett, ed., *Afro-American Religious History: A Documentary Witness* (Durham, N.C., 1985), 145.

British Americans, blending them with Christian belief to create a form of Indian Christianity. Most critically, Occom reimagined the Calibanesque figure of the inarticulate and debased savage, posing "broken" Indian English as a Pentecostal medium of great spiritual power.[5]

African American preacher John Marrant united three cultures in his evangelical ministry, finding in native society a self-authenticating image of the noble savage converted to Christianity. Contributing to a tradition of black-Indian identifications that celebrate the richness of oral traditions, and elaborating on Occom's refiguration of the "savage" speaker, Marrant reimagined the inarticulate Wild Man as a powerful orator.

The symbolism of orality in the works of these evangelists suggests the intercultural adaptations central to the eighteenth-century oratorical revival. Organized around the revivalist's novel forms of oratory and public performance, evangelicalism provided one important arena for cultural exchange where the pre-Revolutionary era's pervasive social hierarchies could be challenged.

II. COMPETING WORDS

In 1749, Jonathan Edwards published the edited diaries of David Brainerd, who in 1747 died in Edwards's Northampton home. Edwards significantly revised Brainerd's journals to produce *The Life of David Brainerd,* cutting out sections, adding others, and summarizing still others, in order to resolve the cultural contradictions of the Awakening and create a new ministerial persona. He portrayed Brainerd as the complement to and completion of the model evangelical subject that he had adumbrated in his two descriptions of Sarah Edwards.[6] With Brainerd's

5. In *New Worlds for All,* Calloway writes that "Indians often reinterpreted Christian messages and adapted Christian rituals to create Indian Christianity or Christianized versions of their traditional religions" (75). For a notable instance of this hybridizing process as it shaped the religion of Handsome Lake, see Anthony F. C. Wallace, *The Death and Rebirth of the Seneca* (New York, 1969).

6. On Edwards's editing practices, see Norman Pettit, introduction to Pettit, ed., *The Life of David Brainerd,* vol. VII of *The Works of Jonathan Edwards* (New Haven, Conn., 1985), hereafter cited as *Life of David Brainerd.* Joseph A. Conforti also discusses Edwards's revisions of Brainerd's original journal in *Jonathan Edwards, Religious Tradition, and American Culture* (Chapel Hill, N.C., 1995), 63–64. Brainerd had begun to prepare his private diary for publication but left the task uncompleted at his death. Edwards took over the project, which first appeared as *An Account of the Life of the Late Reverend Mr. David Brainerd . . .* (Boston, 1749). Extracts from the diaries had already appeared in Philadelphia in 1746 in what was known as Brainerd's *Journal.* Rather than reprint those diary entries that had already been published, Edwards refers the reader to the printed *Journal* throughout the *Life.* The Yale edition, which I use throughout, interpolates the *Journal* passages in brackets.

Life, Edwards resolved the socially destabilizing themes and the deflating narrative trajectory that characterized Sarah Edwards's conversion experience. Jonathan's descriptions of Sarah presented conversion as a disturbingly feminine spiritual penetration by Christ issuing in physical collapse; his account of Brainerd provided the masculine corrective to the feminine passivity that attended spiritual inspiration. Edwards underscored the fact that Sarah's ecstatic fits temporarily interfered with household routines. But in his description of Brainerd, who suffered from tuberculosis, Edwards emphasized the young man's efforts to fit the rhythmic elevation and breakdown produced by his disease to the demands of his missionary work, and celebrated his success in mustering his energies for his chosen task. Brainerd strove to convert the "heathen," a path that Edwards helped to make unavailable to a woman such as Sarah Edwards despite her qualifications as a teacher and minister as well as a pious example.[7]

Edwards's *Life of Brainerd* links Brainerd's missionary dedication to the symbolic redefinition of itinerancy, negotiating its meaning in a dynamic relationship to native American mobility. Choosing between a socially respectable fixed living and an uncertain itinerant life among a marginalized people, Brainerd transformed his social ostracism into a mode of professional performance. He made that choice after being thrown out of Yale in 1742 when, influenced by enthusiast James Davenport, he remarked in a fit of New Light zeal that a certain tutor had "no more grace than a chair." Though he agonized over his expulsion and repeatedly sought to have it overturned so he could complete his degree, Brainerd in an important sense accepted Yale's verdict on his socially marginal state

---

As in his presentations of Abigail Hutchinson and Sarah Edwards, Jonathan Edwards actively modeled his subject in the *Life* into an exemplary evangelical, restricting the extremes of pious elevation and despondency to present a more controlled, less enthusiastic spiritual life. In Brainerd's *Life,* however, he worked from a written account authored by the subject of his own text; such written precursors did not exist in the other instances.

7. *Life of David Brainerd* proved to be one of Edwards's most popular and influential works, attracting wide notice abroad as well as in the colonies and inspiring such famous eighteenth-century missionaries as John Wesley and Francis Asbury. Later, as missionary activity kept pace with European and American imperialism in the nineteenth and twentieth centuries, the *Life* provided a spiritual model for missionaries in India, Australia, New Zealand, China, Africa, Alaska, and South America; see Pettit, introduction to *Life of David Brainerd,* 3–4; Isabel Rivers, " 'Strangers and Pilgrims': Sources and Patterns of Methodist Narrative," in J. C. Hilson et al., eds., *Augustan Worlds* (New York, 1978), 189–203; Conforti, *Jonathan Edwards, Religious Tradition, and American Culture,* 195–196.

In his introduction, Pettit observes that Brainerd's conversion "resembled Sarah's to a remarkable degree," and Jonathan used similar language to describe them (8). Elizabeth D. Dodds reports that, according to Jonathan, Sarah was popular with the Stockbridge Indians (*Marriage to a Difficult Man: The "Uncommon Union" of Jonathan and Sarah Edwards* [Philadelphia, 1971], 159).

and spent his life converting that marginal condition into a position of cultural power. He made choices that dramatically reinforced his exclusion, most importantly in 1743 when he refused a settled, lucrative Congregationalist post to become an Indian missionary.[8]

He first recorded an interest in a missionary life shortly after his expulsion, when he described himself as "willing (if God should so order it) to suffer banishment from my native land, among the heathen, that I might do something for their souls' salvation, in distress and deaths of any kind." Brainerd imagined the "pleasure" of "undergoing the greatest sufferings in the cause of Christ" and like Paul felt "willing to be despised, and to be a gazing stock for the world to behold." Brainerd's grandiosely self-sacrificing ambitions are restated more modestly in a refrain from the Pauline Letter to the Hebrews that echoes through the record of his early itinerancy, asserting his delight in being a "stranger and pilgrim on the earth." Two years later, after several months of ineffective preaching to the Delawares and Susquehannas, he wrote, "I long and love to be a pilgrim; and want grace to imitate the life, labors, and sufferings of St. Paul among the heathen." Brainerd hoped to convert the American "heathen" and usher in Christ's earthly reign, thereby demonstrating his own spiritual power to the skeptical Yale authorities.[9]

Ambitious to imitate Paul, Brainerd not only embraced itinerancy; he flirted with the arrest and imprisonment that provided the circumstances of some of Paul's most effective preaching. Seeking an access of rhetorical authority in captivity, Brainerd traveled to New Haven for Yale graduation after the Connecticut government threatened to detain him for illegal itinerancy. His *Life* exposes the ambivalence of desire and fear that drew him to the institution that had expelled him. Captivity was never very far from Brainerd's mind. One journal entry meditates upon the question "whether I could be resigned if God should let the 'French Indians' come upon me and deprive me of my life, or carry me away captive" and concludes, "My soul seemed so far to rest and acquiesce in God that the sting and terror of these things seemed in great measure gone." When he received a letter warning of danger from the "French Indians" soon afterward, he regarded his

8. The *Life* provides a nuanced instance of the symbolics of itinerancy that Hall explores in *Contested Boundaries*. Calloway notes that most Indian peoples were not the nomads that Europeans represented them to be but horticulturists who moved seasonally. Invasion and disease disrupted native communities, turning many Indian peoples into impoverished and displaced migrants. At the same time, European immigrants motivated by land hunger moved frequently, in striking resemblance to the nomadism that they attributed to native Americans (*New Worlds for All*, 134). For Brainerd's zealous comment, see Pettit, ed., *Life of David Brainerd*, 41–42.

9. Pettit, ed., *Life of David Brainerd*, 159, 173, 184, 259. On the eighteenth-century hero/antihero, see Ronald Paulson, *Breaking and Remaking: Aesthetic Practice in England, 1700–1820* (New Brunswick, N.J., 1989), 168–192.

meditations as providential. His reflections on this occasion were matched by his actions on several proselytizing trips to uninterested and sometimes threatening native communities on the Susquehanna River, when Brainerd courted captivity by disrupting ceremonies and challenging community leaders. Brainerd's fear of a punishing captivity was matched by a barely suppressed longing for the martyrdom that eluded him.[10]

The dynamic of longing and fear in Brainerd's *Life* appears most visibly in those passages where a suspicious self-scrutiny operates in an uncomfortable, shifting psychic balance with the almost flagrant ambition evident in his efforts to imitate Paul's missionary career. Surveying his own complicated motives in an effort to achieve humility, Brainerd sought to eradicate selfishness and replace it with God's image. Brainerd's diary often echoes passages from the journal of Thomas Shepard, which revealed an egotistical, self-justifying impulse lurking within the first-generation minister's seeming selflessness and a matching anguish over his inability to eradicate his ready self-absorption. In a moment that parallels Shepard's struggle with self, Brainerd modifies his open ambition to imitate Paul with a statement at once hopeful and self-disciplining: "And when I long for holiness now, it is not so much for myself as formerly: but rather that thereby I may become an 'able minister of the New Testament' [2 Cor. 3:6], especially to the heathen." Even as he lay dying, Brainerd felt the need repeatedly to reassure his friends of his essential humility. "I don't go to heaven to be advanced, but to give honor to God," he told them, apparently fearful that those around him might view his death as prideful self-advancement rather than an act of pious resignation.[11]

Especially in the early journal entries, native Americans function primarily as externalized images of Brainerd's own "brutish" self, a self threatening in its resistance to conversion and assimilation to the divine image. During Brainerd's first months as a missionary, each time he preached to his native American audience he staged an imaginative confrontation with the collective Other that represented for him his own worst self, an Other that must be converted to godliness for Brainerd to believe in his own holiness. But Brainerd gradually grew more familiar with his audiences and came to recognize individuals rather than types, a process reflected in his increasingly humanized descriptions of individual natives as well as in his adaptations to the cultures of his native proselytes. Competing with the powwows, Brainerd quietly adopted their performance strategies in an effort

10. Pettit, ed., *Life of David Brainerd,* 222. Paul's bondage experiences included his conversion of the jailer in Acts 16:29–34 and his confrontation with Agrippa in Acts 26. Brought captive to the imperial center at Rome, Paul preached "the kingdom of God . . . with all confidence, no man forbidding him" (Acts 28:31). I quote throughout from the King James Version, in keeping with the predominant practice of the writers and preachers treated here.

11. Pettit, ed., *Life of David Brainerd,* 259, 466.

to persuade his listeners and exert authority. Yet he never acknowledged those accommodations, and fears of proximity and contamination marked all of Brainerd's missionary preaching.[12]

Upon arriving at the Mahican town of Kaunaumeek on the Massachusetts–New York border, his first missionary assignment, Brainerd recorded his profound misgivings about his prospects for success:

> I rode to Kaunaumeek, near twenty miles from Stockbridge, where the Indians lived, with whom I am concerned, and there lodged on a little heap of straw: was greatly exercised with inward trials and distresses all day; and in the evening my heart was sunk, and I seemed to have no God to go to. Oh that God would help me!

Summing up subsequent journal entries, Edwards notes that for the rest of the week Brainerd remained "in a dejected, depressed state of mind, and sometimes extremely so," enduring a "nameless and inconceivable" anguish despite the fact that "the Indians kindly receiv[ed] him, and . . . [were] seriously attentive to his instructions." During these early days at Kaunaumeek, Brainerd made few observations about Mahican life or interactions with his "people," as he called them, beyond tentative hopes for conversion followed by fears "that nothing would ever be done for them to any happy effect." Instead, he mentally rehearsed his expulsion from Yale again and again, regretting his "pride, selfishness, bitterness, and party-spirit in times past" and imagining himself "as a beast before God [Ps. 73:22]," "the meanest, vilest, most helpless, guilty, ignorant, benighted creature living."[13]

An entry from two weeks later illuminates the peculiar conjunction of a "nameless" anguish, self-abasement over past enthusiasm, and the weak efforts that he made to convert the Mahicans during his first weeks at Kaunaumeek. He noted that, in his afternoon sermon, he "seemed to be rehearsing idle tales, without the least life, fervor, sense, or comfort: and especially afterwards, at the sacrament, my soul was filled with confusion and the utmost anguish that ever I endured, under the feeling of my inexpressible vileness and meanness." He experienced self-abasement as an exposure of his innermost self: "I should have been ashamed to

12. For a discussion of the dynamic between the collective Other and Brainerd's own holiness, see Richard Slotkin, *Regeneration through Violence: The Mythology of the American Frontier, 1600–1860* (Middletown, Conn., 1973), 198. Noting the scholarly and popular tendency to ignore the Indians in Brainerd's *Journal*, Richard W. Pointer discusses some aspects of this process of adaptation in "'Poor Indians' and the 'Poor in Spirit': The Indian Impact on David Brainerd," *NEQ*, LXVII (1994), 403–426. Pointer traces the ways that Brainerd's "relationships with Indians increasingly shaped everything from his evangelistic method to his psychological health" (418).

13. Pettit, ed., *Life of David Brainerd*, 202–204.

see the most barbarous people on earth," he concluded, "because I was viler and seemingly more brutishly ignorant than they."[14]

Brainerd suffered from the nearly incapacitating performance anxiety registered in this passage throughout his preaching career. His apprehension of the native Americans before him, not as fellow humans, but rather as externalized representations of his own vileness and brutish ignorance, heightened his sense of shame and youthful inadequacy. Such a view of his audience made any concession to native knowledge or culture—even learning their language—deeply problematic, for it suggested that the human endeavor evident in rhetorical accommodation was an accommodation to sin itself. Brainerd adapted his preaching style to audiences unfamiliar with basic Christian dogma only reluctantly, then attributed his adaptation to the Spirit's influence, as in this account of his success at Crossweeksung in 1745: "I was enabled to open the Scripture and adapt my discourse and expressions to the capacities of my people, I know not how, in a plain, easy, and familiar manner, beyond all that I could have done by the utmost study: and this without any special difficulty, with as much freedom as if I had been addressing a common audience who had been instructed in the doctrine of Christianity all their days."[15]

Largely ineffectual at his first two missions, Kaunaumeek and the Forks of the Delaware, Brainerd was sensitive enough to cultural difference to observe how absurd his own beliefs must appear to those who did not share them, even if he did not like to dwell on the observation. Particularly when he intervened in the native rituals that he regarded as idolatrous devil worship, he came close to doubting his own faith and spiritual power. He broke up a Sunday "frolic" to preach, and later lamented that, though the Indians were "sober," he "still saw nothing *special* among them; from whence Satan took occasion to tempt and buffet me with these cursed suggestions, 'There is no God' [Ps. 14:1], or if there be, he is not able to convert the Indians before they had more knowledge, etc." This was as close as Brainerd came to a statement of his faith's blindness to other cultures, and he attributed the insight to the devil. After another feast, his complaints registered less self-awareness: "I knew they must hate to hear me, as having but just got home from their idolatrous feast and devil worship."[16]

Like other missionaries, Brainerd recognized the native powwows as his primary competitors for authority. Not long after his moment of atheistic doubt, he went so far as to invite the powwows to a contest of spiritual power: "I told my

14. Ibid., 206.
15. Ibid., 335.
16. Ibid., 262–263, 276.

people I was a Christian, and asked them why the powwows did not bewitch and poison me." Brainerd deflected any suspicions that he might have crossed the line, at times fine to the point of invisibility even to him, between the Puritan minister's inspired verbal authority and the shaman's ability to control spirits. He believed that the distinction ultimately rested on his almost ritualistic manifestations of self-denial: "I scarcely ever felt more sensible of my own unworthiness than in this action: I saw that the honor of God was concerned in the affair; and I desired to be preserved, not from selfish views, but for a testimony of the divine power and goodness, and of the truth of Christianity, and that God might be glorified." [17]

Christianity and native spirituality again came into focus for Brainerd as competing magics when he instructed his audience "respecting the miracles wrought by Christ in healing the sick, etc., and mentioned them as evidences of his divine mission and the truth of his doctrines." To these claims the Delawares responded by citing "the wonders of that kind" that their powwow "performed by his magic charms." Brainerd feared that this powwow would prove "a fatal obstruction" to any Delaware conversions, but in the end Brainerd's "magic" proved stronger when the powwow himself was converted. [18]

After hearing Brainerd preach at Crossweeksung during "the most remarkable and powerful awakening among the Indians," the powwow "was more effectually awakened and brought under great concern for his soul: And then, he says, upon his feeling the Word of God in his heart (as he expresses it), his spirit of conjuration left him entirely, that he has had no more power of that nature since than any other man living." Having lost his own spiritual power, the shaman longed to hear Brainerd preach, "and seemed desirous to hear the Word of God every day," until during a sermon he had what Brainerd believed to be a saving vision of Christ. Later, when another Indian threatened to bewitch Brainerd, this man "challenged him to do his worst, telling him that himself had been as great a conjurer as he, and that notwithstanding as soon as he felt that Word in his heart which these people loved (meaning the Word of God), his power of conjuring immediately left him." [19]

The competition between two powerful but (for white Christians) incompatible spoken Words marks out one critical site of cultural exchange and displacement in Brainerd's evangelical ministry. In his own personal piety as well as his most successful missionary efforts, he exploited analogous customs and then cordoned off his religious practices as the truly authentic versions of similar per-

17. Ibid., 265–266.
18. Ibid., 392.
19. Ibid., 392, 394–395. For similar accounts among the Moravians, see Jane T. Merritt, "Dreaming of the Savior's Blood: Moravians and the Indian Great Awakening in Pennsylvania," *WMQ*, 3d Ser., LIV (1997), 731.

formances. He often prayed in the woods, a behavior resembling native vision quests undertaken in the solitude of the forest. Brainerd would also on occasion sweat profusely while praying alone or exerting himself in the pulpit. His excessive perspiration might have been related to his tuberculosis, but he identified it as a sign of spiritual endeavor. The strenuous exertions of shamans in healing rituals and the purification ceremonies conducted in sweat lodge ceremonies suggest that Brainerd's native proselytes might have shared his perception that his sweat-streaked face demonstrated sacred power.[20]

The strategic adaptation of such parallels was most evident when, in August 1745, Brainerd at long last initiated a revival, complete with public weeping, crying out, and bodily manifestations. These events were precipitated by the conversion of his translator Moses Tatamy, an important "cultural broker" of property and standing on the Pennsylvania frontier. His conversion and baptism in July dramatically transformed Brainerd's mission, and Brainerd came to rely on Tatamy not only to translate his sermons but to establish an understanding with native communities before he preached to them for the first time.[21] Tatamy might well have been adapting Brainerd's message as he related it, since Brainerd lacked the language skills to supervise his translations. Brainerd warned his translator against "setting himself up as a publick teacher," suggesting his fears that Tatamy would acquire independent authority. Insisting on the purity of his mission, Brainerd rigorously differentiated his revival from a native ceremony. Most of the Delawares were "much affected, and many in great distress for their souls," he wrote, "and some few could neither go nor stand, but lay flat on the ground, as if pierced at heart, crying incessantly for mercy." Brainerd rigidly segregated what he viewed as legitimate expressions of religious emotions from his converts' previous ceremonial behavior: "It was very affecting to see the poor Indians, who the other day were hallowing and yelling in their idolatrous feasts and drunken frolics, now crying to God with such importunity for an interest in his dear Son!" Profuse emotional displays characterized native conversions. Many Indian converts wept

20. On the powerful image of sweat for Nanticoke and Shawnee warriors visiting Bethlehem, see Merritt, "Dreaming of the Savior's Blood," *WMQ*, 3d Ser., LIV (1997), 742. Daniel Gookin described healing rituals on Martha's Vineyard performed by powwows whose "extraordinary strange motions of their bodies" made them "sweat until they foam" (Neal Salisbury, "Red Puritans: The 'Praying Indians' of Massachusetts Bay and John Eliot," *WMQ*, 3d Ser., XXXI [1974], 39).

21. William A. Hunter, "Moses (Tunda) Tatamy, Delaware Indian Diplomat," in Herbert C. Kraft, ed., *A Delaware Indian Symposium* (Harrisburg, Pa., 1974), 71–88. On Tatamy's important role in the revival, see Pointer, " 'Poor Indians' and the 'Poor in Spirit,' " *NEQ*, LXVII (1994), 418–420. Among the Delawares, Mahicans, and Iroquois, community leaders controlled missionary activities (Merritt, "Dreaming of the Savior's Blood," *WMQ*, 3d Ser., LIV [1997], 727), and Tatamy helped gain Brainerd the opportunity to preach.

loudly when they delivered their conversion narratives, perhaps transferring an expressive behavior familiar from native adoption ceremonies to the assimilation ritual that served as the Congregationalist equivalent. Like other New Light ministers, Brainerd eventually felt compelled to tone down his converts' emotional displays, a process that Edwards's editorial practice only served to heighten. Later entries record Brainerd's efforts to constrain enthusiastic expression as he guided his converts away from "passionate" religious responses to more subdued, "rational" ones.[22]

While Brainerd slowly and imperfectly came to perceive parallels between native and Christian spiritual practices and exploit them in his ministry, he retained the demonizing rhetoric that functioned as a verbal stockade to keep Christian belief and ritual within and "idolatrous" native religion without. Yet he allowed the most self-conscious and striking moment of cultural mirroring in his journal to remain un-Christianized, gesturing to a tentative awareness of the cogency of native beliefs through their resemblance to his own beliefs. This episode involved an encounter with "a devout and zealous reformer, or rather restorer, of what he supposed was the ancient religion of the Indians." The meeting took place during Brainerd's initial trip up the Susquehanna River to the island town of Juniata a month after his first successful revival, though he did not record it until his second visit to Juniata the following September.[23] During that later visit, Brainerd quickly despaired of converting the Indians on the island, who had once seemed to him so promising because of their knowledge of English and their exposure to white people in their former Maryland home. Yet they disregarded his efforts to preach to them or teach them about Christianity, preoccupied instead with shaman-led healing ceremonies to combat "a fever and bloody flux." "Their monstrous actions tended to excite ideas of horror" and seemed "peculiarly suited to raise the devil," Brainerd observed, describing the "wild, ridiculous, and distracted motions" in

22. Pointer, " 'Poor Indians' and the 'Poor in Spirit,' " *NEQ*, LXVII (1994), 419; Pettit, ed., *Life of David Brainerd*, 307, 311, 344, 348. James Axtell observes, "Indian confessions seem to have been more lachrymose than most English relations" (*The Invasion Within: The Contest of Cultures in Colonial North America* [New York, 1985], 232). Axtell explains this phenomenon as a sign of a culturally uprooted people's emotional fragility. Elsewhere, however, Axtell notes the howling, bitter crying, and hand wringing that accompanied a captive's adoption in place of a lost relative, just prior to the captive's joyful acceptance into the family (315). Perhaps native converts seamlessly incorporated their own ceremonial practices into the conversion narrative ritual. The Delaware prophet Neolin, active in 1762–1763, preached a new spiritual message and "wept constantly while he preached" (Wallace, *The Death and Rebirth of the Seneca*, 119).

23. Pettit, ed., *Life of David Brainerd*, 329. Larzer Ziff observes of this encounter, "On an island at the junction of Juniata and Susquehanna rivers, David Brainerd had met his double" (*Writing in the New Nation: Prose, Print, and Politics in the Early United States* [New Haven, Conn., 1991], 10).

some detail. In his desperation Brainerd recalled the reformer he had met several
months earlier, describing "his appearance in his pontifical garb, which was a coat
of bears' skins, dressed with the hair on, and hanging down to his toes, a pair of
bearskin stockings, and a great wooden face, painted the one half black, the other
tawny, about the color of an Indian's skin, with an extravagant mouth, cut very
much awry; the face fastened to a bearskin cap which was drawn over his head."
The man approached Brainerd beating a tortoiseshell ceremonial rattle and dancing without allowing "any part of his body, not so much as his fingers, to be seen,"
making it impossible to discern that he was "a human creature." This inhuman
representation of "infernal powers" joined the demonic, the bestial, the Catholic,
and the Indian in a powerful image of native debasement. And it is as an image,
or more accurately a performance, that Brainerd presents this ceremonial dance,
for as he makes clear, he already knows the identity of the man inside the bearskin: "When he came near me I could not but shrink away from him, although it
was then noonday, and I knew who it was, his appearance and gestures were so
prodigiously frightful!"[24]

The terror of the performance subsided as Brainerd engaged the man in dialogue and encountered religious commitments that in many ways resembled his
own. The Indian told Brainerd "that God had taught him his religion, and that
he never would turn from it, but wanted to find some that would join heartily
with him in it; for the Indians, he said, were grown very degenerate and corrupt."
The reformer said further that he "had formerly been like the rest of the Indians,
until about four or five years before that time," when he had a type of conversion experience. "Then, he said, his heart was very much distressed, so that he
could not live among the Indians, but got away into the woods and lived alone
for some months," and in the end "God comforted his heart and showed him
what he should do." The consequences of his "conversion" included serving God
and loving "all men, be they who they would, so as he never did before." He
thought about "leaving all his friends and travelling abroad, in order to find some
that would join with him; for he believed God had some good people somewhere
that felt as he did." Brainerd could be portraying himself: formerly a participant
in communal life, the man became dissatisfied with his society and spent much
time in the woods seeking spiritual guidance; alienated from his community, he
planned to become an itinerant, setting off on a pilgrimage in search of kindred
spirits in other tribes. And like a good New Light, the reformer judged religious
matters according to his own standard of spiritual truth and drew the criticism
of Charles Chauncy's Indian equivalents. "He seemed to be sincere, honest and
conscientious in his own way, and according to his own religious notions, which

24. Pettit, ed., *Life of David Brainerd*, 327, 329.

was more than I ever saw in any other pagan: And I perceived he was looked upon and derided amongst most of the Indians as a precise zealot that made a needless noise about religious matters." This reforming Indian looked to Brainerd "more like true religion than anything I ever observed amongst other heathens."[25]

Brainerd's reformer was an early nativist. From the middle of the eighteenth century, nativist spiritual and political leaders, most famously Pontiac and Tecumseh, advocated intertribal unity and a return to precontact customs. Often these leaders of the "Indians' Great Awakening" argued that the Bible was for Europeans alone since God gave it only to them, that Christianity was the white man's faith, and that Indians should embrace more authentic indigenous forms of spiritual life.[26] Although nativists stressed the return to tradition, emphasized cultural difference, and even developed a theory of separate creations, they nonetheless incorporated elements of Christianity and shared certain spiritual practices characteristic of evangelical revival culture, notably reliance on prophets and dreams. Modeling an intertribal identity comparable to the intercolonial union that the itinerant ministries of the revivalists helped to create, nativist leaders produced a mirror of the Awakening on the frontier of the British Empire.[27]

Brainerd's account of the "reformer" provides one New Light missionary's interpretation of the resemblance between the awakenings of the colonists and the Indians. Perhaps most striking in Brainerd's description is his willingness to perceive the parallel between the New Lights and the nativists and then leave it alone, neither appropriated nor denounced, but respected as a discourse of spiritual revitalization. That willingness suggests a tentative and partial recognition of na-

25. Ibid., 329–330.

26. On the emergence of nativism and pan-Indianism, see Gregory Evans Dowd, *A Spirited Resistance: The North American Indian Struggle for Unity, 1745–1815* (Baltimore, 1992), 23–46, esp. 27; Merritt, "Dreaming of the Savior's Blood," *WMQ*, 3d Ser., LIV (1997), 725–726. Native arguments against the Bible's relevance for themselves were heard with some frequency on the Pennsylvania frontier around the time of Brainerd's activity. In 1751 John Brainerd, David's brother and fellow missionary, recorded one nativist's argument that the Bible was for Europeans alone (Dowd, *A Spirited Resistance*, 30). Merritt quotes a Nanticoke Indian's revelation from the Moravian records at Gnadenhütten that states, "To the Indians, he gave the Sacrifice. . . . To the white people he had given the Bible" (724).

27. On theories of separate creation, see Dowd, *A Spirited Resistance*, 30; on shared and distinct uses of dreams by whites and native Americans, see Merritt, "Dreaming of the Savior's Blood," *WMQ*, 3d Ser., LIV (1997), 724, 737–740. On the significance of dreams and prophecy to the Iroquois, see Wallace, *The Death and Rebirth of the Seneca*, 60–75. Richard White describes Quaker interest in Delaware dreams in *The Middle Ground: Indians, Empires, and Republics in the Great Lakes Region, 1650–1815* (New York, 1991), 330. On the intercolonial evangelical union and its relationship to the Revolution, see Harry S. Stout, "Religion, Communications, and the Ideological Origins of the American Revolution," *WMQ*, 3d Ser., XXXIV (1977), 519–541. For an argument that Brainerd demonizes the nativist, see Ziff, *Writing in the New Nation*, 10–12.

tive systems of belief. Brainerd's recognition of nativism arose as he reflected on the resemblances in religious "discourse." The structure of his account moves from outside to inside. It begins with the "infernal" performance of the nativist's dance, moves through a dialogue about religion, and ends with an acknowledgment of the Indian's "sincere, honest and conscientious" beliefs. The reformer's social position justifies his sacred practice. His itinerancy, his internal standard of belief, and above all his critical relationship to his community legitimate him for Brainerd. Recognizing the qualities that defined New Light subjectivity, Brainerd granted the nativist an interiority and a spiritual authenticity that he denied to the Indians at Juniata, whom he persisted in describing as "led captive by Satan at his will." The reformer's bearskin robe parted to reveal a human subject within, but the Juniata shamans who performed the healing ceremony lacked the opportunity to articulate the meaning of their "wild, ridiculous, and distracted motions." This physical extravagance identified them in Brainerd's mind as the devil's minions. Granting a provisional authenticity and an isolated power to the nativist on the Susquehanna, Brainerd hinted at the emergence of a more positive understanding of native speech among white colonists that gradually complicated, though it did not fully displace, representations dominated by excess and violence, madness and demonism.[28]

Certainly this revisionary moment did not dominate Edwards's *Life*, where it appeared only indirectly through reference to the public *Journal*. Complaining of the "badness of the ink" that Brainerd had used for these entries, and speculating that they were written "with the juice of some berries found in the woods, having no other ink in that wilderness," Edwards referred the reader to the *Journal* for their content. Edwards followed this practice for previously published excerpts throughout the *Life*, but his comments here suggest an active aversion, as if he could not bear to reproduce the words written in such wild ink himself.[29]

Nor did the encounter represent Brainerd's central legacy to future white missionaries, who most often focused on the themes of self-renunciation and strenuous action even in the face of substantial failure that are most evident in the work.[30] Nevertheless, Brainerd's conversation with the nativist leader is significant for its suggestion of some alternative representational and rhetorical possibilities that were opening up within mid-eighteenth-century American evangelicalism. Those possibilities were seized and exploited, not by white missionaries, but by native American and African American converts to the evangelical vision.

28. Pettit, ed., *Life of David Brainerd*, 327, 329–330.
29. Pettit, ed., *Life of David Brainerd*, 325.
30. For a survey of the influence of the *Life* on future generations of missionaries, see Conforti, *Jonathan Edwards, Religious Tradition, and American Culture*, esp. 78, 82.

Reimagining savage speech far more thoroughly than Brainerd, missionaries such as Samson Occom and John Marrant sought to create a rhetorical identity that would afford them a measure of cultural power within white society even as it permitted challenges to the hegemony of that society.

III. SAMSON OCCOM'S PENTECOSTAL INDIAN SPEECH

In a more radical intercultural adaptation of evangelicalism, Samson Occom redefined Indian speech to invent a potent new figure of native American spiritual eloquence and power. The preface to *A Sermon, Preached at the Execution of Moses Paul . . .* , delivered upon the occasion of the execution at New Haven of a Christian Mohegan and expanded for the press in 1772, explained Occom's reasons for agreeing to its publication. There he presented himself to his readers with a combination of studied humility and ambitious hopes for the popularity of his work. "It seems altogether unlikely that my performance will do any manner of service in the world, since the most excellent writings of worthy and learned men are disregarded," he began. Yet he was willing "to suffer my broken hints to appear in the world" because "the books that are in the world are written in very high and refined language; and the sermons that are delivered every Sabbath in general, are in a very high and lofty stile, so that the common people understand but little of them." In contrast to such literary sermons, Occom presented a colloquial idiom that would transcend cultural barriers. He promised that his audience "can't help understanding my talk; it is common, plain, every day talk: little children may understand me. And poor Negroes may plainly and fully understand my meaning; and it may be of service to them. Again, it may in a particular manner be serviceable to my poor kindred, the Indians." In his characterization of his own prose, Occom evokes two stereotypes about native American speech, presenting himself as the Calibanesque speaker of gibberish and as the speaker of a language that is fully transparent and universally accessible. When Occom describes his words as "broken," yet claims that the "common people," children, Negroes, and Indians "can't help understanding my talk," he resolves the paradoxes of Indian speech. Coming from "an uncommon quarter," the sermon achieves great power "because it is from an Indian." "God works where and when he pleases, and by what instruments he sees fit," Occom insisted, revising the Pauline paradox of personal weakness transformed into rhetorical power, "and he can and has used weak and unlikely instruments to bring about his great work."[31]

31. Samson Occom, *A Sermon, Preached at the Execution of Moses Paul, an Indian . . .* (New Haven, Conn., 1772), 3. Describing the sermon's expansion for the press, Occom notes that

Occom imagined Indian English as a kind of Pentecostal speech, a vernacular
that could cross ethnic and class boundaries. His preaching tour of the British Isles
from 1765 to 1768, internationally acclaimed 1772 execution sermon, and *Collection of Hymns and Spiritual Songs* published two years after the sermon all point
to the novel performance mode that Occom created in the course of his career: a
hybridized, evangelical, savage persona, whose liminal position between cultures
permitted a range of identifications across cultures. Contemporary anthropology
held that all cultures and all individuals pass through the savage stage in a developmental trajectory where ontogeny recapitulates phylogeny.[32] All children are
savages in this proto-Romantic model, and thus everyone has a residue of savagism and finds the savage speaker compelling. Seizing on the savage's universal
appeal implicit in this social and psychological theory, Occom transformed a de-
basing model of cultural inferiority into a position of rhetorical power. Through
his persona of the savage speaker whose authentically "broken," rhetorically low-
style words are available to all, Occom rearticulates the Puritan vernacular sermonic ideal in the terms of a distinctive Indian Christianity.

Occom developed this figure of Indian rhetorical power after years spent negotiating cultural barriers and hostile stereotypes such as those visible in Brainerd's
Life.[33] White prejudices and fears of Indian power complicated the display of hu-

---

"about one half of it was not delivered as it was written, and now it is a little altered and enlarged in some places" (3). According to the table of "leading authors, by decade 1701–1790" in
David D. Hall, *History of the Book in America,* forthcoming, Occom's sermon ranked seventh for
the decade 1771–1780.

On European attitudes toward Indian language, see Stephen J. Greenblatt, "Learning to
Curse: Aspects of Linguistic Colonialism in the Sixteenth Century," in Greenblatt, *Learning to
Curse: Essays in Early Modern Culture* (New York, 1990), 16–39; Greenblatt, *Marvelous Posses-
sions: The Wonder of the New World* (Chicago, 1991), chap. 4; David Murray, *Forked Tongues:
Speech, Writing, and Representation in North American Indian Texts* (Bloomington, Ind., 1991),
chap. 2. On the Pauline model of rhetorical power, see Appendix, below.

32. Less successful than his sermon, Occom's hymnal nevertheless appeared in three editions
and remained important to Christian Indian traditions of song well into the twentieth century;
see Bernd Peyer, *The Tutor'd Mind: Indian Missionary-Writers in Antebellum America* (Amherst,
Mass., 1997), 96; Margaret Connell Szasz, "Samson Occom: Mohegan as Spiritual Intermediary,"
in Szasz, ed., *Between Indian and White Worlds: The Cultural Broker* (Norman, Okla., 1994), 61–
78, esp. 73–74. On the anthropological theories, see Roy Harvey Pearce, *The Savages of America:
A Study of the Indian and the Idea of Civilization* (Baltimore, 1965), 49.

33. Brainerd (1718–1747) and Occom (1723–1792) occupied the same geographic and social
spheres for much of Brainerd's short life. Born and raised in a Mohegan town near New London, Connecticut, not far from Brainerd's native Haddam, Occom was a student and colleague
of Brainerd's patron Eleazer Wheelock and received encouragement and financial support from
the Reverend Samuel Buell, Brainerd's companion in evangelical endeavors at Yale and the minister whose preaching awakened Sarah Edwards in 1742. In 1743, Brainerd made a brief visit to
the Montauk mission on Long Island where Occom later worked as a schoolmaster for over a de-

mility essential to his pulpit authority. Attempts to undermine native authority often focused on the question of cultural legitimacy, and Occom routinely faced questions about his authenticity as an Indian and as a Christian, particularly in his role as a strong and articulate defender of native land rights. Occom's opponents questioned his tribal identity, spread rumors suggesting that his conversion was merely staged for the English tour, and accused him of alcoholism. His success in the new international arena of itinerant evangelical celebrities during his 1765 preaching tour of Great Britain sponsored by George Whitefield encouraged him to a new confidence. During the two years he spent traveling the British Isles, Occom preached more than three hundred sermons and raised more than twelve thousand pounds for Moor's Indian Charity School, run by his former teacher Eleazer Wheelock. In Whitefield's international marketplace of charismatic revivalism, Occom had few rivals as a preacher. The tremendous success of his preaching tour and the ultimate failure of the Indian Charity School offer a neat parable about the suasive appeal of intercultural dramatic performance and the social limits to that power.[34]

Though far from the first American Indian to become a celebrity in England, Occom was the first native to preach there. He proved to be an extraordinarily astute manipulator of cultural markers of difference.[35] Staging himself as both an Indian and an evangelical Christian minister, Occom sustained the tension between the two identities, routinely performing the transgression of cultural boundaries. Two portraits of Occom attest to his cultural eclecticism. The earlier portrait, completed by Nathaniel Smibert in the early 1750s, presents Occom outdoors under a tree, dressed in an open-necked white shirt and a blanket. The second portrait was painted during his tour of Britain and shows a more English Occom who nevertheless is manifestly Indian. Seated in a substantial chair, Occom is clad in a minister's well-cut black suit with a white neckcloth. Gesturing toward a large Bible on the desk with his right hand, he seems to trace the line he is read-

---

cade. His mission to the Oneidas was sponsored by the same Society in Scotland for Propagating Christian Knowledge that funded Brainerd's missionary activities.

34. On rumors against Occom's authenticity, see William DeLoss Love, *Samson Occom and the Christian Indians of New England* (Boston, 1899), 135; Murray, *Forked Tongues,* 53–54. Peyer, *The Tutor'd Mind,* 82–88, and Szasz, ed., "Samson Occom," in *Between Indian and White Worlds,* 72–76, both discuss Occom's pro-Indian activities. On Whitefield's involvement in Occom's preaching tour, see Love, *Samson Occom and the Christian Indians of New England,* chap. 8. Occom accused Wheelock of creating an institution "too alba mater [white mother] to Suckle the Tawnees, for She is already adorned up too much like the Popish Virgin Mary." The accusation is a striking reversal of the standard Puritan analogy between Indian and Catholic worship. See Axtell, *The Invasion Within,* 215.

35. Even his name conveys his role as cultural broker, for Occom means "the other side," according to Szasz ("Samson Occom," in Szasz, ed., *Between Indian and White Worlds,* 77).

FIGURE 3. The Reverend Samson Occom. *By Nathaniel Smibert. Permission of Bowdoin College Museum of Art, Brunswick, Maine, bequest of James Bowdoin III*

ing with his forefinger. Despite his apparent attention to the book, however, his face is directed toward the viewer, whose gaze he meets. The pose recalls Jonathan Edwards's pulpit habit of following his sermon text with his finger while looking out at the audience. For Occom, the gesture suggests additional complications related to his cultural heritage. As an Indian he had to perform his literacy for skeptical whites; as a New Light minister he needed to have Scripture at his command, yet he must preach without a script. Pointing at the Book while looking at the audience, Occom demonstrated the literate mastery that enabled him fully to perform, rather than merely read, Scripture. Further elaborating the picture's cultural identifications, a bow and arrow hang on the wall above the Bible roughly parallel with Occom's gesturing arm, as if to suggest that the Bible and the bow and arrow are cultural equivalents, both within Occom's easy reach. In a similar gesture, Occom bound his Bible in a deerskin cover of his own workmanship.[36]

Literacy and orality were among the central signs of cultural identity that Occom manipulated. Converted by James Davenport, the New Light minister who most vigorously encouraged verbal and bodily demonstrations of pious emotion, Occom initially thought that Davenport preached a religion that was "a new thing among mankind, Such as they never heard the like before, so Ignorant was I." While Davenport's oral emphasis and physically expressive delivery appealed to Occom in a way that earlier preachers had not, the attractiveness of what he came to recognize as Christianity was also linked to the charisma of the printed Word. "After I was awakened and converted, I went to all the meetings, I could come at," he wrote in "A Short Narrative of My Life," "and Continued under Trouble of Mind about 6 months; at which time I began to Learn the English Letters; got me a Primer, and used to go to my English Neighbours frequently for Assistance in Reading, but went to no School." Writing for a white audience, he charted his conversion experience as a movement into literacy. Occom described how he "found Serenity and Pleasure of the Soul, in Serving God" just as he "began to Read in the New Testament without Spelling." His experience of reading his way through the New Testament stands in stark contrast to Abigail Hutchinson's similar endeavor. Where Hutchinson read until she found herself surrounded by the "blackness of darkness," Occom's Scripture reading generated a sense of spiritual peace and, eventually, his own ministerial authority.[37]

The cultural politics of oral and literate forms shaped his pedagogy and preaching at the Montauk mission. His 1761 account of Montauk spiritual beliefs reflected the primacy of oral performance in their description of heaven, where good souls "exercise themselves in pleasurable singing and dancing forever." Alert to the difficulty the written word posed for children unaccustomed to literacy technologies, he noted that oral-aural proficiency did not always translate into the visual skills essential for reading. Even "Dull" children "can soon learn to Say over their Letters, they Distinguish the Sounds by the Ear," he observed, "but their

36. For a similar manipulation of cultural signs, see the discussion of the 1740 portrait of Iroquois sachem Hendrick, in Timothy J. Shannon, "Dressing for Success on the Mohawk Frontier: Hendrick, William Johnson, and the Indian Fashion," *WMQ*, 3d Ser., LIII (1996), 14.

37. On this aspect of Occom's conversion, see Occom, letter, Nov. 28, 1765, in Leon Burr Richardson, *An Indian Preacher in England . . .* (Hanover, N.H., 1933), 70; Occom, "A Short Narrative of My Life," in Peyer, ed., *The Elders Wrote,* 731.

FIGURE 4. Samson Occom. *By J. Spilsbury. Courtesy, Dartmouth College Library*

Eyes can't Distinguish the Letters." To address this problem, Occom trained his students in visual recognition using alphabet blocks. The persistent importance of oral performance for native Americans exposed to the culture of the Book became evident when "Some Enthusiastical Exhorters from New England" prejudiced the adults "against Mr. Horton [the Montauk minister], and many of them had left him; by this means he was Discouraged, and was disposed from these Indians." Drawn to exhorters who elevated immediate inspiration over biblical text, the Montauk Indians recognized an oral emphasis closer to their own cultural traditions. After Horton left the mission, however, Occom successfully combatted enthusiasm with Scripture:

> I opposed them not openly but let them go on in their way, and whenever I had an opportunity, I would read Such pages of the Scriptures, and [as?] I thought would confound their Notions, and I would come to them with all Authority, Saying "these Saith the Lord"; and by this means, the Lord was pleased to Bless my poor Endeavours, and they were reclaimed, and Brought to hear almost any of the ministers.

Familiar with "the make and the Disposition of the Indians," Occom recognized the effect of charismatic eloquence in a community resistant to textual authority. He invoked Scripture with just the right degree of personal assertiveness to counter the appeal of enthusiasm, anchoring the words of the text in an authoritative oral performance.[38]

In England as in Montauk, Occom performed the crossing of cultural boundaries as he moved between biblical text and authoritative speech, elaborating the performance semiotic of speech and text. Acclaimed as a preacher in both English and his native Mohegan tongue, he incorporated figurative traditions of native oratory in his English sermons. Sympathetic audiences celebrated Occom for his authenticity during his English tour, praising his "Simplicity" and "guiles" temper. Yet he was also lampooned in the London theater, and he complained to Wheelock of feeling like "a Gazing Stocke, Yea Even a Laughing Stocke, in Strange Countries" for the cause of the Indian school, an experience made more bitter by the school's failure. Occom highlights the difficulty of negotiating social power from his rhetorical successes in "A Short Narrative of My Life," written in 1768 after his return from Britain. There he complains of his unfair treatment during his years at Montauk, when he received from the Boston Board of Commissioners for twelve years' service the same amount that they paid a white missionary for a single year even though Occom saved them money by acting as his own translator. Evaluating that earlier injustice, and expecting more such treatment despite his proven talents, Occom concludes: "So I am ready to Say, they have used me thus, because I Can't Influence the Indians so well as other missionaries; but I can assure them I have endeavoured to teach them as well as I know how;—but I *must* Say, 'I believe it is because I am a poor Indian.' I Can't help that God has made me So; I did not make my self so." The tension between what Occom is "ready to Say"

---

38. Samson Occom, "An Account of the Montauk Indians, on Long-Island," Massachusetts Historical Society, *Collections*, X (Boston, 1809), 106–111, esp. 110; Occom, "A Short Narrative of My Life," in Peyer, ed., *The Elders Wrote*, 15–16.

and what he "must Say" points to the almost unnegotiable restraints that whites placed on Indian self-assertion and the attendant difficulties for native Americans of exercising any sort of agency in white culture. Even the relatively sympathetic Wheelock observed what he called "Insufferable pride" in his native American students and worked incessantly to break them of it. The evangelical Pauline paradigm of rhetorical strength flowing from weakness of itself failed to resolve the problem of colonial hegemony for Occom.[39]

When Occom preached Moses Paul's execution sermon in 1772, he had begun to resolve his unsustainable personal and professional situation created by duplicitous and discriminatory whites through a more exclusive focus on the needs of his own people. Reimagining native speech as an idiom of universal potency, he sought to overcome the constraints placed on his agency and the agency of his "brethren." The task was not an easy one. As an Indian minister preaching to a mixed audience that included prominent white ministers as well as a substantial number of Christian Indians, Occom presented Moses Paul's acts as sinful and criticized the tragic prevalence of drunkenness among native Americans while simultaneously rejecting demonic stereotypes and protecting his own pulpit authority. Even as he embraced the elite white view of drinking as debauchery, Occom recast arguments against it in terms that challenged the hegemonic understanding of native alcohol consumption. In his concluding address to "my brethren and kindred according to the flesh," he argued that drunkenness was not, as many whites believed, a sign of an inevitable Indian degeneracy and eventual disappearance. Rather, alcoholism was the avoidable cause of personal and social decline. For Occom, sobriety was as much a political as a spiritual gesture, demonstrating the rational self-control that whites insisted was impossible for Indians, an argument they used to justify land theft, displacement, and extermination.[40]

As Occom well knew, Indian converts such as Moses Paul and himself were common targets of white suspicion, accused of masquerading as Christians for reasons varying from self-interest to treasonous duplicity. To deflect hostile in-

39. Love, *Samson Occom and the Christian Indians of New England*, 137; Szasz, "Samson Occom," in Szasz, ed., *Between Indian and White Worlds*, 69 (see also 76); Murray, *Forked Tongues*, 55; Occom, "A Short Narrative of My Life," in Peyer, ed., *The Elders Wrote*, 18. On Wheelock's attitudes toward his Indian students, see Axtell, *The Invasion Within*, 211. Dana D. Nelson analyzes this passage from Occom as an instance of the colonial economy of authoritative selfhood in " '(I Speak Like a Fool but I Am Constrained)': Samson Occom's *Short Narrative* and the 'Economies of the Racial Self,' " in Helen Jaskoski, ed., *Early Native American Writing: New Critical Essays* (Cambridge, 1996), 42–65, esp. 58.

40. Occom, "A Short Narrative of My Life," in Peyer, ed., *The Elders Wrote*, 28. Szasz describes Occom's shift around 1773 to a more focused attention to Mohegan and native American needs after his split with Wheelock and missionary leaders ("Samson Occom," in Szasz, *Between Indian and White Worlds*, 72).

terpretations that would uncover an essential, corrupt racial identity beneath his Christian facade, Occom opened his sermon with a discussion of the universality of death and sin. Like Roger Williams in "Christenings Make Not Christians," Occom denied the colonial equivalence between culture and faith. He argued that no people has a monopoly on sinfulness, nor does any nation escape sin. Since Adam fell, all men resemble the European stereotype of the Indian. Turned out of paradise, man has become a "vagabond in God's world . . . yet he is proud, he is haughty, and exalts himself above God, tho' he is wretched and miserable, and poor, and blind and naked. He glories in his shame. Sin has made him beastly and devilish; yea, he is sunk beneath the beasts, and is worse than the ravenous beasts of the wilderness. He is become ill-natured, cruel and murderous; he is contentious and quarrelsome." All men are fallen, Occom asserts, and Satan never discriminates: "Negroes, Indians, English, or of what nation soever, all that die in their sins, must go to hell together, for the wages of sin is death." [41]

In a series of related strategic reversals, Occom's sermon transforms concepts central to evangelicalism and its republican heirs: the identity of the holy community, the nature and value of worldly asceticism, and the racial hierarchies constructed on notions of an ascetic community defined to subordinate and ultimately exclude native Americans. Occom's concluding phrase echoes his sermon text: "For the wages of sin is death, but the gift of God is eternal life through Jesus Christ our Lord" (Rom. 6:23). George Whitefield used this Scripture passage to criticize British and colonial American consumer society; Occom focused on the image of gift to present a more radical critique of the capitalist economy. This opposition between wages and gifts provided Occom with his main lever for opening up cultural categories. Native American gift economies came into routine conflict with European forms of market exchange: the English phrase "Indian giver" reflects fundamentally conflicting cultural attitudes toward goods and their circulation. [42]

41. Samson Occom, *A Sermon*, 10, 17. For an informative discussion of contemporary scholarly skepticism about Indian conversions, see James Axtell, "Were Indian Conversions *Bona Fide?*" in Axtell, *After Columbus: Essays in the Ethnohistory of Colonial North America* (New York, 1988), 100–121.

42. For an important corrective to democratizing views of the Awakening in the Revolutionary era, see Ronald T. Takaki, *Iron Cages: Race and Culture in Nineteenth-Century America* (New York, 1979), 13–15. Frank Lambert discusses Whitefield's language of economy in *"Pedlar in Divinity": George Whitefield and the Transatlantic Revivals, 1737–1770* (Princeton, N.J., 1994), 219. On the conflicting expectations and consequent misunderstandings that arose between Indians and European traders, see Neal Salisbury, *Manitou and Providence: Indians, Europeans, and the Making of New England, 1500–1643* (New York, 1982); see also Wallace, *The Death and Rebirth of the Seneca*, 282; Gregory Evans Dowd, " 'Insidious Friends': Gift Giving and the Cherokee-British Alliance in the Seven Years' War," in Andrew R. L. Cayton and Fredrika J. Teute, eds.,

In his sermon, Occom turned the European hierarchy reflected in that phrase on its head, aligning the wages of a market economy with the body and death. "At the cessation of natural life, there is an end of all the enjoyments of this life; there is no more joy or sorrow; no more hope nor fear, as to the body," he told his audience. Among the activities that end with death, he included "sinful pleasures" like "tavern haunting" and "drunkeness" and such socially acceptable activities as the "contrivance and carrying on any business," "merchandizing and trading," and "buying and selling." Grouping the capitalist's worldly asceticism with the debauchee's promiscuity and drunkenness, Occom rejects financial success as evidence of grace. All of the sinner's activities bear the body's corruption no matter how profitable they may be.[43]

Against the contaminations of the body's wage economy Occom sets the gift economy of grace, developing the familiar opposition between the wages of sin and the gift of grace in a manner that suggests its distinctive significance for his native auditors. Though "there is nothing that we can call our own, but our sins," God gives "heaven and happiness" as "a free gift"; "Christ himself is the gift, and he is the christian's life." Devoured as the saint's "meat and drink," grace is never exhausted. It flows in infinitely replenished streams. The pleasures of sanctity resemble the erotic delights of "a wedding day." Like Paul, the convert is "all alive to God," "willing to spend and be spent" in his service. But spending and being spent, the saint can never hope to repay God. Grace can never be earned.[44]

Functioning like a gift economy, grace offers Occom's Indian audience an escape from the destructive effects of market exchange. In a 1766 letter describing a Mohegan land dispute with the Connecticut government, Occom complained about the effects that conflicting conceptions of property and exchange had on native peoples: "I am afraid the poor Indians will never stand a good chance with the English in their land controversies," he wrote, "because they are very poor, they have no money. Money is almighty now-a-days." In contrast, money is no obstacle in conversion: "He that hath no money may come." Apart from the contested matter of land sales, which Occom's sermon does not address, the most common impact of the money economy on native life took the form of individuals trading all their belongings for liquor. "For the love of strong drink," Occom lamented, "we spend all that we have, and every thing we can get." This is not like the endless "spending and being spent" that grace enables. Human resources are quickly exhausted in such spirituous, rather than spiritual, exchanges. Worse

Contact Points: American Frontiers from the Mohawk Valley to the Mississippi, 1750–1830 (Chapel Hill, N.C., 1998), 114–150. On gift economies, see Marcel Mauss, The Gift: Forms and Functions of Exchange in Archaic Societies, trans. Ian Cunnison (New York, 1967), 55.

43. Occom, A Sermon, 15.
44. Ibid., 19–21, 25.

still, the drunkard has no protection against exchanges even more unequal than market-value trades for alcohol: "If he has any money or any thing valuable, he may loose it all, or may be robb'd, or he may make a foolish bargain, and be cheated out of all he has."[45]

Occom imagined liquid "spirits" as a debased, parodic form of grace. Drunkards were indeed "full of new wine" (Acts 2:13) as hostile observers at the Pentecost thought the apostles to be. But where the apostles spoke in tongues so "every man heard them speak in his own language" (Acts 2:6), the inebriate "cannot bring out his words distinct, so as to be understood." When the drunkard speaks in an incomprehensible tongue, he resembles the misguided Corinthians whom Paul chided for speaking unintelligibly and thus barbarically: "Therefore if I know not the meaning of the voice, I shall be unto him that speaketh a barbarian, and he that speaketh *shall be* a barbarian unto me" (1 Cor. 14:11). Since the drunkard's speech cannot circulate, he remains trapped in his debased condition outside any community, a barbarian in the eyes of others: "He is of no service to himself, to his family, to his neighbours, or his country." The babbling inebriate's condition resembles that of the debtor. Neither has the necessary currency—linguistic or monetary—to escape his isolated condition within the spirituous exchange economy.[46]

Occom worried that, incomprehensible and isolated, the native drunkard reinforced white America's most unflattering stereotypes about the nonsensical language and anarchic individualism of "Satanic" Indians. Christianity offered a substitute for the liquor that circulated, not in the gift economy of true divine grace, but rather in an exchange economy that mired native Americans in debt and its linguistic equivalent, unintelligible babble. Imagined as an alternative to market exchange, Protestantism, as Occom construed it in an early form of Indian Christianity, suggested a route out of the exploitative system of white trade.[47] As he turned away from his hopes of success within white society and became more fo-

---

45. Ibid., 23, 29–30; Peyer, *The Tutor'd Mind*, 74. Nelson discusses Occom's resistance to his own commodification by whites in his "Short Narrative," in " '(I Speak Like a Fool but I Am Constrained),' " in Jaskoski, ed., *Early Native American Writing*, 55–56.

46. Occom, *A Sermon*, 30.

47. Occom's strategy mirrored the practices of David Brainerd's native converts who embraced Brainerd's spiritual message but resisted the work ethic that he tried to inculcate in them; see Pointer, " 'Poor Indians' and the 'Poor in Spirit,' " *NEQ*, LXVII (1994), 418. Calloway notes that Indians sometimes used Christianity to resist aspects of white culture, a strategy evident in Occom's sermon *(New Worlds for All,* 69). Occom's plan for the Brothertown community indicates his commitment to native autonomy; see Love, *Samson Occom and the Christian Indians of New England,* chap. 12. See also Calloway's discussion of the "Indian-oriented" faction that developed around Occom in the New Stockbridge church in *The American Revolution in Indian Country: Crisis and Diversity in Native American Communities* (Cambridge, 1995), 105.

cused upon native American problems and needs, then, he began to recast the terms of Christianity for his own community in ways that both adapted to and challenged white assumptions. Braiding together native metaphors of gift-giving with Christian metaphysics, Occom's sermon presents his interpretation of Christian belief as an alternative to individual death and cultural extinction for native peoples. At the same time, Occom's "broken" but widely accessible Indian English circulated with the gift's freedom, equally available to "common people," whether European, African, or native American.

IV. JOHN MARRANT, "SAVAGE" SPEAKER

Samson Occom's Christian "savage" persona was only one of a number of Revolutionary-era efforts by ethnic minorities to create intercultural identifications that would counter the representational force of an independent American nation that restricted citizenship to whites. The preaching career of John Marrant, Indian missionary and the first ordained African American minister, presents a sustained critique of the Revolution's exclusionary nationalism. He offered instead an expansive, inclusive version of a spiritual imperium cleansed of racial hierarchies. Marrant articulated that vision of a universal awakening at the end of his best-selling captivity narrative when, anticipating his career as a missionary to the Indians of Nova Scotia, he prayed that

> vast multitudes of hard tongues, and of a strange speech, may learn the language of Canaan, and sing the song of Moses, and of the Lamb; and, anticipating the glorious prospect, may we all with fervent hearts, and willing tongues, sing Hallelujah; the kingdoms of the world are become the kingdoms of our God, and of his Christ.

Here Marrant imagines a universal Christian culture characterized by a cosmopolitan oratory, its expressive forms dominated by speech and song.[48]

Marrant's embrace of the possibilities of an orally oriented Christianity began

48. See John Marrant, *A Narrative of the Lord's Wonderful Dealings with John Marrant . . . ,* in Adam Potkay and Sandra Burr, eds., *Black Atlantic Writers of the Eighteenth Century: Living the New Exodus in England and the Americas* (New York, 1995), 67–74, esp. 95; Sidney Kaplan and Emma Nogrady Kaplan, *The Black Presence in the Era of the American Revolution, 1770–1800,* rev. ed. (Amherst, Mass., 1989), 111–116. Marrant's narrative was first published under this title in London in 1785 and it became one of the three most popular captivity narratives of the eighteenth and nineteenth centuries. It went through numerous editions; for a partial list, see 70–73. William Aldridge, a white British evangelical minister, served as Marrant's amanuensis and editor. Marrant exercised the greatest control over the fourth edition (also 1785), which Potkay and Burr reprint.

with his conversion by George Whitefield around 1770 in Charleston, where as a free black youth he trained as a musician and a carpenter. Entering a Whitefield revival meeting intent on disrupting it, Marrant was startled when Whitefield instead made him a participant in his divine drama by applying a damning text directly to the young troublemaker. Marrant made his way into the crowded room where Whitefield was about to preach and lifted his french horn to his shoulder to blow it just as Whitefield "was naming his text, and looking round, as I thought, directly upon me, and pointing with his finger, he uttered these words, 'Prepare To Meet Thy GOD, O Israel.'" Singled out in this manner as the subject of the text, Marrant found that the "Lord accompanied the word with such power, that I was struck to the ground, and lay both speechless and senseless near half an hour. . . . I was constrained in the bitterness of my spirit to halloo out in the midst of the congregation, which disturbing them, they took me away."[49]

Converted by Whitefield's dramatic preaching, his proselytes often imagined their lives as holy theater, an effect clearly evident in Marrant's narrative. Like David Brainerd, Marrant modeled his life in part on Paul, whose oratorical feats in captivity were the standard by which evangelical missionaries evaluated their own successes. When Marrant converts first his would-be executioner and later the Cherokee "king," he reenacts Paul's bondage experiences.[50] Marrant's Pauline revision of the captivity narrative hinges on a far more thorough identification with his captors than that achieved by David Brainerd, enabling him to transform himself into a savage speaker. Marrant learns Cherokee from an Indian companion before he is taken captive. As a consequence, his experience reverses the typical captive's plunge into an alien linguistic world, where the silent, isolated prisoner communicates through pantomimic gestures. In traditional captivity narratives such as the "Narrative of the Captivity and Restoration of Mrs. Mary Rowlandson" (1682), the prisoner experiences Indian bondage as bondage to sin and release as redemption. Rowlandson punctuated her tale with the numerous Scrip-

49. Marrant, *A Narrative of the Lord's Wonderful Dealings*, in Potkay and Burr, eds., *Black Atlantic Writers of the Eighteenth Century*, 78.

50. That Marrant identified with Paul (rather than his editor's identifying him that way) is evident from Marrant's own words in Marrant, *A Journal of the Rev. John Marrant* . . . (London, 1790), which includes numerous Pauline references; see esp. 3, where Marrant paraphrases 1 Cor. 1:26–29. He relies heavily on Pauline Scripture throughout the account of his missionary career in his journal.

Benilde Montgomery focuses on alternative scriptural identifications in the narrative, including Lazarus and Christ; see "Recapturing John Marrant," in Frank Shuffelton, ed., *A Mixed Race: Ethnicity in Early America* (Oxford, 1993), 105–115. Like Montgomery, I find "a gathering of transethnic contacts that manages to retain the powerful stamp of all three" (113) in Marrant's narrative. In contrast, see Thomas M. Hatley, *The Dividing Paths: Cherokees and South Carolinians through the Era of Revolution* (New York, 1993), 237.

ture texts that sustained her during her captivity. Marrant's narrative reformulates these conventions into a tale of hidden eloquence released in captivity, and producing earthly power. Praying for his life in fluent Cherokee, Marrant first learns he is a talented preacher and finds his calling. After the converted king releases him from his prison and takes him into the newly Christianized tribe, Marrant adopts Cherokee dress and serves as the king's counselor.

Marrant shared Samson Occom's dream of a verbal power that could overcome cultural boundaries. He might well have known of the famous native American preacher through their mutual association with the countess of Huntingdon and their common Indian missionary work. Like Occom's widely comprehensible, "broken" Indian English, the captive Marrant's infusion of confidence as he prays in Cherokee recalls the Pentecostal moment when linguistic barriers fell away: "I prayed in English a considerable time, and about the middle of my prayer, the Lord impressed a strong desire upon my mind to turn into their language, and pray in their tongue. I did so, and with remarkable liberty, which wonderfully affected the people." The linguistic mastery or "liberty" evident in Marrant's spontaneous prayer astonishes his audience, persuades the executioner of the Lord's reality and presence, and ultimately saves Marrant's life when he converts the king. Seeking to create more ethnically inclusive alternatives to the dominant culture, Occom and Marrant created rhetorical parallels between America's native and African peoples. Where Occom identified the enslavement of Africans with similar political oppressions affecting native Americans, Marrant associated oral "liberty" with the eloquence of an Indian tongue.[51]

---

51. Marrant, *A Narrative of the Lord's Wonderful Dealings*, in Potkay and Burr, eds., *Black Atlantic Writers of the Eighteenth Century*, 85. Theophus Smith discusses the role of "style-switching" between ethnically marked elements in African-derived traditions of spirit possession found in contemporary African American churches, a practice that resembles the style-switching and ecstatic behavior that Marrant describes here; see *Conjuring Culture: Biblical Formations of Black America* (New York, 1994), 118–119. For Occom's correspondence with Phillis Wheatley and African American minister Lemuel Haynes, see Peyer, *The Tutor'd Mind*, 100, 330 n. 128.

On the continuing identification of African American spirituality with native American culture, see Joseph Roach, *Cities of the Dead: Circum-Atlantic Performance* (New York, 1996), 202–211. Michael P. Smith's photo essay *Spirit World: Pattern in the Expressive Folk Culture of African-American New Orleans* (New York, 1992) about black evangelical churches in the South includes several photographs of Pentecostals channeling native American spirits and dressing in elaborate quasi-Indian robes.

Not all interactions between native Americans and African Americans resulted in such harmony. On the southern frontier where Marrant proselytized, escaped slaves were sometimes assimilated into native societies. Other African Americans were betrayed, taken captive, or killed by their Indian captors; see Peter H. Wood, *Black Majority: Negroes in Colonial South Carolina from 1670 through the Stono Rebellion* (New York, 1974), 260–263.

The release of Marrant's oral powers takes place in a peculiar, gender-inflected dynamic with biblical text. The Cherokee king's daughter is first attracted to him, not by his prayer, but by the Bible in his hand. Fascinated with the book, "she took . . . it, and having opened it, she kissed it, and seemed much delighted with it," a response reminiscent of the one that Thomas Harriot attributed to the Roanoke Indians. Upon the king's request, Marrant reads from the English Bible "in the most solemn manner I was able . . . and when I pronounced the name of Jesus, the particular effect it had upon me was observed by the king." Though Marrant's evident emotion fails to convince the king of the Lord's reality, the young man's response to the text fascinates the king's daughter, who "took the book out of my hand a second time; she opened it, and kissed it again; her father bid her give it to me, which she did; but said, with much sorrow, the book would not speak to her." Failing to make the book speak to her, the "princess" cries out during Marrant's prayer and falls dangerously ill.[52]

As bearer of the Book and speaker of the written Word, Marrant acquires text's charisma. When Marrant claims for himself the literate European's privileged relationship to the book displayed before a nonliterate people, he revises prior figurations linking blackness with textual silence in order to claim the text's voice as his own. Marrant's literacy allows him to disrupt the identification of black bodies with black marks devoid of meaning when he gives voice to Scripture. In order to achieve this figural revision, "Marrant restructures the trope such that it is the Cherokee who assume the perilous burdens of negation."[53] More specifically, the Cherokee princess assumes the burden of negation, for she alone among the observers regrets the book's silence and inscrutability, much as Abigail Hutchinson regretted the blurring of the letters of the Bible. Her father the king has little interest in Marrant's textual medium. He is more concerned with competing sources of authority, asking Marrant "why I read those names with so much reverence." Marrant responds, "Because the Being to whom those names belonged made heaven and earth, and I and he," but the king denies the assertion, refusing to acknowledge text's superior spiritual authority. When the princess cries out during Mar-

---

52. Marrant, *A Narrative of the Lord's Wonderful Dealings,* in Potkay and Burr, eds., *Black Atlantic Writers of the Eighteenth Century,* 86.

53. Henry Louis Gates, Jr., *The Signifying Monkey: A Theory of Afro-American Literary Criticism* (New York, 1988), 145. Marrant primarily revises James Albert Ukawsaw Gronniosaw's *Narrative of the Most Remarkable Particulars in the Life of James Albert Ukawsaw Gronniosaw . . .* (1770), in Potkay and Burr, eds., *Black Atlantic Writers of the Eighteenth Century,* 27–63, esp. 34. Gronniosaw portrayed his envy of his captor's ability to make the book talk and concluded that his black skin prevented the book from speaking to him. For Gates, Marrant's revision of Gronniosaw puts him at the head of a black tradition in English literature "not because he was its first author but because he was the tradition's first revisionist" (*Signifying Monkey,* 145).

rant's prayer, the king sees not evangelical conviction but witchcraft. He views Marrant's amuletlike book and his ability to exert control over others merely by speaking as proof of a malign magical power.[54]

The Cherokee king was not alone in perceiving a resemblance between evangelical preaching and culturally shared forms of magic. The evangelical's sense of divine power operating through the spoken word closely resembled magical beliefs and occult practices that had a pervasive presence in the colonies. Many native American and African magical practices resembled European occult beliefs, particularly in their shared fear of and fascination with the spoken charm or curse that strips its object of personal agency. Such views of the spoken word made evangelical preaching a particularly rich arena for cultural hybridism. Evangelicalism provided one of the most important sites of exchange between culturally diverse forms of magic and American Christianity.[55]

Certainly in Marrant's account the king sees the evangelist's powerful speech rather than his possession of text as the greatest challenge to Cherokee cosmology and kingly authority. Like a hostile powwow who casts spells producing illness and even death, Marrant's prayer causes the king's daughter suffering that no Cherokee shaman can mitigate. To the princess, however, Marrant's verbal power lies not in his spoken charms but in his ability to make text speak. Fascinated, perhaps, by the similarity between the book's black marks and its owner's black skin, which could suggest a privileged access to text, Marrant's princess appears to fall ill in response to her own exclusion from the printed word. Marrant's imprisonment for witchcraft simultaneously performs the imprisonment of voice within the book.

Dragged from prison to make the princess well and threatened like John the Baptist with dismemberment if he fails, Marrant responds, not with Scripture, but with extemporaneous prayer:

> We went to prayer; but the heavens were locked up to my petitions. I besought the Lord again, but received no answer: I cried again, and he was intreated. He said, "Be it to thee as though wilt;" the Lord appeared most lovely and glorious; the king himself was awakened, and the others set at liberty.

---

54. Marrant, *A Narrative of the Lord's Wonderful Dealings,* in Potkay and Burr, eds., *Black Atlantic Writers of the Eighteenth Century,* 86.

55. Jon Butler documents a widespread interest in magic and the occult at all social levels in the seventeenth century and an increasingly "folklorized" or lower-class occult tradition continuing into the eighteenth and nineteenth centuries; see *Awash in a Sea of Faith: Christianizing the American People* (Cambridge, Mass., 1990), chap. 3, esp. 92. See also Raboteau, *Slave Religion,* 33; John W. Roberts, *From Trickster to Badman: The Black Folk Hero in Slavery and Freedom* (Philadelphia, 1989), esp. 77–78.

Marrant makes no mention of his prayer's effects on the king's daughter. Her illness provides the narrative route to a masculine oral authority equal to the king's. When Marrant converts the king, the princess disappears from the narrative. Marrant's narrative treatment of the Cherokee princess reflects common evangelical attitudes toward women and Scripture, notably the view evident in Jonathan Edwards's treatment of Abigail Hutchinson. Marrant stages his ability fully to vocalize biblical text, the source of his masculine verbal authority, against the backdrop of a woman's failed efforts to make text speak. Liberated, clad in the "habit of the country," and speaking "their tongue in the highest stile," Marrant exercises absolute power in the community, demanding even that the king "take off his golden ornaments, his chain and bracelet, like a child."[56]

Marrant so thoroughly assimilates to Cherokee culture that his family fails to recognize him when he returns home. Praying over dinner, he appears to his family as "a wild man . . . come out of the woods, to be a witness for God, and to reprove our ingratitude and stupefaction." Marrant's ethnically unspecified "wild man" recalls the European Wild Man, a figure common to intellectual and popular culture throughout the medieval and Renaissance periods and incorporated into the figure of the American frontiersman. The Wild Man of legend and literature dwells alone beyond the pale of civilization, his inarticulateness separating him from the rest of humanity. Like Caliban before Miranda teaches him to speak, the Wild Man has no language. Taking up this richly ambiguous figure, Marrant's narrative invokes the Christian wild man John the Baptist in order to reimagine the inarticulate Wild Man as the eloquent savage. Marrant performs the role of the skin-clad, locust-eating Baptist when he leaves his family and friends to go "over the fence . . . which divided the inhabited and cultivated parts of the country from the wilderness," whence he travels "in the desert all day without the least inclination of returning back." Sleeping in trees, fasting or grazing on grass, and drinking the dew from leaves, Marrant is reduced to a near animal-like condition, sustained only by his constant communion with the Lord.[57]

56. Marrant, *A Narrative of the Lord's Wonderful Dealings*, in Potkay and Burr, eds., *Black Atlantic Writers of the Eighteenth Century*, 87. A similar reliance on oral power characterizes Marrant's *A Journal of the Rev. John Marrant*, where he records a competition between himself and another man, an "Arminian," or Wesleyan Methodist. While the Arminian "read Mr. Wesley's society book" and drew the church order from it, Marrant preached "the Gospel of Christ" (39) and ultimately triumphed.

57. Marrant, *A Narrative of the Lord's Wonderful Dealings*, in Potkay and Burr, eds., *Black Atlantic Writers of the Eighteenth Century*, 81, 89. On the Wild Man of legend and literature, see Greenblatt *(Learning to Curse, 21)*. Marrant might have been influenced by tales of white South Carolina evangelist Hugh Bryan, who in the 1740s lived barefoot in the woods recording prophecies and was accused of plotting a slave rebellion that would destroy Charleston; see Morgan, *Slave Counterpoint, 423–424.*

Through the course of his adventures, Marrant blends and blurs numerous identities: Paul, John the Baptist, African American evangelist, eloquent Indian. Marrant's identity resembles the West African and African American trickster figure Esu-Elegbara, messenger of the gods, god of communication, and figure for the power of multiplicity and temporal fluidity. John the Baptist plays a parallel role in Christian culture, serving as God's messenger and articulating the contradictions between human and eternal time. Marrant's experiences in a wide range of black Atlantic communities in North America and England might have familiarized him with African traditions of multiplicity as well as Christian conceptions of temporal discontinuity. Like the indeterminate Esu and the liminal Baptist, Marrant performs the elision of racial and religious as well as temporal contradiction in the service of an unbounded, uncontainable spiritual energy that emerges in the wilderness.[58]

That energy permits the crossing of boundaries in the creation of the narrative as well. Marrant's original narrative was "taken down from his Relation, arranged, corrected and published, By the Rev. Mr. Aldridge"—that is, William Aldridge, a Methodist minister and associate of the countess of Huntingdon. Maintaining the narrative's authenticity while admitting his editorial as well as scribal role, Aldridge claimed, "I have always preserved Mr. Marrant's ideas, tho I could not his language; no more alterations, however, have been made, than were thought necessary." Marrant's narrative, then, is triply hybridized in that it is an act of textualized speech, an African American tale recorded and edited by a white Englishman, and a narrative of intercultural evangelism. One factor is offered as a guarantee of Marrant's authenticity across all of these complexly interrelated distinctions of medium and ethnicity: the display of powerful feeling. Aldridge explicitly predicates the very existence of the "Narrative" on Marrant's talent for emotional expression. Anticipating that readers will be skeptical about the account's more marvelous events, Aldridge justifies his belief that the incidents related are strictly true with a reference to Marrant's visible feeling: "He appeared to me to feel most sensibly, when he related those parts of his Narrative, which describe his happiest moments with God, or the most remarkable interpositions of Divine Providence for him; and I have no reason to believe it was counterfeited." Marrant persuaded Aldridge that he spoke divine truth by displaying intense emotion, which Aldridge then sought to capture in the recorded narrative. During his captivity and throughout his later career as the first African American minister and missionary, Marrant's manipulation of the performance semi-

---

58. Esu-Elegbara: Gates, *Signifying Monkey,* 37. See also Smith, *Conjuring Culture,* 151. The Baptist's complex sense of temporality is evident in his description of the Messiah, "After me cometh a man which is preferred before me: for he was before me" (John 1:30).

otic of speech and text proved central to his preaching success, for his expressive talents enabled him to convey persuasive feeling across boundaries of medium and culture.[59]

Marrant's "Narrative" situates him in the cosmopolitan culture of eighteenth-century evangelism. He articulated his internationalist resistance to a racially exclusive American identity in a 1789 sermon that he delivered to the African Lodge of the Honorable Society of Free and Accepted Masons in Boston, whose grand master was Prince Hall, one of the first black abolitionist leaders. Marrant delivered his address on the Festival of Saint John the Baptist, a patron saint of the Masons. In the sermon, Marrant explicitly celebrates the Baptist as one who upheld his duty to "the whole family of mankind in the world." He proposes that Masonic organizational principles, like the Baptist's Christianity, are truly universal: "Men of all nations and languages, or sects of religion, are and may be admitted and received as members, being recommended as persons of a virtuous character." Marrant fails to recognize the tension between Masonry and evangelical Christianity on the one hand and tolerance of religious difference on the other. For him the Christian faith and Masonry offered two mutually reinforcing vehicles of international brotherhood.[60]

Marrant celebrates the Masonic fraternity for providing its members with a freedom of movement and access akin to the physical, cultural, and spiritual mobility of evangelicalism:

> They have a free intercourse with all Lodges over the whole terrestrial globe; wherever arts flourish, a man hath a free right (having a recommendation) to visit his brethren, and they are bound to accept him; these are the laudable bonds that unite Free Masons together in one indissoluble fraternity—thus in every nation he finds a friend, and in every climate he may find a house.

59. Marrant, *A Narrative of the Lord's Wonderful Dealings*, in Potkay and Burr, eds., *Black Atlantic Writers of the Eighteenth Century*, 76. On authenticating strategies in slave narratives, see Robert B. Stepto, *From behind the Veil: A Study of Afro-American Narrative*, 2d ed. (Urbana, Ill., 1991), chap. 1. Though Marrant could read and write, he might not have been able to compose in a polished literary vein. Marrant demonstrated competent literacy in his missionary journal of 1790. But Jeremy Belknap remarked that he believed Prince Hall had edited Marrant's 1789 Masonic sermon before it was published, suggesting that Marrant might never have achieved a high level of literary sophistication; see Potkay and Burr, eds., *Black Atlantic Writers of the Eighteenth Century*, 74. Gates discusses the problem of partial literacy for Africans who sought the legitimating force that full literacy bore in the white comminuty (*Signifying Monkey*, 127–132).

60. Marrant, "A Sermon Preached on the 24th Day of June 1789, Being the Festival of St. John the Baptist . . ." (Boston, 1789), Marrant, *A Narrative of the Lord's Wonderful Dealings*, both in Potkay and Burr, eds., *Black Atlantic Writers of the Eighteenth Century*, 106–122, esp. 115, 117. On Prince Hall, see Kaplan and Kaplan, *The Black Presence in the Era of the American Revolution*,

This free intercourse is facilitated, Marrant notes, by the "signs and tokens" that Masons have used to converse with each other from the time of Babel. Theories of native American gestural communication in many ways resemble Marrant's claims for evangelical Christianity and Freemasonry, which he describes as "like a universal language." Such a view of embodied language transformed the speaker's physical presence from a mark of difference into a locus of understanding. In contrast to writers such as John Smith, who characterized the gestural forms of native orators as signs of madness or violence, Marrant celebrates gesture as a mode of intercultural exchange. Even as the elocutionary revival in eighteenth-century British oratory and rhetorical theory drew upon Cicero and Quintilian to emphasize the physical component of public speech as an avenue for reaching broader audiences, Masonic "signs and tokens" inspired John Marrant with still broader visions of "free intercourse . . . over the whole terrestrial globe" as lodges of different nations and colors dwelt together in "perfect harmony."[61]

The themes of cultural hybridism and intercultural communication that are central to Marrant's narrative and sermon reflect in part the dramatic, orally oriented preaching style of George Whitefield. In the years after the Great Awakening, as independent black churches like Richard Allen's African Methodist Episcopal Church formed and a distinctive black Christian culture emerged, African American preachers like Marrant created new modes of oral performance that drew on their African heritage as well as white evangelical preaching. The influence of white evangelicalism on African American spiritual life has been widely explored; less familiar are the multivalent cultural influences inscribed in Marrant's "Narrative," native American as well as white and black. Marrant's *Jour-*

202–214; Steven C. Bullock, *Revolutionary Brotherhood: Freemasonry and the Transformation of the American Social Order, 1730–1840* (Chapel Hill, N.C., 1996), 159.

61. Marrant, *A Narrative of the Lord's Wonderful Dealings,* in Potkay and Burr, eds., *Black Atlantic Writers of the Eighteenth Century,* 111, 114, 117. Developed for communication between communities and as an accompaniment to spoken narrative or formal oratory, native American sign languages fascinated European linguistic theorists from the time of first contact. On native American sign languages, see introduction to D. Jean Umiker-Sebeok and Thomas A. Sebeok, eds., *Aboriginal Sign Languages of the Americas and Australia,* I (New York, 1978), xiii–xxxii; *The Jesuit Relations,* quoted in Axtell, *The Invasion Within,* 88. On the early Renaissance revival of universal language theories, see Dilwyn Knox, "Ideas on Gesture and Universal Languages c. 1550–1650," in John Henry and Sarah Hutton, eds., *New Perspectives on Renaissance Thought: Essays in the History of Science, Education, and Philosophy* (London, 1990), 101–136. On Cicero and Quintilian, see Appendix, below. Jay Fliegelman discusses the elocutionary revolution in *Declaring Independence: Jefferson, Natural Language, and the Culture of Performance* (Stanford, Calif., 1993), 28–35. On the historical and conventional nature of gesture, see Keith Thomas, introduction to Jan Bremmer and Herman Roodenburg, eds., *A Cultural History of Gesture* (Ithaca, N.Y., 1991), 1–14.

nal reflects his ongoing preoccupation with evangelicalism's intercultural possibilities during his years as a missionary in Nova Scotia. There, he preached to a congregation "of white and black, and Indians, when groans and sighings were heard, through the congregation, and many were not able to contain." In the ethnically mobile oral world opened up by extemporaneous evangelical oratory, native American rhetorical influences as well as African and European speech forms played a role in the development of evangelical preaching.[62]

Marrant's preaching career contributed to an emerging performance tradition marked by elaborations of Samson Occom's Pentecostal savage speaker. Like Occom, African American preachers such as Marrant embraced the Pauline tradition of personal weakness transformed into rhetorical power. Simultaneously, they revised the figure of the violent savage, whose bodily extravagance resists meaning. This dual revision began with the characteristic features of Whitefieldian oratory — its extemporaneousness, its physical expressivity, its Pauline models — and recast them in forms that directly addressed the speaker's marginalization. Occupying and transforming the role of savage speaker, Occom and Marrant sought to convert a position of cultural impotence into one of power.

However, the possibilities and limitations of such intercultural exchange for transforming white perspectives emerge in Edwards's *Life of David Brainerd*. Brainerd's ability to see past the nativist reformer's bearskin robes and ceremonial gestures in order to construct an interior spiritual life for the man depended upon Brainerd's perception of a form of subjectivity that resembled evangelical self-understanding. Even as his own preaching changed to reflect native American influence, he cast those natives who did not display the nativist's alienation from his community and attachment to ancient traditions in the role of the mere savage — the physically extravagant, the violent, the uninterpretable, the demonic. The performative possibilities that Occom discovered within the figure of the savage speaker, and that Marrant developed in his identification with the Cherokees and in his recasting of the inarticulate Wild Man as the powerful orator, offered important, though ultimately limited and imperfect, correctives to the savagism that Brainerd continued to embrace.

62. Marrant, *A Journal of the Rev. John Marrant*, 12.

3 Negotiating Power

I. REPUBLICANISM AND THE ELOQUENT INDIAN

Diplomatic eloquence drew the attention of the English-speaking public to native speech traditions long before Occom sought to recast the figure of the "savage" speaker as a figure of Pentecostal power. When Occom traveled to England in 1765, he followed in the footsteps of Iroquois and Cherokee ambassadors who had been making the journey since early in the century. English and Anglo-American interest in native oratory, and native challenges to the figure of the violent savage speaker, first focused on the eloquence of the native diplomat. English celebration of Indian eloquence had its initial official occasion in 1710, when Queen Anne received a delegation of Iroquois "Kings" in St. James's Palace. Native Americans had appeared in England both voluntarily and under compulsion for a century and a half before the "Kings" arrived, notably when Pocahontas was received with some fanfare at court in 1616. Although natives had preceded them across the Atlantic in ones and twos, the "Kings" composed the first formal delegation representing the political and military interests of their people in the English court. Already a popular stage figure in plays such as John Dryden and Robert Howard's *Indian-Queen* (1664), Dryden's *Indian Emperour* (1665), and Thomas Southerne's stage adaptation of Aphra Behn's novel *Oroonoko* (1694), the eloquent Indian made his first formal diplomatic appearance as the English began to imagine the imperial wars that would eventually force France out of Canada. Seeking to triumph over the French in the struggle for control of the continent, the English and Anglo-Americans created new political, performance, and representational strategies for negotiating with the Iroquois.[1]

1. For the most complete account of this diplomatic mission, see Richmond P. Bond, *Queen Anne's American Kings* (Oxford, 1952), 33, 106–107. Joseph Roach situates the mission in the circum-Atlantic world of performance of the treaty council and the English stage in *Cities of the Dead: Circum-Atlantic Performance* (New York, 1996), chap. 4. Benjamin Bissell notes the visit's importance for the emerging literary trope of the noble savage in *The American Indian in English Literature of the Eighteenth Century* (New Haven, Conn., 1925), chap. 3. See also Eric Hinderaker,

Colonial military leaders arranged for the four men, Mohawks Theyanoquin (or Hendrick), Sagayeanquaprahton (Brant), Ohneeyeathtonnoprow (John), and Mahican Elowohkaom (Nicholas) to appear at court with full diplomatic pomp.[2] Arriving in London in the queen's carriages, they were received at court under the care of the master of ceremonies and were ushered into their audience with Anne by the lord chamberlain. There Hendrick delivered a speech, which was read to the queen in English, stating the Iroquois commitment to their English allies and the need to reduce French power in Canada. The "Kings" employed a handful of the metaphors and symbols characteristic of the Iroquois treaty council, describing how they had "hung up the *Kettle*, and took up the *Hatchet*" in preparation for the abortive attack on Canada, whose abandonment by the English prompted their visit. They also offered what quickly became the most familiar gesture of the treaty council: "As a Token of the Sincerity of the Six Nations, We do here, in the Name of All, present Our *Great Queen* with these BELTS *of* WAMPUM." Anne was familiar enough with Indian diplomacy to reciprocate with gifts for her visitors. Hendrick's speech, widely reprinted in broadsides and newspapers in England and the colonies, made the Indian oration a newly prominent and popular genre.[3]

Hendrick's speech to the queen introduced the traditions of the Iroquois treaty council to England. In the councils conducted on North American soil between the powerful Iroquois and the British colonists, we see the complex evolution of performance genres that began with contact between the peoples of Europe and the Americas and that came to prominence in the English-speaking world through these councils. From the first council the English colonists held with the Iroquois (1664) to the great intercolonial treaty at Lancaster, Pennsylvania (1744), to the 1794 treaty that marked the end of the new republic's willingness to negotiate within the historic framework of the treaty council, England and English America recognized Iroquois power and autonomy by adopting their style of diplomacy. Colonial Americans and native Americans together engaged in long-standing Iroquois rituals of negotiation whose methods of conduct the Iroquois

---

"The 'Four Indian Kings' and the Imaginative Construction of the First British Empire," *WMQ*, 3d Ser., LIII (1996), 487–526.

2. Daniel K. Richter offers a brief account of these men in *The Ordeal of the Longhouse: The Peoples of the Iroquois League in the Era of European Colonization* (Chapel Hill, N.C., 1992), 368 n. 29.

3. See Bond, *Queen Anne's American Kings*, 1–3, 94–96, esp. 94. The speech was initially published as a broadside entitled *The Four Indian Kings Speech to Her Majesty* (1710). On Hendrick's continuing role as a cultural mediator, see Timothy J. Shannon, "Dressing for Success on the Mohawk Frontier: Hendrick, William Johnson, and the Indian Fashion," *WMQ*, 3d Ser., LIII (1996), 13–42.

FIGURE 5. Tee Yee Neen Ho Ga Row, Emperour of the Six Nations. *Engraving by J: Simon after John Verlest. 1710. King Hendrick, depicted here, and his three companions posed for court painter John Verlest during their visit to Queen Anne. Courtesy, the John Carter Brown Library at Brown University*

substantially controlled throughout the eighteenth century. Council oratory was a prominent feature of these diplomatic rituals, and through the publicity attending them native eloquence came to be celebrated in the English-speaking world.

As the English sought to challenge French authority in New York and Canada after 1664, the importance of Iroquois diplomatic forms to that territorial project generated interest in Indian oratory that was a complex mix of the political and the aesthetic. Along with the writings of John Smith and the stage figure of the eloquent savage, French texts provided a model for interpreting native speech traditions. Most notably, Louis Armand de Lom d'Arce, baron de Lahontan, praised the verbal artistry of the natives of New France in *New Voyages to North-America*. His work was published in English in 1703, the same year that the first French edition appeared. Two subsequent London editions, both from 1735, suggest persistent English interest in the French work.[4]

The intertwined political and aesthetic sources of English and Anglo-American interest in native speech traditions shaped the first extended history of a native American people written in English. In *History of the Five Indian Nations,* Cadwallader Colden drew on the work of Lahontan and other French precursors as well as his own experience with the Iroquois, notably among the Mohawks who had adopted him into the tribe. He produced a narrative with an avowed political motive: to raise English awareness of the importance of the Iroquois as a buffer to and weapon against French power in Canada. Colden was a Scottish-born New York official prominent in Indian affairs and a member of the transatlantic republic of letters. He corresponded extensively with scientists and intellectuals, including John Bartram and Benjamin Franklin, both of whom shared his fascination with native America. Members of the republic of letters were beginning to appreciate native American eloquence as a model for colonial political identity. This is visible in Colden's *History* (1727), which appeared on both sides of the Atlantic. The first edition, published in New York, surveyed Iroquois history, culture, and political life, developing an image of the republican Indian. A subsequent, significantly expanded version was published in three London editions in 1747, 1750, and 1755. Here Colden added treaty texts (including the Lancaster treaty) and other significant documents to the narrative of the first edition, exemplifying Iroquois eloquence and negotiating skill. The later editions were offered for sale in the colonies and were extracted "in all the Magazines, and in the Monthly Review." Critical of British imperial policy and hoping to play a central role in

4. On the publication history of Lahontan's work, see James Constantine Pilling, *Bibliography of the Algonquian Languages* (Washington, D.C., 1891), 288–295. Gordon Sayre discusses Lahontan in *Les Sauvages Américains: Representations of Native Americans in French and English Colonial Literature* (Chapel Hill, N.C., 1997), 31–48; see also James Axtell, *The Invasion Within: The Contest of Cultures in Colonial North America* (New York, 1985), 75, 87–88.

persuading British officials to cultivate a more active involvement with the Iroquois, Colden echoed French comparisons between ancient and New World culture. "The Greeks and Romans, Sir, [were] once as much Barbarians as our *Indians* now are," he wrote in his dedication, identifying the Iroquois with ancient republicans.[5]

Colden correctly noted that for the Iroquois the treaty council constituted the legitimate public domain between themselves and the colonists. The colonial governments likewise often preferred to negotiate within a treaty setting defined as public. The shaping of such a public domain is visible in the Philadelphia treaty of 1742, where Onondaga sachem Canassatego reinterpreted the hierarchy between the Delawares and the Six Nations in a manner that would have important consequences for both colonial-Iroquois and Iroquois-Delaware relations. Canassatego employed metaphors of gender to imagine a masculine public domain in which legitimate land sales could take place. Though Indian women attended treaty councils and sometimes played influential roles, they had a limited power to speak publicly or conduct public business. "We conquered You, we made Women of you," Canassatego told the assembled Delawares; "you know you are Women, and can no more sell Land than Women." Canassatego impressed the importance of conducting land sales openly upon the subordinate Delawares when he contrasted their method of selling land "in the Dark" to that of the Six Nations, who "give publick Notice, and invite all the *Indians* of their united Nations, and give them all a Share of the Present they receive for their Lands." Though it had disastrous effects on relations between the Iroquois and the Delawares, Canassatego's definition of the treaty council as the appropriate public domain for land sales suited the Pennsylvania government, which preferred dealing with a single, cooperative, masculine, and self-defined "publick" political power to dealing with decentralized native leaders scattered throughout the backcountry.[6]

5. Alice Mapelsden Keys, *Cadwallader Colden: A Representative Eighteenth Century Official* (New York, 1906), 8 9; Benjamin Franklin to Cadwallader Colden, Oct. 25, 1753, in Leonard W. Labaree et al., eds., *The Papers of Benjamin Franklin* (New Haven, Conn., 1959–1962), V, 80 (Franklin was involved in the arrangements to offer the London edition of 1747 for sale in the colonies); Cadwallader Colden, *The History of the Five Indian Nations . . .* , 2 vols., 3d ed. (London, 1755), I, vii. This edition offers the most complete version of Colden's expanded text. For a modern analysis of the power of eloquence among indigenous peoples that stresses the circulation of linguistic and other signs as an alternative to Western systems of power, see Pierre Clastres, *Society against the State: The Leader as Servant and the Humane Uses of Power among the Indians of the Americas* (New York, 1977), chap. 2.

6. *The Treaty Held with the Indians of the Six Nations at Philadelphia, in July, 1742* (Philadelphia, 1743), reprinted in Carl Van Doren and Julian P. Boyd, eds., *Indian Treaties Printed by Benjamin Franklin, 1736–1762* (Philadelphia, 1938), 35. Jane Merritt traces the shifting meanings of gendered metaphors with particular reference to Iroquois-Delaware relations in "Meta-

At Philadelphia, Canassatego identified the Iroquois treaty council as the primary public forum for negotiations between native Americans and colonial Americans in a speech whose rhetorical power manifested the central importance of oratory to that public domain. Reputed a "famous orator," the Onondaga leader used his eloquence to realize his ambitions as a power broker between the colonies and other native communities in the Covenant Chain. From the colonial side, Colden wrote his *History* to urge the colonial and British governments to pursue just such a policy with the Iroquois. Crucial to this diplomatic endeavor was a portrait of Iroquois political order recognizable to the leaders of British American policy. "The People of the *Five Nations* are much given to *Speech-making*," Colden observed, "ever the natural Consequence of a perfect Republican Government: Where no single Person has a Power to compel, the Arts of Persuasion alone must prevail." Like Canassatego, Colden identified publicity with eloquence when he observed that the best Iroquois speakers "gain the Esteem and Applause of their Countrymen," which is their only form of distinction, in "publick Councils and Treaties with other Nations." Colden placed particular emphasis on the "republican" form of Iroquois government operating through persuasive eloquence rather than coercion.[7]

Colden's description of Iroquois eloquence did not account for Canassatego's manipulations at Philadelphia, but it did echo the political discourse of classical republicanism that emerged into prominence with the publication in the early 1720s of the widely influential *Cato's Letters* of Thomas Gordon and John Trenchard. Ambivalent about eloquence because of its potential for abuse, Trenchard and Gordon nonetheless acknowledged its central role in republican government. They particularly celebrated the Roman state, where "he who spoke best, that is,

---

phor, Meaning, and Misunderstanding: Language and Power on the Pennsylvania Frontier," in Andrew R. L. Cayton and Fredrika J. Teute, eds., *Contact Points: American Frontiers from the Mohawk Valley to the Mississippi, 1750–1830* (Chapel Hill, N.C., 1998), 77–81. Although in practice native women continued to occupy a range of public roles, as Indians negotiated with Euro-Americans authority was redefined in masculine terms. For Canassatego's distorted claims in this speech and the effects on Iroquois-Delaware relations, see Francis Jennings, *The Ambiguous Iroquois Empire: The Covenant Chain Confederation of Indian Tribes with English Colonies from Its Beginnings to the Lancaster Treaty of 1744* (New York, 1984), 343–346; Jennings, " 'Pennsylvania Indians' and the Iroquois," in Daniel K. Richter and James H. Merrell, eds., *Beyond the Covenant Chain: The Iroquois and Their Neighbors in Indian North America, 1600–1800* (Syracuse, N.Y., 1987), 90.

7. The crucial work on the Covenant Chain between the British, the Iroquois, and the tribes allied with the Iroquois is Jennings, *The Ambiguous Iroquois Empire*, 8–9, chap. 2. Maryland secretary Witham Marshe described Canassatego as a "famous orator" ("Witham Marshe's Journal of the Treaty Held with the Six Nations . . . ," in Massachusetts Historical Society, *Collections,* 1st Ser., VII [1801; Boston, 1846], 171–201 [hereafter cited as MHS, *Colls.*]). For Colden's comments, see Colden, *History of the Five Indian Nations,* I, 15.

with most reason and truth, had the most voices."[8] Classical republican thought stimulated public interest in political oratory, and parliamentary deliberations began to appear in the *Gentleman's Magazine* and the *London Magazine* in the 1730s and 1740s. Reproduced from memory often supplemented with a heavy dose of imagination, yet claiming to be authentic reports, these magazine versions of parliamentary speeches fostered the growth of rhetorical culture on both sides of the Atlantic. Print culture propelled a rhetorical revival in Britain and the colonies. Written speeches reported as the actual words spoken in Parliament were particularly influential in America, where colonial political culture in the early eighteenth century increasingly took its cues from a distant metropolis. Yet the cultural relationship between Britain and its colonies was more reciprocal than such a formulation suggests. Well before Jean-Jacques Rousseau popularized the figure of the noble savage in Europe, the same English magazines that published parliamentary speeches printed the eloquent words of American Indian orators. Midcentury theorists of classical republicanism imagined that true citizenship was attainable only among savages, a speculation provoked by the dominant role that persuasion played in governing native societies. One major figure in the elocutionary movement, Thomas Sheridan, was a savage Irishman as well as an actor; similarly, the Scottish rhetoricians who led the oratorical revival were from a provincial culture sometimes viewed as savage. Native Americans and the peoples of the British Isles were linked in the rhetorical and political literature celebrating eloquence as Britain's imperial provinces taught a new style of political performance to the metropolis. Eventually, the American colonies would use their own savage eloquence to speak back to the imperial center as oratory became the defining republican genre of the Revolution.[9]

8. John Trenchard and Thomas Gordon, *Cato's Letters; or, Essays on Liberty, Civil and Religious, and Other Important Subjects,* ed. Ronald Hamowy, 2 vols. (Indianapolis, Ind., 1995), II, 729. The *Letters* were reprinted in the American colonies quickly and often. In *The Origins of American Politics* (New York, 1970), Bernard Bailyn notes that "James Franklin began reprinting the *Letters* in his *New England Courant* eleven months after the first of them appeared in London" (54). Numerous subsequent publications followed, and the *Letters* quickly became part of the basic vocabulary of colonial politics.

9. See Samuel Johnson, *Debates in Parliament,* 2 vols. (London, 1787); Benjamin Beard Hoover, *Samuel Johnson's Parliamentary Reporting: Debates in the Senate of Lilliput* (Berkeley, Calif., 1953). On the printing of native American oratory, see Bissell, *The American Indian in English Literature,* 57–69; Bond, *Queen Anne's American Kings,* 40. On parliamentary eloquence, see Adam Potkay, *The Fate of Eloquence in the Age of Hume* (Ithaca, N.Y., 1994), 36–40. On Rousseau's *Essai sur l'origine des langues* in the context of native American oratory, see Nicholas Hudson, *Writing and European Thought, 1600–1830* (Cambridge, 1994), 138–142. On the views of theorists of classical republicanism, see J. G. A. Pocock, *The Machiavellian Moment: Florentine Political Thought and the Atlantic Republican Tradition* (Princeton, N.J., 1975), 501; Potkay, *The Fate of Eloquence in the Age of Hume,* chap. 5.

The leaders of Britain's "elocutionary revolution" placed new emphasis on the performance dimensions of oratory, celebrating gesture, facial expression, and vocal tone as primary bearers of meaning and fundamental tools of persuasion. Colonial American viewers reevaluated the physical drama of native oratory in light of the new style of performance, praising the gestures and movements of Indian speakers that so fascinated and disturbed early English observers such as John Smith. Noting the heightened forms of elegant speech that their best speakers cultivated in "Study and Exercise," Colden describes linguistic and performance features such as the prevalence of metaphors and the "Gutturals and strong Aspirations" that make their delivery "very sonorous and bold." "The speakers whom I have heard," Colden notes as he confesses to an ignorance of their languages, "had all a great Fluency of Words, and much more Grace in their Manner, than any Man could expect, among a People intirely ignorant of all the liberal Arts and Sciences."[10]

Eighteenth-century narratives like Colden's deployed classical comparisons to celebrate the drama of Indian oratory, reframing native eloquence in keeping with the emerging admiration for vigorous, even theatrical, delivery. A notable instance of the aestheticization of native performance appears in an account of the Treaty of Lancaster, where leaders from three colonies celebrated the oration of the Iroquois warrior Gachradodow. Observing that at the time of the treaty Gachradodow was "about forty years of age, tall, straight-limbed, and a graceful person," Maryland secretary and Scotsman Witham Marshe noted that "his action, when he spoke, was certainly the most graceful, as well as bold, that any person ever saw; without the buffoonery of the French, or over-solemn deportment of the haughty Spaniards." One member of the audience commented that "he had never seen so just an action in any of the most celebrated orators he had heard speak," and another insisted that Gachradodow "would have made a good figure in the forum of old Rome." Classical republicanism and the elocutionary revolution permitted such warm appreciations of native eloquence, particularly when the colonists wished to project a republican image of America to the British.[11]

---

10. Colden, *History of the Five Indian Nations,* I, 15–16. On the elocutionary revolution, see Jay Fliegelman, *Declaring Independence: Jefferson, Natural Language, and the Culture of Performance* (Stanford, Calif., 1993), 28–35.

11. Marshe, "Witham Marshe's Journal," in MHS, *Colls.,* 1st Ser., VII, 200. Marshe quotes the comments of Edmund Jennings, a member of the Maryland council, and George Thomas, lieutenant governor of Pennsylvania.

II. IROQUOIS AND AMERICAN PUBLICS

In 1744, Benjamin Franklin sent his London bookseller William Strahan two hundred copies of the printed treaty proceedings between three colonial governments and the Iroquois held earlier that year at Lancaster, Pennsylvania. "The Method of doing Business with those Barbarians may perhaps afford you some Amusement," he suggested to Strahan, who advertised the book in the May 1745 issue of the *London Magazine*. As Pennsylvania's official printer, Franklin had begun printing the colony's treaties with the Iroquois in 1736. When he printed his last treaty in 1762, he had produced thirteen folio volumes of treaty records. Only the Lancaster treaty seemed significant enough in political and aesthetic terms for Franklin to send to London. The treaty aroused substantial interest not only in London but throughout the British colonies. In June 1745, Franklin sent twenty-five copies of the treaty to his partner James Parker in New York, and in the fall of 1744 and again in 1745 he shipped a total of eighty-one copies to Jonas Green in Annapolis. Franklin was not the only colonial printer to sense public interest in this treaty. That same year, William Parks of Williamsburg reprinted the Lancaster treaty, making it the only Franklin treaty to appear in a second colonial edition. As James N. Green observes, "All in all we have perhaps 1000 to 1500 copies in two editions available in quantity through the middle colonies, the Chesapeake, and England, a really extraordinarily wide distribution for an original American book at that time."[12]

Franklin's efforts reflect the interest in relations with the Iroquois that had been building alongside tensions with France and that climaxed at the Lancaster proceedings shortly after King George's War was declared. The negotiations at Lancaster were important more for the role in which they cast the Iroquois than for their substance. The treaty determined the route of the road through Virginia that the Iroquois used to carry on a war against the Catawbas, addressed the murder of several warriors killed by Virginia frontiersmen and the murder of a white trader by an Indian, and provided the League with generous compensation for lands

---

12. Labaree et al., eds., *The Papers of Benjamin Franklin*, II, 411, 416. See also George Simpson Eddy, ed., *Account Books Kept by Benjamin Franklin*, II (New York, 1929), 118; C. William Miller, *Benjamin Franklin's Philadelphia Printing, 1728–1766: A Descriptive Bibliography* (Philadelphia, 1974), 191–192; John Bartram, *Observations . . . in His Travels from Pensilvania to Onondago . . .* (London, 1751), reprint as *Travels in Pensilvania and Canada* (Ann Arbor, Mich., 1966). Canassatego's prominence in these negotiations doubtless accounts for his transformation into the hero of a romantic novel by John Shebbeare, *Lydia; or, Filial Piety* (London, 1755), which is discussed in Bissell, *The American Indian in English Literature*, 89–96. Parker: Miller, *Benjamin Franklin's Philadelphia Printing*, 191–193. Green: Leo Lemay, typescript edition of Franklin's accounts; James Green to author, Aug. 21, 1998. Green also notes that the treaties printed for the colonial governments were given away for free.

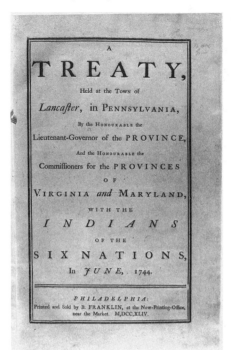

that they claimed in Maryland and Virginia by right of conquest over other native peoples. Under other circumstances, Maryland and Virginia would have been considerably less willing to compensate the Iroquois for dubious land claims. But the treaty proceedings were designed above all to assure Iroquois attachment to the British Empire and to cast the Six Nations as a powerful ally able to maintain not only their own neutrality but the neutrality of such affiliated peoples as the French-allied Praying Indians of Canada. The desire to elevate the Iroquois in the opinion of the English-speaking world is evident in colonial secretary Richard Peters's letter to Pennsylvania proprietor Thomas Penn. Peters, who edited the printed treaty, observed of the events portrayed there that "the Indians really appear superior to the Commissioners in point of sense and argument" and predicted that "it will raise people's opinions of the wisdom of the Six Nations." [13]

What English and colonial American readers found when they opened Franklin's printed treaty was a textual account of an event whose basic form followed performance conventions that had evolved within the Iroquois League since the late fifteenth century. By the end of the seventeenth century, these conventions had become the predominant framework for conducting forest diplomacy, shap-

13. Van Doren and Boyd, eds., *Indian Treaties Printed by Benjamin Franklin*, xl.

ing both the extensive negotiations that the League held with other native communities and with the colonial powers and also influencing the negotiations of non-Iroquois native peoples. Parts of the treaty proceedings were conducted before crowds numbering in the hundreds, and they reached a more extended colonial and transatlantic audience in textual form. The printed treaties, themselves hybrid Iroquois-European creations, were also hybrid verbal forms that represented the spoken word as text.[14]

For the Lancaster treaty, Franklin created the effect of performance on the printed page by employing a playlike format that emphasized the theatrical dimensions of the proceedings, giving them a European form that sometimes conflicted with Iroquois traditions. The treaty text opens "in the Court-House in the Town of *Lancaster*," then offers a list of participants resembling the dramatis personae of a playbill. The colonial delegates are named, as is the interpreter Conrad Weiser, but the native participants are presented collectively as "the Deputies of the *Onandagoes, Senecas, Cayogoes, Oneidas* and *Tuscaroraes.*"[15] The printed treaty omits an account of the march into Lancaster of 250 Iroquois, including the deputies of the Six Nations, their followers, attendants, wives, and children, conducted "in very good order" and led by Canassatego, who greeted the colonial representatives at the courthouse with a song in his own tongue inviting them to renew earlier treaties. The text instead begins with their entry into the courthouse, where Pennsylvania lieutenant governor George Thomas "bid them welcome into the Government" and offered "Wine, Punch, Pipes and Tobacco." The bulk of the treaty records consists of the words delivered by colonial and native leaders with no physical description, lending the printed treaty the feel of a complex if somewhat static stage drama similar to a declamatory play such as Joseph Addison's influential *Cato.* For readers unfamiliar with Iroquois practices, Franklin provided explanations in parentheses and footnotes. Through such strategies, the

14. On the Iroquois treaty council, see Paul A. W. Wallace, *The White Roots of Peace* (Philadelphia, 1946); Francis Jennings et al., eds., *The History and Culture of Iroquois Diplomacy* (Syracuse, N.Y., 1985); Richter, *The Ordeal of the Longhouse,* chap. 2; Matthew Dennis, *Cultivating a Landscape of Peace: Iroquois-European Encounters in Seventeenth-Century America* (Ithaca, N.Y., 1993), chap. 3.

15. Lawrence C. Wroth describes the treaty councils as the first genuinely American genre and asserts their aesthetic value as a quasi-dramatic form in "The Indian Treaty as Literature," *Yale Review,* XVII (1928), 749–766. On treaty proceedings as theater, see also A. M. Drummond and Richard Moody, "Indian Treaties: The First American Dramas," *Quarterly Journal of Speech,* XXXIX (1953), 15–24; Carl Van Doren, introduction to *Indian Treaties Printed by Benjamin Franklin,* vii–xviii; William N. Fenton, "Structure, Continuity, and Change in the Process of Iroquois Treaty Making," in Jennings et al., eds., *The History and Culture of Iroquois Diplomacy,* 3–36; Roach, *Cities of the Dead,* chap. 4. For the proceedings, see *A Treaty, Held at the Town of Lancaster, in Pennsylvania, by the Honourable the Lieutenant-Governor of the Province . . .* (1744), in Van Doren and Boyd, eds., *Indian Treaties Printed by Benjamin Franklin,* 43.

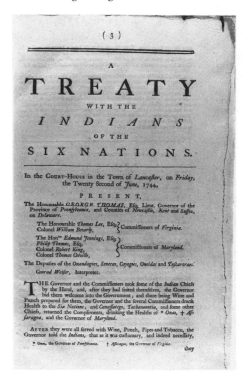

printed treaty format emphasizes colonial control over the proceedings, though the content of the treaty shows that such control was quickly compromised and that power was actively negotiated throughout the council meeting. In the first instance of contestation, Canassatego rejected the request of the Virginia delegates that they be allowed to speak before the delegates from Maryland. Such disputes over treaty protocol provided the Iroquois leaders with their most visible opportunities to control the direction of the proceedings and produced tension between the textual form of the treaty and the negotiations it presented.[16]

Conflicts over the forms and strategies of intercultural communication punctuate the Lancaster proceedings. Treaty protocol had its basis in the Iroquois Condolence Council, a ritual with roots in the founding of the League that provides

16. On the Iroquois procession, see Marshe, "Witham Marshe's Journal," MHS, *Colls.*, 1st Ser., VII, 179; see also Fenton, "Structure, Continuity, and Change," in Jennings et al., eds., *The History and Culture of Iroquois Diplomacy*, 18. Franklin's two previous treaties begin with a paragraph establishing the issues to be negotiated and offering a sketchy description of the Iroquois arrival, though nothing as rich in detail as Marshe recorded in his journal. On the subsequent proceedings, see Van Doren and Boyd, eds., *Indian Treaties Printed by Benjamin Franklin*, xxxviii–xxxix, 43.

solace to a grieving party and, in laying grief to rest, permits discussion to begin. These rites, which had been performed in a meeting at Onondaga earlier in the year, established the very possibility of communication. This was an issue of special concern at Lancaster, where the Iroquois leadership made the means and truthfulness of communication into central issues of negotiation. Once communication had been established, a number of symbolic practices drawn from Iroquois precedent governed the process of negotiation. Both sets of speakers employed a set of metaphors and symbols drawn from Iroquois political rhetoric, including most famously the chain, the fire, the hatchet, the kettle, the rope, the tree, and terms of kinship.[17] Orators on both sides laced their performances with the presentation of black-and-white wampum strings and belts, which the colonists had come to accept as an alternate form of "writing." These rows of polished and strung shells served a variety of symbolic functions, as mnemonic devices designed to recall an earlier treaty or embody a message, as reinforcements of a particular point, or as signifiers of agreement to a provision. Along with wampum, an exchange of gifts (bundles of skins from the natives, trade goods from the colonists) marked a successful agreement.[18]

So did the giving of the "Yo-hah" with which the assembled Iroquois manifested the consensus behind specific treaty provisions. Describing the impressive and unfamiliar cry, Witham Marshe noted that it was made "on presenting wampum to the Indians in a treaty, and is performed thus: The grand chief and speaker amongst them pronounces the word *jo-bah!* with a loud voice, singly; then all the others join in this sound, *woh!* dwelling some little while upon it, and keeping exact time with each other, and immediately, with a sharp noise and force, utter this sound, *wugh!*" Marshe particularly remarked that it was "performed in great order, and with the utmost ceremony and decorum." Franklin observed in a footnote to the printed treaty that "the *Yo-hah* denotes Approbation, being a loud Shout or Cry, consisting of a few Notes pronounced by all the *Indians* in a very musical Manner." A vocal manifestation of Iroquois political order at its most successful, the cry quite literally gave voice to the League's ability to achieve consen-

17. On the Condolence Council, see Fenton, "Structure, Continuity, and Change in the Process of Iroquois Treaty Making," in Jennings et al., eds., *The History and Culture of Iroquois Diplomacy*, 18, 22. On the rites conducted at Onondaga, see "Conrad Weiser's Report on Journey to Onondaga," in W. Stitt Robinson, ed., *Virginia Treaties, 1723–1775* (Frederick, Md., 1983), vol. V of *Early American Indian Documents*, 43–44; Paul A. W. Wallace, *Conrad Weiser, 1696–1760: Friend of Colonist and Mohawk* (Philadelphia, 1945), 163–165. On the speakers' metaphors, see "Glossary of Figures of Speech in Iroquois Political Rhetoric," in Jennings et al., eds., *The History and Culture of Iroquois Diplomacy*, chap. 6.

18. On the various roles of wampum and gift giving, see Michael K. Foster, "Another Look at the Function of Wampum in Iroquois-White Councils," in Jennings et al., eds., *The History and Culture of Iroquois Diplomacy*, 99–114; Richter, *Ordeal of the Longhouse*, 48.

sus. The cry impressed the colonists with its harmony, unity, and power even as it generated a disparate orthography.[19]

Weiser appears in the printed treaty primarily in his role as a technician of communication technologies. He translates and interprets texts for the Iroquois; he returns the "Yo-hah" for the colonists, adapting the collective practice of the Iroquois into a single-voiced official assent. Occasionally the text incorporates some aspect of the translation process, often in an explanatory mode. When Canassatego repeats "to the Interpreter the Substance of what the Governor had spoke, in order to know if he had understood him right," a parenthetical explanation states that this is "a Method generally made use of by the *Indians*." Later, Weiser twice explains the meaning of a metaphor in Canassatego's history of the Covenant Chain. When Weiser is not clarifying or participating in Iroquois diplomatic practices, the printed treaty ignores his work as translator. It identifies the need for mediation with the opacity of Iroquois negotiating practices and their lack of textual skill and portrays the speeches themselves as mutually transparent.[20]

As Pennsylvania's agent, Weiser became the most famous translator and negotiator in the colonies, trusted by the Iroquois and relied upon by colonial governments. Weiser was a Palatine German who immigrated to the New York frontier as a child and was adopted by the Mohawks as a teenager. A "white Indian" who lived literally on the Pennsylvania frontier and figuratively on the borderland between colonial and native societies, he spoke both English and Iroquois as second tongues. Iroquois leaders regarded Weiser as "the Guardian of all the Indians" and designated him Tarachiawagon, or Holder of the Heavens, a name taken from an Iroquois deity who disclosed future events of public importance and protected the people. In one incarnation, as Hiawatha, Tarachiawagon founded the League and established peace among the warring Iroquois societies. Bestowing this honorific upon Weiser, the Iroquois sacralized his diplomatic role and identified him with the ideals of a spiritually cleansed Iroquois-colonial public arena. Weiser's career as an interpreter mirrors in the political realm the intercultural domains of evangelical missionaries and reflects a comparable liminality. He was drawn to

19. Marshe, "Witham Marshe's Journal," MHS, *Colls.*, 1st Ser., VII, 185; Van Doren and Boyd, eds., *Indian Treaties Printed by Benjamin Franklin*, 46. Merritt discusses colonial attempts to capture native speech in writing, and native resistance to those efforts, in "Metaphor, Meaning, and Misunderstanding," in Cayton and Teute, eds., *Contact Points*, 67–68.

20. Van Doren and Boyd, eds., *Indian Treaties Printed by Benjamin Franklin*, 46, 51. Nancy L. Hagedorn describes the multifaceted work of interpreters, elaborating the silences of the printed treaty, in "'A Friend to Go between Them': The Interpreter as Cultural Broker during Anglo-Iroquois Councils, 1740–1770," *Ethnohistory*, XXXV (1988), 60–80. She notes that Weiser and other interpreters assisted colonial negotiators in writing speeches.

the more experimental spiritual movements that flourished on the frontier during the Great Awakening years when the Lancaster treaty was held, and for a time he participated in the religious commune at Ephrata.[21]

Weiser and Canassatego formed a close political alliance that shaped imperial relations. At the 1742 Philadelphia treaty, Canassatego praised Weiser's work and urged the colony to compensate him well for his efforts. Testifying to Weiser's skill and honesty, Canassatego claimed him to be "equally faithful in the Interpretation of whatever is said to him by either of us, equally allied to both." Canassatego imagined Weiser's identifications as perfectly split, telling the colonial representatives, "When we adopted him, we divided him into Two equal Parts: One we kept for our selves, and one we left for you." Reflecting colonial prejudices against native standards of cleanliness, and parodying white imputations of cultural contamination from contact with Indians, Canassatego urged the government to provide Weiser with new shoes and clothes, for "he is become as nasty as an *Indian*." Weiser routinely turned to Canassatego for consultation to strategize a resolution of conflicts and deferred to Canassatego's superior command of Iroquois diplomatic forms. At a 1743 conference at the Iroquois capital of Onondaga preliminary to the Lancaster treaty, Weiser asked Canassatego "to speak for me in Open Council, as I would tell him, Article by Article . . . because . . . it required some Ceremonies with which I was not acquainted." Canassatego's confidence in Weiser's translations of deeds and treaties mirrored Weiser's trust in the Onondaga's ceremonial skill and integrity. At the Lancaster treaty the following year, Virginian Thomas Lee so distrusted Weiser's close relationship with the Iroquois that he sought to replace him. When Weiser learned of the Virginian's distrust and removed himself from the Iroquois councils, Canassatego demanded his presence, insisting that "they had a Right to one half of him." Canassatego further insisted that, if the colonists and the League were indeed to become "one Body, and one Soul," in the language of Iroquois diplomacy, they would achieve that union in the dual person of Conrad Weiser.[22]

The proceedings at Lancaster got off to a rocky start, for the "seven flaming fine Gentlemen" who composed the Virginia delegation and their Maryland counterparts were unused to negotiating with native Americans. These southern delegates lacked any commitment to the emerging view of Indian orators as exemplary re-

21. See Wallace, *Conrad Weiser*, esp. 50–59, 194–195; "Conrad Weiser's Report," in Robinson, ed., *Virginia Treaties*, vol. V of *Early American Indian Documents*, 47; Joseph S. Walton, *Conrad Weiser and the Indian Policy of Pennsylvania* (Philadelphia, 1900), esp. chap. 7; E. G. Alderfer, *The Ephrata Commune: An Early American Counterculture* (Pittsburgh, 1985).

22. Van Doren and Boyd, eds., *Indian Treaties Printed by Benjamin Franklin*, 37, 46; "Conrad Weiser's Report," in Robinson, ed., *Virginia Treaties*, vol. V of *Early American Indian Documents*, 44; Wallace, *Conrad Weiser*, 189.

publicans, viewing them instead as debased savages. The Virginians in particular resisted the advice of Weiser and Pennsylvania's other experienced negotiators that they should defer to native terms and practices. Their recalcitrance threatened to disrupt the proceedings with their "narrowness and haughtiness," warned Pennsylvania's Richard Peters, who later celebrated the conduct of the Iroquois in his letter describing his version of the treaty proceedings. Weiser found it necessary to admonish Marshe and his companions "not to talk much of the Indians, nor laugh at their dress, or make any remarks on their behaviour" to avoid an incident that might disrupt the negotiations. Lieutenant Governor Thomas, who served as a mediator between the southern colonies and the Iroquois, issued a similar mandate to Marshe's superiors, advising them to make "Allowances" for Iroquois "Prejudices and Passions" and to provide "a Present now and then for the Relief of their Necessities." "Every Advantage you gain over them in War will be a weakening of the Barrier of those Colonies," he insisted, making such a seeming victory over the Iroquois instead "Victories over yourselves and your Fellow Subjects." Only an alliance with the Iroquois, Thomas suggested, would allow the English colonies to maintain their identity in the face of French aggression.[23]

Thomas's warnings did not deter the Maryland commissioners from trying to establish the negotiations on their own terms. They deployed the figure of the violent and impassioned savage that Thomas had already evoked, contrasting the "rash Expressions" of a League message sent "as if you designed to terrify us" with the Maryland council's own self-described cool consideration of the issue at hand: a dispute over land that the Iroquois had seized from a group of southern Potomack Indians. Confronted with threatening Iroquois demands for compensation, the delegation claimed, the council's calm analysis of the situation had produced the conference in order to resolve the conflict without violence. Insisting that, as subjects of the English king, they "possess and enjoy the Province of *Maryland* by virtue of his Right and Sovereignty thereto," yet offering "a Quantity of Goods" to prevent "every Misunderstanding," the delegation concluded with a testimony of their sincerity following Iroquois precedent: "We have now freely and openly laid our Bosoms bare to you; and that you may be the better confirmed of the Truth of our Hearts, we give you this Belt of Wampum." As Maryland's representatives portrayed the situation, their sincere and rational discourse provided the terms for resolution of a conflict produced by savage speech.[24]

Responding to Maryland's efforts to define the terms of the dispute, the Iro-

---

23. Julian P. Boyd, "Indian Affairs in Pennsylvania, 1736–1762," in Van Doren and Boyd, eds., *Indian Treaties Printed by Benjamin Franklin,* xxxvii, 45; Marshe, "Witham Marshe's Journal," MHS, *Colls.,* 1st Ser., VII, 180.

24. Van Doren and Boyd, eds., *Indian Treaties Printed by Benjamin Franklin,* 48, 49.

quois postponed their reply until the next day, enforcing the Iroquois convention of conferring after each statement of position. In contrast with the stereotype of savage speech, Iroquois treaty council rhetoric emphasized reserve and restraint. Those qualities stood in marked and sometimes frustrating contrast to European verbal ideals of loquacity and quickness. Benjamin Franklin remarked on these different speech conventions, noting the value placed upon fluency both in the British House of Commons, "where scarce a Day passes without some Confusion that makes the Speaker hoarse in calling *to order*," and in polite conversation, "where if you do not deliver your Sentence with great Rapidity, you are cut off in the middle of it . . . and never suffer'd to finish it." Already in 1744 British standards of eloquence influenced the colonies. Arriving at Lancaster, the haughty Virginians found much to admire in the Pennsylvania lieutenant governor's "spirit, cheerfulness, and lively conversation." [25]

Liveliness was not valued in the same way among the Iroquois, particularly in a diplomatic setting. The stately drama of an Iroquois oration could convey a rich range of meanings, from studied assertion to sly humor to angry denunciation. But the formal restraints on treaty oratory precluded the quick retort or the witty rejoinder valued among the English. "Every sudden Repartee, in a publick Treaty, leaves with them an Impression of a light inconsiderate Mind," Colden observed, though they shared the English appreciation for "brisk witty Answers" in private conversation. Remarking on the "great Order and Decency" characteristic of native councils, Franklin described their proceedings: "He that would speak, rises. The rest observe a profound Silence." Silence followed the conclusion of a speech for several moments, allowing the orator time to remember anything he might have forgotten. European observers routinely commented upon the importance of silence and attentive listening in native societies. Diplomatic conventions emphasizing restraint and gravity were shaped by the deliberative rigors of consent-based government. Ambassadors articulated positions previously established in private discussions. A claim asserted, a rebuke made, or an offer tendered in a speech to the assembled treaty participants would be debated in private and a response given at the next treaty session. While League negotiators insisted upon these diplomatic conventions, colonists often grew restive under the slow pace of negotiation that such constant consultation necessitated. Iroquois diplomats retorted that the rush to get down to business threatened to preempt the "drawing together of minds" that must precede true agreement. [26]

25. Benjamin Franklin, "Remarks concerning the Savages of North America" (1783), in Franklin, *Writings* (New York, 1987), 969–974, esp. 971; Van Doren and Boyd, eds., *Indian Treaties Printed by Benjamin Franklin*, xxxvii.

26. Colden, *History of the Five Indian Nations*, I, 20; Franklin, "Remarks concerning the

Such pauses could be put to effective use. Before the Lancaster conference dispersed on the first day of negotiations, Canassatego seized the opportunity to assert his own priorities in a manner that subtly revealed a central tension of the negotiations. Reminding the colony's representatives of their inexperience in Iroquois diplomacy, and underscoring the uneasy mutual dependence that Lieutenant Governor Thomas had already sketched out for the visiting commissioners, Canassatego chose this moment at the end of the day's proceedings to educate the Maryland delegation. "If you have made any Enquiry into *Indian* Affairs," he told the southern diplomats, "you will know, that we have always had our Guns, Hatchets and Kettles, mended when we came to see our Brethren."[27] Canassatego made their repair a symbol of shared responsibility for maintaining the balance of power: the colonies and the Iroquois would collaborate in making war if they did not collaborate in making peace. From the beginning of the treaty, Canassatego and the Iroquois delegation made the technologies of war and peace—weapons and language—the central symbols of intercultural relations in the negotiations.

The following day opened with Canassatego's rejection of Maryland's bid to claim the diplomatic upper hand. Tall, robust, and energetic, with "a manly countenance, mixed with a good-natured smile" and "a surprising liveliness in his speech" despite his sixty or so years, Canassatego conveyed a mature authority and demonstrated the force of the spoken word. He began by repeating the commissioners' description of events, an Iroquois practice designed to verify understanding. But in this act of repetition Canassatego substantially reinterpreted Maryland's account, wresting the agency behind the treaty away from the colony and placing it with the Iroquois. "You say we [asserted our land claim] in such Terms as looked like a Design to terrify you; and you tell us further, that we must be beside ourselves, in using such a rash Expression as to tell you, We know how to do ourselves Justice if you still refuse," he began, focusing immediately on the issue of communication and the stereotype of the passionate savage that the Maryland delegation had evoked. Canassatego explained the reason for the tone of their message: "It is true we did say so, but without any ill Design; for we must inform you, that . . . we were resolved to use such Expressions as would make the greatest Impressions on your Minds, and we find it had its Effect; for you tell us, 'That your wise Men held a Council together, and agreed to invite us, and to enquire of our Right to any of your Lands . . . and to assure us of [the governor's] Willingness to remove whatever impedes a good Understanding between

Savages," in Franklin, *Writings*, 970; Foster, "Another Look at the Function of Wampum," in Jennings et al., eds., *History and Culture of Iroquois Diplomacy*, 103. See also Hagedorn, " 'A Friend to Go between Them,' " *Ethnohistory*, XXXV (1988), 60–80.
    27. Van Doren and Boyd, eds., *Indian Treaties Printed by Benjamin Franklin*, 49.

us.' " "This shews that your wise Men understood our Expressions in their true Sense," he insisted. An act of successful communication and not a threat of violence had produced the conference, Canassatego claimed, and Iroquois rhetorical skill would ensure a successful outcome.[28]

In appealing to the Maryland commissioners "to remove whatever impedes a good Understanding between us," Canassatego evoked one of the most potent metaphors of Iroquois diplomacy: the road of communication, which could become blocked by the logs, brambles, and boulders of misunderstanding and needed periodically to be swept clear of obstacles through the work of a treaty council.[29] In the Lancaster proceedings, the road to understanding was blocked by events that took place on literal roads whose use had generated the conflicts that the negotiators worked to resolve. These roads became particular loci of conflict and anxiety where disputes over territory and goods, cultural differences over justice and hospitality, and the meaning and practice of mobility came into focus. They included the route to Allegheny where three Delawares were alleged to have killed trader John Armstrong — an event that introduced conflicting cultural expectations about who should be punished for the murder and how punishment should be determined — and the road through Virginia that Six Nations warriors took as they traveled south to battle with the Catawbas.

Disputes about the latter road focused on the inhospitality of frontier whites who refused to follow the practice of providing food to travelers. The generous displays of the colonists at formal occasions such as the treaty council contrasted strikingly with the absence of everyday generosity to native travelers. The contrast was rendered all the more striking at the Lancaster treaty when, immediately before the feast, the Iroquois asserted that, although "it is always a Custom among Brethren or Strangers to use each other kindly," they had found that "you have some very ill-natured People" who refused to provide food. The speaker demanded that "the Persons in Power may know that we are to have reasonable Victuals when we are in want." The Iroquois custom of hospitality to travelers both violated colonial market expectations and demanded a constant and widely shared goodwill that the colonists did not actually feel toward natives. The clash between native gift economies and profit-oriented colonial markets in food and drink proved to be a persistent source of tension in treaty negotiations. It also provided colonial writers with a critique of the market's moral limitations, as Jefferson's fascination with Logan's speech or Franklin's observations in "Remarks con-

28. Marshe, "Witham Marshe's Journal," MHS, *Colls.*, 1st Ser., VII, 179, Van Doren and Boyd, eds., *Indian Treaties Printed by Benjamin Franklin*, 50–51.

29. "Glossary of Figures of Speech in Iroquois Political Rhetoric," in Jennings et al., eds., *History and Culture of Iroquois Diplomacy*, 121.

cerning the Savages of North-America" (1783) suggest. The participants at the Lancaster conference reflected on these and other cultural differences between the colonists and the Iroquois as they debated the location, uses, and meanings of the actual roads that produced so many metaphoric logs, brambles, and boulders in the road of communication.[30]

More open reflection on cultural differences took place as treaty participants discussed and debated the technologies of communication that informed the negotiations at the most fundamental level. Without a shared understanding of those technologies, no true agreement would be possible. Canassatego first raised the problem in his long speech responding to the Maryland delegates. Addressing Maryland's claim that "our *Great King of* ENGLAND, and his Subjects, have always possessed the Province of *Maryland* free and undisturbed from any Claim of the *Six Nations* for above one hundred years past," Canassatego asked, "What is One Hundred Years in Comparison of the Length of Time since our Claim began? since we came out of this Ground?" "You came out of the Ground in a Country that lies beyond the Seas, there you may have a just Claim," he continued, "but here you must allow us to be your elder Brethren, and the Lands to belong to us long before you knew any thing of them." Collapsing the difference between numerous native peoples with discrete identities and shifting territorial claims, Canassatego asserted native priority of rights to the land when confronted with colonial claims and obscured the novelty of the Iroquois claim to this territory.[31]

Canassatego described the initial Iroquois decision to share the land with Europeans as a response to intriguing and useful new technologies: "It is true, that

---

30. Van Doren and Boyd, eds., *Indian Treaties Printed by Benjamin Franklin*, 64. Jefferson included the already famous speech attributed to the Shawnee chief Logan in his *Notes on the State of Virginia* (1787), in Jefferson, *Writings* (New York, 1984), 188–189. On the long-lived appeal of the speech, see Roy Harvey Pearce, *The Savages of America: A Study of the Indian and the Idea of Civilization* (Baltimore, 1965), 79. On Jefferson's attraction to the speech, see Fliegelman, *Declaring Independence*, 97–98.

Franklin's "Remarks" sets out to explore native standards of civility and ends with a lengthy account of an exchange between Canassatego and Conrad Weiser in which Canassatego offers an unflattering comparison of native hospitality with white mercenary concerns:

> If a white Man in travelling thro' our Country, enters one of our Cabins, we all treat him as I treat you; we dry him if he is wet, we warm him if he is cold, and give him Meat and Drink that he may allay his Thirst and Hunger, and we spread soft Furs for him to rest and sleep on: We Demand nothing in return. But if I go into a white Man's House at Albany, and ask for Victuals and Drink, they say, where is your Money? and if I have none, they say, get out, you Indian Dog.

Benjamin Franklin, *Writings* (New York, 1987), 974.

31. Van Doren and Boyd, eds., *Indian Treaties Printed by Benjamin Franklin*, 48, 51. Jennings treats these land claims skeptically in *The Ambiguous Iroquois Empire*, 359–360.

above One Hundred Years ago the *Dutch* came here in a Ship, and brought with them several Goods; such as Awls, Knives, Hatchets, Guns, and many other Particulars, which they gave us; and when they had taught us how to use their Things, and we saw what sort of People they were, we were so well pleased with them, that we tied their Ship to the Bushes on the Shore." He then narrated the stages of Iroquois relations with the Dutch foregrounding Iroquois agency in gradually strengthening the chain uniting them as "one People," a process that he figured as moving the rope tying the Dutch ship from the bushes to a tree, then to "a strong and big Rock," then to "the big Mountain," and eventually replacing rope with wampum to make the chain stronger. When the English took over New Holland, the English governor of New York offered to replace the wampum chain binding the colony to the Iroquois, for wampum "was liable to break and rot, and to perish in a Course of Years." A silver chain "would be much stronger, and would last for ever." "This we accepted," Canassatego observed, "and fastened the ship with it, and it has lasted ever since." [32]

The substitution of silver for wampum, and of English agency for Iroquois control, stood metonymically in Canassatego's oration for a series of technological transformations. The English colonists insisted that the new technologies marked a clear improvement in native circumstances, but the Iroquois maintained that they had proved much more ambiguous. For the Onondaga ambassador, differences over technology stood for differences in understanding the value of native ways of life. "We have had some small Differences with the *English*," he observed,

> and, during these Misunderstanding, some of their young Men would, by way of Reproach, be every now and then telling us, that we should have perished if they had not come into the Country and furnished us with Strowds and Hatchets, and Guns, and other Things necessary for the Support of Life; but we always gave them to understand that they were mistaken, that we lived before they came amongst us, and as well, or better, if we may believe what our Forefathers have told us.

Hatchets and knives of stone and bows and arrows had served "our Uses as well then as the *English* ones do now," he insisted. Other English technologies had constrained the Iroquois more than metalwork had liberated them. "We are now straitened, and sometimes in want of Deer, and liable to many other Inconveniencies since the *English* came among us," he continued, pointing to the secretary, "and particularly from that Pen-and-Ink Work that is going on at the Table." Writing, Canassatego insisted, was neither the symbol of cultural superiority nor the ultimate arbiter of territorial disputes that the English so often tried to make it. A

---

32. Van Doren and Boyd, eds., *Indian Treaties Printed by Benjamin Franklin*, 51, 52.

flawed linguistic medium, it blocked rather than fostered understanding between the Iroquois and the English, particularly as the written word served colonial claims to native territory. Canassatego overturned English claims of textual authenticity and stability, highlighting instead colonial manipulation and duplicity using written deeds.[33]

Behind the Onondaga's words hovered Pennsylvania's 1737 Walking Purchase of Delaware land, in which false documents played a significant role and the letter of the deed rather than the spirit of the agreement was observed.[34] In addition, Canassatego told the story of the Dongan deed of 1686 to illustrate the peculiar and deceptive uses to which "Pen-and-Ink Work" had been put in English relations with the Iroquois. In the 1680s, the governor of New York had warned the Iroquois not to sell territory to Pennsylvania. Instead, he urged them to put their land "into his Hands," "that we might always have our Land when we should want it." But when he sailed to England, the governor "carried our Land with him, and there sold it to our Brother *Onas* [the Iroquois term for the Pennsylvania governor] for a large Sum of Money." Belatedly informed of the sale, the Iroquois would have remained uncompensated for their territory but for the generosity of the Pennsylvanians who "paid us for our Lands over again." Canassatego's narration emphasized the absurdity of imagining that land could be abstracted from its physical existence and conveyed in a document. He told the story in response to the Maryland delegation's assertions that the Susquehanna Indians had yielded the disputed land "by a Treaty above ninety Years since." Canassatego's tale both undermined the authority of the written document and educated the southern diplomats in the protocols of generous dealings that he hoped would govern the current proceedings. The appeal prepared the ground for successful Iroquois demands that they be amply compensated.[35]

But Canassatego failed to weaken the authority of the written treaty in the minds of the colonial negotiators. Insisting that a treaty "being in Writing, is more certain than your Memory," the colonial representatives claimed that the use of documents "is the Way the white People have of preserving Transactions of every Kind, and transmitting them down to their Childrens Children for ever, and all Disputes among them are settled by this faithful kind of Evidence, and must be the Rule between the Great King and you." "We are all Subjects, as well as you, of the Great King beyond the Water," Thomas told them, and imperial diplomacy was founded on documents.[36]

33. Ibid., 52.

34. On the Pennsylvania Walking Purchase, see Jennings, *The Ambiguous Iroquois Empire*, 332–333, 336–339, 388–397.

35. Van Doren and Boyd, eds., *Indian Treaties Printed by Benjamin Franklin*, 49, 52.

36. Ibid., 61, 78.

The Iroquois themselves found numerous uses for texts. Writing had become a familiar feature of the cultural frontier by the mid-eighteenth century. Canassatego demonstrated his familiarity with textual technologies of land transfer when he told the Maryland delegates, "We have had your Deeds interpreted to us, and we acknowledge them to be good and valid," but they did not apply to the land at issue. Deceived and manipulated through writing though they had been, native leaders employed it of necessity and could even use the technology to their advantage. Canassatego had already, in his famous speech to the 1742 treaty council at Philadelphia, publicly embraced the authority of written deeds against the testimony of the Delaware Indians. "Your Cause is bad; your Heart far from being upright; and you are maliciously bent to break the Chain of Friendship with our Brother *Onas* and his People," he informed the Delawares. "We have seen with our Eyes a Deed sign'd by nine of your Ancestors above *Fifty* Years ago for this very Land, and a Release sign'd, not many Years since, by some of yourselves and Chiefs now living, to the Number of fifteen or upwards." Asserting textual authority strategically for his own purposes, Canassatego accepted the authenticity of written deeds to align himself with English power and to subordinate the Delawares more completely to the Iroquois.[37]

Canassatego's manipulation of textual power represents one end of a spectrum of native relationships with the written word while his critique of its inauthenticity represents the other. Rearticulating the performance semiotic of speech and text, he expressed the complex relationship of native leaders to culturally marked verbal media. Recognizing the usefulness of writing, Iroquois leaders conducted business with colonists and other native communities through letters, for instance when, at the urging of colonial authorities at Albany, they "desired a Letter might be sent to the *Catawbas* and *Cherikees,* to desire them to come and confirm the Peace," or when the Conoy Indians sent a written message to Virginia's governor.[38]

Despite its usefulness, the medium generated uncertainty and anxiety, heightened by the fact that natives depended largely on whites to conduct their correspondence. Representatives of several colonies encouraged their native negotiating partners to send Indian children to colonial schools to learn the skills that would permit them to act on behalf of their people. Dangers from disease and maltreatment as well as the psychological damage done by cultural deracination contributed to native refusals. At Lancaster, Canassatego firmly rejected the Vir-

37. Ibid., 35, 52. On the increasing use of written documents by Pennsylvania Indians, see Merritt, "Metaphor, Meaning, and Misunderstanding," in Cayton and Teute, eds., *Contact Points,* 82, 84–85. On the importance of Canassatego's speech in the historiography of the Iroquois, see Jennings, *The Ambiguous Iroquois Empire,* 22–23; Wallace, *Conrad Weiser,* 131–132.

38. Van Doren and Boyd, eds., *Indian Treaties Printed by Benjamin Franklin,* 64.

ginia delegation's proposal that a few Iroquois children be sent to Williamsburg to "learn Languages, and to write and read." "We love our Children too well to send them so great a Way," he informed them.[39]

A widespread distrust of literacy heightened such reluctance. The Iroquois delegates at Lancaster made repeated references throughout the proceedings to letters that had never been written, had gone astray or remained unanswered, or whose authenticity could not be confirmed, suggesting that lapses in communication and even active deception accompanied reliance upon the written word. Gachradodow countered the inappropriate confidence of the colonists in the authority of documents to promote peace, informing them that the Catawbas had responded to their letter with insults. Canassatego reproached the lieutenant governor of Pennsylvania for failing to write the English king a letter that the Iroquois had requested in hopes of resolving their dispute with Maryland. The possibility of misunderstanding in written exchanges appeared clearly in the discrepant accounts of the letter from the Conoy Indians. While the colonists maintained that the letter ceded land because "the settling of the white People all round them had made Deer scarce," Canassatego paraphrased the Conoys' letter differently. In his account, the letter revealed that the Conoys felt "ill used by the white People" and expected some compensation. Yet, he asserted, they "never have received any Answer."[40]

The colonists' insistence upon textual authority threatened the negotiations directly when the Virginia delegation made assertions based on a letter, allegedly written a year earlier at Onondaga, that ceded all claims to the territory under dispute. The Iroquois representatives flatly denied its existence. "Let us see the Letter," Tachanoontia demanded, "and inform us who was the Interpreter, and whose Names are put to that Letter." Surely, if such a letter had been written, "some of our Council would easily remember it." The Virginia delegation could only produce a letter forwarded from the New York commissioners for Indian affairs. That letter, along with the ample treaty documentation that the Virginians brought forth, met with the equivalent of a collective shrug from the Iroquois. Contested textual evidence paled beside the light of reputation: "All the World knows we conquered the several Nations" inhabiting the disputed land, Tachanoontia asserted. The "Right of Conquest" took precedence over the text-based claims that the Virginians advanced in the name of the "Great King" across the sea. The colonists could no more sustain a paper claim to territory than they could capture the "Yo-hah" in English orthography. In the end, the Iroquois succeeded in forcing

---

39. Ibid., 76. Franklin recounted this exchange, embellishing it substantially, in "Remarks concerning the Savages," in Franklin, *Writings,* 969–970.

40. Van Doren and Boyd, eds., *Indian Treaties Printed by Benjamin Franklin,* 67–68.

the haughty Virginians to provide the generous compensation that Canassatego had set out as a negotiating standard in his opening speech.[41]

Competitions for discursive power were enacted at the treaty council in the shifts between the spoken and written words, as the Iroquois and the colonists disputed the degree of power and authenticity that each medium would hold in their interactions. Three moments illustrate this underlying dynamic most directly. At the end of the formal dinner in the courthouse, Gachradodow stepped to "an elevated Part of the Court-House," where he gave a speech "with all the Dignity of a Warrior, the Gesture of an Orator, and in a very graceful Posture." His elaborate performance foregrounded the force of the spoken word as he enacted a ritual naming of the Maryland governor, who was given an Iroquois title comparable to those that the governors of Pennsylvania and Virginia already possessed. The name that the Iroquois diplomats chose for the governor of Maryland, perhaps as a subtle parody, recalled the Maryland delegation's early attempt to control the terms of the negotiations. Gachradodow announced that they had agreed to call him "*Tocarry-hogan,* denoting Precedency, Excellency, or living in the middle or honourable Place betwixt *Assaragoa* [the governor of Virginia] and their Brother *Onas,* by whom their Treaties might be better carried on."[42] This act of oral definition in the naming ceremony was followed directly by the signing of the land deed granting Iroquois territory to the government of Maryland. First the commissioners ordered Conrad Weiser to interpret the deed; then, witnessed by a number of colonial representatives, Canassatego and thirteen other sachems made their marks and impressed their seals on the document. Manifesting the complexities of the performance semiotic, Gachradodow's speech foregrounding Iroquois control of treaty council protocol was followed by the signing of the written deed granting native land, the primary symbol of colonial power.

The second moment highlighting the complex symbolism of verbal form at the treaty occurred in the resolution to the Virginia dispute. Canassatego asked the delegation to fulfill his earlier request to "represent their Case to the King." The commissioners had claimed that "this Dispute is not between *Virginia* and you; it is setting up your Right against the Great King . . . our common Father, [who] will do equal Justice to all his Children." If that was true, then the King would have to learn the Iroquois position. Canassatego did not propose traveling to England himself, as his predecessor Hendrick and the other Iroquois ambassadors

41. Ibid., 55, 56.

42. Ibid., 65. The name for Pennsylvania's governor, "Onas," or "Feather," translated the name of the respected William Penn and simultaneously punned on the tool of writing. "Assaragoa" (or "Assaryquoa"), that is, "Sword or Big Knife," was a reference to the cutlass that an earlier Virginia governor gave them; see "Persons Participating in Iroquois Treaties," in Jennings et al., eds., *History and Culture of Iroquois Diplomacy,* 230, 246.

had done. Instead, he relied on the Virginians to represent the Iroquois case to the British monarch. The Virginians promised to "make such a Representation faithfully and honestly," and to guarantee their faith they provided "a Writing, under their Hands and Seals, to that Purpose." Despite the possibilities of manipulation that attended textual communication, Canassatego accepted the "Paper, containing a Promise to recommend the *Six Nations* for further Favour to the King" and gave it to Weiser for safekeeping. Canassatego's strategy for maintaining Iroquois power depended upon his acceptance of the ability of this "Writing" to bind Virginia, which reflects his faith in Weiser.[43]

Competitions for power were again enacted through the symbolism of speech and text at the signing of a deed granting land to Virginia. The deed, translated by Weiser and marked and sealed by the Iroquois leaders, recognized "the King's Right to all the Lands that are, or shall be, by his Majesty's Appointment in the Colony of *Virginia*." Earlier the Virginia commission went back "into old Times" and asserted that "the Great King holds *Virginia* by Right of Conquest, and the Bounds of that Conquest to the Westward is the Great Sea." It is unclear whether the Iroquois leaders understood the nature of Virginia's claim, which extended to the Pacific Ocean. Either way, their ability to manipulate textual symbols depended on Weiser.[44]

Canassatego's trust in Weiser, however misplaced it might have been, led him to imagine a diplomatic realm where the Iroquois and the English could achieve a reciprocity that would benefit both peoples. During the first half of the century, the English colonists and their most important native allies projected upon one another mirror images of political power that would be mutually sustaining. The Iroquois League occupied a mediating position between the French and English colonies, a position enhanced by Iroquois claims to control the allegiances of a number of important tribes such as the Delawares and the Shawnees on the frontier of English settlement and the Praying Indians in French-controlled territory. At the start of an imperial war, the English colonies felt urgently the need to ensure the Six Nations' commitment to the English cause. For Benjamin Franklin, intercolonial interests further amplified the treaty's importance. Franklin hoped that the joint diplomatic action of three colonies established a precedent for a future American union. The Iroquois leaders themselves urged such a union upon the colonies. In 1736, Iroquois speaker Kanickhungo repeated back to the colonies their own advice to the Iroquois "to strengthen ourselves by entring into firm Leagues of Friendship and Alliance with several other Nations of *Indians* around

43. Van Doren and Boyd, eds., *Indian Treaties Printed by Benjamin Franklin*, 61–62, 69, 78. The paper is printed in Robinson, ed., *Virginia Treaties*, 88.

44. Van Doren and Boyd, eds., *Indian Treaties Printed by Benjamin Franklin*, 60, 69; Jennings, *The Ambiguous Iroquois Empire*, 361.

us."[45] Such a union invested the Iroquois League with its substantial strength, Canassatego later asserted. "We heartily recommend Union and a good Agreement between you our Brethren," he exhorted at the end of the Lancaster negotiations, reflecting the Iroquois agenda of extending and consolidating their power. "We are a powerful Confederacy; and, by your observing the same Methods our wise Forefathers have taken, you will acquire fresh Strength and Power." Franklin echoed Canassatego's words six years later when he wrote, with an evident sense of colonial superiority, "It would be a very strange Thing, if six Nations of ignorant Savages should be capable of forming a Scheme for such an Union . . . and yet that a like Union should be impracticable for ten or a Dozen *English* Colonies." Despite Canassatego's projection of shared obligation, the Lancaster treaty proved to be the summit of Iroquois power over the colonies.[46]

Canassatego's vision of a shared Iroquois-English public domain had already begun to crumble in 1749 when the Onondaga sachem arrived at Weiser's doorstep on his way to a treaty in Philadelphia with a host of almost three hundred native followers, only to have Weiser rebuke him for traveling with such a large and unruly cortege. The treaty had already been completed with the partial representation of the Seneca leaders, Weiser informed him. Canassatego responded that the Senecas could not speak for the League and insisted that he could not exclude anyone who wanted to accompany him to a treaty meeting. Canassatego viewed the size of his party as evidence of his political power; Weiser and the Pennsylvania authorities saw it as an unnecessary expense. The dispute came close to producing a complete rupture between Pennsylvania and the League. Canassatego's inclusive understanding of diplomacy masked the deterioration of the common public arena created by the Covenant Chain between the colonists and the Iroquois. In Philadelphia, Canassatego revealed his slipping hold on power when he commented to the delegates that "white People are no more obedient to you than our young Indians are to us." A year later, as Weiser made his way to Onondaga for renewed negotiations, he received word that his old ally was dead, the result of either execution or murder. Tahashrouchioony, a younger, Roman Catholic man with ties to the French, took over leadership of the Iroquois, and when Weiser arrived he was told that "all the Belts of Wampum belonging to the Publick from

45. For more on Franklin's political life and its ties with colonial Indian relations, see Gerald Stourzh, *Benjamin Franklin and American Foreign Policy* (Chicago, 1954), 48. For Kanickhungo's comment, see Van Doren and Boyd, eds., *Indian Treaties Printed by Benjamin Franklin*, 8.

46. Franklin to James Parker, Mar. 20, 1750, in Franklin, *Writings*, 442–446, esp. 444; Van Doren and Boyd, eds., *Indian Treaties Printed by Benjamin Franklin*, 78. On the Lancaster treaty as the both the "summit" of Iroquois power and the beginning of the rapid slide down the "slope" that ended with the British defeat of France and their native allies in 1763, see Jennings, *The Ambiguous Iroquois Empire*, chap. 18. See also Richard L. Haan, "Covenant and Consensus: Iroquois and English, 1676–1760," in Richter and Merrell, eds., *Beyond the Covenant Chain*, 57.

the several English Governors that remained unanswered at the Death of Canassatego, and found in his Possession, were by [Tahashrouchioony's] orders burned with him." Canassatego's public domain of diplomatic power in relation to the English empire, symbolized by the destroyed wampum belts, deteriorated rapidly after his death. The loosening of League authority over its own members made negotiation far more difficult. The Iroquois and English publics that for a time constituted a mutually reinforcing set of alliances crumbled, and the League itself splintered during the Revolutionary war. These allied communities experienced widespread resistance to collective authority that culminated, though with very different consequences, for both the colonies and the Iroquois in the American Revolution.[47]

Even as centralized Iroquois authority crumbled, the colonial experience of Iroquois diplomacy, and of native American speech traditions in general, helped to model the rhetorical revival that defined important aspects of Revolutionary public culture. Many American political leaders encountered the native diplomacy that was a basic feature of colonial and early national life. In practice, colonial treatment of native leaders often continued to reflect the suspicious and condescending attitudes of the southern delegates at Lancaster rather than the celebratory view of Pennsylvania secretary Richard Peters. Yet at the same time, praise for the savage republican speaker became a regular feature of colonial political discourse aimed at British imperial policy.[48] Thomas Jefferson described a common experience of the major colonial capitals when he wrote to John Adams in 1812 that "before the Revolution [southern Indians] were in the habit of coming often, and in great numbers to the seat of our government [Williamsburg]." Jefferson's interest in native eloquence began in his youth and persisted into old age. He particularly celebrated the oratory of the Cherokee warrior Outacity, whose "sounding voice, distinct articulation, [and] animated action" inspired "awe and veneration." As early as the mid-eighteenth century, the Indian oration even provided a model for the celebratory rhetoric of pseudo-Indian groups such as the Schuylkill Fishing Company of Pennsylvania and the Tammany societies, organizations for white men that functioned as social and political centers.[49]

47. Colin G. Calloway, *The American Revolution in Indian Country: Crisis and Diversity in Native American Communities* (Cambridge, 1995), 21 n. 88 (see also prologue); Jennings, *The Ambiguous Iroquois Empire*, 364.

48. The two subjects of Chap. 4, below, James Otis of Massachusetts and Patrick Henry of Virginia, had either family or personal experience with native diplomacy and governance. See John J. Waters, Jr., *The Otis Family in Provincial and Revolutionary Massachusetts* (Chapel Hill, N.C., 1968), 40, 180; Henry Mayer, *A Son of Thunder: Patrick Henry and the American Republic* (Charlottesville, Va., 1991), 150–151, 264–265.

49. Jefferson to Adams, June 11, 1812, in Lester J. Cappon, ed., *The Adams-Jefferson Letters: The Complete Correspondence between Thomas Jefferson and Abigail and John Adams* (1959;

When joined to republican thought, such celebrations of native eloquence helped to shape a view of natural liberty linked to the figure of the savage speaker who exerts power through persuasion rather than commands, a view that emerged at the center of Revolutionary ideology. Sketching the Iroquois polity as an ideal republican order with "absolute Notions of Liberty," Colden insisted that all Iroquois offices were won by merit and carried no remuneration. "Here we see the natural Origin of all Power and Authority among a free People," he asserted in a thinly veiled commentary on colonial officeholding that marked the difference between "natural" power and the "artificial Power or Sovereignty" brought by "the Laws and Constitution of a Country."[50]

Attempting to debunk such a view of native life, tory Peter Oliver insisted that Indian communities did not exist in a "perfectly ideal" condition of natural liberty but rather possessed "civil Government" led by "Kings and wise Men of Council, their *Sachems* and *Sagamores,* on whom they rely for their Conduct." These leaders filled the role that written laws supplied to "more refined Nations." Writing after the Revolution, Oliver sought to dismantle the patriot concept of natural liberty focused on an imagined scene of communal self-presence achieved through speech. He sketched a mythic assembly in order to critique the relationship between speech and political representation that was fundamental to Whig thought: "Where will be found a *Blackheath* large enough for them to assemble upon in full Synod? Or, when assembled, how long a Time must it take for the Sound of every Proposal to reverberate in its full Weight? I think it might be readily answered, that it would take such a length of Time, that each Individual would be a Governor without having any one Subject to govern."[51] Yet Oliver's skepticism points to the significance of this image for the patriot movement. Evocative of a purer, more primitive political order, whether of Greeks and Romans, ancient Britons, or contemporary native Americans, such an image of a community fully present to itself in spoken debate deeply shaped the rhetoric and political culture of Revolutionary America.

Chapel Hill, N.C., 1988), 305–308, esp. 307. In *Declaring Independence,* 99, Fliegelman notes that Jefferson's attraction to Outacity's eloquence did not extend to the verbal power of Patrick Henry. On the role of pseudo-Indian rhetoric among the Schuykill Fishing Company and the Tammany societies, see Philip J. Deloria, *Playing Indian* (New Haven, Conn., 1998), 13, 32–33.

50. Colden, *History of the Five Indian Nations,* I, 2–3, 11. See also Deloria, *Playing Indian,* chaps. 1, 2.

51. Douglass Adair and John A. Schutz, eds., *Peter Oliver's Origin and Progress of the American Rebellion: A Tory View* (San Marino, Calif., 1961), 5, 8. Oliver's previously unpublished manuscript is dated 1781 (ix).

4 The Oratorical Public Culture of Revolutionary America

I. MEDIUM AND MESSAGE IN REVOLUTIONARY PUBLIC CULTURE

In February 1761, the American Revolution began—or so John Adams came to believe. Writing fifty years later, Adams portrayed the argument of prominent Boston lawyer James Otis, Jr., against writs of assistance as the first salvo in the war of words that escalated into actual warfare and ultimately led to American independence. Sketching the scene, which took place in a Boston courtroom, as a moment of pure, almost primal eloquence that shaped a new community and a new patriot identity, Adams celebrated Otis's dramatic performance for the scope and force of his words and the passion of their delivery. In a moment of Pentecostal power, Otis's speech transfixed and transformed his audience:

> Otis was a flame of Fire! With the promptitude of Clasical Allusions, a depth of Research, a rapid Summary of Historical Events and dates, a profusion of legal Authorities, a prophetic glare of his eyes into futurity, and a rapid Torrent of impetuous Eloquence, he hurried away all before him; American Independence was then and there born.

Adams cast the impact of Otis's passion in terms that drastically collapse the sequence of events leading to war with Britain: "Every man of a crowded audience appeared to me to go away, as I did, ready to take up arms against writs of assistance."[1]

---

1. L. Kinvin Wroth and Hiller B. Zobel, eds., *Legal Papers of John Adams,* II (Cambridge, Mass., 1965), 107; John Adams to William Tudor, Mar. 29, 1817, in Charles Francis Adams, ed., *The Works of John Adams, Second President of the United States . . . ,* X (Boston, 1856), 247–248. Adams overstated the event for posterity, but Otis's argument did have an impact throughout the colonies. He reiterated it regularly as writs of assistance continued to be a source of controversy in colonial politics. For a later case in which Otis was involved, see George Gregerson Wolkins, "Daniel Malcom and Writs of Assistance," in Massachusetts Historical Society, *Proceedings,* LVIII (1925), 5–84. See also Joseph R. Frese, "James Otis and Writs of Assistance," *NEQ,* XXX (1957), 496–508; Robert J. Taylor et al., eds., *Papers of John Adams,* 10 vols. (Cambridge, Mass., 1977–1996), I, 152–153.

Adams's mythic narrative of Revolutionary origins points to the new prominence of political eloquence in colonial public life. Distinguishing their art from
its antecedents in the pulpit, the courtroom, and the legislature, Revolutionary-
era political leaders broke the elite frame of Assembly or court chamber in order
to address a wider public. Lawyers such as Otis played a crucial role in the rise of
the partisanship that characterized radical politics, transforming narrow legislative and legal arguments into broad and stirring assertions of colonial rights. The
very nature of legal practice accustomed lawyers to the strategies of partisan argumentation. The prosecution of popular causes such as the Writs of Assistance case
allowed whig lawyers to present themselves as public servants, overcoming public
suspicion of their profession. Newly sophisticated and professionalized attorneys
spoke *to* laypeople, and increasingly they claimed to speak *for* them. "I . . . now
appear not only in obedience to your order," Otis told the Massachusetts court in
1761, "but also in behalf of the inhabitants of this town . . . and out of regard to
the liberties of the subject."[2]

Lawyers transformed themselves into political orators in part by adapting
the impassioned spiritual rhetoric of the Great Awakening.[3] Similar performance
techniques facilitated the adaptation of pulpit forms to the political arena. A colonial lawyer prepared for a courtroom argument in much the same way that a minister prepared to preach a sermon. He read and synthesized the relevant documents; perhaps he sketched an outline. In court, he spoke without a prepared text,
as lawyers still do.[4] The improvisational delivery that lawyers shared with evangelical preachers did not guarantee an inspired performance, however. Addressed
to a judicial audience, the technicalities of legal argumentation made for dry fare,

2. Richard Brown, *Knowledge Is Power: The Diffusion of Information in Early America, 1700–
1865* (New York, 1989), 84, 101–102; Wroth and Zobel, eds., *Legal Papers of Adams,* II, 139.

3. Colonial ministers themselves were initially uneasy with the public dispute and division
that signaled an intensifying imperial conflict. Their experiences with the schisms of the Great
Awakening made them reluctant to engage in controversy. The patriot clergy eventually did become a major force in Revolutionary politics, but the impact of evangelical eloquence had been
felt much earlier in the performances of political orators. There is an extensive literature on the
New Light influence on Revolutionary politics. For works concerned with the impact of evangelical preaching on political oratory, see Alan Heimert, *Religion and the American Mind: From
the Great Awakening to the Revolution* (Cambridge, Mass., 1966); Rhys Isaac, *The Transformation
of Virginia, 1740–1790* (Chapel Hill, N.C., 1982); Harry S. Stout, "Religion, Communications, and
the Ideological Origins of the American Revolution," *WMQ,* XXXIV (1977), 519–541; Stout, *The
New England Soul: Preaching and Religious Culture in Colonial New England* (New York, 1986),
part 5; Donald Weber, *Rhetoric and History in Revolutionary New England* (New York, 1988).

4. George V. Bohman notes that the preparation of a written speech was rare, limited to judicial charges to grand juries, eulogies, and Boston Massacre orations; see "The Colonial Period,"
in William Norwood Brigance, ed., *A History and Criticism of American Public Address,* I (New
York, 1943), 3–54.

the antithesis of New Light passion. Otis's Writs of Assistance speech worked to change both the language and the audience for legal eloquence.

In his diary for 1758, Adams asks, "Of what use to a Lawyer is that Part of oratory, which relates to the moving of the Passions?" He concludes, in a moment that anticipates his admiration for Otis's speech, passion "may be used to rouse in the Breasts of the Audience a gallant Spirit of Liberty," especially "on any Instance of arbitrary Conduct in an Officer or Magistrate." Otis, who had been briefly drawn to evangelicalism after hearing Whitefield speak in 1740, fulfilled this ideal, leading Adams to insist that in Otis he saw "Isaiah and Ezekiel united."[5] Evangelical passion alone did not define Revolutionary eloquence, either in Adams's mind or in colonial society. A new ideal of gentility modeled on British civil society required the colonial lawyer to unite thorough legal training, broad literary and general knowledge, and urbane manners. The qualities that Adams attributed to Otis's speech—breadth of knowledge, copiousness, quasi-sacred authority, and above all the power to induce passion in others—characterized the emerging tradition of partisan political speech.[6] What Otis accomplished in Massachusetts, Patrick Henry achieved in a somewhat modified fashion in Virginia. Both men broke new ground as the performance artists of their era, introducing political oratory as a newly important genre of public discourse to their respective regions.

As the careers of Otis and Henry suggest, the role of oratory in colonial political life changed dramatically in the context of Revolutionary conflict. Its expanded audience mirrored the comparable expansion of print culture. Print and oratory often complemented each other in the intensifying political activities of the colonists. At the same time, competing rhetorics of textuality and orality marked Revolutionary debates in complex ways. Otis and Henry proved so central to the emergence of political oratory because they spent their public lives de-

5. L. H. Butterfield, ed., *The Earliest Diary of John Adams* (Cambridge, Mass., 1966), 74; John J. Waters, Jr., *The Otis Family in Provincial and Revolutionary Massachusetts* (Chapel Hill, N.C., 1968), 112; Adams, ed., *Works of John Adams*, X, 272.

6. Remarking on the novel expectations and ideals for lawyers in midcentury, Brown notes that Otis's Writs of Assistance speech inaugurated "a new form of public speaking and a new role for lawyers" (*Knowledge Is Power*, 102). These professional ideals crystallized in the mid-eighteenth century and increasingly dominated the legal profession in the nineteenth century, when Daniel Webster represented the pinnacle of eloquent achievement (chap. 4). Robert Ferguson discusses the significance of lawyers as public figures in the post-Revolutionary period in *Law and Letters in American Culture* (Cambridge, Mass., 1984). On the emergence of civil society in the colonies and its replication of British forms, see David S. Shields, *Civil Tongues and Polite Letters in British America* (Chapel Hill, N.C., 1997); Richard L. Bushman, "American High-Style and Vernacular Cultures," in Jack P. Greene and J. R. Pole, eds., *Colonial British America: Essays in the New History of the Early Modern Era* (Baltimore, 1984), 345–383.

FIGURE 8. James Otis, Jr. *By Joseph Blackburn. 1755. Coll. Mrs. Carlos A. Hepp.*
Reproduction courtesy Frick Art Reference Library, New York City

fining the symbolic meanings of linguistic media. Both men privileged oral forms
and overturned textual precedents to produce a community fully present to itself.
Clearing away textual authority to make room for their acts of oral creation, they
spoke a new public realm into being. Their careers trace the interaction of symbolic meanings and institutional changes as an oratorical public sphere emerged
in self-conscious tension with textual modes of publicity.

II. SPEECH, PRESENCE, AND REPRESENTATION

The political literature of the Revolutionary period offers a sustained engagement with the problems of representation. The well-known disputes over whether the colonies were or could be adequately represented in Parliament were simply the most sophisticated formulations of a wider range of issues. These included basic problems of communication and understanding between colonies an ocean away from the mother country as well as the extreme vulnerability of personal reputations at such a distance. Defining a colony in *The Rights of the British Colonies Asserted and Proved* (1764), James Otis emphasized the issues of distance and separation. A colony, he wrote, is "a settlement of subjects, in a *territory disjoined* or remote from the mother country." This remoteness exposed the details of the colonial condition to the vicissitudes of heavily mediated communication. Lamenting the misapprehensions about the colonies held not only by the average British citizen but also by the highest government officials, Otis related a tale about a British secretary of state who thought New England was an island. Such misunderstandings made imperial governance deeply problematic. They could be corrected, Otis held, if the colonies had representation in Parliament. Under those circumstances, "persons of the first reputation among their countrymen" could be sent "truly to represent them."[7] But Parliament never seriously pursued this possibility. As tensions grew between Britain and its American colonies, the difficulty in understanding the political climate half a world away increasingly made independence seem inevitable. When in 1776 Thomas Paine reflected on the absurd condition that the colonists had "to be always running three or four thousand miles with a tale or a petition, waiting four or five months for an answer, which when obtained requires five or six more to explain it in," he was only repeating what Otis and others had been saying with varying degrees of directness for a decade or more.[8]

Proximity and distance, presence and absence, and their relationship to all levels of representation preoccupied James Otis. They structured the whole range of his public performances, from his 1760 publications on language and literature to the career-shaping 1761 Writs of Assistance case, to his political pamphlets and activities as Boston's representative. Throughout his career, Otis thought about

7. James Otis, *The Rights of the British Colonies Asserted and Proved* (1764), in Charles F. Mullett, ed., "Some Political Writings of James Otis," in *University of Missouri Studies,* IV (1929), 301–347, esp. 319, 327 (hereafter cited as Mullett, ed., "Political Writings of Otis"). Thomas Hutchinson, *The History of the Colony and Province of Massachusetts-Bay,* ed. Lawrence Shaw Mayo, 3 vols. (Cambridge, Mass., 1936), III, is punctuated by charges and countercharges of misrepresentation; see esp. 213, 219–220, 228.

8. Thomas Paine, *Common Sense,* in Paine, *Collected Writings* (New York, 1995), 28.

social and political issues in terms of the modes and processes of representation: Through what channels is knowledge conveyed? What verbal medium or institutional structure communicates most effectively? What social consequences arise from the choice of a particular medium or institution? In answering these questions, he returned again and again to the relationship between the written and spoken words. Speech for Otis reflected proximity and presence, the immediacy of community that authorizes legitimate political power. In keeping with his essentially logocentric understanding of speech, Otis viewed writing as a medium derivative at best, destructive of fundamental rights at worst.[9]

Otis's privileging of speech reflected larger tendencies in the patriot movement and was reflected, in turn, in the portraits that contemporary historians drew of him. Virtually every account of Otis represents him as a figure whose verbal pyrotechnics dominated and disrupted colonial politics for almost a decade. Tory representations, including the histories of Thomas Hutchinson and Peter Oliver and the letters of Massachusetts governor Francis Bernard, return again and again to his uncivil, scurrilous speech, his flare for the dramatic, and his ability to manipulate others with his emotional outbursts. In contrast, whigs portrayed him in the image of the classical orators: passionate but controlled, he denounced corruption and guided the people toward their true interests. Turned one way, then, Otis embodied the patriot orator; turned another, the demagogue.[10]

Otis's engagement with the oral extended far beyond his talent for strategically disruptive interjections or his flare for persuasive oratory, however. The pervasive oral texture of his thought had a broad basis in his philosophy of language. That philosophy, in turn, had implications for his political theory of fundamental rights, which influenced the entire course of Revolutionary and early national politics. Otis's two published literary treatises, "The Rudiments of Latin Prosody" and "A Dissertation on Letters" (both 1760), emphasize musicality, pronunciation, and delivery as the most significant features of language. Otis's preoccupation with the nature of spoken language put him at the forefront of European linguistic thought, together with Thomas Sheridan and Jean-Jacques Rousseau.[11]

9. The standard biography of Otis remains William Tudor, *The Life of James Otis, of Massachusetts . . .* (1823; New York, 1970). See also the hostile interpretation in Clifford K. Shipton, "James Otis," in *Sibley's Harvard Graduates,* XI (Boston, 1960), 247–287. Waters places Otis in a multigenerational family context in *The Otis Family.* The most useful work for understanding Otis's place in the early patriot movement is John C. Miller, *Sam Adams: Pioneer in Propaganda* (Boston, 1960). On logocentrism and its relationship to phonocentrism, see Jacques Derrida, *Of Grammatology,* trans. Gayatri Chakravorty Spivak (Baltimore, 1976), chap. 1.

10. The doubling of the patriot orator and the demagogue is an instance of Thomas Gustafson's Thucydidean moment *(Representative Words: Politics, Literature, and the American Language, 1776–1865* [Cambridge, 1992], 13–14).

11. James Otis, "The Rudiments of Latin Prosody," "A Dissertation on Letters . . . ," both in

After midcentury, fears that the spread of literacy and the rise of the press were contributing to the decline of deference and traditional face-to-face society stimulated a novel fascination with the powers of orality among European elites. The elocutionary movement addressed these fears, privileging the physical and vocal dimensions of speech and returning the textualized word to the human body. Otis's contributions in the elocutionary vein met with approval in Britain, where "some of the most learned men of the day spoke well of it." In the American colonies, his work took on alternative, more democratic meanings than the traditional significances attached to orality in Britain.[12]

Otis's "Rudiments," as well as his lost treatise on Greek prosody, sought to revive and purify the oral dimension of the dead classical languages. In "A Dissertation," his more significant work, he explored the relationships between body and voice and between speech and writing. "The bountiful Author of Nature," he began, "has furnished us with a power of forming a number of simple, and distinct vocal sounds, called *articulate*. . . . To form adequate ideas, and a just distribution of the vowels, and consonants, no regard must be had to the characters that represent them; nor should any thing else be attended to, but the sound of the vowels, and their modifications." Otis described the human voice as the world's most beautiful instrument capable of producing certain sounds, which then form speech. Speech provides the original that writing seeks to copy.[13]

For writing to capture the fullness of meaning, human or divine, vocal sounds

---

Otis, *The Rudiments of Latin Prosody, with A Dissertation on Letters . . .* (Boston, 1760). A treatise on Greek prosody never appeared in print and was destroyed when Otis burned his manuscripts before his death.

Sheridan delivered his popular *Course of Lectures on Elocution* in 1758 and 1759; it appeared in print in 1762. Rousseau began to develop his critique of the influence of writing on speech around the same time. Otis wrote in a general climate of concern among British and European intellectuals over the impact of textual forms on spoken language; see Nicholas Hudson, *Writing and European Thought, 1600–1830* (Cambridge, 1994), 103–110, 127–142.

12. Hudson observes, "The view that writing was incapable of the expressive powers of speech, and that its dominance had undermined the happiness and morality of people in modern society, was a prominent and fashionable opinion in the 1760s and 1770s" (*Writing and European Thought*, 92). Jim Mitchell notes a correlate shrinking of the print market in Europe, where "printing did not increase steadily during the century but almost everywhere suffered during the middle decades of the century a contraction so severe that the level of output achieved during the first third of the century was not regained, if at all, until near the end of the century"; see "The Spread and Fluctuation of Eighteenth-Century Printing," *Studies on Voltaire and the Eighteenth Century*, CCXXX (1985), 305–321, esp. 318. On Otis's elocutionary contributions, see Shipton, "James Otis," in *Sibley's Harvard Graduates*, XI, 249.

13. Otis, "A Dissertation," in *Rudiments of Latin Prosody*, 3–4; see also Otis, "Rudiments," ibid., 16, 20. Otis never defended the significance of properly articulating ancient poetry. He simply assumed that the poetry remains "barbarous" (59) unless pronounced as the author's contemporaries did.

must be reflected accurately in alphabets. This is not the case in English or other European languages, Otis complained. The Latin alphabet does not visually represent the sounds that the letters stand for; moreover, the same letter often represents multiple sounds. If scholars were to perfect the alphabet, they would have to pay close attention to vocal mechanisms, for instance by studying Otis's extensive descriptions of how the organs of the throat and mouth form each letter. The most important rule in language, Otis maintained, is "to study and follow nature," by which he meant taking the spoken word, with its basis in the body, as the standard for writing.[14]

In the last third of the "Dissertation," Otis shifted his attention from the mechanics of speech at the level of articulation to the components of pronunciation, by which he meant those parts of oratory that were coming to be known as elocution — vocal tone and pitch, gesture and posture, facial expressions — as well as the ethical aspects of rhetoric. Otis recommended the ancients for an understanding of delivery, referring repeatedly to Cicero, Quintilian, and Longinus. Like John Adams, another admirer of Cicero, Otis understood the passions as central to the orator's art. The eloquent speaker must first feel intensely. He then conveys his own sincere emotions to his audience "by proper variations of tone" and through the image of them "painted in the face."[15] Such emotive expression requires firm self-control, Otis observed, which in turn may necessitate the study of moral and religious philosophy. Alluding to Quintilian, he insisted that "the great and fundamental principle of rhetoric, as well as of every thing else valuable in human life, is *integrity*. A perfect understanding of a subject, without the proper affections flowing from the love of *truth*, will produce but a phlegmatic declaimer, at best but a dry reasoner." Passion in the service of truth makes an orator great. Success with an audience requires the rigorous self-effacement, the ardent dedication to the good of others that he claimed to personify in the Writs case: "He that would command the affections of his hearers, must not in shew and pretence only, but in truth, annihilate self-love and with his whole heart and soul pursue the good of others, and even *that* without much parade or pomp, lest he appear rather in the disagreeable light of a haughty dictator, than like a kind and sincere friend." Like the Puritan ethos of ministerial self-effacement, self-sacrifice called for the speaker to subordinate the self to a higher cause. Otis enacted this impera-

---

14. Otis, "A Dissertation," in *Rudiments of Latin Prosody*, 43. Writing has its own basis in the body, which Otis chose to ignore. Jonathan Goldberg discusses Renaissance writing manuals and their attention to the hand as a tool of writing in *Writing Matter: From the Hands of the English Renaissance* (Stanford, Calif., 1990).

15. Otis, "A Dissertation," in *Rudiments of Latin Prosody*, 52, 59. In classical rhetoric, Otis noted, elocution meant diction, or the proper ordering of words for rhythm and balance, a concern common to both spoken and written rhetoric; see 45.

tive quite directly in 1769, when he was badly beaten by Boston customs agents whom he had challenged to a duel after accusing them of communicating unflattering accounts of the colonies and their leaders to high British officials.[16]

While Otis recommended classical rhetoric on the nature and uses of the passions in oratory, he situated that tradition in the modern context of polite letters. Echoing Condillac, Otis lamented that the classical art of declamation had been lost forever, corrupted by artifice and exaggeration. The best model and training ground for modern orators was polite conversation, a genre modeled on British precedents and well known to Otis from his membership in numerous Boston literary and social clubs:

> Study the most easy, natural ways of expressing yourself, both in the tone of your voice and gesture of your body. These are best learned, or rather finished, by observation of the best company, where all is free and easy, yet the most exact propriety and decency is preserved. And the nearer the pronunciation in public, comes to the freedom and ease of a sensible well-bred man in private conversation, (provided we make the proper allowances for different occasions and subjects) the more just and natural will it generally be.[17]

The "just and natural" qualities that Otis attributed to "private conversation" suggest the political values already attached to a style of speech that he adapted for public discourse and that he used as a yardstick for measuring the translation of classical political eloquence into a modern idiom. The rhetorical values that Otis sketched in the "Dissertation," embracing the not altogether compatible traditions of ancient eloquence and modern civility, provide us with his expressly articulated terms for his political career.[18]

An unarticulated third rhetorical model was that of the opposition leader. Historically, the leader of the opposition in Massachusetts, as in England, employed wild and unpredictable behavior to keep the government off balance, and Otis adopted similar strategies.[19] Otis maintained his role as opposition leader through

16. Otis, "A Dissertation," in *Rudiments of Latin Prosody,* 55, 56.

17. Otis, "A Dissertation," in *Rudiments of Latin Prosody,* 56. American clubs often functioned as training grounds for orators. See, for instance, the numerous descriptions of speechifying in Dr. Alexander Hamilton, *The History of the Ancient and Honorable Tuesday Club,* ed. Robert Micklus, 3 vols. (Chapel Hill, N.C., 1990), and the formation of a Boston club for intellectual discussion and oratorical practice in L. H. Butterfield, ed., *Diary and Autobiography of John Adams,* 4 vols. (Cambridge, Mass., 1961), I, 251–252.

18. On the conflict between ancient eloquence and polite style in Britain, see Adam Potkay, *The Fate of Eloquence in the Age of Hume* (Ithaca, N.Y., 1994), esp. chap. 2.

19. On Boston opposition leaders who laid the groundwork for the style of leadership adopted by Otis and Samuel Adams, see John J. Waters and John A. Schutz, "Patterns of Massachusetts Colonial Politics: The Writs of Assistance and the Rivalry between the Otis and Hutch-

the combination of eloquence and abuse he directed at the government in his newspaper pieces, pamphlets, and Assembly and town meeting speeches. Governor Bernard, one of his chief victims, concluded, "The Troubles of this Country take their rise from, and owe their Continuance to one Man . . . James Otis, Esq." Otis compounded the "original System of Humbling the Government and weakening its Authority, by constant Opposition to the Governor" with "a malitious virulent and unrelenting Animosity against the persons employed in the Government." Neither polite nor passionate in the controlled classical sense, Otis's impetuous, often bitter, and occasionally tearful outbursts and hard-hitting newspaper attacks appealing to "the affections of his hearers" regularly disrupted the subdued, rational tone the Tory government sought to achieve in Boston politics.[20] The conflict between passion, in both its classical and oppositional forms, and polite "freedom and ease" runs just below the surface of Otis's text. The temperateness of polite society suited the aspirations to gentility of the rising lawyer class of which he was a member, while passionate eloquence proved central to the radical movement, as opposition political strategies were dressed in the prestigious and legitimating language of classical oratory. Moreover, for Otis, whose volatility eventually degenerated into madness, polite speech might work both to contain his eruptions and to deflect charges of demagoguery.

The improvisational talents that Otis brought to bear in his conversation and oratory were not always as successful in his writing. Otis's prose style in his political pamphlets reflects his privileging of the oral in his works on language. He composed his pamphlets rapidly, as if seeking to capture the impulses of his mind with the directness of speech. He then refused to revise. Commenting on the stylistic inadequacies of Otis's pamphlets, biographer William Tudor described how they were composed in "carelessness, haste, and a disdain of revising thoughts, thrown off with the rapidity of a powerful, impatient spirit." Otis sought to create

---

inson Families," *WMQ*, 3d Ser., XXIV (1967), 565; David W. Conroy, *In Public Houses: Drink and the Revolution of Authority in Colonial Massachusetts* (Chapel Hill, N.C., 1995), chap. 4. The explosive style that John Wilkes used to lead the British radical movement provided inspiration for colonial leaders; see Peter Shaw, *American Patriots and the Rituals of Revolution* (Cambridge, Mass., 1981), chap. 3 (see also the discussion of Otis in chap. 4).

20. Shipton, "James Otis," in *Sibley's Harvard Graduates*, XI, 270; Otis, "A Dissertation," in *Rudiments of Latin Prosody*, 56. Tories typically contrasted their own allegedly rational discourse with the emotional dissimulations of their opponents; see, for instance, Peter Oliver, "Address to the Soldiers of Massachusetts Bay Who Are Now in Arms against the Laws of Their Country," in the *Boston Weekly News-Letter*, Jan. 11, 1776, reprinted in Douglass Adair and John A. Schutz, eds., *Peter Oliver's Origin and Progress of the American Rebellion: A Tory View* (San Marino, Calif., 1961), 158. On Thomas Hutchinson's unsuccessful attempt to use rational debate to resolve tensions, see Bernard Bailyn, *The Ordeal of Thomas Hutchinson* (Cambridge, Mass., 1974), chap. 4.

the oral effect of the extemporaneous and evanescent in his writing; that evanescence became a reality when he burned his manuscripts in his final years.[21]

Otis's greatest institutional innovation suggests the privileged place that the spoken word held in his thought: with his support, Massachusetts became the first colony to establish a public gallery in its Assembly in 1766. Pennsylvania followed suit in 1770, and after 1789 the chambers of Congress offered public accommodations. Thomas Hutchinson observed that the Massachusetts gallery gave the radicals "great additional weight and influence over the people. . . . [A] speech, well adapted to the gallery, was oftentimes of more service to the cause of liberty than if its purport had been confined to the members of the house." Peter Oliver reported the uses to which the Boston patriot leaders put the "Gallery Men" who assembled to hear the debates: "There was a Gallery at a Corner of the Assembly Room where *Otis, Adams, Hawley,* and the rest of the Cabal used to crowd their Mohawks and Hawcubites, to echo the oppositional Vociferations, to the Rabble without doors." [22] Oliver's description of radicals echoing speeches from the gallery, like Benjamin Franklin's calculations of the numbers listening to George Whitefield, indicates the power of oral techniques of amplification. Though the Revolutionary era saw the first extensive use of print to mobilize political opposition, word-of-mouth transmission continued to be both important and successful.

What spoken eloquence lost in range when compared to print it gained in immediacy. The virtues of presence attached to oral communication had theoretical as well as technological value in a political debate that hinged on colonial problems of distance from the mother country.[23] Opponents recognized the

21. Tudor, *Life of James Otis,* 172. See also Adams, ed., *Works of John Adams,* X, 277. Miller describes a process in which Samuel Adams edited and revised Otis's drafts when they collaborated in *Sam Adams: Pioneer in Propaganda,* 88.

22. For Otis's role in opening the Massachusetts gallery, see Shipton, "James Otis," in *Sibley's Harvard Graduates,* XI, 269. J. R. Pole discusses the reasons for opening the Massachusetts Assembly and the implications for conceptions of representation in *Political Representation in England and the Origins of the American Republic* (Berkeley, Calif., 1966), 69–71. See also Gordon S. Wood, "The Democratization of Mind in the American Revolution," in *Leadership in the American Revolution* (Washington, D.C., 1974), 63–89, esp. 73–74. For Hutchinson's remarks, see Hutchinson, *History of the Colony and Province of Massachusetts-Bay,* ed. Mayo, III, 120; on the "Gallery Men," see Adair and Schutz, eds., *Peter Oliver's* Origin and Progress, 110.

23. Much modern scholarship has characterized the Revolutionary period as a time of transition from an oral, face-to-face culture to a print-based society; see Bernard Bailyn, *Pamphlets of the American Revolution, 1750–1776,* I (Cambridge, Mass., 1965); Michael Warner, *The Letters of the Republic: Publication and the Public Sphere in Eighteenth-Century America* (Cambridge, Mass., 1990); Larzer Ziff, *Writing in the New Nation: Prose, Print, and Politics in the Early United States* (New Haven, Conn., 1991).

Conroy critiques the print argument based on the importance of tavern society to Revolu-

symbolic significance of speech to the patriot movement. Echoing language used against the Puritans and the New Lights, Oliver wove together witchcraft, religious enthusiasm, and uncontrolled passion and pride as explanations for the "rebellion." He united these themes through prominent images of consuming orality and transgressive speech. Describing a conflict between Bernard and the Assembly over council elections, Oliver vituperated, "nothing less would satisfy their Voraciou[s]ness than the swallowing down all legal Government, and substituting a Democracy in its Place. Now, the whole Pack opened, and *Otis* hallooing them: Ribaldry and Scurrility were open mouthed. Such Language prevailed in the lower House of Assembly, that would have disgraced a *Billingsgate* Convention." Similar images dominate his text.[24]

The symbolic dimensions of writing and speech structured Otis's thought not only in his proposals for institutional reform but at the highest levels of political theory in his analysis of fundamental law. Two stories, one from early in Otis's legal career, the other from its end, reveal the intellectual path along which linguistic theory and practice merged with law and politics. John Adams recorded the first anecdote in his diary for 1759, quoting Otis: "It makes me laugh to see Pratt lugg a Cart load of Books into Court to prove a Point as clear as the Sun. The Action is as dead as a Hubb." Tudor relates the second anecdote, attributing it to the time after Otis's madness forced him to cease his legal practice. Speaking as amicus curiae, he observed "that since the declaration of Independence we had become a new nation, whose judicial decisions, he hoped and wished, might be founded in sound reason; and that no decisions from the books . . . ought to prevail against the dictates of reason and common sense." In both anecdotes, Otis sets the unwritten spirit of the law over its dead letter.[25]

The view of parliamentary power that emerges in his pamphlets emphasizes the legislative body's technical right to rule the colonies in any way it chooses, but nevertheless stresses the importance of measuring Parliament's codified law against an unwritten, higher standard: "There must be in every instance [of legislation], a higher authority, viz. GOD. Should an act of parliament be against any of *his* natural laws, which are *immutably* true, their declaration would be contrary to eternal truth, equity and justice, and consequently void: and so," Otis concluded hopefully, "it would be adjudged by the parliament itself, when convinced of their mistake." Like the Latin alphabet in the "Dissertation," which only roughly approximates the primary spoken word, codified law must be constantly measured

---

tionary mobilization in *In Public Houses,* 189 n. 38. Brown discusses the persistent importance of oral transmission through conversation or lectures in *Knowledge Is Power,* esp. 288–289.

24. Adair and Schutz, eds., *Peter Oliver's* Origin and Progress, 57–58.

25. Butterfield, ed., *Diary and Autobiography of John Adams,* I, 90; Tudor, *Life of James Otis,* 480.

against an unwritten divine law. Only when Parliament scrutinizes its legislation in these terms does it govern justly.[26] Parliament must be self-regulating, in Otis's theory, for he appears never to have accepted a written constitution as a distillation of fundamental values. British citizens, he insisted, had no use for "codes, pandects, novels, decretals of Popes, and the inventions of the D——l" while they could depend on the natural law embodied in the British Constitution. Otis repeatedly characterized the higher law as ineffable and thus uncodifiable.[27]

Otis made his most powerful symbolic use of speech and writing in his Writs of Assistance speech of 1761, his greatest claim to popular fame. For all of Adams's nostalgic enthusiasm, when the hearing was scheduled, the speech seemed little more than routine. Writs of assistance were general search warrants that the superior courts of the colonies issued to customs officials to facilitate their enforcement of the Navigation Acts. These documents permitted the bearer to search any suspect interior for untaxed goods without probable cause. Francis Bernard arrived as governor of the colony with instructions to step up customs enforcement using these writs, among other things. When they came up for renewal upon the death of George II in October 1760, some members of the Massachusetts customs and merchant communities opposed their continued issuance as a way to block intensified customs scrutiny, and a hearing was scheduled before the superior court.[28]

The hearing took place in the council chamber of the Old Town House in Boston. Drab, poorly executed portraits of colonial governors were "hung up in obscure corners of the room" while the "more than full length" representations of the despised Stuart kings Charles II and James II, vividly colored and richly real-

---

26. *Rights of the British Colonies*, in Mullett, ed., "Political Writings of Otis," 334. In "Reason in Madness: The Political Thought of James Otis," *WMQ*, 3d Ser., XXXVI (1979), 194–214, James R. Ferguson writes: "The concept of a benevolent and self-regulating sovereign authority enabled Otis to affirm the absolute and uncontrollable power of Parliament and at the same time to insist that there were principles of law distinct from and superior to the institutions of government. He appealed to those principles not to limit the sovereign powers of legislation or taxation, and not to justify disobedience, but only to enable Parliament to channel the exercise of its power in the proper directions" (202–203).

27. Otis, *A Vindication of the British Colonies* (1765), in Mullett, ed., "Political Writings of Otis," 385–407, esp. 407. Despite this resistance, however, his argument set American political thought on the path to the formulation of a written constitution and the development of judicial review; see Gordon S. Wood, *The Creation of the American Republic, 1776–1787* (Chapel Hill, N.C., 1969), esp. 293–295.

28. The details of the case are exhaustively elaborated in M. H. Smith, *The Writs of Assistance Case* (Berkeley, Calif., 1978). See also the editorial note preceding Adams's records of the case in Wroth and Zobel, eds., *Legal Papers of Adams*, II, 106–123; Frese, "James Otis and Writs of Assistance," *NEQ*, XXX (1957), 496–508; Waters and Schutz, "Patterns of Massachusetts Colonial Politics," *WMQ*, 3d Ser., XXIV (1967), 543–567; Waters, *The Otis Family*, esp. 118–125.

ized, hung "in splendid golden frames . . . on the most conspicuous sides of the apartment."[29] Chief Justice Thomas Hutchinson and four other judges, attired in new scarlet robes and "immense judicial Wiggs," gathered to hear the arguments, together with the barristers seated at a long table. Adams observed wryly that the justices and barristers "were not seated on ivory Chairs, but their dress was more solemn and more pompous than that of the Roman Senate, when the Gauls broke in upon them."[30]

Adams cast Otis in the role of the barbarian Gaul, though with his smooth-shaven, plump features, urbane presence, and careful, unostentatious dress, he scarcely looked the part. At thirty-six, Otis was a relatively young but well-respected figure on the Boston legal scene and the owner of an impressive law library that Adams frequented. Otis had recently resigned as acting advocate general of the Admiralty Court because his ties to local merchants made him unwilling to meet Governor Bernard's demands for stricter customs enforcement. His teacher and mentor Jeremiah Gridley spoke first at the hearing, summoning his "great Learning, his great Parts and his majestic Manner" to defend the writs on the grounds of precedent and through an analogy with the government's rights of taxation. He made a thorough and ultimately persuasive case, but "stiffness and affectation" marred his "bold, spirited Manner of Speaking." Oxenbridge Thacher responded to Gridley's argument from precedent, claiming that he had made a thorough search of the books without finding "any such Writ as this Petition prays." "Sensible, but slow of Conception and Communication," Thacher's delivery struck Adams as "queer, and affected." "He is not easy," Adams concluded.[31]

When Otis rose to speak after Thacher, the contrast could not have been more

---

29. Adams remembered that the royal portraits had arrived without frames during Governor Pownall's administration but had been stowed away until Governor Bernard "had them cleaned, superbly framed, and placed in council for the admiration and imitation of all men." For Adams, this display registered a shift in political climate; see Adams to William Tudor, Mar. 29, 1817, in Adams, ed., *Works of John Adams*, X, 244–249, esp. 245. The reference to portraits of colonial governors is from Adams's Apr. 15, 1817, letter to Tudor (250).

30. See Adams, letter to William Tudor, Dec. 18, 1816, Adams, ed., *Works of John Adams*, X, 233, 245.

31. Butterfield, ed., *Diary and Autobiography of John Adams*, I, 83, 84. Adams's records of the case, which include his original notes and the abstract he created from them, are available in Wroth and Zobel, eds., *Legal Papers of Adams*, II, 123–144, esp. 138.

Adams offered these descriptions of Gridley and Thacher in a diary entry for April 1759, where he evaluated the mental powers and courtroom presence of the most prominent Boston lawyers. In his nostalgic 1817 reminiscence for Tudor, Adams was more flattering: "Mr. Gridley argued with his characteristic learning, ingenuity, and dignity. . . . Mr. Thacher followed him on the other side, and argued with the softness of manners, the ingenuity and cool reasoning, which were remarkable in his amiable character" (Adams, ed., *Works of John Adams*, X, 247).

dramatic. Otis fairly vibrated with energy and insight. "Quick and elastic," with an "Apprehension . . . as quick as his Temper," Otis "springs, and twitches his Muscles about in thinking," Adams noted. In a speech that lasted more than four hours, Otis made a wide-ranging, thorough, and passionate argument centering on the claim that customs officers who used a writ of assistance to discover smuggled goods violated the fundamental property rights of British citizens: "A Man, who is quiet, is as secure in his House, as a Prince in his Castle, not with standing all his Debts, and civil Prossesses of any kind."[32] Otis held that the fundamental law of private property served as a primary standard against which all statutory law should be measured. "ALL PRECEDENTS ARE UNDER THE CONTROUL OF THE PRIN-CIPLES OF THE LAW," he thundered. According to the letter of the law, Otis was in the wrong, and ultimately he lost the case when Chief Justice Hutchinson enforced the precedents that Gridley cited. But although his argument failed in the narrow technical sense that writs of assistance continued to be issued, he succeeded in transforming Anglo-American political theory, introducing the concept of funda-mental principles of law that preexist and sanction codified law. As a champion of fundamental law, Otis critically shaped the developing argument against par-liamentary authority in the colonies, including the chief controversy—taxation without representation.[33]

Otis organized the most significant oration of his career around the contrast between two types of legal writs, the special writ and the general writ of assis-tance. A special writ would be issued only on oath for a particular purpose; in con-trast, writs of assistance were universal, perpetual, and transferable. Passed from one customs agent to another, from one location to another, they had nothing to bind them to a specific location or situation. "Writs in their nature are temporary things," he insisted, "when the purposes for which they are issued are answered, they exist no more; but these monsters in the law live forever, no one can be called to account." The writ of assistance represented the most threatening aspects of text-based law for Otis, in his own terms, the monstrousness of it. Like acts of

---

32. Butterfield, ed., *Diary and Autobiography of John Adams*, I, 84; Wroth and Zobel, eds., *Legal Papers of Adams*, II, 125. Adams reconstructed Otis's speech from notes that he made dur-ing the hearing, probably with the intention of publishing it on the British model. He recorded Josiah Quincy's response to his abstract in his diary for April of the same year, suggesting that he wrote it up soon after the February hearing (see Butterfield, ed., *Diary and Autobiography of John Adams*, I, 210). Smith, *Writs of Assistance Case*, discusses the composition process on 312–386.

33. Wroth and Zobel, eds., *Legal Papers of Adams*, II, 144. Otis's influence is discussed in Charles Howard McIlwain, *The American Revolution: A Constitutional Interpretation* (New York, 1924), 153–156; Bernard Bailyn, *The Ideological Origins of the American Revolution* (Cambridge, Mass., 1967), 176–181; Wood, *Creation of the American Republic*, 262–263, 292–295; Bailyn, *Ordeal of Thomas Hutchinson*, 55–56; James R. Ferguson, "Reason in Madness," *WMQ*, 3d Ser., XXXVI (1979), 194–214.

Parliament, such writs could be issued far from the community where they were employed. Moreover, they could be fully anonymous; they required no personal oath to guarantee the legitimacy of the complaint against an individual believed to hold smuggled goods. And finally, they were never returned. A writ of assistance issued to one individual could be transferred to others and used in situations remote from that which occasioned its issuance.[34] In the symbolic terms of Western linguistic theory, impersonality, transferability, and permanence characterize text; they contrast with the oral qualities of presence, immediacy, and evanescence.[35] When Otis approved of a special writ but not a general one, he insisted on linking specific legal texts to their oral origins by requiring that they maintain their basis in oath and judicial oversight, much as he insisted that writing derive from speech in the broader linguistic context of the "Dissertation."

Writs of assistance presented a form of pure textuality that threatened to reduce society to a Hobbesian state of nature. "What a scene does this open!" Otis exclaimed to the court. "Every man prompted by revenge, ill humour or wantonness to inspect the inside of his neighbour's house, may get a writ of assistance; others will ask it from self defence; one arbitrary exertion will provoke another, until society will be involved in tumult and in blood." Otis warned that, with a writ of assistance, "every man may . . . spread terror and desolation around him, until the trump of the arch angel shall excite different emotions in his soul." Observing that the writs allowed power even to "MENIAL SERVANTS," Otis queried, "What is this but to have the curse of Canaan with a witness on us, to be the servant of servants, the most despicable of God's creation." Otis evoked Scripture as he sketched the writ's power to disrupt society. The scriptural references mark the shift from his argument about precedents based on "look[ing] into the books" to the psychological experience of those who bore or were under the authority of such writs. The allusions occurred, that is, as Otis drew his auditors' attention from the letter of the law to its spirit. Scripture provided him with a higher textual authority than that of the law while shifting the terrain of his argument from legal precedent to the interiority of the law's subjects.[36]

Relating a Gothic tale of revenge evocative of the novels of Charles Brockden Brown, Otis described how a customs agent was called before a constable for an impious act and retaliated by using his writ to search the houses of his prosecu-

34. Wroth and Zobel, eds., *Legal Papers of Adams,* II, 143. After the Writs case failed, the General Court passed a bill seeking to remedy precisely these characteristics of the writ, but Governor Bernard vetoed the legislation; see Smith, *Writs of Assistance Case,* 425–426.

35. Walter J. Ong presents this contrast in *Orality and Literacy: The Technologizing of the Word* (London, 1982), chaps. 3, 4. Geoffrey Galt Harpham offers a useful analysis of the symbolic dimensions of such beliefs in *The Ascetic Imperative in Culture and Criticism* (Chicago, 1987), 3–18.

36. Wroth and Zobel, eds., *Legal Papers of Adams,* II, 139, 142, 143.

tors.[37] A writ-bearing agent such as this one could vengefully or viciously expose private interiors while his own motivations remained masked behind an anonymous text, unconstrained by personal oath or judicial scrutiny. Otis later amplified this conspiracy rhetoric in a fashion that echoed through the colonies. He accused the British Parliament and ministry of tyrannically plotting to enslave the colonies, a mental and moral debasement whose contours he perceived beneath the seeming legitimacy of legislative enactment in such statutes as the Sugar and Stamp Acts and the Townshend Acts. Like the writs, these acts masked the intentions of their authors while exposing the colonists to regulation. Anonymous and impersonal, such legal texts disrupted individual integrity, community harmony, and imperial relations. Only language modeled on and tied to the spoken word, Otis believed, could guarantee privacy, natural rights, and proper representation to the colonists.[38]

The most violent and thorough exposures of colonial interiors were those performed, not by writ-wielding customs agents, but by Boston mobs. The violated buildings were the warehouses and domiciles of leading tories, notably those of stamp master Andrew Oliver and his brother-in-law Governor Thomas Hutchinson. During the Stamp Act riots of August 1765, Oliver's and Hutchinson's homes were ripped open and their contents carted off or thrown in the street, their insides stripped and dismantled. Amid the money, plate, and jewelry that looters scattered about as they carried away their prizes were Hutchinson's books and papers, his draft *History,* and the historical papers he had been gathering for a public archive. These papers provided a symbolic and emotional link between Hutchinson and the Bay Colony; they represented his deep interest in his home colony and dedication to writing as a filial act of commemoration. They also signified his social status as the scion of one of Massachusetts's oldest and most prominent families. Their destruction suggests that they had some public significance for the radicals as well: they stood as a symbol of Hutchinson's claims to represent the Bay Colony and its history.[39]

The evisceration of his home was only the first in a series of episodes that involved the exposure of Hutchinson's papers. In 1773 and again in 1776, radical

37. The writings of Charles Brockden Brown often reveal an anxiety over textuality that closely parallels Otis's fears. See, for instance, the role of diaries and letters in *Wieland* (1798) and *Edgar Huntly* (1799). Brown trained as a lawyer before making literature his career.

38. On the pervasive use of conspiratorial rhetoric, see Gordon S. Wood, "Conspiracy and the Paranoid Style: Causality and Deceit in the Eighteenth Century," *WMQ,* 3d Ser., XXXIX (1982), 401–441.

39. Bailyn, *Ordeal of Thomas Hutchinson,* 35. See also Adair and Schutz, eds., *Peter Oliver's Origin and Progress,* 30. Robert Blair St. George discusses the New England tradition of house destruction and the specific instance of Hutchinson's house in *Conversing by Signs: Poetics of Implication in Colonial New England Culture* (Chapel Hill, N.C., 1998), chap. 3.

leaders obtained and published Hutchinson's letters, editing them to heighten the impression of a conspiracy against the colony. The most serious of these incidents was the 1773 publication of severely edited versions of letters that Hutchinson had written to Thomas Whately, which Massachusetts agent Benjamin Franklin obtained in London and sent back to Boston. When they appeared in print, they precipitated a crisis that hastened the Revolution and ended Hutchinson's career as governor. Hutchinson insisted that the published letters misrepresented him. The editors took passages out of context and made silent revisions that distorted his meaning, he asserted to anyone who would listen. But patriots thought they had undeniable textual proof that Hutchinson had conspired with the British government to "enslave" the colony.[40]

Texts destroyed Thomas Hutchinson, as he had long feared they would. Throughout his political career, he fretted openly to correspondents about the possibility that a letter would end up in the wrong hands ("Letters are liable to miscarry," he wrote in 1758), revised again and again to avoid misunderstanding, used cipher and vowelless script to deter unintended readers. Yet despite his fears, he lived his life absorbed in texts and writing. In London, he eschewed dinner parties, the theater, and public gardens, and instead spent most of his time composing the final volume of his *History.* Even while an active public figure, he spent much time with a pen in hand, keeping up a diary, composing, revising, and copying letters and other documents, writing his history. Nothing could be further from Otis's manner of rapid and unmodified composition. Hutchinson's speeches to the Massachusetts Assembly similarly reflect the kind of careful composition that Otis and his patriot contemporaries increasingly viewed as proof of dissimulation. In her patriot play *The Adulateur,* Mercy Otis Warren portrayed Rapatio, a character modeled on Hutchinson, speaking of his toady Gripeall's use of "A speech prepar'd." This was a specimen "of modern composition" that he "must correct." Warren makes such textual manipulation a symbol of Rapatio/Hutchinson's masked power.[41]

As Warren's play suggests, Thomas Hutchinson and James Otis made conflicting political choices based on social expectations and values symbolized by their attitudes toward written and spoken forms of language. Otis's radical politics of orality were set against Hutchinson's conservative politics of textuality in the political arenas of Revolutionary Boston. The imperial politics that Hutchinson identified with the social authority of writing were challenged and ultimately defeated within the oratorical public sphere that Otis helped to create.

40. Bailyn describes these incidents fully in *Ordeal of Thomas Hutchinson,* chap. 7, 334–340.
41. Ibid., 221–222; Mercy Otis Warren, *The Plays and Poems of Mercy Otis Warren* (Delmar, N.Y., 1980), 26.

III. THE TRANSFORMATIVE SPEECH OF PATRICK HENRY

New Englanders such as Otis and Hutchinson inherited a certain hostility toward nonverbal icons from their Puritan ancestors.[42] This legacy made the contrast between speech and writing both so stark and so richly significant in the
Revolution's sacralized political context. In Virginia and the other southern colonies, material objects were regarded with less suspicion. The leaders of Virginia's
Anglican church lacked the iconoclastic drive of their northern brethren. They
used gestures and postures, clothing and objects to figure social meanings that in
the North were borne by linguistic forms. The wider range of acceptable signifiers
meant that the contrast between voice and text carried a lighter load of symbolic
significance in the South.

Early southern society invested textually marked social distinctions with symbolic meaning primarily through performance. Vital legal and spiritual knowledge entered communal life in oral performance settings such as the church or the
courtroom.[43] The oral recitation characteristic of traditional gentry culture weakened the role of the written word itself, focusing attention instead on the reciter
and eliciting deference toward him. Read aloud, legal and scriptural texts entered
the communal consciousness as components in "patterned forms of communal
action," where the emphasis was on the iconic, hierarchical performance rather
than on the verbal medium. Not all of these gentry performances relied in a significant way on words. Gambling, horse racing, dancing, and other displays of
elite power concentrated on the heroic or elegant body, not on spoken or written
language. Language was simply one code, one set of icons among many.[44]

In the decades before the Revolution, evangelical missionaries from the North

---

42. Neil Harris, *The Artist in America: The Formative Years, 1790–1860* (Chicago, 1982), 2.

43. David D. Hall comments that, while "everyone in the Chesapeake accepted the prem-
ise that written or printed documents embodied political legitimacy," assertions of sovereignty
such as those attending the issuance of a royal charter "involved the performance of such texts
in a public setting"; see "The Chesapeake in the Seventeenth Century," in Hall, *Cultures of Print:
Essays in the History of the Book* (Amherst, Mass., 1996), 97–150, esp. 104. A. G. Roeber has argued that the workings of Virginia courts remained substantially oral well into the eighteenth
century *(Faithful Magistrates and Republican Lawyers: Creators of Virginia Legal Culture, 1680–
1810* [Chapel Hill, N.C., 1981], chap. 3).

44. Describing the limited importance of words in Virginia patriot culture, Isaac writes,
"Verbal pronouncements, whether in spoken or written addresses, did not emerge in Virginia
in 1774 as the most effective means of alleviating widespread anxieties or seeking to realize aspirations. Rather, it was through participation in patterned forms of communal action that broad
mobilization proceeded most effectively"; see *Transformation of Virginia*, 248. Dell Upton notes
the central role of reading in the Anglican services of Virginia in *Holy Things and Profane: Anglican Parish Churches in Colonial Virginia* (New York, 1986), 9–10. He describes the iconic display
of the Ten Commandments on church walls (120–121).

carried new modes and symbols of literacy to the southern colonies, where they took root through the influence of such leaders as Presbyterian Samuel Davies and Separate Baptist Shubal Stearns. Evangelicals cultivated new forms of communal articulateness. The novel authority that itinerant ministers claimed for popular oral culture arose in tandem with a more broadly literate attentiveness to the meaning of Scripture. Appealing to private conscience in biblical interpretation, evangelicals invested literacy with a degree of spiritual and social significance largely new to the South. The intense verbalism of southern New Lights reproduced certain features of New England Puritanism that had been reinvigorated in the Great Awakening: Scripture reading, discussion groups, personal testimony, colloquial preaching. But a different social organization distinguished the verbal dynamics in the southern colonies, particularly as the significant number of African American converts came to shape those dynamics, heightening the importance of the oral and infusing it with African elements. For eighteenth-century southerners, control over spoken and written language bore the symbolic significance of a primary cultural schism between the classically influenced, Anglican gentry culture and the popular culture of nongentry whites and African Americans who joined the evangelical churches.[45]

Changes in political oratory during the Revolutionary era both signaled and contributed to the transformations in Virginia society. Traditionally, most of the secular eloquence in the colony took place within the House of Burgesses, where members cultivated their skills in deliberative oratory and the governor delivered periodic addresses on political objectives. Only rarely did a speaker imagine an audience for his words beyond the walls of the legislative chamber.[46] In Virginia as in Massachusetts, patriot eloquence inspired popular passion and political action, disrupted established hierarchies and institutions, and drew on the uncodifiable rules of natural law and feeling for its insights. The plays of Virginia burgess Robert Munford, a whig leader and collaborator with Patrick Henry, reveal the suspicion that attended the efforts of patriot leaders to address a broader pub-

45. On classical and evangelical cultures, see Rhys Isaac, "Preachers and Patriots: Popular Culture and the Revolution in Virginia," in Alfred F. Young, ed., *The American Revolution: Explorations in the History of American Radicalism* (DeKalb, Ill., 1976), 125–156. On Euro-African cultural hybridization in southern evangelicalism during the eighteenth century, see Mechal Sobel, *The World They Made Together: Black and White Values in Eighteenth-Century Virginia* (Princeton, N.J., 1987), esp. chaps. 14, 15.

46. Richard Beale Davis, *Intellectual Life in the Colonial South, 1585–1763*, 3 vols. (Knoxville, Tenn., 1978), III, 1619–1620. Charles S. Sydnor offers the classic description of traditional gentry politics in *American Revolutionaries in the Making: Political Practices in Washington's Virginia* (New York, 1952). Gordon S. Wood describes the gradual popularization of Virginia politics in the middle decades of the eighteenth century in *The Radicalism of the American Revolution* (New York, 1992), 142–145.

lic. High-flown patriot oratory registered imposture for Munford. In *The Patriots* (written in 1776 or 1777), eloquent speech provides no accurate index to social and political legitimacy. The thoughtful Meanwell warns against the radical eloquence of Tackabout, who is called "the prettiest spokenest man I ever saw" and who, it turns out, is a disguised tory. Tackabout describes his exercise of eloquence in terms that resemble hostile descriptions of Otis's radical oratory: "I have damn'd the ministry, abus'd the king, vilified the parliament, and curs'd the Scotch. I have raised the people's suspicions against all moderate men; advised them to spurn at all government: I have cried down tories, cried up whigs, extolled Washington as a god, and call'd Howe a very devil. I have exclaimed against all taxes, advised the people to pay no more debts; I have promised them success in war, a free trade, an independent dominion. In short, I have inspired them with the true patriotic fire, the spirit of opposition." His verbal pyrotechnics persuade the people that he speaks for them while the moderates who truly act in the people's best interests are themselves falsely accused as tories. "Men who aim at power without merit," the true patriot Meanwell observes, "must conceal the meanness of their souls by noisy and passionate speeches in favour of every thing which is the current opinion of the day; but real patriots are mild, and secretly anxious for their country, but modest in expressions of zeal. They are industrious in the public service, but claim no glory to themselves." [47]

Thomas Jefferson shared Munford's uneasiness with the novel role of popular eloquence in Virginia's political life. Particularly in his descriptions of Patrick Henry, the native son who became the nation's most famous patriot orator, Jefferson registered profound ambivalence about the uses of political speech. Writing in 1805 to Henry's biographer William Wirt, Jefferson celebrated Henry as "the man who gave the first impulse to the ball of revolution" and called him "the greatest orator that ever lived." Elsewhere, he rhapsodized that Henry spoke "as Homer wrote." Jefferson described Henry's ability "to attain a degree of popularity with the people at large never perhaps equalled" and attributed it to his "consumate knolege of the human heart." But that knowledge was hardly of the romantic sort that Wirt later attributed to Henry in his *Sketches of the Life and Character of Patrick Henry* (1818), where Wirt imagined his hero as a Shakespeare of the platform, an artist of nature. According to Jefferson, Henry "was avaritious and rotten hearted. His two great passions were the love of money and of fame." These traits, Jefferson implied, were what allowed Henry insight into the populace at large. [48]

47. Courtlandt Canby, ed., "Robert Munford's *The Patriots*," *WMQ*, 3d Ser., VI (1949), esp. 450, 462–464. See also Jay B. Hubbell and Douglass Adair, "Robert Munford's *The Candidates*," *WMQ*, 3d Ser., V (1948), 217–257.

48. Stan V. Henkels, ed., "Jefferson's Recollections of Patrick Henry," *PMHB*, XXXIV (1910),

Jefferson represented the great orator as a figure of pure voice, passionate and self-aggrandizing, lacking the stabilizing force of text read or written. According to Daniel Webster, Jefferson observed that, like music, Henry's speeches evoked passion and pleasure but conveyed an indeterminate meaning: "When he had spoken in opposition to *my* opinion, had produced a great effect, and I myself been highly delighted and moved, I have asked myself when he ceased, 'What the Devil has he said,' and could never answer the enquiry." Henry's "imagination was copious, poetical, sublime; but vague also," and he was useless for most legislative business. Jefferson had nothing but contempt for Henry's lack of interest in literature and history and for his ignorance of legal and legislative procedure. He returned to these failings insistently whenever he wrote or talked about Henry. "He was a man of very little knowledge of any sort, he read nothing and had no books. . . . He wrote almost nothing, he *could not* write," Jefferson told Webster. Skeptical of Wirt's assertion that Henry read Livy annually, Jefferson emphasized his poverty of reading, then in a conciliatory tone noted that Henry "drew all natural rights from a purer source, the feelings of his own breast." [49]

Henry fostered precisely the image of himself as a man of vocal power that Jefferson sketched. In contrast to the formidably learned Otis, who came to favor oral modes from an immersion in literate discourse, Henry presented himself as a poorly educated, self-made man of the people, a leader with sources of knowledge deeper and truer than mere books. In Philadelphia for the Continental Congress in 1774, where he was already famous as the Virginia Demosthenes, he told John Adams that "he had no public Education. At fifteen he read Virgill and Livy, and has not looked into a Latin Book since. His father left him at that Age, and he has been struggling thro Life ever since." [50] The Henry legend sustains his self-depiction as a leader drawing on the inner resources of intuition and insight rather than external supports such as texts or paternal inheritance for his power. The story of his licensing for the bar captures important aspects of the legend. Henry studied law for just a few weeks before presenting himself to the legal eminences of Williamsburg to be examined for a license. John Randolph quickly abandoned questions on municipal law, where Henry's deficiencies were obvious, turning instead to the laws of nature and nations and to general history, at which he did

---

385–418, esp. 387; Thomas Jefferson, "Autobiography," in Jefferson, *Writings,* ed. Merrill D. Peterson (New York, 1984), 3–101, esp. 6.

49. Charles M. Wiltse and Harold D. Moser, eds., *The Papers of Daniel Webster: Correspondence,* I (Hanover, N.H., 1974), 372–373, 390; Henkels, ed., "Jefferson's Recollections of Patrick Henry," *PMHB,* XXXIV (1910), 409.

50. Butterfield, ed., *Diary and Autobiography of John Adams,* II, 151. Jay Fliegelman discusses the Revolutionary rebellion against fathers in *Prodigals and Pilgrims: The American Revolution against Patriarchal Authority, 1750–1800* (Cambridge, 1984), esp. chap. 4.

better. Testing him next on the common law, Randolph pressed him on a point, pretended to disagree with him, and forced Henry to defend his reasoning. Then he pulled down his lawbook and said to Henry, "Behold the force of natural reason; you have never seen these books, nor this principle of law; yet you are right and I am wrong. . . . I will never trust to appearances again." Years later, Edmund Randolph confirmed Henry's textual weakness and intuitive strength: "In black-letter precedents he was never profound, in general principles he had no reason to shrink from a struggle with any man." Rational and intuitive, rather than acquired, knowledge sustained Henry throughout much of his career.[51]

The rhapsodic power of speech that made Henry a great orator flowed from sources different from, even antithetical to, textual knowledge. Judge Peter Lyons, a frequent court opponent of Henry's, described how his colleague's courtroom eloquence disrupted his own ability to write, so rapt was he in Henry's performance. Lyons claimed that "he could write a letter, or draw a declaration or plea at the bar, with as much accuracy, as he could in his office, under all circumstances, *except when Patrick rose to speak;* but that whenever *he* rose . . . he was obliged to lay down his pen, and could not write another word, until the speech was finished."[52] As Lyons's tale suggests, Henry's mesmerizing speech competed successfully with legal forms and precedents. During the course of his legal and legislative career, Henry sought through his performances to dismantle elite textual authority in favor of the spectacular authority of the popular orator speaking universally accessible truths in a colloquial idiom. His role in the ideology of Revolution paralleled that of James Otis. Nineteenth-century critic E. L. Magoon observed, "James Otis and Patrick Henry were, above all others, best fitted for the emergency to which they were born, because they dared to say more in public than any other men." Unlike Otis, however, Henry never theorized orality in treatises on language and politics. In keeping with the southern emphasis on embodied

51. William Wirt, *Life of Patrick Henry,* rev. ed. (Philadelphia, 1836), 35; Edmund Randolph, *History of Virginia,* ed. Arthur H. Shaffer (Charlottesville, Va., 1970), 168. Henry's self-created public image should be understood in the context of the emergent persona of the patriot lawyer. Led by Henry in the 1763 Parsons' Cause case, Virginia lawyers began to redefine themselves as Country representatives of the people, in contrast to the corrupt, Court-oriented justices and colonial government. Henry's emphasis on his lack of learning reflects the widespread popular distrust of the technical legal language and book-law that had characterized public contempt for the legal profession. See Roeber, *Faithful Magistrates and Republican Lawyers,* chap. 4.

52. Wirt, *Life of Patrick Henry,* 56; see also Henry Mayer, *A Son of Thunder: Patrick Henry and the American Republic* (Charlottesville, Va., 1991), 58. Lyons might have adapted a well-known story about Cicero. In the version of Princeton's John Witherspoon, "Caesar came to the judgment seat determined to condemn [C. Ligarius], and even took the pen in his hand to sign his condemnation, but that he was interested by Cicero's eloquence and at last so moved that he dropped the pen and granted the orator's request" ("Lectures on Eloquence," in Thomas Miller, ed., *The Selected Writings of John Witherspoon* [Carbondale, Ill., 1990], 257).

action, Henry displayed the power and primacy of the spoken word in dramatic enactments that staged the triumph of voice over black-letter law books, parliamentary acts, and established forms of governance.[53]

Otis identified the symbolic power of voice as the representational power of synecdoche, the ability of a part to stand for a whole (the voice for the individual, the individual for the colony or nation). This representational power flowed from the spoken word's proximity to and separation from the body, its autonomy as well as its immediacy and presence. For Henry, the symbolic power of voice was a metaphoric, transformative power. Speech could effect the metamorphosis of self and society. Virtually every description of Henry begins with his physical and cultural limitations and seeks to analyze the transformation that occurred as he spoke. His tall, lean frame and awkward movements did not suggest great dramatic talent. St. George Tucker observed that, upon first attending the House of Burgesses as a young man in 1773, he looked at Henry "with no great prepossession." Edmund Pendleton and Richard Henry Lee were far closer to the beau ideal of the orator. Tucker soon afterward realized his error when he witnessed "that almost supernatural transformation of appearance, which . . . [was] invariably wrought by the excitement of his genius."[54] William Wirt portrayed Henry's "supernatural transformation" through allusions to Moses descending from Sinai: "His countenance shone" with the appearance of "supernatural inspiration." Edmund Randolph was less mystical but equally fascinated by Henry's mutations. "Not always grammatical, and sometimes coarse in his language," Randolph remarked, "he taught his hearers how to forget his inaccuracies by his action, his varying countenance and voice." Jefferson similarly observed that "his pronunciation, was vulgar and vicious, but it was forgotten while he was speaking." That transformative power registered linguistically in his "intrepidity of metaphor," primarily scriptural and natural, whose boldness Randolph compared favorably to that of the elder Pitt.[55]

The mutation of self that Henry achieved in his speeches occurred in dramatic tension with certain singularly static elements of his performance. Just as Jonathan Edwards stared at the bell rope while delivering "Sinners in the Hands of an Angry God," so Henry fixed his eyes on the Assembly moderator "without straying in quest of applause." His voice, too, created the impression of variety in uniformity, its harmonious monotony diversified by "a dramatic versatility of

53. E. L. Magoon, *Orators of the American Revolution*, 3d ed. (New York, 1849), 32.

54. Wirt, *Life of Patrick Henry*, 108, 110. This letter is reprinted in William Wirt Henry, *Patrick Henry: Life, Correspondence, and Speeches*, I (New York, 1891), 163–164. Henry identifies Wirt's anonymous correspondent as Tucker.

55. Wirt, *Life of Patrick Henry*, 43, 50; Randolph, *History of Virginia*, ed. Shaffer, 168, 179–180; Jefferson, in Wiltse and Moser, eds., *Papers of Daniel Webster*, I, 372.

action and of countenance." "His was the only monotony which I ever heard reconcilable with true eloquence," Randolph remarked, struggling to describe adequately the puzzling mixture of stasis and transformation that Henry achieved. The overall effect was of a dramatic metamorphosis governed by a few fixed performance elements such as the stare and the monotone.[56]

A comparable metaphoric structure of controlled transformation governed evangelical conversion. The familiar stages of conversion provided a framework for the violation of boundaries and conventions that portended the emergence of a newborn self characterized by uncontainable speech. More than any other Revolutionary orator, Henry enacted the transfer of that model of transfigured, vocal, public selfhood into the political domain.[57] He organized his most famous oration, the "Liberty or Death" speech to the Virginia Convention on March 23, 1775, as a semisecularized variant of the evangelical sermon. Randolph compared Henry on this occasion to Paul preaching at Athens. Seeking to convict, convert, and assure the hesitant legislators and the public that military preparation was essential for the preservation of Virginia's political liberties, he "transferred into civil discussions many of the bold licenses which prevailed in the religions." These included not only the basic conversion structure but also the wealth of scriptural references and the animated, extempore delivery for which evangelical preachers were known. An eyewitness described Henry's elaborate theatrics, including slavelike gestures of submission and bondage, the shattering of chains, and the plunging of an invisible dagger into his breast. The dynamic elements of his performance were held in check by his restrained gaze, which only heightened his appeal as a dramatic spectacle. He never looked around to solicit the audience's attention, Randolph noted, yet "every eye [was] fixed upon him."[58]

56. Randolph, *History of Virginia*, ed. Shaffer, 180. Fliegelman describes Henry's appeal as a yoking of the artful and the natural, the beautiful and the sublime, in a spectacle of self-control (*Declaring Independence: Jefferson, Natural Language, and the Culture of Performance* [Stanford, Calif., 1993], 94–107, esp. 101–104).

57. On "Whitefieldian uncontainability" (99) and its connection to democratic personality, see Nancy Ruttenberg, *Democratic Personality: Popular Voice and the Trial of American Authorship* (Stanford, Calif., 1998), 97–100, 185–188. Isaac describes Henry's oratorical merging of evangelical and gentry cultures in "Preachers and Patriots," in Young, ed., *The American Revolution*, 152–154. See also Kenneth Cmiel, *Democratic Eloquence: The Fight over Popular Speech in Nineteenth-Century America* (New York, 1990), 52.

58. Randolph, *History of Virginia*, ed. Shaffer, 179, 212. David A. McCants persuasively identifies the conversion structure in the "Liberty or Death" speech in *Patrick Henry, The Orator* (New York, 1990), 57–63. Charles L. Cohen analyzes the jeremiadic elements of the speech and argues for its basic thematic and tonal authenticity as reconstructed by St. George Tucker in "The 'Liberty or Death' Speech: A Note on Religion and Revolutionary Rhetoric," *WMQ*, 3d Ser., XXXVIII (1981), 702–717.

Another legend held that Henry concluded his speech by plunging a paper cutter toward his

The uncontainable and transformative power of Henry's speech registered in numerous ways: in the success of his motion to mobilize for armed conflict, in the plea of Colonel Edward Carrington to be buried on the spot outside Henrico Parish Church where he heard the speech, in the words "Liberty or Death" painted or sewn on the coats of the burgesses and the Culpeper County militia in the summer of 1775, in the popular oral accounts that circulated about the speech, and in the countless schoolroom recitations of Henry's words over the next two centuries. The multiplication and dissemination of Henry's speech generates a mimetic dynamic to produce an expansive national identity figured as voice. "Henry was his pure self," Edmund Randolph wrote. "After every illusion had vanished, a prodigy yet remained. It was Patrick Henry, born in obscurity, poor, and without the advantages of literature, rousing the genius of his country and binding a band of patriots together to hurl defiance at the tyranny of so formidable a nation as Great Britain. This enchantment was spontaneous obedience to the workings of the soul." [59]

But to what "soul" did Henry's eloquence foster obedience? The cult of personality that Whitefield produced in the transatlantic evangelical community and that Henry transformed into a quasi-sacred national political phenomenon obscured just this question. Was that soul God? A proto-Emersonian oversoul? An extrainstitutional popular spirit or public opinion? Henry himself? The tangled strands of identity and power that were woven into a Henry oration produced a potent mimetic impulse while obscuring the nature of hegemonic authority. Henry performed the expansion of the one, through the imitative response of the crowd, to encompass the many. In the early republic, he became an embodiment of the national motto, "E pluribus unum." [60]

The same interplay of singularity and multiplicity, of stasis and transformation, that characterized Henry's speech performances structures the single most important instance of textual production in his career: the composition, passage, publication, and preservation of the Stamp Act Resolves. In the history of the

---

breast (703 n. 4). See also John Roane's description quoted in Moses Coit Tyler, *Patrick Henry* (1898), rev. ed. (Ithaca, N.Y., 1962), 147–149.

59. Randolph, *History of Virginia*, ed. Shaffer, 212. McCants relates the Carrington and Burgess stories in *Patrick Henry, the Orator*, 57–58. For the Culpeper County militia, see Henry, *Patrick Henry: Life, Correspondence, and Speeches*, I, 319. For the oral traditions about Henry's speeches, see Cohen, "The 'Liberty or Death' Speech," *WMQ*, 3d Ser., XXXVIII (1981), 715.

Compare Ruttenberg's observations about Whitefield: "This is the conversional moment: when the enlarged self . . . converges, at the height of spiritual ecstasy, with the mimetically enlarged voice of the crowd, and the oppositional, divisive voice of the scoffers is reborn as the all-encompassing voice of the people" (*Democratic Personality*, 101).

60. Christopher Looby, *Voicing America: Language, Literary Form, and the Origins of the United States* (Chicago, 1996), chap. 5.

resolves, we see text invested with a malleability and responsiveness to context akin to spoken improvisation. Several versions of these resolves survive, numbering from four to seven resolutions that vary in wording. The controversy over the authenticity of these different texts casts into relief the competing attitudes toward written and spoken language in Revolutionary Virginia. The Stamp Act itself sought to regulate texts, requiring that a wide variety of legal documents as well as almanacs, newspapers, and pamphlets be written or printed on stamped paper, marking them as part of an imperial system.[61] It promised to have its biggest impact on lawyers, printers, and their customers, restricting access to text-based forms of law, news, and information. Henry drew up his resolutions protesting the act as unconstitutional, he later remembered, "alone, unadvised, and unassisted, on a blank leaf of an old law-book," as if writing new law. He took his stand against the act on May 29, 1765, when to a thinly attended House he made an eloquent argument for passing the resolutions and succeeded in winning passage of five. The next day, in Henry's absence, the House voted to retain all but the fifth resolution, which was removed from the record and replaced with a fresh sheet containing only the first four. The defeated fifth resolution (as distinct from the resolution numbered five in published versions) has never been firmly identified. It and two others that Henry prepared were never entered in the official record, and the editor of the *Virginia Gazette* refused to print the resolves at all. But the full resolves did appear in newspapers throughout the colonies outside Virginia where Henry and his associates circulated them. These accounts of the resolves, particularly the more daring but rejected sixth and seventh, and not the four resolves finally passed in the House, inspired the other colonies to acts of defiance.[62]

There is one text here (the full seven resolves), yet there are several (that erased from the House records, that finally entered in the House records, that preserved by Henry, those published in the newspapers). The treatment of the manuscript text as single yet multiple resembles a common practice of oral performers. In many performances the singer, orator, or tale-teller selects familiar elements of a well-known piece from which to build a performance. Beginning with a few crucial components, the performer in part selects and in part improvises a version of a song, speech, or poem. Recorded on tape, the performer will often insist that today's execution of the piece is identical with yesterday's rendering, although

---

61. See Edmund S. Morgan and Helen M. Morgan, *The Stamp Act Crisis: Prologue to Revolution* (1953; Chapel Hill, N.C., 1995). For the items taxed, see 72. For the Virginia Resolves, see 92–103.

62. Henry left the note from which the quotation was taken sealed up with a copy of the resolves among his papers; see Wirt, *Life of Patrick Henry*, 74–76, esp. 76. For the events surrounding the Stamp Act Resolves, see Mayer, *A Son of Thunder*, 81–92. On the newspaper accounts of the resolves, see Morgan and Morgan, *Stamp Act Crisis*, 102.

those expecting a print-text standard of identity would disagree. Although in theory writing provides too fixed a medium for such improvisations, in practice documents can be subject to just such alterations. Multiple, competing versions of a text may exist, each with its own distinct claims to authenticity.[63]

Henry's use of the resolve texts resembles oral composition: winning a vote on five and then losing one, circulating the full seven, then years later recording a particular set of five that might or might not have been the same as those originally passed. When Jefferson helped Wirt sort through the variants in 1814, he disagreed with Henry's own record of the mysterious fifth resolution, speculated that Henry sealed up his copy "long after the transaction" when he found the resolutions numbered six and seven too radical, and complained that "those engaged in public affairs so rarely make notes of transactions passing within their knowledge. Hence history becomes fable instead of fact." Jefferson's own careful preservation of his original text of the Declaration of Independence and his insistence on its authenticity over the amended and published version reveal his investment in text as evidence of historical truth and authorial subjectivity. This was an investment in a particular kind of textual authority that Patrick Henry did not share. Remaking writing in the image of speech, he insisted on texts that were not fixed and abstract but transformative and context-dependent.[64]

Given Jefferson's celebration of fixed textual authority, it is ironic that he authenticated a crucial component of the oral tradition that grew up around Henry during his life. There are two accounts of Henry's famous speech to the House on the Stamp Act Resolves, one recorded soon after the event in the journal of an anonymous French traveler and lost for more than a century, the other part of the Henry legend to which Jefferson attested five decades afterward. The Frenchman recorded Henry saying that "he had read that in former times tarquin and Julus had their Brutus, Charles had his Cromwell, and he Did not Doubt but some good american would stand up, in favour of his Country." Called down for trea-

---

63. Although the strategy of oral composition described here is widely practiced, it is not exclusive. The degree of fixity and improvisation in oral composition varies between cultures and between genres and even pieces; see Ruth Finnegan, *Oral Poetry: Its Nature, Significance, and Social Context* (Bloomington, Ind., 1992), chap. 3, esp. 79–80. Henry's circulation of the measures was heir to the English system of scribally published political speeches and documents that Harold Love discusses in *The Culture and Commerce of Texts: Scribal Publication in Seventeenth-Century England* (Amherst, Mass., 1998). Love notes the strong practical and symbolic relationship of scribal publication to oral performance on 147–148. Hall discusses the political and legal uses of scribal publication in "The Chesapeake in the Seventeenth Century," in Hall, *Cultures of Print*, 101–115.

64. Letter, Aug. 14, 1814, in H. A. Washington, ed., *The Writings of Thomas Jefferson . . .* , VI (New York, 1854), 367, 370. See also Jefferson's inclusion of the original and revised texts in his "Autobiography," in Jefferson, *Writings*, ed. Peterson, 19–24.

FIGURE 9. Patrick Henry before the Virginia House of Burgesses. *By Peter F. Rothermel.*
1851. Rothermel's painting portrays the legendary moment of defiance that became part of the
nineteenth-century image of Henry. Courtesy, Red Hill, The Patrick Henry National
Memorial, Brookneal, Virginia

son, Henry responded "that if he had afronted the speaker, or the house, he was ready to ask pardon, and he would shew his loyalty to his majesty King G. the third, at the Expence of the last Drop of his blood." But, he continued, he had spoken in the "heat of passion" for "the Interest of his Countrys Dying liberty." He concluded by begging for pardon.[65]

The other, much more dramatic account of this speech circulated as part of the Henry legend when Wirt quizzed Jefferson in 1814. This is the famous Wirt version that Jefferson authenticated:

> Cesar had his Brutus — Charles the First, his Cromwell and George the Third — ('Treason! cried the speaker — 'Treason, treason,' echoed from every part of the house. . . . Henry faltered not for an instant; but rising to a loftier attitude, and fixing on the speaker an eye of the most determined fire, he finished his sentence with the firmest emphasis) — *may profit by their example.* If *this* be treason, make the most of it.[66]

Both the Frenchman's version and the version of Virginia legend make the improvisational moment when Henry responded to charges of treason the climax of the drama. The differences in tone that the two accounts record — restraint of passion tinged with irony on the one hand, bold assertion on the other — register the evolution from colonial subordination to post-Revolutionary triumph over England. The metamorphosis of the speech in these accounts reveals once again the metaphoric structure of controlled transformation that organized Henry's career. Embodying that oral dynamic in a series of famous performances, Henry represented for Americans their Revolution figured as vocal assertion.

During the American Revolution, whig political oratory figured a public sphere from which text had been symbolically (but not actually) evacuated. In the speeches of James Otis and Patrick Henry, the living word triumphed over the dead letter of British law. Otis's radical politics of representative orality and Henry's transformative speech projected scenes of communal self-presence in which the relationship between the one and the many were variously negotiated. Their performances reveal the cultural and political significances attached to orality and textuality rather than the reified meanings so often ascribed to

---

65. "Journal of a French Traveller in the Colonies, 1765," *AHR,* XXVI (1920–1921), 745. Mc-Cants argues for the authenticity of the French traveler's version while observing that the conventional nature of the apology did not detract from Henry's daring; see *Patrick Henry, the Orator* 50

66. Wirt, *Life of Patrick Henry,* 83. In response to Wirt's question about the veracity of the legend, Jefferson wrote, "I well remember the cry of treason, the pause of Mr Henry at the name of George the III, and the presence of mind with which he closed his sentence, and baffled the charge vociferated" (Washington, ed., *Writings of Jefferson,* VI, 364–371, esp. 368–369).

these terms. They also suggest the danger of assuming a modernizing trajectory from speech into print: vernacular political oratory emerged as a formal genre with a national audience in tandem with the expansion of print culture. American patriot orators created novel modes of nationalist identity based on their public performances. Through the public self-creation that occurs in the space of appearance, the orator enacts a public role that others then perform and modify. Generations of children reciting the "Liberty or Death" speech offer an example of this; more immediately, John Adams's self-conscious imitation and adaptation of James Otis's patriot identity suggest how public roles are taken up and transformed. The specificity of bodily experience that such performances entailed stands in contrast to the disembodied abstractions of print-based publicity.[67] Throughout the nineteenth century, as Americans wrote the history of their own Revolution in biographies of its great orators, and as elocution became a popular form of training and entertainment that involved the recitation of famous speeches, oratorical performance provided a crucial site where national identity became concretely embodied.

67. On the space of appearance in the American Revolution, see Hannah Arendt, *On Revolution* (New York, 1963), chap. 1. For a discussion of the orator as a public figure in the French Revolution, see Dorinda Outram, *The Body and the French Revolution: Sex, Class and Political Culture* (New Haven, Conn., 1989), 76–83.

The abstractness of the republican public domain shaped by print culture is the subject of Michael Warner, *The Letters of the Republic: Publication and the Public Sphere in Eighteenth-Century America* (Cambridge, Mass., 1990); for elaborations and complications of this model, see Dana D. Nelson, *National Manhood: Capitalist Citizenship and the Imagined Fraternity of White Men* (Durham, N.C., 1998), chap. 1; Bruce Burgett, *Sentimental Bodies: Sex, Gender, and Citizenship in the Early Republic* (Princeton, N.J., 1998), introduction, chap. 1.

5   *The Body of the Nation*

I. "WORDS OF REPROACH" AND "WRITTEN REASON"

On the icy evening of March 5, 1770, the streets of Boston rang with the clamor of bells and loud cries of "Fire!" Inhabitants rushed from their houses into the snow-covered streets and headed toward the town's major congregating points, where they gradually learned that there was, in fact, no blaze. Fights had broken out between the townspeople and the British soldiers stationed there, and someone reacted with the call-out signal for a fire. Firefighter John Coburn's experience of that evening was typical. Coburn testified in his deposition before town officers, "On the evening of the 5th of March instant, being alarmed by the cry of fire and ringing of bells, [I] ran out of my house with my bags and buckets; upon going to Mr. Payne's door, he told me it was not fire, it was a riot." [1]

Venturing out into the street, Coburn and merchant Edward Payne heard rumors that soldiers were assaulting and wounding citizens. They returned to their residences near the customhouse and watched as a group of civilians gathered around the sentinel, urging him, "Fire, fire, damn you, why don't you fire." Coburn grew nervous and retired inside his house, but Payne remained standing with others in his door to watch the scene unfold. A relief guard arrived to protect the sentry, with Captain Thomas Preston in command. The cries and taunts of fire continued, "some crying fire because the bells rung, some, no doubt, fire to the soldiers, daring them to it." All at once, the soldiers did open fire on the crowd, apparently in response to someone's order. One bullet struck Payne and wounded him in the arm. All told, five civilians were killed and seven more wounded in

---

1. Robert Blair St. George discusses the providential meanings of fire in New England in *Conversing by Signs: Poetics of Implication in Colonial New England Culture* (Chapel Hill, N.C., 1998), 246–250. The Massacre depositions are printed in Frederic Kidder, *History of the Boston Massacre, March 5, 1770* . . . (Albany, N.Y., 1870), 60. Kidder collected the major published documents dealing with the Boston Massacre and the subsequent trials, favoring the patriot perspective. The other major source for Massacre documents, which includes previously unpublished records, is L. Kinvin Wroth and Hiller B. Zobel, eds., *Legal Papers of John Adams,* III (Cambridge, Mass., 1965).

FIGURE 10. The Bloody Massacre Perpetrated in King Street on March 5th, 1770, by a Party of the 29th Regt. *By Paul Revere. 1770. Courtesy, American Antiquarian Society*

the volley of gunfire, shot down by British soldiers in what the patriot leadership quickly labeled the Boston Massacre.[2]

Two trials were held in Boston to explain the causes for the violence and punish those responsible for the killings. Efforts to sort out what happened in front of the

2. Kidder, *History of the Boston Massacre*, 81, 162.

customhouse on King Street focused on the sources and significances of the word "fire," called out repeatedly that night in many contexts and voices. At the trial of Captain Preston, the court sifted through testimony about what orders Preston gave his men and when he gave them, in an effort to clarify the blurred voice of British authority. Did Preston order the soldiers to fire, or did he rather instruct them to hold their fire? When did he issue the orders, before or after shooting began? If Preston's voice was not the one his men heard telling them to open fire, whose was it? Was there, in fact, an intentional speech act that led to the killings? Or did the soldiers begin shooting without an order, perhaps confused or provoked by the frenzied shouts of the crowd?

Trial testimony placed Preston in front of his men, negotiating with the townspeople in an effort to defuse tensions, when the shots were fired, and the jury acquitted him. Despite that verdict, Paul Revere's print *The Bloody Massacre* immortalized the image of Preston giving the order to fire at passive, retiring civilians. Locating unambiguous authoritative speech at the root of the conflict, *The Bloody Massacre* bore the satisfying clarity of the patriot explanation of the shootings: they were the result of a high-level army conspiracy to punish Bostonians for their hostile reception of the troops and for their general uppityness toward the British ministry. Unlike Revere's print, the inconclusive trial testimony concerning the source, substance, and timing of the call to fire left a mystery at the heart of the night's events. Eventually that mystery was solved when Hugh Montgomery, one of two soldiers convicted of manslaughter in the second Massacre trial, related to his attorneys how someone had knocked him down "and rising again, in the agony from the blow he said Damn you, fire and immediately he fired himself and [the] rest followed." But the myth of Preston's agency persisted. Montgomery's sudden, angry, pain-filled call to his fellows lacked both the intentional clarity and the authority of rank that the patriot conspiracy theory required.[3]

The trials and confessions do not exhaust the ambiguities of the cries of "fire" that echoed through the Boston streets that March night. The revelation of the source of certain mysterious voices only shrouded the unexplained voices more deeply in uncertainty. Some patriots speculated that the original cry of "fire" was the watchword that the soldiers had established to draw the townspeople into the streets, where they could be assaulted.[4] Tories offered countertheories of town

3. Hiller B. Zobel, *The Boston Massacre* (New York, 1970), 300.

4. See Samuel Adams's contention in one of his "Vindex" papers addressing the Massacre in Harry Alonzo Cushing, ed. *The Writings of Samuel Adams*, II (New York, 1906), 94. The soldiers, Adams asserted, had formed "a general combination . . . to put in execution some wicked and desperate design" (98). Adams's charge was not entirely unfounded, for several soldiers posted handwritten notices on the morning of the fifth warning the "Rebellious People in Boston" that they were "Determend to Joine to Gether and Defend them Selves against all Who shall Oppose

conspiracy, insisting that the cries of fire and the ringing of bells were patriot signals to bring out the mob for a preconcerted assault on the soldiers. Several witnesses testified to seeing a man attired like a council member in a red cloak and white wig, haranguing a group of citizens to take action against the soldiers. The story of this anonymous figure filled the role in tory mythology that the Revere print filled for the patriots: it portrayed intentional acts of elite speech controlling crowd actions. Whig leaders, in turn, deflected tory charges, denying the existence of the man in the red cloak and white wig and claiming that, if the townspeople were responsible for the shouts and the bells, it was "from an apprehension of some of the inhabitants, that the Soldiers were putting their former threats into execution, and that there would be a general massacre." Although historians have generally traced the warning cries to the civilians, the questions of source and motivation remain unresolved and ultimately unresolvable.[5]

As mentioned in Chapter 4, above, James Otis and Patrick Henry shaped an oratorical public sphere in which the patriot voice sounded with immediacy and power, resonating with the authority of a community fully present to itself. The events surrounding the Boston Massacre revealed a patriot voice that could be opaque and incoherent in its multiplicity. What people heard when they listened to accounts of that night were not the formal pronouncements of political leaders.[6] Instead, they heard the taunts, threats, and conciliatory phrases of soldiers, camp followers, apprentices, sailors, working men, and merchants. Popular speech studs the records, not in the form of extended eloquence, but rather as brief ver-

---

them." Dirk Hoerder discusses the posted notice in *Crowd Action in Revolutionary Massachusetts, 1765–1780* (New York, 1977), 224.

5. Cushing, ed., *Writings of Samuel Adams,* II, 94. Zobel resolves these ambiguities by asserting the control of the whig leadership *(Boston Massacre,* 180). Jesse Lemisch and Pauline Maier criticize Zobel for his present-minded orientation and privileging of order and authority in Lemisch, "Radical Plot in Boston (1770): A Study in the Use of Evidence," *Harvard Law Review,* LXXXIV (1970), 485–504; Maier, "Revolutionary Violence and the Relevance of History," *Journal of Interdisciplinary History,* II (Summer 1971), 119–135. Hoerder unfolds the autonomous sources of popular action and the relationship between popular forces and whig leaders in *Crowd Action,* 223–234, and Hoerder, "Boston Leaders and Boston Crowds, 1765–1776," in Alfred F. Young, ed., *The American Revolution: Explorations in the History of American Radicalism* (De-Kalb, Ill., 1976). For a reading of the Massacre as a patriot moral drama created to have special persuasive force, see Kurt W. Ritter, "Confrontation as Moral Drama: The Boston Massacre in Rhetorical Perspective," *Southern Speech Communication Journal,* XLII (1977), 114–136. E. P. Thompson sketches English backgrounds to colonial crowd actions in "The Moral Economy of the English Crowd in the Eighteenth Century," *Past and Present,* no. 50 (Feb. 1971), 76–136.

6. Hoerder states, "None of those who sometimes attempted to lead or incite crowd action was on the scene" and concludes that the riot took place without a clear plan. Rather, "there was a tacit agreement between some sections of the people and the soldiers to fight it out" *(Crowd Action,* 234).

bal clashes marked by their emotional intensity and the repetitive, conventional language of insult and injury. The words collected in the depositions and trial testimony are staccato in their rhythms and explosive in their delivery. They echo with the elongated vowels and drawn-out articulation of pleas and wails, or they reverberate with the intensity of the speaker's desire to avoid tragedy. Huzzas and cheers perforate the verbal fabric of the scene. Lacking an originating text, popular speech lacks a clear source. Its origins are unknowable and perhaps unknowing. The justices of the peace controlling the collection of town depositions and the judges and lawyers running the trials fostered such an image of popular speech in their interrogations and written records. These elites did not include any analysis the townspeople or soldiers might have offered on the larger causes behind the Massacre. Such an omission leaves the threats and taunts disturbingly free from specific context and opens them to explanations stressing either simplistic psychological factors or the machinations of large-scale conspiracy.[7]

The production of Peter Carr's deathbed speech as testimony in the soldiers' trial reveals the forms of interpretive control exercised upon popular speech. Carr, an immigrant Irishman and leather breeches maker, was fatally wounded on the night of the fifth but did not die until several days later. In that time he spoke to several people about the events of the Massacre. Their testimony about his deathbed words provided dramatic but contradictory insight into a victim's view of that night. The laconic reports of testimony by Catherine Field, Carr's landlady, and John Mansfield, a neighbor or fellow resident of the Field household, recounted bare statements of fact. Field remembered: "He said on his death bed, he saw a parcel of boys and negroes throwing snow balls at the guard. He thought the first or second man from the sentinel box was the man that shot him." Though Mansfield "was often at his bed side," the trial records report only that he heard Carr say "he thought he knew the man that shot him."[8]

Physician John Jeffries was able to report a longer exchange with Carr that differed both in substance and in tone from the reports of Field and Mansfield. Jeffries interrogated his dying patient, hoping to quiet his own fears about the direction the conflict with Britain was taking.[9] His report of Carr's responses em-

---

7. Michael Schudson explores the aforementioned features of popular speech as they came to characterize party politics in the nineteenth century in "Was There Ever a Public Sphere? If So, When? Reflections on the American Case," in Craig Calhoun, ed., *Habermas and the Public Sphere* (Cambridge, Mass., 1992), 143–163. Greg Dening describes similar limitations on the testimony of the *Bounty* sailors tried for mutiny; see *Mr. Bligh's Bad Language: Passion, Power, and Theatre on the Bounty* (Cambridge, 1992), pp. 39, 11

8. Kidder, *History of the Boston Massacre,* 212. It is impossible to tell from the trial transcript whether Field and Mansfield gave their testimony in response to specific questions, although Field's testimony in particular reads this way.

9. Jeffries's commitment to the patriot cause was shaken by the Massacre, and he eventually

phasized the assaults that civilians made on soldiers. Jeffries told the court that he asked Carr "whether he thought the soldiers would fire," and Carr responded that "he thought the soldiers would have fired long before." Jeffries's account continued:

> I then asked him whether he thought the soldiers were abused a great deal after they went down there; he said he thought they were. I asked him whether he thought the soldiers would have been hurt if they had not fired; he said he really thought they would, for he heard many voices cry out, kill them. I asked him then, *meaning to close all,* whether he thought they fired in self-defence, or on purpose to destroy the people; he said he really thought they did fire to defend themselves; that he did not blame the man, whoever he was, that shot him.

Jeffries's tone of interrogation reveals his investment in clearing the soldiers. Speaking for Carr, he continued:

> He told me also, he was a native of Ireland, that he had frequently seen mobs, and soldiers called upon to quell them; whenever he mentioned that he always called himself a fool, that he might have known better; that he had seen soldiers often fire on the people in Ireland, but had never seen them bear half so much before they fired in his life.

Jeffries's report of Carr's deathbed speech set him outside the community of native Bostonians and outside the bounds of the law. Repeated "in Court, by the mouth of another, in favour of the prisoners," Carr's words contributed importantly to the lesser convictions and acquittals that the jury handed down to the soldiers.[10]

Both defense attorney John Adams and loyalist justice Peter Oliver cited Jeffries's account of Carr's words as proof that the soldiers acted upon adequate provocation. Adams went further, interpreting the account as proof that Carr and Crispus Attucks, another nonnative Bostonian, "sall[ied] out upon their thought-

---

sided with the British; see Clifford K. Shipton, *Sibley's Harvard Graduates,* XV (Boston, 1970), 420.

10. Kidder, *History of the Boston Massacre,* 213 (emphasis added); Cushing, ed., *Writings of Samuel Adams,* II, 120. In his "Vindex" papers, Samuel Adams discussed the problems of evidence that Jeffries's narration of Carr's words raised. Adams pointed out the eagerness that motivated Jeffries's inquiries and the time that elapsed before he was called upon to repeat Carr's answers in court, remarked that Carr was not on oath in his conversations with Jeffries, and noted how Carr's account diverged from that of other witnesses, particularly on the issue of whether the crowd pelted the relief squad with snowballs and oyster shells. Adams pointed to the "pains and anxiety occasioned by a mortal wound" under which Carr suffered as a factor that might well have shaped his answers, particularly his willingness to forgive his killer. Moreover, Adams insisted on the significance of the other witnesses to Carr's deathbed speech and noted particularly "that *Car* gave *them* a very different account from that which he gave to his doctor" (144).

less enterprises, at the head of such a rabble of negroes, etc., as they can collect together," for which "the good people of the town" take the blame. Even Robert Treat Paine, the prosecuting attorney, accepted Jeffries's construal of Carr's words and Adams's scapegoating strategy, though in his position Paine identified Carr not as head of the mob but as a sympathizer with the soldiers. "His Country and behaviour" as he stood removed from the crowd suggested to Paine that his allegiances lay with the army, composed as it was of a significant number of Irish soldiers.[11] Different as Adams's and Paine's explanations for Carr's role in the riot were, they both set him apart from "true" Bostonians on the basis of his Irish background. The words that Jeffries posthumously attributed to Carr exculpated the soldiers and acted as a symbolic wedge between the "people of Boston" and outsiders such as the victim himself.

In his summation, a forensic oration justly remembered for its rhetorical sophistication and persuasiveness, John Adams pursued Jeffries's strategy of representing the Massacre victims as violent outsiders. Called upon to defend the soldiers despite his patriot sympathies, Adams insisted that he would use "no Art or Address" but only "Fact, Evidence and Law" in his defense arguments. Though he habitually spoke extempore, during the first day of his two-day summation he spent much of the time "read[ing] to them . . . from Books" in both Latin and English. Adams explained to the court the reason for his unusually heavy reliance on textual authorities: "I have endeavored to produce the best authorities, and to give you the rules of law in their words, for I desire not to advance anything of my own. I choose to lay down the rules of law, from authorities which cannot be disputed." Presenting himself as a vessel conveying the common law to the jurors without contamination or adulteration, Adams insisted that the voicing of law was a fundamental freedom: "If we cannot speak the law as it is," he asked, "where is our liberty?" By characterizing the law as abstract and above debate, and himself as its conduit, Adams sought to protect himself from the political dangers of defending the soldiers, casting himself instead as the defender of the community's freedom.[12]

11. Kidder, *History of the Boston Massacre*, 258; Wroth and Zobel, eds., *Legal Papers of John Adams*, III, 279. According to Zobel, "the average man in the Twenty-ninth was over thirty, medium tall, and Irish," many spoke with Irish accents, and many were Roman Catholics; see *Boston Massacre*, 93–94.

12. James M. Farrell discusses the classical background to Adams's speech in *"Pro Militibus Oratio:* John Adams's Imitation of Cicero in the Boston Massacre Trial," *Rhetorica,* IX (1991), 233–249. On Adams's time spent reading, see L. H. Butterfield, ed., *Diary and Autobiography of John Adams,* 4 vols. (Cambridge, Mass., 1961), III, 293, 295. On Adams's extempore oratory, see 310, where he claimed that he "never wrote a Speech beforehand, either at the Bar or in any public Assembly, nor committed one to writing after it was delivered." For Adams's comments on textual authorities and the law, see Kidder, *History of the Boston Massacre*, 241, 242.

Adams was not alone in recognizing that the jury's interpretation of the evidence would depend on their understanding of the law at issue. In his concluding remarks to the jury, Justice Edmund Trowbridge distinguished three types of law: Jewish law, "unwritten" common law, and "written" statutory law. Common law reinterpreted "Mosaical law" to create "the settled and established rules, and ancient customs of the nation, approved for successions of ages." It represented "the result of the wisdom and experience of many ages" and consisted of "the general customs or immemorial usage of the English nation." Trowbridge figured the common law as a living tradition based on the spoken word of learned judges and identified with English nationhood. He presented biblical and statutory laws as excessively textual, divorced from their original speech communities and cast in a derivative written form. The debates and proceedings in the colonial legislatures that produced statutory law did not constitute a legitimating speech community for Trowbridge. Neither did the assertions of Bostonians who invoked the Bible, urging that "whosoever sheddeth man's blood, by man shall his blood be shed." [13] Only the common law captured the integrity of an elite oral tradition that Trowbridge insisted must provide the legal framework for the trial. Common law, imagined as a succession of originative speech acts, united the colonies with the oral community of the English nation. Trowbridge worked to bridge the abyss that James Otis saw looming between England and America with the trope of the common law founded in and sustaining a speech community governed by elites. Like Justice Trowbridge, Adams claimed that law guaranteed liberty in that it represented the efforts of "the greatest and best characters the English nation ever produced" to construct an interpretive framework for understanding and judging complex events. But while the tory Trowbridge described the common law as "unwritten law," Adams characterized it as "written reason" and stressed its textuality through acts of reading that gave voice to legal texts.[14]

13. Kidder, *History of the Boston Massacre*, 227, 260, 264. Trowbridge was an associate of Thomas Hutchinson. Gary B. Nash describes the role that the tory "Junto" of which Trowbridge was a member played in the Boston politics of the 1760s in "Social Change and the Growth of Prerevolutionary Urban Radicalism," in Young, ed., *The American Revolution*, 3–36, esp. 21–27. Scriptural definitions of justice circulated through Boston during the trial. Defense attorney Josiah Quincy, Jr., warned the jurors not to invoke "disconnected passages of Scriptures, applied in a manner foreign to their original design or import" (227) in their deliberations.

14. Kidder, *History of the Boston Massacre*, 232, 259. Trowbridge manifested a traditional form of legal thought that J. G. A. Pocock has described in "Time, Institutions, and Action: An Essay on Traditions and Their Understanding," in Pocock, *Politics, Language, and Time: Essays on Political Thought and History* (New York, 1971), 233–272.

Adams spoke specifically of Chief Justice Sir Matthew Hale, but he referred to Fortesque as "of equal character" (Kidder, *History of the Boston Massacre*, 233). The value of the common law as Adams saw it derived in large measure from the characters and status of the men who formu-

The significance of Adams's textual symbolism became evident in the second half of his summation, where he developed a contrast between the elite text of the law and the "insolent, scurrilous, or slanderous" speech of the crowd. Strategically deploying text to discipline the perceived excesses of popular speech, Adams made acts of linguistic differentiation and control central to his defense strategy. He noted dryly the reluctance of witnesses to call the people assembled in King Street a mob. "We have been entertained with a great variety of phrases, to avoid calling this sort of people a mob," he observed. "Some call them shavers, [s]ome call them geniuses." Such slang terms conveyed an ambivalence that Adams firmly rejected: "The plain English is, gentlemen, most probably a motley rabble of saucy boys, negroes and mulattoes, Irish teagues and outlandish jack tars; and why we should scruple to call such a set of people a mob, I can't conceive, unless the name is too respectable for them." When Adams labeled the King Street crowd a mob, he relied on the authority, not of legal precedent, but of linguistic norms.[15] Yet even while asserting the authority of "plain English," Adams himself used the familiar, derogatory terms for Irishmen and sailors. The tension between vernacular and genteel speech marked an ambivalence in Adams's thought over the proper modes of political discourse. From a young age, Adams manifested a "regularizing spirit" in tension with an attraction to linguistic multiplicity. As a youth he learned several styles of handwriting, then consciously adopted a single style. His Humphrey Plough-jogger letters from the 1760s were written in the persona of a partially literate Massachusetts farmer, drawing on the political power of a popular idiom. Fifteen years after the Plough-jogger letters, Adams unsuccessfully proposed a national language academy, urging Congress to form "the first public institution for refining, correcting, improving, and ascertaining the English language." Adams hoped that a purified language would become "the principal means of advancement through the various ranks and offices of society."[16]

----

lated it. His view in this respect was not far different from that of Trowbridge. Unlike the tory justice and like James Otis, however, Adams measured common law against divine and moral law; see 235.

15. Kidder, *History of the Boston Massacre*, 249, 255. The definitions listed in the *Oxford English Dictionary* suggest the ambivalence of a term like "shaver," which means both "one who pillages or plunders" and, more neutrally, " 'fellow,' 'chap.' " "Mob" was derived from the Latin *mobile vulgus*.

16. Adams, "To the President of Congress" (Sept. 5, 1780), in Charles Francis Adams, ed., *Works of John Adams, Second President of the United States . . .* (Boston, 1852), VII, 249–251. On his handwriting, see Peter Shaw, *The Character of John Adams* (Chapel Hill, N.C., 1976), 8. For discussions of Adams's academy proposal in the context of early national language theories, see Dennis E. Baron, *Grammar and Good Taste: Reforming the American Language* (New Haven, Conn., 1982), 16–18; Thomas Gustafson, *Representative Words: Politics, Literature, and the American Language, 1776–1865* (Cambridge, 1992), 306; David Simpson, *The Politics of American En-*

Adams's dreams of a democratic medium under the control of a national academy sprang from the same set of social assumptions that led him to insist on terming the King Street crowd a mob: "plain English" as defined from above, rather than the disparate and volatile conventions of popular speech, should be the medium of politics, law, and society. The act of "proper" denomination mirrored the scapegoating content of his speech. Linguistic distinctions both reflected and created social distinctions. The name of "mob" set the crowd in symbolic as well as actual opposition to the law. Adams portrayed the law as texts deriving from the best minds and maintaining "a steady, undeviating course" despite "vicissitudes of government, fluctuations of the passions, or flights of enthusiasm."[17] He characterized the mob in contrast as lower class and foreign in origin, impure through its mixture of people, motivated by oral aggression, and physically mobile, a quality linked philologically to the term "mob" itself. He dwelled upon the crowd's social composition, noting that "many of these people were thoughtless and inconsiderate, old and young, sailors and landmen, negroes and mulattoes." Adams characterized the "mob" as outsiders from the political community: boys too young to own property or exercise power, sailors without a permanent residence, Irish immigrants, "negroes and mulattoes." He sought to save the soldiers from murder convictions while purifying the Boston body politic whose capacity for self-government had been called into question after a series of collective actions by a "mixed" crowd.[18]

Distinguishing the "mob" from Boston proper, Adams focused on the single member of the crowd who represented in his mind its most threatening tendencies: Crispus Attucks, the heroically proportioned mulatto sailor of African American and Natick Indian derivation who died with two bullets in his chest. Building his dramatic narrative to a climax, Adams marked out Attucks as the

---

glish, 1776–1850 (New York, 1986), 29–32; Kenneth Cmiel, *Democratic Eloquence: The Fight over Popular Speech in Nineteenth-Century America* (New York, 1990), 40.

17. Kidder, *History of the Boston Massacre,* 258.

18. Kidder, *History of the Boston Massacre,* 236. Such a portrait of the crowd was a common whig strategy for disavowing or disguising leadership involvement in collective action. See, for example, the reference to "Boys and Negroes" as perpetrators in Zobel, *Boston Massacre,* 158. Adams's comment may reflect a working-class reality. Quoting this passage, Peter Linebaugh and Marcus Rediker interpret the Boston Massacre as one manifestation of the "many-headed hydra" that constituted an "Atlantic working class" composed of sailors, slaves, and others with shared interests and common strategies of resistance in "The Many-Headed Hydra: Sailors, Slaves, and the Atlantic Working Class in the Eighteenth Century," in Colin Howell and Richard Twomey, eds., *Jack Tar in History: Essays in the History of Maritime Life and Labour* (Fredericton, New Brunswick, 1991), 11–36, esp. 21. Adams's partner in the case, Josiah Quincy, Jr., repeatedly referred to the people assembled in King Street as "mixed." See Kidder, *History of the Boston Massacre,* 177, 222.

direct cause of the tragedy. Attucks, he asserted, "appears to have undertaken to be the hero of the night." The real armed force on the street that night was, not the passive, frightened relief squad, but Attucks and his troop of twenty or thirty sailors, which Adams described as an "army with banners." They represented the "unlawful assembly" that jurors should fear and hate, as he imagined the soldiers did:

> Now to have this reinforcement coming down under the command of a stout mulatto fellow, whose very looks was enough to terrify any person, what had not the soldiers then to fear? He had hardiness enough to fall in upon them, and with one hand took hold of a bayonet, and with the other knocked the man down: this was the behavior of Attucks: to whose mad behavior, in all probability, the dreadful carnage of that night is chiefly to be ascribed.[19]

The "mad behavior" of a black sailor substituted in Adams's account both for the order to fire that whig conspiracy theorists attributed to Captain Preston and for the speech of the bewigged council member in tory narratives. The tragedy was produced, not by the eloquence of elites, but by Attucks's curses and exclamations. Figuring the link between verbal aggression and physical violence, Attucks represented the "savage" speaker haunting patriot speech. This was, not the Pentecostal savage speaker of Samson Occom or John Marrant, but the self-mutilating savage of the Drake narrative or the mad savage of John Smith. Describing Adams's rhetorical strategy in his defense, Thomas Hutchinson observed, "He being a Representative of the Town and a great Partisan wishes to blacken the people as little as may be consistent with his Duty to his Clients." In "blackening" the mob by putting Attucks at its head, Adams sought to avoid "blackening" the town, or soiling its reputation. His scapegoating strategy singled out "a Carr from Ireland" together with "an Attucks from Framingham" as the mob leaders who just "happen[ed] to be here," thus making the two Massacre victims who were neither Anglo-American nor native Bostonians responsible for their own fates and the deaths of others. Adams portrayed the Massacre as a contingent act of violence produced by uncontrolled savage speech, not an intentional consequence of organized conspiracy and elite eloquence.[20]

Adams's lurid description of Attucks as mob leader echoed and amplified broader themes of racial identity and difference circulating during the occupation of Boston. Early in the occupation, *A Journal of the Times*, the patriot news-

19. Kidder, *History of the Boston Massacre*, 257-230.

20. Wroth and Zobel, eds., *Legal Papers of John Adams*, III, 26. See Kidder, *History of the Boston Massacre*, 258, for the Carr reference. On figurations of the Irish as "black," see Noel Ignatiev, *How the Irish Became White* (New York, 1995), chap. 2.

sheet designed to publicize Boston's ordeal, recorded the shock of Bostonians at one feature of military discipline: "To behold Britons scourg'd by Negro drummers, was a new and very disagreeable spectacle." The presence of blacks in the army engaging in the battles between soldiers and townspeople drew repeated hostile comment. One Bostonian asked a black soldier what he had to do with "white people's quarrels." The encouragements that soldiers offered to enslaved people to join the British in resisting their masters further complicated the issue. In the alleged words of three officers, "if the Negroes could be made freemen, they should be sufficient to subdue these damn'd rascals." [21] Such allegiances disrupted the fraternal bond between white American and white Briton, and united white Britons with blacks against white Americans. The British appeal to enslaved Africans created a potential internal threat to white colonists. At the same time, the army's removal from the frontiers in Louisbourg and West Florida left those colonies exposed to assaults by native Americans. Part black and part Indian, Attucks represented both threats to the colonies. As patriot leaders sought to negotiate the separation from Britain and to create a non-English identity for themselves, they foregrounded British allegiance as complicity with black and red threats to white colonists, distinguishing themselves both from their British enemies and from African Americans and native Americans. Already in 1764, James Otis challenged English conceptions that the colonies were populated "with a compound mongrel mixture of *English, Indian* and *Negro.*" In reality, he insisted, the northern colonies consisted of "freeborn *British white subjects.*" After 1770, many colonists were ready to drop "British . . . subjects" from Otis's description, as the meaning of "American" became "freeborn" and "white." [22]

21. Oliver Morton Dickerson, *Boston under Military Rule, 1768–1769: As Revealed in "A Journal of the Times"* (Boston, 1936), 3, 18 (see also 6) (hereafter cited as *Journal of the Times*); see esp. 16 for a complaint lodged against Captain John Willson for inciting "certain Negro slaves . . . to cut their master's throats, and to beat, insult, and otherwise ill treat their said masters, asserting that now the soldiers are come, the Negroes shall be free, and the Liberty Boys slaves." Peter H. Wood discusses how British offers of freedom inspired black resistance and provoked deep anxiety among white Americans throughout the Revolutionary period in "'Liberty is Sweet': African-American Freedom Struggles in the Years before White Independence," in Alfred F. Young, ed., *Beyond the American Revolution: Explorations in the History of American Radicalism* (DeKalb, Ill., 1993), 149–184.

On the Bostonian's remark, see John Hill's deposition in Kidder, *History of the Boston Massacre,* 50.

22. On the native American threat, see Dickerson, *Journal of the Times,* 9, 22–23. Francis Jennings notes the role that Indian policy played in precipitating the colonial revolt against Great Britain, first in bringing British troops to the continent, then in providing the rationale for taxation, and finally as a symbol of British savagery in turning against the colonists; see "The Indians' Revolution," in Young, ed., *The American Revolution,* 319–348, esp. 337. For Otis's comments, see James Otis, *The Rights of the British Colonies Asserted and Proved* (1764), in Charles F. Mul-

For Adams, Attucks represented corporeal danger to Boston, both through his representation of the threats that enslaved blacks and hostile Indians posed to white colonists and through the violence that he allegedly directed against the soldiers. Attucks embodied a third type of threat for Adams as well, the threat of verbal aggression escalating into physical assault: "This man with his party cried, do not be afraid of them, they dare not fire, kill them! kill them! knock them over! and he tried to knock their brains out." [23] Describing the taunts and threats of the crowd, he noted that "such words of reproach stimulate in the veins and exasperate the mind," exciting the soldiers' violent reaction. Adams's analysis of the powers of speech to stimulate passion and escalate conflict into violence here mirrors his lifelong fascination with the orator's ability to govern human emotion. Adams struggled to control his own sharp tongue and declined an invitation to "harrangue" the town meeting, claiming, "That way madness lies." His comment referred to the mental illness that plagued James Otis's final years, linking his deterioration to verbal aggression. To defend himself against the consequences of "mad" speech, Adams self-consciously embraced genteel language, reserved his eloquence for his class peers, and criticized those who did not share his verbal ideal.[24] The mob's "scurrilous language" stood in Adams's mind for the potential of passionate speech to disrupt rather than order society. "Savage" vitriol figured the disintegrative possibilities of rhetoric in all its forms.

On one telling occasion, however, Adams did experiment with a sensationalist rhetoric of revenge, although in a written form rather than in savage speech. An unpublished letter to Thomas Hutchinson blaming him for the events of March 5,

---

lett, ed., "Some Political Writings of James Otis," in *The University of Missouri Studies*, IV (1929), 301–347, esp. 319. See also Ronald T. Takaki, *Iron Cages: Race and Culture in Nineteenth-Century America* (New York, 1979), 5; Jared Gardner, *Master Plots: Race and the Founding of an American Literature, 1787–1845* (Baltimore, 1998), chap. 1.

The heavy Irish presence in the army complicated the process of symbolic transformation of identity in certain ways. The problematic ethnicity of many soldiers as white but non-English enhanced patriot claims to be the true inheritors of the English tradition. On the Little English patriotism of the American patriot leaders' ally John Wilkes, see Linda Colley, *Britons: Forging the Nation, 1707–1837* (New Haven, Conn., 1992), 105–117.

23. Kidder, *History of the Boston Massacre*, 257.

24. Kidder, *History of the Boston Massacre*, 249; Butterfield, ed., *Diary and Autobiography of John Adams*, III, 290–291. The connections that Adams made between the socially marginal people who composed the Boston crowd and his fear of violent language are evident in a diary entry where Adams commented on the continual "cursing and damning and God damning" of Admiral Montagu. Montagu's language would shame "a Coachman, a Jack Tar before the Mast," even "a Porter, a Shew Black or Chimney Sweeper," and was identical, Adams claimed, to "Otis's when he is both mad and drunk" (Butterfield, ed., *Diary and Autobiography of John Adams*, II, 71–72). On Adams's struggle to maintain verbal self-discipline, see Shaw, *Character of John Adams*, 14.

1770, appears in Adams's diary for July 1773, apparently authored by Adams himself:

> You will hear from Us with Astonishment. You ought to hear from Us with Horror. You are chargeable before God and Man, with our Blood. — The Soldiers were but passive Instruments, were Machines, neither moral nor voluntary Agents in our Destruction more than the leaden Pelletts, with which we were wounded. — You was a free Agent. You acted, coolly, deliberately, with all that premeditated Malice, not against Us in Particular but against the People in general, which in the Sight of the Law is an ingredient in the Composition of Murder. You will hear further from Us hereafter.[25]

The letter is signed "Chrispus Attucks." Deflecting attention from his own role in vilifying Attucks, and obliquely compensating for his defense of the soldiers and his "blackening" of popular action, Adams adopted the identity of the man he had made a scapegoat for the Massacre in order to put forth another theory of elite conspiracy with Hutchinson at its center. Blending Gothic horror and law in the rhetoric of legal sensationalism that Otis developed before Adams's admiring eyes in the Writs of Assistance case, Adams took the style a step further into Gothicism with the fictive signature. Ventriloquizing the spirit of the mulatto Attucks, he adopted the mask of resistance common to radical protest in the colonies, where blackface and Indian garb were common strategies of self-concealment among whites. Masquerading as "Chrispus Attucks," Adams ventured briefly into what was for him the dark but potent terrain of popular politics involved in sensational Gothic visions of blood and vengeance.[26]

II. AUTHORITATIVE BODIES

In a retrospective letter on the Revolution, John Adams characterized the events following the Massacre in the idealizing idiom of classical republicanism.

25. Butterfield, ed., *Diary and Autobiography of John Adams,* II, 84–85.

26. The Boston Tea Party was the most famous radical protest to involve such disguises. Philip J. Deloria describes colonial American uses of Indian disguise in resistance movements in *Playing Indian* (New Haven, Conn., 1998), chap. 1. For other instances, see Zobel, *Boston Massacre,* 215; Pauline Maier, "Popular Uprisings and Civil Authority in Eighteenth-Century America," *WMQ,* 3d Ser., XXVII (1970), 3–35, reprinted in *In Search of Early America: The William and Mary Quarterly, 1943–1993* ([Williamsburg], Va., 1993), 138–162, esp. 140, 143. Alan Taylor describes the continuing use of such ethnic masquerades in rural land disputes in *Liberty Men and Great Proprietors: The Revolutionary Settlement on the Maine Frontier, 1760–1820* (Chapel Hill, N.C., 1990), 190–194; Taylor, "Agrarian Independence: Northern Land Rioters after the Revolution," in Young, ed., *Beyond the American Revolution,* 221–245, esp. 222.

Distinguishing the Massacre "mob" from the thousands of people who assembled in Old South Church the morning after the killings, Adams celebrated the sober "discussions, deliberations, and debates" of "the most virtuous, substantial, independent, disinterested, and intelligent citizens," formed into "a regular deliberative body."[27] Just as Adams made Crispus Attucks stand in for the "mob," so he presented Samuel Adams as the representative for the town in negotiations with Lieutenant Governor Thomas Hutchinson. Called upon to remove the troops from Boston, Hutchinson promised to order the transfer of one regiment, but not both. Samuel Adams responded firmly. Rising "with an air of dignity and majesty" and speaking "with a self-recollection, a self-possession, a self-command, a presence of mind that was admired by every man present," he "stretched forth his arm, though even then quivering with palsy, and with an harmonious voice and decisive tone said, 'If the Lieutenant-Governor or Colonel Dalrymple, or both together, have authority to remove one regiment, they have authority to remove two, and nothing short of the total evacuation of the town by all the regular troops, will satisfy the public mind or preserve the peace of the province.'" John Adams identified the instant "when Samuel Adams stretched out his arm, and made his last speech" as "the critical moment" in the negotiations. When he described the display of self-mastery in Samuel Adams's forward-thrust arm, an intentional gesture made in defiance of the shaking caused by palsy, he memorialized the symbolic transformation of the unpredictable, fragmented, and shifting popular body into the orator's unified and dominating physical presence. With this gesture, Samuel Adams converted violent physical action of the sort that Crispus Attucks represented into the rhetorical action that accompanies persuasive oratory.[28]

John Adams's retrospective narrative simplified and collapsed, and thereby gave dramatic emphasis to, the unification and consolidation of a Boston patriot

27. Adams to William Tudor, Apr. 15, 1817, in Adams, ed., *Works of John Adams*, X, 249.

28. Ibid., 252, 253. Peter Oliver portrayed a version of Samuel Adams's insistence that, if Dalrymple could "order the Removal of one [regiment], he could of both" (Douglass Adair and John A. Schutz, eds., *Peter Oliver's* Origin and Progress of the American Rebellion: A Tory View [San Marino, Calif., 1961], 90). Like John Adams, Oliver foregrounded Samuel Adams's leadership, although in an accusatory rather than a celebratory mode. Thomas Hutchinson, in contrast, portrayed a largely anonymous committee speaking for "the unanimous voice of the people assembled" *(The History of the Colony and Province of Massachusetts-Bay*, ed. Lawrence Shaw Mayo, 3 vols. [Cambridge, Mass., 1936], III, 198). Though he does identify Adams as the committee's "prolocutor" (199), he gives him much less prominence than either Oliver or John Adams, in keeping with the less personalized tone of his *History*.

Still another account of these events eliminates Samuel Adams altogether. James Allen's "A Poem" describes "the city-senate" in debate, ruled by the ghostly voices of "Our FATHER's spirit"; see *Orations Delivered at the Request of the Inhabitants of the Town of Boston, to Commemorate the Evening of the Fifth of March, 1770* (Boston, 1785), 199 (hereafter cited as *Orations*).

FIGURE 11. Samuel Adams. *By John Singleton Copley. c. 1772. Deposited by the City of Boston. Permission of Museum of Fine Arts, Boston*

community under the direction of whig leadership in the aftermath of the Massacre. His narrative points to an important truth: the prominent role that whig leaders played in winning the removal of troops from Boston helped establish their popular authority. From 1771 to 1783, Boston's whig leaders used the annual Boston Massacre orations to establish hegemony over the local populace by focusing on the figure of the orator. The Boston Massacre orations presented an altered model of power and order in the town, staging the verbal skill and physical courage of the whig leadership before "immense crowds of people." The patriot leadership enhanced its authority through the incarnational logic that increasingly governed their relationship to the townspeople as the body of the people became identified with the orator's body, their voice with his voice.[29]

The annual oration created a distinctive colonial identity from the experience of suffering and death at the hands of British soldiers. The town meeting defined the mission of the oration, calling for a speech that would "impress upon our minds the ruinous tendency of standing Armies in Free Cities, and the necessity of such noble exertions in all future times, as the Inhabitants of the Town then made, whereby the dangers of Conspirators against the public Liberty may be still frustrated." For thirteen years, Joseph Warren, John Hancock, and other established or aspiring whig leaders delivered speeches that guided Bostonians in their recollections of the horrors of March 5, 1770, and projected future horizons of imperial conflict and national independence. Jonathan Austin captured the re-iterative aspect of the construction of memories in his 1778 oration, insisting that "from the fifth of March 1770, through every degree of violence and barbarity, to the present day, it is but one connected scene."[30] Each year the oration provided new narrative formulations and contextualizations that incorporated the unfolding events of the war. Throughout the years of mounting tension and conflict, the performances kept the shock of these deaths fresh for the Boston public and, in their printed versions, transmitted that shock to those who did not attend the event and to citizens of other colonies. Using print to disseminate opposition political speech, whig leaders further elaborated the role of memory that the commemoration made central to patriot identity. The task of warning against standing armies, the shared patriot identities of the orators, and their self-conscious efforts to shape a tradition through repeated references to past orators and orations, all contributed to the emergence of a coherent invented tradition.[31]

29. James Spear Loring, *The Hundred Boston Orators*... (Boston, 1852), 27. Tracing the transformations in the relationship between the lower-class members of Boston crowds and the whig leadership, Hoerder foregrounds the Boston Massacre as a turning point; see "Boston Leaders and Boston Crowds," in Young, ed., *The American Revolution*, 260–261. See also Hoerder's *Crowd Action*, 223–235.

30. *A Report of the Record Commissioners of the City of Boston: Containing the Boston Town Records, from 1770 to 1777* (Boston, 1887), 48; *Orations*, 109.

31. For the narrative revisions, see, for example, the speeches of Peter Thacher (1776), Jonathan Austin (1778), William Tudor (1779), all in *Orations*, 77, 110, 114, 117–119. The Boston Massacre orations are some of the very few Revolutionary political speeches to survive in printed form, although pulpit oratory often circulated in print. On the complementary relationship of celebrations and printed accounts, see David Waldstreicher, *In the Midst of Perpetual Fetes: The Making of American Nationalism, 1776–1820* (Chapel Hill, N.C., 1997), 10–13.

In March 1783, Dr. Thomas Welsh summed up the legacy of the Boston Massacre orations for his Boston audience, foregrounding the importance of the Massacre narrative to nation formation. The passing on of the Boston Massacre story was essential to the consolidation of an invented American tradition, Welsh suggested:

> Let the stranger hear and let the listening youth be told, — *that on the evening of the fifth of March, seventeen hundred and seventy, under the orders of a mercenary officer, murder, with her polluted weapons, stood trampling in the blood of our slaughtered countrymen.*[32]

Welsh rehearsed what had become the central narrative of the Massacre commemoration. Untroubled by the outcome of the trials that substantially exonerated Preston and his men, Welsh repeated the myths of Preston's agency and British conspiracy behind the killings. The orations sustained a coherent narrative of tyrannous and depraved British leadership, which was the narrative that Welsh urged his audience to pass on to the stranger and the listening youth.

In Welsh's speech, the Boston Massacre narrative played midwife in the birth of a nation:

> Imagination cannot well conceive what mingling passions then convulsed the soul and agonized the heart! — those pangs were sharp indeed which ushered into life, *a nation!* — like *Hercules* she rose brawny from the cradle, the snakes of *Britain* yet hung hissing round her horrible, and fell! — at her infant voice they hasted — at the dread of her rising arm they fled away.

The classical image of an Amazonian America chasing away the British with her "infant voice" and "rising arm" figured the American victory as an act of vocal power. Welsh's image of young America as a potent speaker was just one of many moments when patriots and loyalists alike portrayed the Revolution as an exertion of voice. As with Samuel Adams's eloquent gesture and authoritative speech, the powerful voice and body of young America incarnated multiple competing actions and intentions in a unified speaking figure.[33]

Colonizing the bodies of the dead and the voices of the mob, the Massacre orators performed their control over the people on the metaphoric stage of memory. Oratory and memory have long been intimately linked, both functionally and symbolically, and orations commemorating important events provide occasions for defining a community's identity through its relationship to a particular ver-

32. *Orations,* 177.

33. Ibid. Christopher Looby discusses pervasive vocal images of Revolutionary and early national identity in *Voicing America: Language, Literary Form, and the Origins of the United States* (Chicago, 1996), esp. 16–28.

sion of the past. In the American colonies, and particularly in New England, significant occasions were imbued with sacred meaning through the words of a minister. In election sermons, fast and Thanksgiving Day sermons, and funeral and execution sermons, the clergy interpreted contemporary events and individual lives for the community.[34] Organized around the spectacle of the solitary orator, the Boston Massacre celebrations adapted the sacred technologies of the pulpit to patriot political needs. In doing so, they broke with the rituals of past Boston political commemorations. The yearly Pope Day festivities of November 5 or the banquets celebrating the Stamp Act action of August 14, 1765, often included toasts and speeches, foregrounding popular action or the display of social hierarchy. As events they were more diffuse and varied than the orations. The presence of significant numbers of women in the audience at the orations also created a different dynamic than at those earlier, more masculine-oriented events. Through the orations the patriot leaders staged a new political relationship with the Boston public based upon reiteration and interpretation of a sacralized "text": the causes and consequences of the events of March 5.[35]

Delivered in churches and introduced with a prayer, the orations drew upon sacred themes and styles to evoke an aura of divine legitimacy. Martyrdom, sacrifice, bloodshed, and Redemption organized the symbolic terrain where the emerging nationalist politics of commemoration drew upon the language of Christian righteousness. In the first oration, James Lovell called forth a redemptive cosmology, urging his audience, "Make the bloody 5th of *March* the Æra of the resurrection of your birthrights." The next year Joseph Warren made oblique reference to Herod's massacre of the Innocents when he reproached "those troops, who polluted your streets with INNOCENT BLOOD." Such adaptations of sacred themes to the Revolutionary cause punctuate the orations.[36]

34. On commemoration and the invention of tradition more generally, see Eric Hobsbawm, introduction, in Hobsbawm and Terence Ranger, eds., *The Invention of Tradition* (Cambridge, 1983), esp. 6–7. Classical rhetoricians first developed the arts of memory to enable orators to remember their speeches; see Frances A. Yates, *The Art of Memory* (Chicago, 1966), 2–6. On election sermons, see Harry S. Stout, *The New England Soul: Preaching and Religious Culture in Colonial New England* (New York, 1986), 167–174.

35. On Pope Day celebrations, see Peter Shaw, *American Patriots and the Rituals of Revolution* (Cambridge, Mass., 1981); Hoerder, "Boston Leaders and Boston Crowds," in Young, ed., *The American Revolution,* 239; Loring, *The Hundred Boston Orators,* 23. On Stamp Act dinners, see Hoerder, "Boston Leaders and Boston Crowds," in Young, ed., *The American Revolution,* 245. On women attending the orations, see Alfred F. Young, "The Women of Boston: 'Persons of Consequence' in the Making of the American Revolution, 1765–76," in Harriet B. Applewhite and Darline G. Levy, eds., *Women and Politics in the Age of the Democratic Revolution* (Ann Arbor, Mich., 1990), 181–226, esp. 203.

36. *Orations,* 11, 26. Catherine L. Albanese provides the best discussion of the orations as

An oration typically began with a celebratory description of a new American society forming from isolated individuals, only to expel the British soldiers from the recently created paradise. Warren opened his 1772 oration with the observation that "man is formed for *social life*" and went on to note, "Our reason approves that wise and generous principle which actuated the first founders of civil government; an institution which hath its origin in the *weakness* of individuals, and hath for its end, the *strength and security* of all." The soldiers of a standing army violate the strength and security of civil government by introducing immorality and a reliance on "arms as the only arbiters by which every dispute is to be decided." John Hancock noted two years later that soldiers in standing armies were often "unfit to live in civil society." The soldiers' flawed sociability, manifested in their immoral and aggressive behavior, justified both their expulsion from Boston and their exclusion from town sympathies. They represented the corrupt British identity that colonial patriots rejected with increasing firmness.[37]

While criticizing the imperfect humanity of British soldiers, the orators sought to elicit the humanizing effects of sympathy toward the soldiers' victims. In the first and most restrained of the orations, James Lovell observed, "The humane, from having often thought, with pleasing rapture, on the endearing scenes of social life, in all its amiable relations, will lament, with heart-felt pangs, [the victims'] sudden dissolution, by indiscretion, rage and vengeance." Later orators amplified Lovell's quiet rhetoric of sensibility. Joseph Warren set the aggressively sentimental and sensational tone of subsequent orations in his 1775 performance:

> APPROACH we then the melancholy walk of death. Hither let me call the gay companion; here let him drop a farewel tear upon that body which so late he saw vigorous and warm with social mirth—hither let me lead the tender mother to weep over her beloved son—come widowed mourner, here satiate thy grief; behold thy murdered husband gasping on the ground, and to complete the pompous show of wretchedness, bring in each hand thy infant children to bewail their father's fate—take heed, ye orphan babes, lest, whilst your streaming eyes are fixed upon the ghastly corpse, *your feet slide on the stones bespattered with your father's brains.*

Parodying Warren's sensational address as an exercise in *"enthusiasm"* in a mock Boston Massacre oration, tory Thomas Bolton ridiculed the "true *puritanic whine*," which he found "so remarkably flat and productive of horror." Bolton imagined Warren and other leading whigs as *"sachems,* or *Indian chiefs"* rhetori-

---

sacralizing, mythic events; see *Sons of the Fathers: The Civil Religion of the American Revolution* (Philadelphia, 1976), 71–74, esp. 73.

37. *Orations,* 17, 50.

cally manipulating the people.[38] Bolton's portrayal of them as savage speakers notwithstanding, the patriot leaders found Warren's emotional rhetoric effective. Later orators frequently echoed this passage, prompting the "streams of sensibility" that the audience shed in a display of feeling at once cathartic, inflaming, and unifying. The orators evoked the unquiet shades of the victims to stimulate both sympathy and horror and thus draw clear community boundaries.[39]

The spirits of the dead proved central to the rhetoric of the orations, for they marked additional boundaries—the interfaces of past and present, of death and life—that the speakers sought to keep fresh in their audience's memory. "The baleful images of terror croud around me—and discontented ghosts, with hollow groans, appear to solemnize the anniversary of the FIFTH OF MARCH," Warren intoned in 1775. The unquiet dead haunted the perpetrators of the murders: "Do not the injured shades of Maverick, Gray, Caldwell, Attucks and Carr, attend you in your solitary walks, arrest you even in the midst of your debaucheries, and fill even your dreams with terror?" Hancock inquired. Alternatively, the specters urged patriots to action: "Yes, ye injured shades!" Jonathan Austin apostrophized in 1778; "we will still weep over you, and if any thing can be more soothing, WE WILL REVENGE YOU."[40]

Such spectral presences united Boston patriots in an effort to "see" the horrific past in their imaginations and respond to it through political and martial action. Negotiating the competing experiential and epistemological claims of absence and presence in the work of commemoration, Boston Massacre orators evoked an absence in the flesh that registered as a ghostly presence in the mind of the townspeople. Conjuring up past horrors and the absent dead like a morbid Prospero, the orator created mental images in the audience that substituted for more cor-

---

38. Ibid., 8, 64–65. The orators drew on the varied theories of sensibility that dominated British philosophy after Locke to describe the natural formation of society as a consequence of innate sociability. For a useful discussion of the varieties of sensibility in the context of revolutionary thought, see Chris Jones, *Radical Sensibility: Literature and Ideas in the 1790s* (London, 1993), esp. chap. 1; Andrew Burstein, *Sentimental Democracy: The Evolution of America's Romantic Self-Image* (New York, 1999), esp. chap. 3. For Bolton's comments, see Thomas Bolton, "An Oration," in David Potter and Gordon L. Thomas, eds., *The Colonial Idiom* (Carbondale, Ill., 1970), 301–304, esp. 301, 303.

39. Jonathan Mason, Jr. (1780), in *Orations,* 135. For other sentimental displays, see esp. the speeches of Benjamin Hichborn (1777), Mason (1780), and Thomas Dawes, Jr. (1781), all in *Orations,* 85–97, 129–144, 145–159.

The orations were related to the popular literature of horror that emerged in the second half of the eighteenth century, in which witnesses to an atrocity refused identification with the criminal, isolating him or her as a moral monster; see Karen Haltunnen, "Early American Murder Narratives: The Birth of Horror," in Richard Wightman Fox and T. J. Jackson Lears, eds., *The Power of Culture: Critical Essays in American History* (Chicago, 1993), 67–101.

40. *Orations,* 64, 48, 108.

poreal monuments. The role of matter in sustaining memory remained problematic for the heirs of the Puritans. The town meeting established the commemorative oration only after a proposed monument to the victims had temporarily come to naught.[41] No permanent monument was built for several years, but transparencies were displayed near the Massacre site on the night following the oration. These large paintings, heavily varnished and illuminated from behind, included an image of the unbuilt monument as well as soldiers firing, victims falling, and Liberty grieving. Such displays reproduced in the visual field the mental images staged through the orator's rhetoric, suggesting the cautious, reiterative use to which the descendants of the iconoclastic Puritans put physical representations — and also suggesting the subordination of such representations to verbal images.[42]

The pervasive imagery of voice that characterizes the orations further articulates the orators' thematic engagement with issues of mediation and structures of authority. Several speakers figure the Massacre itself and the subsequent commemorations as episodes in the creation of a united patriot purpose through the exercise of voice. Referring to the "enslaved" colonists, John Hancock looked forward to the day when patriotic endeavor transformed "the hoarse complaints and bitter moans of wretched slaves, into those cheerful songs, which freedom and contentment must inspire." Later orators imagined the history of the Revolution as a story to be passed on to posterity. Jonathan Austin urged fathers, "Ring in their [sons'] young ears the dreadful tale of murders, rapes, and massacres." George Minot observed that the audience's "united voices" made the oration sacred, while Thomas Welsh celebrated the orators who "by their voices declared, in strains of manly eloquence" the destructive powers of standing armies.[43]

The Bible provided the orators with striking oral images of blood crying out in a testimony against violence and in a promise of future good deriving from physical sacrifice. Joseph Warren first used the image to invoke these meanings. In the peroration of his 1772 oration, Warren employed the image of speaking

41. On changing attitudes toward the dead and death, see Terry Castle, "The Spectralization of the Other in *The Mysteries of Udolpho,*" in *The Female Thermometer: Eighteenth-Century Culture and the Invention of the Uncanny* (New York, 1995), 120–139; David E. Stannard, *The Puritan Way of Death: A Study in Religion, Culture, and Social Change* (New York, 1977), 147–161. Michael Kammen discusses American ambivalence about monuments, and their attendant slowness to construct them, in *Mystic Chords of Memory: The Transformation of Tradition in American Culture* (New York, 1991), 33.

42. For the transparencies, see Loring, *The Hundred Boston Orators,* 25, 59. Kenneth Silverman describes transparencies in *A Cultural History of the American Revolution . . .* (New York, 1987), 96. Neil Harris discusses distrust of images and the preeminence of the verbal in *The Artist in America: The Formative Years, 1790–1860* (Chicago, 1982), 2.

43. *Orations,* 55, 111, 161, 171. For tropes of storytelling, see also Mason (1780), Thomas Welsh (1783), both in *Orations,* 138, 177.

blood to link the "INNOCENT BLOOD" of the Massacre victims with the blood the Puritan fathers shed as they conquered the wilderness: "The voice of your Fathers blood cries to you from the ground . . . MY SONS, SCORN TO BE SLAVES!" Ventriloquizing the patriarch's blood through a sustained exhortation, Warren called on his auditors to protect their fathers' legacy of liberty. Four years later, Peter Thacher adapted the trope of speaking blood more directly from the Cain and Abel story while repeating Warren's celebration of an ancestral legacy that motivates patriotism. Recounting the series of open conflicts with the British that began at Lexington and Concord, Thacher described what impelled the colonists as they "sprang to arms": "We felt ourselves inspired with the spirit of our ancestors; we heard our brethren's blood crying to us for vengeance; we rushed into the midst of battle."[44] Through the trope of speaking blood, Warren and Thacher both evoked biblical sanction for their incitements to further violence and placed their audiences in a tradition that celebrated physical suffering for communal values. They also intensified the embodied quality of voice. Breath figures spirit as it moves invisibly between the outer atmosphere and the body's interior. Blood, hidden within the body's interior, is revealed to have a visible material existence when the individual's physical surface is violated and that interior is exposed. The trope of speaking blood links voice to memory and imbues it with a permanence akin to writing; it also associates voice with the scene of physical wounding when the individual body's surface is violated and collective identity takes shape around the sacrifice.

Through its evocation of ghosts, its imagery of speaking blood, and its ambivalence toward physical artifacts, the annual celebration placed the negotiation of material absence and presence at the heart of patriot commemoration. Central to this project were the wounded survivors of the Massacre who were displayed on a platform during the oration to solicit charity. They functioned as ghostly doubles of the orator, whose implicit offer of himself as a willing sacrifice to British violence intensified his physical presence. In the years before the war began, the

44. *Orations*, 26, 27, 78. The primary scriptural sources for the metaphor of speaking blood are Gen. 4:10, where the Lord upbraids Cain for slaying Abel ("What hast thou done? the voice of thy brother's blood crieth unto me from the ground"), and Paul's reworking of this moment in Heb. 12:24, where he refers to Jesus' blood of the new covenant "that speaketh better things than *that of* Abel." Abel's speaking blood made him an appropriate figure in memorial literature. For instance, John Norton entitled his biography of John Cotton *Abel Being Dead Yet Speaketh . . .* , in Cotton, *The New England Way* (London, 1658).

For readings of the sacrificial role of blood across cultures, see Rene Girard, *Violence and the Sacred*, trans. Patrick Gregory (Baltimore, 1977), 33–38; Mary Douglas, *Purity and Danger: An Analysis of Concepts of Pollution and Taboo* (London, 1966). On the belief that Christ's blood unites parts into a whole, see Piero Camporesi, *Juice of Life: The Symbolic and Magic Significance of Blood*, trans. Robert R. Barr (New York, 1995), 15–16.

annual oration provided a setting in which patriot sacrifice was not just verbally inculcated but directly acted out. Physical courage and self-command were required of the first orators. They offended the tories, the governor, and the British army, and they ran substantial risks. Angry British soldiers were often present in the audience, creating an atmosphere of latent aggression that threatened to explode into open battle. According to tradition James Lovell, the first Boston Massacre orator, responded with a grandiose flourish to his father's warning that his life would be in jeopardy if he accepted the invitation to speak: "Is that the case, father?" he is reported to have said. "Then my mind is decided, my resolution is fixed, that I will attempt it at every hazard."[45] The commemoration threatened a more literal repetition of the events of March 5 than that of mere memory. In the face of this threat, the orators provided the people not only with an interpretation of past events but also with an ideal body in the present. Exercising a Samuel Adams–like control over his body in the face of imminent threats from British soldiers, the orator incarnated the ideal patriot and projected a diverse community transfigured into a unified nation.

The orators performed the patriot hero's part, staging for their auditors the gruesome realities of wounding, suffering, and death and recuperating them in the framework of heroic martyrdom. The disabled men, in contrast, embodied the wounds of occupation borne by the town. John Hancock's oration elaborated the implications of their presence most fully. Hancock characterized the condition of Christopher Monk, an apprentice shot in the back and badly crippled, as a warning of the consequences of standing armies:

> Unhappy Monk! cut off in the gay morn of manhood, from all the joys which sweeten life, doom'd to drag on a pitiful existence, without even a hope to taste the pleasures of returning health! yet Monk, thou livest not in vain; thou livest a warning to thy country, which sympathises with thee in thy sufferings; thou livest an affecting, an alarming instance of the unbounded violence which lust of power, assisted by a standing army, can lead a traitor to commit.

"FOR us he bled, and now languishes," Hancock continued, transforming Monk from a cautionary example against standing armies into a Christlike sacrificial embodiment of the colonies. "The wounds by which he is tortur'd to a lingering death, were aimed at our country!" The spectacle of Monk's wounded state, Hancock hoped, would evoke the quasi-sacred emotion of patriotism, "which impels us to sacrifice every thing dear, even life itself, to our country." Here Hancock anticipated the wounds that further military conflict might soon mark on the

45. Loring, *The Hundred Boston Orators,* 32.

bodies of those present. He contained the potential fearful effects of that imagined wounding through the language of patriotic sacrifice.[46]

The violent doubling of male bodies functions as a sign of ritual breakdown and the need to reestablish clear cultural boundaries. The Boston Massacre commemorations focused on male bodies that mirrored one another in two discrete pairings: British soldiers opposing American patriots in life and in memory, and heroic orators transfiguring wounded massacre victims through speech. The two paired groups reflected different aspects of the symbolic process that went into constructing an American national identity. The opposition between the soldiers and the patriots used male bodies to mark the emergence of a new system of difference. A second mutation of the reigning systems of difference transformed the monarchical ideology of the king's two bodies that structured English political thought at least through Blackstone's *Commentaries* of 1765. Monarchical ideology imagined the king as both mortal individual and representative of the eternal body politic. The doubled bodies of orator and wounded man split that pairing apart in a republican modification of the relationship between the personal body and the body of the nation. In the emerging republican conception of the body politic, the heroic orator incarnates the eternal nation while the wounded victim of martial violence experiences the particularity of individual suffering occasioned by the wars that protect and enhance the state. When these two roles merge, the image of the national body condenses with peculiar force in the person of the orator-victim.[47]

A dramatic instance of this convergence occurred in 1775, when Dr. Joseph Warren delivered his second Boston Massacre oration at the Old South Church in March only to be killed at Bunker Hill two months later. Warren delivered his oration to an overflowing crowd. The pulpit stairs and pulpit area itself were filled with soldiers who threatened to attack the assembled whig leadership if Warren "said anything against the King." Warren occupied the radical wing of the patriot leadership, and in his printed oration he came closer to calling openly for a break with Great Britain than any previous speaker when he insisted that *"anarchy itself,* that bugbear held up by the tools of power . . . is infinitely less danger-

46. *Orations,* 48–49.

47. Girard, *Violence and the Sacred,* 68–88; Ernst H. Kantorowicz, *The King's Two Bodies: A Study in Mediaeval Political Theology* (1957; Princeton, N.J., 1981), 3–6. For an interpretation of the significance of war and self-sacrifice to American liberalism, see Steven Watts, *The Republic Reborn: War and the Making of Liberal America, 1790–1820* (Baltimore, 1987). In his great novel on the problem of union, Melville explored a similar set of thematic issues through the mutilated figure of Ahab; see Sharon Cameron's discussion in *The Corporeal Self: Allegories of the Body in Melville and Hawthorne* (Baltimore, 1981), 28–29.

ous to mankind than *arbitrary government.*" The assertiveness of his speech was set in counterpoint to his bodily restraint. Clad in a toga, he stood in a "Demosthenian posture, with a white handkerchief in his right hand" and "began and ended without action." A patriot witness reported the tense moment when a captain seated on the pulpit stairs "held up one of his hands in view of Warren, with several pistol bullets on the open palm, and, with a vehement and fierce exclamation, endeavored to alarm the audience with the cry of fire." As on the night of the Massacre, when shouts and orders echoed one another creating pervasive indeterminacy, "fire" proved a remarkably volatile syllable. A loyalist observer offered a competing account of this moment, focusing on the interpretative ambiguities of language. Not "fire," but "O fie, fie!" was the cry of the soldiers, this author insisted. It was a cry of reproach against Warren's radicalism that the assembled citizens misinterpreted as a threat against themselves.[48]

Warren's response to the British captain's threatening gesture proved crucial to the performance. "Warren observed the action" of holding up the bullets "and, without discontinuing his discourse, dropped a white handkerchief upon the officer's hand" to cover them. His understated gesture dispersed potential violence through rhetorical action, just as Samuel Adams's outstretched arm averted battle in John Adams's memory. The orator's ability to react immediately, manifesting his self-possession in both mind and body, prevented physical conflict. The political-leader-as-orator commanded others through his display of self-command.[49] Warren's decision to perform without action—or with the barest hint of action when he dropped the handkerchief over the bullets—places him in the self-effacing performance tradition of Jonathan Edwards's pulpit oratory and Patrick Henry's patriot eloquence. Just as Edwards rigidly controlled his bodily motions to produce the purest spiritual response, so Henry and Warren, limiting their movements in a crowded building, focused the audience's attention on their radical message. The atmosphere of violence in the Old South Church altered the performance dynamic in important ways, however. Warren staged a spectacle of bodily integrity threatened with violation, more literally performing Henry's plea for liberty or death. Fatally shot at Bunker Hill just weeks later, Warren's body became the object of intensive communal interpretation that fulfilled the implications of this moment.

48. *Orations*, 58–59. In existing accounts, the violence that the officers planned is described variously as seizure and murder. Herbert S. Allan reports the different versions of the story in *John Hancock: Patriot in Purple* (New York, 1948), 167–168. Allan quotes Hutchinson's diary record of the condition upon which the soldiers were to act.

49. Loring, *The Hundred Boston Orators*, 60. On the orator's display of self-control, see Jay Fliegelman, *Declaring Independence: Jefferson, Natural Language, and the Culture of Performance* (Stanford, Calif., 1993), 103–107.

FIGURE 12. The Death of General Warren at the Battle of Bunker's Hill, 17 June 1775. *By John Trumbull. 1786. Courtesy, Yale University Art Gallery, Trumbull Collection*

On the Massacre anniversary following Warren's death, Peter Thacher invoked the image of speaking blood when he identified Warren as the first and foremost hero and martyr among the patriot dead whose memory provoked "sensations of indignant wrath" in the breast of the patriot soldier. That soldier, Thacher continued, "will listen to the voice of their blood, which cries aloud to heaven, and to him for vengeance" and "sacrifice whole hecatombs of their murderers to their illustrious *manes.*" The British had buried Warren's body in an unmarked and undistinguished grave, and when Thacher spoke, the fate of Warren's corpse had become something of a cause célèbre. There was public outrage that British soldiers had proposed to cut off his head, and discomfort with the undistinguished site of Warren's burial. Seeing an opportunity to strengthen the patriot cause through the ritual means used so successfully with the funerals of the Massacre victims, whig leaders arranged to have Warren's corpse identified and reinterred with full Masonic pomp in King's Chapel on March 8, 1776. In his sermon on this occasion, Perez Morton addressed Warren's remains: "ILLUSTRIOUS RELICKS! What tidings from the grave?" he began. "Art thou risen again to exhibit thy glorious wounds, and thro' them proclaim salvation to thy country!" Morton's Christic imagery makes Warren's wounds into mouths proclaiming political redemption. His eulogy reveals with special clarity how elite leaders reembodied the voices of the "mob" as an expression of a unified nation. In contrast to John Adams's savage

Attucks whose union of words and blows set him outside the Boston patriot community, Morton's Warren represented the patriot union of speech and violence. In contrast to Hancock's Christlike Monk who merely suffered for his country, Morton's Warren actively redeemed it. The hierarchical meanings invested in male bodies are recorded in Morton's apology to Warren's corpse: "Though thy body has long laid undistinguished among the vulgar dead, scarce privileged with earth enough to hide it from the birds of prey. . . . thy memory has been embalmed in the affections of thy grateful countrymen; who, in their breast, have raised eternal monuments to thy bravery!" The anxiety that attended the fate of Warren's body suggests the ritual significance of elite bodies as incarnations of the body politic.[50]

Warren's death in 1775 made him one of the first figures in an emerging national symbolic and helped to translate a local idiom of martyrdom into a national political language.[51] That translation had begun the previous year, when the Continental Congress assembled to attempt a collective colonial response to British occupation of Boston. Urging restraint on patriot leaders in the besieged city, the delegates warned that if hostilities broke out Boston would become a figurative wound on the body politic. "They dread the Thoughts of an Action because, it would make a Wound which could never be healed," John Adams explained to Bostonians eager to take offensive measures. George Washington echoed Adams's image of the unsuturable wound in a letter to a British lieutenant expressing fear that the ministry would press their measures to the point of open conflict and bloodshed in Massachusetts. Such actions would create "a vital wound" in "the peace of this great Country, as time itself cannot cure or eradicate the remembrance of," he warned. The rhetoric of bodily violation that circulated among the delegates entered the official record when, on October 7, Congress as a whole stated officially in a resolution that the city of Boston and province of Massachusetts "are considered by all America, as suffering in the common cause."[52] The

---

50. *Orations*, 81. Perez Morton's oration on this occasion is printed with the Massacre orations in *Orations*, 187–200, esp. 187. On the outraged response to the treatment of Warren's corpse, see Shipton, *Sibley's Harvard Graduates*, XIV (Boston, 1968), 526.

51. In 1776, Congress named their largest ship after him and in 1777 voted to establish a monument to him. Ship: Rhode Island Delegates to Nicholas Cooke, June 21, 1776, in Paul H. Smith, ed., *Letters of Delegates to Congress, 1774–1789* (Washington, 1976–), IV, 287. Monument: Worthington Chauncey Ford, ed., *Journals of the Continental Congress, 1774–1789*, I (Washington, D.C., 1904), 242–243.

Lauren Berlant develops the idea of a National Symbolic in *The Anatomy of National Fantasy: Hawthorne, Utopia, and Everyday Life* (Chicago, 1991), 5.

52. Adams to William Tudor, Oct. 7, 1774, in Smith, ed., *Letters of Delegates to Congress*, I, 157; Ford, ed., *Journals of the Continental Congress*, I, 57. In draft letters to Gage composed at this time, both John Adams and Samuel Adams warned that violence between the inhabitants of Massachusetts and the British army would produce "A Wound which could never be healed!"

language of suffering, wounding, and martyrdom, voiced by the delegates from Massachusetts, echoed by delegates from other colonies, and transcribed in the congressional record, proved the tool for forging a united resistance to British authority. The spectacle of besieged and suffering Boston came to occupy the role in the colonial Imaginary that the display of the Boston Massacre victims and their unhealable wounds played in that city's annual commemoration ceremonies: as unifying objects of patriot sensibility. Articulated in the terms of the Boston Massacre orators, a chain of identifications began with the wounded male body and moved through the suffering city to the not-yet-incarnate nation.[53]

(Smith, ed., *Letters of Delegates to Congress,* I, 158, 160). Washington's similar phrasing occurs in a letter to Robert Mackenzie, a lieutenant in one of the British regiments stationed at Boston; see 166–167

53. This relationship appears with great clarity in John Burk's play *Bunker-Hill; or, The Death of General Warren: An Historic Tragedy in Five Acts* (1797; New York, 1970). A concluding pageant staged around Warren's bier includes, among a number of standards, one with the phrase, "Boston, Parent of the Revolution."

6 Forms of State

I. DOCUMENTS AND DEBATES

In the contemporary United States, the Declaration of Independence and the Constitution have achieved a symbolic clarity and stability that they did not have for the generation that implemented the new government. Now figured as secular Scripture, these foundational texts promise an immutable, if ever-elusive, source of national meaning. Yet the Declaration and the Constitution achieved their current status gradually and in competition with other modes of national embodiment. During the years of national founding, alternative forms of national identity associated with the power of voice fulfilled or challenged the plenitude of constitutional meaning.[1] Americans continued to develop the performance semiotic of speech and text that earlier represented competing hierarchies of authenticity and power during the Great Awakening, in diplomatic and missionary interactions with native Americans and African Americans, and as a feature of the political strife with Great Britain. Where the relationship between textual and spoken expression was complementary, political speech both completed and transformed the founding documents. As always, where the relationship involved challenge or attempted displacement, proponents of the spoken word set living speech against the text's dead letter while opponents identified voice, often figured as demonic or Babel-like, as disrupting the text's full and stable meaning. Employing these symbolic meanings of foundational documents and the representative power of voice, political orators in the post-Revolutionary period recast the performance

1. Christopher Looby observes that "the spoken word in America retained (and perhaps even amplified) its charismatic authority even after the making of the written Constitution." He goes on to note, "Despite recent arguments that the legitimacy of constitutional authority was intimately dependent upon the *textuality* of that instrument (which is true enough), the widespread cultural investment of authority in vocal forms like political oration and sermons created a counterpoint of anxiety about the sufficiency of textuality as a ground of authority, and inspired a widespread enchantment with vocal forms as necessary supplements to if not alternative grounds for authority." See *Voicing America: Language, Literary Form, and the Origins of the United States* (Chicago, 1996), 43–44.

semiotic of speech and text in ways that contributed to the shape and meaning of new governing institutions.

"Who shall write the history of the American revolution? Who can write it? Who will ever be able to write it?" The anxious tone of John Adams's questions to Thomas Jefferson in 1815 was prompted by the publication of Carlo Botta's *Storia della guerra americana*. Adams admired Botta's history of the Revolution but ultimately found it inadequate. For Adams, the absence of crucial records rendered the task of writing an authentic history of the American Revolution impossible. "The most essential documents, the debates and deliberations in Congress from 1774 to 1783 were all in secret, and are now lost forever," he lamented. Following the precedent of classical historians, Botta filled this absence with speeches that he invented for his heroes. His efforts included an oration attributed to Richard Henry Lee in support of the Declaration of Independence that Adams dismissed as "a splendid morcell of oratory." The inauthenticity of Botta's fictive orations provoked Adams's anxiety over national memory, not least because Adams regretted the loss of his own great impromptu effort on behalf of independence. Since the Continental Congress debated secretly and kept only limited records to foster the public image of unanimity among the delegates, the actual orations were lost to posterity. Adams noted that, with the possible exceptions of Pennsylvania Farmer John Dickinson and Princeton president John Witherspoon, "the Orators, while I was in Congress from 1774 to 1778 appeared to me very universally extemporaneous, and I have never heard of any committed to writing before or after delivery." The extemporaneous performance of the speeches and the secrecy of congressional proceedings created a peculiar difficulty for those such as Adams who viewed debate and deliberation as the essence of political action. Without the written traces of these speeches, Adams insisted, the true spirit of the Revolution could never be captured. Jefferson agreed. Only the "external facts" of the Revolution could be recorded. "All it's councils, designs and discussions, having been conducted by Congress with closed doors, and no member, as far as I know, having even made notes of them," Jefferson replied, "these, which are the life and soul of history must for ever be unknown." The interior of the Revolution, the evanescent speech that Jefferson figured as its life and soul, was forever lost, leaving behind only its dead body to molder in the pages of the history books.[2]

2. Adams to Jefferson and Thomas McKean, Jul. 30, 1815, Jefferson to Adams, Aug. 10[-11], 1815, in Lester J. Cappon, ed., *The Adams-Jefferson Letters: The Complete Correspondence between Thomas Jefferson and Abigail and John Adams* (1959; Chapel Hill, N.C., 1988), 451–452. Hannah Arendt shared Adams's fascination with these novel modes of publicity, finding the value of revolutionary action in "the speech-making and decision-taking, the oratory and the business, the thinking and the persuading, and the actual doing." Arendt based her interpretation to a significant extent on the writings of Adams, for instance when she quotes Adams on the delights of

But text could also capture the essence of the Revolution. Many of Jefferson's contemporaries were surprised, perhaps none more so than Adams, at the preeminent place that the Declaration of Independence eventually came to occupy in the political culture of the new republic. Fetishizing the text qua text, Americans divorced the document from its origins in congressional deliberation. John Trumbull's painting of the moment when the Declaration was signed provides an important instance of the fetishizing impulse. The Declaration looms large in Jefferson's autobiography as well, its prominence there mirroring the preeminence granted the framing and signing of the document in Revolutionary mythology.[3] But in contrast with Trumbull's painting, which isolates the document itself as the center of congressional attention and activity, the full set of notes that Jefferson included in his autobiography sets the Declaration within the deliberative process. Printed with underlinings and marginal emendations, the text of the Declaration suggests the integrity of his original text but also reveals its transformation through collaborative editing. Although Jefferson later described these revisions as "mutilations" of his carefully composed document, he recognized that the alterations were the product of a valuable exchange. The debate reports sandwiching the Declaration foreground this collaborative creation and capture fragments of the extempore speeches surrounding the document's acceptance.[4]

Adams defended the cause of independence in an extemporaneous rejoinder to Declaration opponent John Dickinson that led Jefferson to identify Adams as the Declaration's "ablest advocate and defender." The unrecorded speech gained

---

Revolutionary participation: "It is action, not rest, that constitutes our pleasure" *(On Revolution* [New York, 1963], 33–44).

3. Jay Fliegelman, *Declaring Independence: Jefferson, Natural Language, and the Culture of Performance* (Stanford, Calif., 1993), 21; Larzer Ziff, *Writing in the New Nation: Prose, Print, and Politics in the Early United States* (New Haven, Conn., 1991), 113–116; Michael Warner, *Letters of the Republic: Publication and the Public Sphere in Eighteenth-Century America* (Cambridge, Mass., 1990), 104–106; Jacques Derrida, "Declarations of Independence," *New Political Science*, XV (1986), 7–17. For a useful reading of the Declaration, see also Garry Wills, *Inventing America: Jefferson's Declaration of Independence* (New York, 1978). Jefferson's notes on the Declaration in his autobiography make a disproportionate bulge in his otherwise chronologically balanced narrative; see Julian P. Boyd, ed., *The Papers of Thomas Jefferson*, I (Princeton, N.J., 1950), 299–301.

4. On "mutilations," see Fliegelman, *Declaring Independence*, 5. The tension that numerous critics have identified between Jefferson the creative literary genius, who produced the elegant periodic sentences of the Declaration, and Jefferson the copyist, who synthesized various sources into a whole that was then revised, originates in the text's collaborative creation as recorded in Jefferson's notes. On the clash between classical synthesis and Romantic originality in critiques of Jefferson, see Fliegelman, *Declaring Independence*, 164–178; Ziff, *Writing in the New Nation*, 115; Pauline Maier, *American Scripture: Making the Declaration of Independence* (New York, 1997), chap. 3.

FIGURE 13. The Congress Voting Independence. *By Robert Edge Pine and/or Edward Savage. Unlike Trumbull, Pine and Savage depict the Declaration emerging in the context of congressional debate. Permission of the Historical Society of Pennsylvania*

a reputation as Adams's greatest oration. Adams himself regretted the ephemerality of his rhetorical achievement, noting that it was one of only a very few of his speeches he had given that he wished had been "literally preserved." Jefferson described the speech in terms that elevate its power to move the audience over its artfulness. "He was not graceful nor elegant, nor remarkably fluent but he came out occasionally with a power of thought and expression, that moved us from our seats." [3]

Adams's awkward but impassioned speech presented a striking contrast with the preceding speech by Dickinson. Adams observed that Dickinson "had prepared himself apparently with great Labour and ardent Zeal" to bear his testimony against independence with "formality." Dickinson had in fact written and revised the beginning and end of this important speech, while the middle section consisted of fragmentary notes from which he improvised in an effort to manifest his grasp of the issues and his sincerity. Despite such efforts at spontaneity, Adams's emphasis on the "formality" of Dickinson's speech, a term weighted with the evangelical critique of formal religion, suggests its overall effect.[6]

5. Peter Shaw, *The Character of John Adams* (Chapel Hill, N.C., 1976), 98.

6. L. H. Butterfield, ed., *Diary and Autobiography of John Adams,* 4 vols. (Cambridge, Mass.,

Called on to answer Dickinson's address, Adams made the most of the contrast between prepared speech and impromptu performance. His display of hesitance and lack of grace and fluency reveal Adams's particular grasp of the importance of performance style. The performance semiotic of speech and text involved strategic, contextual choices about the use or rejection of text. At the Boston Massacre trial, Adams violated his habitual practice of impromptu delivery, reading from law books to establish a contrast between his text-based arguments, which were saturated with the stability of written discourse, and the volatility and violence of mob speech. Speaking on behalf of the Declaration before Congress, Adams employed his improvisational talents to effect in an arena where his eloquent words could not be confused with the harangues of the Boston town meeting, much less the impassioned shouts of Crispus Attucks and his companions. His awkwardness and spontaneity conveyed the authenticity of his expression in response to Dickinson's polished performance. Years later, Adams recollected this very difference between the two orations. "I began by saying . . . that I had confidence enough in the plain Understanding and common Sense that had been given me, to believe that I could answer" Dickinson's arguments "notwithstanding the Abilities which had been displayed and the Eloquence with which they had been enforced." Alluding to Thomas Paine's famous pamphlet, Adams set the display of abilities and eloquence against "plain Understanding and common Sense" to distinguish his natural performance from Dickinson's artfulness.[7]

Outside the walls of Congress, the speech of the "mob" or the "demagogue" continued to represent a potential threat to the emerging order. Connecticut Wits David Humphreys, Joel Barlow, John Trumbull, and Lemuel Hopkins elaborated the figure of the corrupt politician and demagogue in their collaborative poem *The Anarchiad* (1786–1787). Written in response to Shays's Rebellion and designed to encourage the adoption of a stronger national government, *The Anarchiad* was published serially as nonsequential fragments of an ancient work whose damaged manuscript had been recently recovered from an Indian burial mound. Portraying persistent fears of "savage" speech, the poem uses mock-heroic language to describe the efforts of Anarch to rule native America. One fragment presents the local politician Wronghead celebrating his own demagoguery. Describing himself as "busied, daily, planning pop'lar schemes, / And nightly rapt in demo-

---

1961), III, 396. Dickinson's compositional approach is described and his speech reproduced from his notes in J. H. Powell, ed., "Speech of John Dickinson Opposing the Declaration of Independence, 1 July, 1776," *PMHB*, LXV (1941), 458–481. For an analysis of sermon composition that links the use of text fragments to evangelicalism and Revolution in the eighteenth-century New England pulpit, see Donald Weber, *Rhetoric and History in Revolutionary New England* (Oxford, 1988), esp. 11–13.

7. Butterfield, ed. *Diary and Autobiography of John Adams*, III, 397.

cratic dreams," Wronghead reveres "fair discord as a goddess." He rails "at Congress, Courts, and legal powers," declaims against "trade, great men and lawyers' fees" to please "vulgar ears," and deploys *"cant pretense of Liberty"* to great effect. The Wits' portrait of Wronghead incorporates the standard characteristics of the demagogue: the attack on authority, the language of liberty, the leveling impulse. Emptied of political substance, the demagogue's rhetoric appears as a self-interested attack on all social order and the restraints it imposes.[8]

When the Wits and other Shaysite opponents sought to discredit the figure of popular voice, they ran counter to the Revolution's most robust rhetorical legacy. Shaysite rhetoric resounded with themes and images that had mobilized colonial resistance to the British only a decade earlier. The language of localism, of immediacy and presence that the protesters embraced was the language that Otis had refined in the 1760s. Even the resistance to the disruptive textuality of writs remained the same: on one occasion, a sheriff trying to serve a writ was forced to eat it, consuming the words of a distant authority.[9] When they presented their proposals for reform to their social superiors, however, the leaders of the resistance turned not to the images and practices of popular voice but to the written petition. Anxieties of form governed their choice of medium. The petition introduced a degree of mediation in acts of political protest directed against the authority of their social superiors.

Led by Captain Wheeler, an armed contingent that attempted to shut down the Worcester Court faced the local judge named Ward in September 1786. The confrontation suggests the social regimes of language governing the Shaysites' preference for petitions in conveying their grievances. On this occasion, Judge Ward followed the sheriff into the midst of the armed protesters while they pressed their bayonets at him. Ward's act was designed to impress the crowd with his courage. Turning to Captain Wheeler, the judge "asked who commanded these people; and on Wheeler's not answering, he repeated it again; at last Wheeler answered, but did not own the command." Wheeler's silence stood in stark relief against the judge's verbal boldness and confident presentation of self in a threatening setting. Like the patriot orator represented by Joseph Warren, Judge Ward united physical courage and rhetorical power with social authority. Ward sought to enforce his

8. David Humphreys et al., *The Anarchiad: A New England Poem* (1861), ed. Luther G. Riggs (Gainesville, Fla., 1967), 29–30.

9. See David P. Szatmary, *Shays' Rebellion: The Making of an Agrarian Insurrection* (Amherst, Mass., 1980), 124–125. On hostility to writs and their agents during Shays's Rebellion, see also Alan Taylor, "Regulators and White Indians: The Agrarian Resistance in Post-Revolutionary New England," in Robert A. Gross, ed., *In Debt to Shays: The Bicentennial of an Agrarian Rebellion*, in *Publications of the Colonial Society of Massachusetts*, LXV (Charlottesville, Va., 1993), 145–146.

authority through oral eloquence, announcing that he would "speak to the grievances they complained of, in their paper they sent to the Court." The protesters
asked him to reduce his comments to writing, but Ward refused, asserting instead
that, "if they would take away their bayonets, and let him stand on some emi-
nence, where he might be seen and heard by all the people, he would speak, and
not otherwise." [10]

The judge succeeded in attaining a position on the courthouse steps, where
he addressed the assembled forces for close to two hours, during which time he
"answered all the reports he had heard, and proved the fallacy of them." He refused to answer questions from the audience unless the speaker would give his
name, denying anonymity to the assembled men and enforcing conditions of face-
to-face address. Concluding his long speech, Ward demonstrated his understanding of the power of an authoritative performance when he turned to Wheeler and
"told him that he had better take his men away; that they were waging war, which
was treason; and that the consequence would be (here he made a short pause, and
then added in a strong voice) the Gallows." Ward labored to transform the protest
into a scene of deference to authority through the power of his spoken word,
but his efforts did not succeed. The next day, after requesting to see the court's
proposal in writing, the Shaysites refused the compromise and made further demands that closed the courts completely. Unable to match Ward's performance
of authority, the protesters sought repeatedly to textualize the exchange. Written
negotiation created a distance between themselves and Ward that allowed them to
consider the court's proposals in a social space quarantined from the aura of the
judge's personal authority. Captain Wheeler fell silent in Judge Ward's presence,
but text permitted assertive expression that transgressed status lines. Ultimately,
however, the protesters' inability to talk back to their social superiors revealed to
them the insecurity of their position and contributed to their defeat when confronted with government forces.[11]

As this episode suggests, the political challenge for those white male citizens
whom Massachusetts Ratifying Convention representative Amos Singletary described as "us poor illiterate people" was not actual literacy, which was widespread.[12] Rather, it was the creation of institutions and rhetorical strategies for
legitimating popular political speech, a process that could take place only as popu-

10. This incident is reported in the *Hampshire Gazette* (Northampton, Mass.) for Sept. 27,
1786.

11. Ibid. Bob Gross generously shared his Shays materials with me. On the increasing assertiveness of petition language and the connection between petitions and "a tentative but discern-
ible lower-class ideology" in the Revolutionary era, see Ruth Bogin, "Petitioning and the New
Moral Economy of Post-Revolutionary America," *WMQ*, 3d Ser., XLV (1988), 391–425.

12. Bernard Bailyn, ed., *The Debate on the Constitution* (New York, 1993), part 1, 906.

lar orators succeeded in separating their performances from their historical associations with uncontrolled passions and crowd actions. These difficulties were evident in the constitutional ratification conventions, which were designed to create a space outside existing forms of government where a simulacrum of "the people" could materialize. The framers never proposed direct popular participation in these debates but called instead for specially elected representatives. Though participation was restricted, the state conventions were open to the public, and substantial numbers of people attended them. The representational nature of the proceedings split "the people." They became both performers of and witnesses to their own act of creation. The state conventions assembled in a courthouse, church gallery, or theater, where the audience performed synecdochically the role of the large, vague, dispersed body that the delegates also stood for, creating an oddly doubled effect of popular presence. The ratification conventions provided each state with the occasion for placing electoral representation in what Federalist leaders hoped would be the service of national power. The imaginary body of "the people" materialized in thirteen discrete scenes of oratorical performance. The material form of that body was negotiated through the imagery and performance of voice and text. Delegates disputed the social and political significance of stability and flexibility, passion and reason, permanence and transience, and popular will and fundamental law, through the symbolism of verbal form.

Oral and textual modes provided a complex set of meanings through which the new republic defined the nature of mediation intrinsic to representational government. Participants on both sides revealed their sophisticated grasp of the meanings attached to linguistic form. Ancient images of oral powers with the potential to nurture or to destroy structured many arguments about the Constitution.[13] Central aspects of the ratification debates revolved around the meanings articulated through images and practices of oral potency, linked to bodily metaphors of pregnancy and ingestion. An Antifederalist commonplace warned that the national government would "swallow up" the states. The Constitution's supporters responded with celebrations of a national government that leading Pennsylvania Federalist James Wilson described as "a new body, capable of being encreased by the addition of other members;—an expanding quality peculiarly fitted to the circumstances of America." When coupled with images of dismemberment that in Wilson's speech explicitly echoed Revolutionary fears that the

13. These symbolic linkages between speech and oral consumption could be turned many ways. Similar patterns of oral imagery identifying oratorical skill with voracious, and often cannibalistically vicious, appetite marked white discourse about American Indians and later became identified with the West; see Michael Paul Rogin, *Fathers and Children: Andrew Jackson and the Subjugation of the American Indian* (New York, 1975), 114–124; Anne Norton, *Alternative Americas: A Reading of Antebellum Political Culture* (Chicago, 1986), chap. 7.

colonies must "UNITE OR DIE," Federalist figures of dilation worked to create the sense that the national body must be either magnified or ripped apart. Antifederalists figured the states as self-contained entities, in danger of losing their distinct existences in the formation of a larger whole.[14]

The prevalence of oral imagery in the constitutional debates reflects the common belief that the success of the government depended on an unwritten ethic of virtuous citizenship at least as much as the establishment of written rules. Virtuous speech and action would necessarily supplement the text of the Constitution. The classical republican preoccupation with virtue interpolated moral requirements into a document whose fundamental amorality arose from its institutional and procedural emphasis. Expressing a widespread understanding of the new government, the Reverend Samuel Miller of New York insisted that the basis of political legitimacy resides "not in the words and letters of the *Constitution;* but in the temper, the habits, and the practices of the people."[15]

While the virtue of the people as a whole preoccupied cultural guardians, many viewed that virtue less as an end in itself than as a means to produce virtuous elected representatives who would embody the national meaning encoded in the Constitution. Delegates to the constitutional conventions debated the identity of the genuine people and the appropriate forms for conveying their real sentiments. The Federalists insisted that popularly elected representatives would always reflect the authentic popular will. Antifederalists were less confident. Amos Singletary looked to the day when those who held congressional power possessed money and learning that distanced them socially from ordinary citizens as fully as the British Parliament had been geographically distant from the American colonies. Differences in language marked that social distance. Singletary warned his fellow delegates,

> These lawyers, and men of learning, and monied men, that talk so finely and gloss over matters so smoothly, to make us poor illiterate people swallow down the pill, expect to get into Congress themselves; they expect to be the managers of this Constitution and get all the power and all the money into their own

14. James Wilson, "Opening Address," in Bailyn, ed., *Debate on the Constitution,* part 1, 791–803, esp. 793, 798. In 1786, the New England states began making plans to form a union for trade protection against Great Britain, which they hoped would include Pennsylvania. The potential for such regional associations fueled concerns over dismemberment; see Charles Page Smith, *James Wilson: Founding Father, 1742–1798* (Chapel Hill, N.C., 1956), 216–217. Isaac Kramnick discusses the different Federalist and Antifederalist attitudes toward national expansion in "The 'Great National Discussion': The Discourse of Politics in 1787," *WMQ,* 3d Ser., XLV (1988), 3–32, esp. 9–10.

15. Michael Lienesch, *New Order of the Ages: Time, the Constitution, and the Making of Modern American Political Thought* (Princeton, N.J., 1988), 163–164.

hands, and then they will swallow up all us little folks, like the great *Leviathan,* Mr. President, yes, just as the whale swallowed up *Jonah.*[16]

Singletary's metaphors of orality linked elite eloquence both to force-feeding ("swallow down") and to greedy incorporation ("swallow up"). Recognizing the hegemonic potential of oratory, he sought to unmask Federalist pretensions to the high ground of disinterested, rational debate. In Singletary's view, the learned, polished performances of the Federalist orators at the Massachusetts Ratifying Convention revealed their hunger for power and their urge to dominate their social inferiors, not their superior ability to govern. In an assembly resounding with high oratory, Singletary pressed his warning against elite speech. Worried about the fate of the Constitution in their critical state, Massachusetts Federalists "mobilized all the rhetorical talent available" to achieve success. Yet that high oratory proved alienating rather than persuasive to the many delegates who viewed such displays as suspect efforts to intimidate and dominate social inferiors.[17]

First among the rhetorical talent, whose ability to "talk so finely and gloss over matters so smoothly" Singletary rightly feared, was Fisher Ames, the rising Federalist orator who achieved national celebrity with his congressional eloquence in the 1790s. Ames shared his opponents' valuation of language as a crucial element in the debates over the Constitution.[18] But Ames portrayed the rhetorical dangers facing the new nation in terms that differed strikingly from Singletary's fears of verbal dissimulation. Ames feared, not the artful deceptions of fine talk or technical phrasing, but the perils of speech whose immediacy and evanescence threatened to dissolve society into incoherence. Early in the convention, Ames addressed those dangers in an oration defending the concept of representation underlying the Constitution's electoral process. Antifederalists objected to the less frequent, and therefore less popular and direct, federal elections called for in the founding document, where biennial elections to the House of Representatives substituted for the annual elections common to many state legislatures and the Continental Congress. Ames characterized his opponents' view of representation as "but an image, a copy, fainter and more imperfect than the original, the people." Annual elections were necessary to sustain the accuracy of such an image. Ames argued instead that the people achieve true sovereignty only through their elected representatives. "The representation of the people is something more than

16. Bailyn, ed., *Debate on the Constitution,* part 1, 906.

17. Ibid., 889 n. 1, 1190. See also Michael Allen Gillespie's discussion in "Massachusetts: Creating Consensus," in Gillespie and Michael Lienesch, eds., *Ratifying the Constitution* (Lawrence, Kans., 1989), 138–167, esp. 147–148.

18. See Thomas Gustafson, *Representative Words: Politics, Literature, and the American Language, 1776–1865* (Cambridge, 1992), chap. 8, on this theme in the constitutional debates.

the people," he insisted. Annual elections introduced volatility to government and created a blurred and shifting portrait of the popular will. A more stable representation would permit a magnified and enhanced image of the popular will to manifest itself in the legislative actions of elected officials.[19]

For Ames, this magnification required the passage of time both to permit the representative's acquisition of "a just knowledge of the true interests of the union" and to encourage the temporal mediation of popular desire. "A democracy is a volcano, which conceals the fiery materials of its own destruction," he famously warned, expressing classical republican distrust of pure democracy as an unstable and therefore fatally flawed system. Yet he remained confident that "the people always mean right, and if time is allowed for reflection and information, they will do right." Not "the first wish, the momentary impulse of the publick mind," but rather "the sober, second thought of the people shall be law." Against "the loud clamours of passion, artifice and faction," Ames set the "due deliberation" of independent representatives who need not fear immediate loss of office.[20]

The deliberations of representatives projected an accurate magnified image of the people. That expanded image, in turn, produced a literal enlargement of population. Ames articulated his nationalist vision of future magnitude in a language of nurturance that contrasts strikingly with Singletary's image of force-feeding. "The time I hope, will come," he prophesied, "when this excellent country will furnish food, and freedom, (which is better than food, which is the food of the soul) for fifty millions of happy people." While Singletary invoked cannibalistic metaphors of ingestion, Ames figured the federal government as a source of physical and spiritual sustenance for a swelling national body. The dilation of the time that the national legislature spent deliberating laws mirrored the temporal dilation necessary for physical reproduction. Ames identified congressional debate with national expansion through the unarticulated feminine figure of pregnancy and parturition.[21]

Similar images of expansion saturated Federalist discourse. In a famous discussion of representation in *Federalist No. 10* that probably influenced Ames, James Madison distinguished between a pure democracy, where citizens participate directly in governance, and a republic based on representation, whose effect is "to refine and enlarge the public views, by passing them through the medium of a chosen body of citizens, whose wisdom may best discern the true interest of their

19. Ames's speech is reprinted in Bailyn, ed., *Debate on the Constitution,* part 1, 891–895, esp. 892.

20. Ibid., 894–895.

21. Ibid., 894. Shirley Samuels discusses the symbolic importance of female bodies in early republican discourse and iconography in *Romances of the Republic: Women, the Family, and Violence in the Literature of the Early American Nation* (New York, 1996), chap. 1.

country, and whose patriotism and love of justice will be least likely to sacrifice it to temporary or partial considerations." Such amplification of the "public voice, pronounced by the representatives," whom Madison described as "the most diffusive and established characters," corresponded in Madison's vision to the amplification of the body of the nation. The second advantage of republicanism over democracy, Madison argued, was that representation permitted the extension of a republic over a "greater number of citizens and extent of territory" than the less spacious terrain to which Montesquieu limited republican governments. Against the pregnant image of an American federal republic, Madison and the Federalists repeatedly set the dangers of dismemberment into multiple, competing nations should the Constitution fail.[22]

Such physical images lent themselves to dramatic performances that placed the orator's body at the juncture of local and national bodies. In one of the Federal Convention's most famous moments, Virginia's George Mason forcefully conveyed his opposition to the Constitution when he announced that "he would sooner chop off his right hand than put it to the Constitution as it now stands." Mason presented self-mutilation as preferable to signing a document he believed would harm his constituents, linking the amputation of his hand to the action of signing against his conscience. Edmund Randolph echoed and revised Mason's assertion at the Virginia Ratifying Convention: "The Union is the anchor of our political salvation," he insisted, "and I will assent to the lopping of this limb (meaning his arm) before I assent to the dissolution of the Union."[23] For both Mason and Randolph, the orator referred to his body in a powerfully concrete fashion to symbolize the relationship between different levels of abstract political being, the states and the nation. Just as the Boston Massacre orators staged their willingness to incarnate the consequences of political action, so these Virginia leaders offered themselves as referents for the physical imagery of nation making.

Complex figures of voice and body were matched by elaborate symbolisms of text in the constitutional debates. Federalists imagined the Constitution as a textual medium that would filter and clarify the popular voice until it spoke in the pure idiom of the public good. Attentive to the danger of making "the Constitution like Religious Creeds, embarrassing to those bound to conform to them and more likely to produce dissatisfaction and scism, than harmony and union," the Philadelphia delegates framed a document that sought to blend stability with

22. *Federalist No. 10*, in Alexander Hamilton et al., eds., *The Federalist: A Commentary on the Constitution of the United States* (New York, n.d.), 59, 60, esp. 59, 60. Kramnick describes competing conceptions of representation in "The 'Great National Discussion': The Discourse of Politics in 1787," *WMQ*, 3d Ser, XLV (1988), 11–15.

23. Adrienne Koch, ed., *Notes of Debates in the Federal Convention of 1787 Reported by James Madison* (New York, 1987), 566; Bailyn, ed., *Debate on the Constitution*, part 2, 600.

flexibility through a mixture of express measures and strategic silences. But Antifederalists saw certain of the document's silences as evidence of tyrannous intent and sought in particular a complete textualization of individual rights. Benjamin Rush tried to calm Pennsylvania Antifederalist fears that the Constitution lacked a bill of rights by drawing a familiar analogy: "I believe, Mr. President, that of all the treaties which have ever been made, William Penn's was the only one, which was contracted without parchment; and I believe, likewise, it is the only one that has ever been faithfully adhered to." Objecting to a bill of rights as an "idle and superfluous instrument," Rush insisted that "there is no security but in a pure and adequate representation." [24] His impatient dismissal of the need for written guarantees of basic rights resonated later in the debates, when Rush scandalized his audience by attributing the Constitution to the God who "had fulminated the ten commandments from Mount Sinai." While for Rush the Constitution was the Scripture that the people's representatives would interpret for their constituents' benefit, Antifederalists viewed the textualization of rights as a necessary protection against the government. For Patrick Henry, a bill of rights contained "poor little humble republican maxims," conventional wisdom that had to be written down to be preserved. James Wilson, in contrast, insisted that text could never adequately embody fundamental rights: "Who will be bold enough to undertake to enumerate all the rights of the people," he asked. Responding to Wilson's sublime rhetoric of indefinable rights, Pennsylvania delegate Robert Whitehill spoke reproachfully of the "mystery" attending the proposed government. "Surely, Sir," he insisted, "our language was competent to declare the sentiments of the people, and to establish a bar against the intrusions of the general government." Only the written word could guarantee individual rights against the encroachments of powerful elites. For Henry and Whitehill as for the Shaysites, text provided a popular weapon of self-defense in the struggle between the many and the few.[25]

Text figured stability and reinforced social hierarchy for the Constitution's supporters, while for the Antifederalists it provided the necessary medium for the protection of the vulnerable against the privileged, one that the less fortunate could employ to establish an equality of rights if not of means. The final document as amended in the first congress blended these two purposes in a lasting synthesis. The symbolic potency of the Constitution in American political culture stems in important ways from its reconciliation of these two sets of meanings identified with text: the stability of government and the protection of immutable individual rights. The problem of republican speech never achieved a resolution of its conflicting meanings comparable to that accomplished in the text of the Constitution.

24. Koch, ed., *Notes of Debates*, 270; Bailyn, ed., *Debate on the Constitution*, part 1, 816–817.
25. Bailyn, ed., *Debate on the Constitution*, part I, 808, 811, 814, 869, part 2, 623.

No single forum persuasively integrated the diverse meanings of authority and resistance, hierarchy and democracy, amplification and evanescence attached to the spoken word. Modern Americans continue to articulate their persistent sense of difference and conflict through the exercise of voice and the elaboration of its imagery.

II. PERFORMING THE PRESIDENCY

Having broken free from the forms of empire and monarchy, Americans faced a pressing set of questions. Where did sovereignty reside in the complex new federal system? And how was that sovereignty to be performed? As national leaders sought to resolve these questions, a tension emerged between representative authority, particularly the charismatic, quasi-monarchical power of President Washington, and the textual authority of the Constitution. The federal convention that produced the Constitution identified the supplementary relationship between that document and elected representatives in its discussion of the need to fill national offices with "Continental Characters," men of sufficient stature and knowledge to overcome regional biases and transfigure discrete local communities into a unified nation. Two concepts organize this enactment: performativity, or the power of words themselves to effect a result, an idealized moment when language and action unite fully in an agent; and performance, or the pervasive theatricality that opens a space between intention and realization, calling into question the possibility of their full union. "Can we perform a single national act?" James Wilson asked the Pennsylvania Ratifying Convention of the existing system. He answered his own question in the negative: "The powers of our government are mere sound." Performance, not performativity, characterized national speech. Seeking to connect words to effective action, Wilson, Madison, and other Federalists proposed a system that would produce men of "continental reputation."[26] Under the proposed Constitution, ideal representatives would project an image of the "people." Individual citizens would see themselves mirrored in the enlarged, national proportions that such men made visible. To those who doubted that divisive local interests could be transcended, Wilson anticipated that "Continental Characters will multiply as we more and more coalesce." The president in particular could be "justly stiled THE MAN OF THE PEOPLE." Transcending regional interests, he "will watch over the whole with paternal care and affection," Wilson promised. The widespread expectation that George Washington would be elected the first president gave substance to Wilson's paternalistic rhetoric.

26. Ibid., part 1, 864; Koch, ed., *Notes of Debates*, 306.

The nation's preeminent "Continental Character" and father figure, Washington would be called upon to perform the roles of constitutional supplement and symbol of the incarnate nation.[27]

The apparent inevitability of Washington's selection as the nation's first president often masks the stages of his emergence as a national symbol. His early career established his reputation on both sides of the Atlantic as a colonial agent of the British imperial army who possessed not only substantial military talents, most notably knowledge of native American modes of warfare and negotiation, but also a flair for self-dramatization and a rising resentment of colonial subordination.[28] Transforming himself in the 1770s and 1780s from a disaffected agent of empire and a leading representative of powerful Virginia into the preeminent figure of a national identity, Washington negotiated conflicts between local symbolic practices and the slowly forming national Imaginary. The tensions between entrenched local and emerging national modes of identification were particularly apparent in his initial appointment as commander in chief of the Continental army in June 1775, when the imperial conflict that was not yet a war for independence remained confined to the Massachusetts Bay area. Washington's selection as the leader of a Continental force met resistance from some New Englanders who

27. Koch, ed., *Notes of Debates,* 578; Bailyn, ed., *Debate on the Constitution,* part 1, 825. Bruce Burgett discusses Washington as a figure of corporate nationalism in *Sentimental Bodies: Sex, Gender, and Citizenship in the Early Republic* (Princeton, N.J., 1998), 68–73. Discussions of elected representatives and the formation of a national character were often linked in debates over the Constitution and figured in terms of embodiment. Rufus King of Massachusetts articulated the relationship between national embodiment and sovereignty in terms that recall the logic of the king's two bodies when he observed that the states "did not possess the peculiar features of sovereignty, they could not make war, nor peace, nor alliances nor treaties. Considering them as political Beings, they were dumb, for they could not speak to any foreign Sovereign whatever. They were deaf, for they could not hear any propositions from such Sovereign. They had not even the organs or faculties of defence or offence, for they could not of themselves raise troops, or equip vessels, for war." In contrast, a fully unified national government would go beyond confederation to achieve consolidation: "A Union of the States is a Union of the men composing them, from whence a *national* character results to the whole." See Koch, ed., *Notes of Debates,* 152.

On the historical difficulty of transferring the logic of the king's two bodies to nonmonarchical forms of government, see Edmund S. Morgan's discussion of "the People's Two Bodies" under Cromwell, in *Inventing the People: The Rise of Popular Sovereignty in England and America* (New York, 1988), chap. 4.

28. Washington won transatlantic recognition for his role in the Seven Years' War. His youthful ambition to cut a dashing figure on the imperial scene is evident in a passage from a letter to his brother that appeared in the *London Magazine:* "I heard Bulletts whistle," he wrote in 1754, "and believe me, there was something charming in the sound" (George Washington, *Writings,* ed. John Rhodehamel [New York, 1997], 48). Paul K. Longmore describes Washington's self-modeling in *The Invention of George Washington* (Berkeley, Calif., 1988).

felt that one of their own should be given the command. In an address to the Massachusetts legislature shortly after his appointment, Washington sought to overcome local objections to his leadership. Echoing the sacrificial idiom of the Boston Massacre orators, which John Adams later deployed in Congress to motivate Continental support on Boston's behalf, Washington presented himself as an embodiment of New England's values: "In exchanging the Enjoyments of domestic Life for the Duties of my present honourable, but arduous Station," he insisted, "I only emulate the Virtue and public Spirit of the whole Province of Massachusetts Bay, which with a Firmness, and Patriotism without Example in modern History, has sacrificed all the Comforts of social and political Life, in Support of the Rights of Mankind, and the Welfare of our common Country." Washington transcended local identities to transfigure the suffering of a part into the patriotism of the whole. Imaged as both Moses and Christ, Washington became at once a leader of the nation and a sacrificial offering on its behalf.[29]

While Washington modeled himself on suffering Boston, however, others were already imagining him as the colonial double of George III. One rumor portrayed Washington exclaiming that "he wished to God! the Liberties of America were to be determined by a single Combat between himself" and George III.[30] This rumor, like the story that circulated at the same time in which Washington offered to raise an army at his own expense and march to the defense of Boston, pointed to the popular longing that he directly replace the British monarch. Washington Irving captured that longing in *Rip Van Winkle,* when he described the hotel sign where King George's face "was singularly metamorphosed" into that of "GENERAL WASHINGTON" after the Revolution. Irving's story neatly captures Washington's role in the new republic's complex rearticulation and transformation of monarchical forms. Monarchical substitutions mixed uneasily with sacrifice and martyrdom in the nation's emerging symbolic register.[31]

29. "Address to the Massachusetts Provincial Congress," in Philander D. Chase et al., eds., *The Papers of George Washington: Revolutionary War Series,* I (Charlottesville, Va., 1985), 59–60. For a discussion of Washington as both Moses and Christ, see Jay Fliegelman, *Prodigals and Pilgrims: The American Revolution against Patriarchal Authority, 1750–1800* (Cambridge, 1982), chap. 7. Fliegelman writes, "Washington had become America's new center and circumference — a naturalized version of both the Old Testament father and New Testament savior" (198–199).

30. Ezra Stiles, quoted in Longmore, *Invention of George Washington,* 139.

31. Washington Irving, "The Legend of Sleepy Hollow," in *History, Tales, and Sketches* (New York, 1983), 779. Washington's kinglike position in the renegotiation of political forms, as well as the biblical and classical aspects of Washington's persona, has been examined in many works, notably Looby, *Voicing America,* 93–95; Longmore, *Invention of George Washington,* 184–201; Fliegelman, *Prodigals and Pilgrims,* chap. 7; Barry Schwartz, *George Washington: The Making of an American Symbol* (New York, 1987), 28–36; Garry Wills, *Cincinnatus: George Washington and the Enlightenment* (Garden City, N.Y., 1984). Simon P. Newman examines the conflicting Feder-

Washington's status as a national icon soon provoked suspicion as well as adulation. John Adams echoed his Puritan ancestors when he warned the Continental Congress against idolatry in a speech delivered after Washington's success at the battle of Princeton in 1777: "I have been distressed to see some of our members disposed to idolise an image which their own hands have molten. I speak here of the superstitious veneration which is paid to General Washington." The superior authority belonged to Congress itself, Adams insisted. By the time he served as the first vice president, Adams had grown far less suspicious of "superstitious veneration" and become one of the strongest public advocates of monarchical forms. Despite Adams's change of heart, however, the problem of political formalism remained central to debates over the exercise of authority in the new republic.[32]

Washington quickly proved attentive to the importance of linguistic forms in the new government. Already as a youth he showed heightened awareness of the symbolic dimensions of the written word, particularly as a negotiation of political power and social authority. In the same bound volume of school exercises that contained his "Rules of Civility," he collected "forms of Writings" that included such frequently used legal texts as a lease, an indenture, and a will. His own writings reveal his awareness of the symbolic dimensions of text in both their form and their content. Aspiring to prominence, Washington cultivated a correct, direct, and forceful prose style and on the eve of the Revolution replaced his ornate early penmanship with a clear and simple hand. His handwriting and prose style mirrored the public character of calm, dispassionate commitment that he created for himself, reinforcing the effect of sincerity and transparency. Even the periodic lapses of self-control that disrupted his poise and manifested themselves in his writing when "anger . . . tangled his words and twisted his syntax" bolstered the impression of transparent sincerity.[33]

Washington's relationship to the forms and meanings of textuality shaped his public image as it emerged in his portraits. His first portrait, Charles Willson Peale's 1772 *George Washington,* portrays the soldier with his hand over his heart, suggesting his commitment to the dictates of his conscience. The words "Order of March" appear clearly on the document in his pocket, recalling his own "plan

---

alist and Republican attitudes toward this substitution of Washington for George III in "Principles or Men? George Washington and the Political Culture of National Leadership, 1776–1801," *Journal of the Early Republic,* XII (1992), 477–507, esp. 480.

32. George W. Corner, ed., *The Autobiography of Benjamin Rush: His "Travels Through Life" Together with His Commonplace Book for 1789–1813* (Princeton, N.J., 1948), 141.

33. Longmore, *Invention of George Washington,* 6, 8, 121; see also 72. On Washington's search for self-mastery as part of his public persona, see 14, 36, 80. As Washington's secretary of state, Thomas Jefferson commented upon Washington's fits of passion "when he cannot command himself" in *The Anas,* in Andrew A. Lipscomb and Albert Ellery Bergh, eds., *The Writings of Thomas Jefferson,* I (Washington, D.C., 1903), 265–492, esp. 382.

FIGURE 14. George Washington in the Uniform of a British Colonial Colonel. *By Charles Willson Peale. 1772. Courtesy, Washington and Lee University, Lexington, Va.*

of the order of march and order of battle" that he devised for his 1758 campaign to take Fort Duquesne. Subsequent images pictured Washington with texts that were not his own. Noël Le Mire's 1780 portrait sets the commander in chief in a biblically evocative Oriental setting complete with turbaned servant. Reproducing Peale's gesture of the hand hidden in the waistcoat, Le Mire places it lower than the heart in a conventional gesture of natural social elevation. In his other

FIGURE 15. George Washington. *By Nöel Le Mire. 1780. Courtesy, Anne S. K. Brown Military Collection, Brown University Library*

hand Washington holds forth a sheaf of official papers, the Declaration of Independence topmost. Additional scrolls await his attention on the carpet-covered table behind him, while beneath his feet lie torn and tattered British proclamations. *His Excellency George Washington* (1783) similarly positions the general atop texts of the Stamp Act and the Boston Port Bill while with his free hand he gestures toward a scroll that reads "American Freedom established by Valour and Perseverance." Later artists often chose to portray famous moments in Washington's career using representations of texts that typified his ability to return power to the people and their representatives, including his resignation from command of the army and his Farewell Address.[34]

Gilbert Stuart's famous Lansdowne portrait offers perhaps the most ambiguous instance of textual imagery in a Washington portrait. Painted in 1796, the year when Congress passed Jay's Treaty with Great Britain after heated controversy, Thomas Paine published his hostile *Letter to Washington,* and the president issued his Farewell Address, Stuart's painting conveys a serene image of presidential power transcending the controversies that surrounded Washington during his second administration. The Lansdowne portrait images the president in a richly expressive context reflecting the adoption of monarchical forms in the portraiture of the republican court. Surrounded by the symbols of his federal authority, including the chair of state from which he has risen, Washington stands clad in the simple black velvet attire characteristic of his presidential style, holding the sword of military power in his left hand and gesturing over a writing table with his right. On the table beneath his arm are scrolls, writing implements, and books that include the *Federalist* and the *Journals of Congress.* Among the books on the floor under the table is a copy of the Constitution. Two pieces of red drapery— one half-covering the table, the other providing a backdrop behind the president's head—are lifted to expose parallel views of the Constitution and the sun-tinged sky. In striking contrast to the hand over the heart of the 1772 Peale portrait, Washington's arm and outstretched hand are positioned between these two exposed tableaux, suggesting his mediatory role between the books on the floor and table and the natural or divine authority of the sun and sky. More subtly than the anonymous European print *George Washington Giving the Laws,* which portrays him as Moses, Stuart images the president as the locus of national authority, literally standing above the Constitution in a direct relation to a higher power.

34. David Steinberg offered insights into the Peale and Le Mire portraits in a personal communication of Aug. 23, 1998. For other related images, see John James Bartlett, *General Washington's Resignation* (1799); John Trumbull, *Resignation of General Washington* (1824–1828); and Canova's statue of Washington.

FIGURE 16.
George Washington. *By Gilbert Stuart.
c. 1797. Permission of National Portrait
Gallery, Smithsonian Institution*

Washington's gesturing arm in the Lansdowne portrait unifies and transcends the meaning of the texts beneath it.[35]

Representations such as Stuart's negotiated the relationship between textual embodiments of sovereignty and its physical embodiment in the president. That negotiation took place more directly in the tense debates over governmental procedures in the first administrations. Texts, most notably the Constitution but also more mundane forms of governance, were frequently situated between the executive and legislative branches that respectively represented the one and the many. Washington proved such a powerful national symbol because of his ability to represent unity through his "internal consistency and reliability," his ability "to be one thing." At times, however, his embodiment of unified power too much resembled its precedents in monarchical forms of sovereignty.[36]

35. Wills interprets this painting very differently, characterizing Stuart's Washington as subordinate to the laws and symbols of the Union; see *Cincinnatus*, 171–172. Schwartz is more attentive to the "tension between monarchical and republican strains in American political culture" evident in the portrait. He further comments on the tradition of monarchical state portraiture whose form Stuart adopted in *George Washington*, 54.

36. Wayne Fields, *Union of Words: A History of Presidential Eloquence* (New York, 1996), 7. On August 5, 1789, Washington wrote asking James Madison, "Would an Oral or written communi-

An early debate over the form of federal writs suggests how Washington threatened to preempt the founding document while filling its gaps. As written judicial orders from a federal court, federal writs provided an important textual site for the determination of the relationship between unitary and multiple forms of sovereignty. The decision not to designate the president as author of these writs drew critical comment from Federalists John Adams and Fisher Ames. Adams insisted that, since the only mode of proceeding against the president was by impeachment, he was effectively beyond "the power of a common justice" and thus could be appropriately identified as the author of a writ. Senator William Maclay of Pennsylvania, a leading republican proponent, retorted that the president "is not above the laws." English writs were issued in the king's name because of a legal fiction perpetuating the former practice of "his being personally in court." In a government that explicitly separated the executive and judicial branches, however, the president could not be personally in court. In Maclay's view, the effort to have the president identified in the text of writs was "a part of their old system of giving the President . . . every appendage of royalty." Echoing James Otis's argument in the Writs of Assistance speech against the textual circulation of sovereign power, Maclay warned against inscribing presidential authority at the head of federal writs.[37]

Washington's two administrations oversaw the implementation of practices and policies of everyday governance that the Constitution left undefined, including everything from presidential forms and titles to the modes of address appropriate in a republic, to the structures of interaction between the president and the other branches of government. The acrimonious debates that occurred over such matters reveal that Washington's relationship to the text of the Constitution was far from one of comfortable subordination. Maclay repeatedly held up the Constitution in congressional debates as a source of authority against what he perceived to be the aristocratic encroachments of the Washington administration. Others found the Constitution inadequate to the task Maclay assigned it. Expressing the persistent uneasiness about the locus of national identity that surrounded the new government, Henry Knox insisted in 1793, "It is the President's character, and not the written constitution, which keeps it together."[38]

---

cation be best?" in soliciting Senate advice and consent on foreign treaties (Huntington Library, San Marino, Calif., HM 1500).

37. Maclay's *Journal* provides an account of events in the first Senate from the perspective of an increasingly disaffected insider who believed that aristocratic forces were triumphing over true republicanism; see *The Journal of William Maclay, United States Senator from Pennsylvania, 1789–1791* (1890; New York, 1965), 163–164.

38. Thomas Jefferson recorded Knox's statement in the notes that comprise *The Anas*, in Lipscomb and Bergh, eds., *The Writings of Thomas Jefferson*, IX, 344.

As the individual with greatest claim to authoring the nation, first as head of the Continental army and later as chair of the Constitutional Convention, repository of its notes, and initial signer of the Constitution, Washington called into question the origins of the document itself. Supreme Court justice John Marshall later concluded of Washington's relationship to the Constitution, "Had the influence of character been removed, the intrinsic merits of the instrument would not have secured its adoption." At the convention, Washington acted as neutral moderator. Silent until its final moments, explaining that "his situation . . . restrained him from offering his sentiments," he generated an aura of authority over the Constitution that his active commitment to a particular position would have dissipated.[39]

Such reluctance to speak marked Washington's public persona and was often cited as evidence of his appealing modesty. Jefferson celebrated Washington's tendency throughout his legislative career to speak rarely, and then never "ten minutes at a time, nor to any but the main point which was to decide the question." His reticence set him in contrast to the wordy legislators who unnecessarily prolonged debate, and it contributed to his image as an American Cato. Adams, too, remarked on Washington's reticence but characteristically interpreted it in a more hostile fashion: "Secrecy! Cunning! Silence! *voila les grands sciences des temps modernes*," he exclaimed to Benjamin Rush in 1806.[40] The familiar image of Washington, his mouth firmly closed, could suggest to his detractors not only sphinxlike mystery but a monarchical style of authority found in courtly politics. Gilbert Stuart captured such an ambivalent image in his "Athenaeum" portrait of 1796. In a calmer moment, Adams observed that "the Examples of Washington, Franklin and Jefferson are enough to shew that Silence and reserve in public are more Efficacious than Argumentation or Oratory," for an orator "makes himself too familiar with the public." Avoiding offense and creating an air of enigmatic authority, Washington's reserve permitted him a certain disengagement from partisan conflict.[41]

39. John Marshall, *Life of Washington*, 2 vols. (1804–1807; Philadelphia, 1848), II, 127, quoted in Robert H. Wiebe, *The Opening of American Society: From the Adoption of the Constitution to the Eve of Disunion* (New York, 1985), 42; Koch, ed., *Notes of Debates*, 655.

40. Thomas Jefferson, *Writings*, ed. Merrill D. Peterson (New York, 1984), 53; John A. Schutz and Douglass Adair, eds., *The Spur of Fame: Dialogues of John Adams and Benjamin Rush, 1805–1813* (San Marino, Calif., 1966), 59.

41. Eric Hinderaker discusses silence as a monarchical language of power in "The 'Four Indian Kings' and the Imaginative Construction of the First British Empire," *WMQ*, 3d Ser., LIII (1996), 495. Both painted and sculpted busts of Washington tend to focus attention on his firmly closed mouth; see Schwartz, *George Washington*, illustrations 29–32; Wills, *Cincinnatus*, illustrations 28, 35. George Mercer noted this feature while suggesting one practical reason for it in his 1760 description: "His mouth is large and generally firmly closed, but which from time to time

On the occasions when he did speak formally, Washington manifested a distinct lack of poise. William Maclay captured Washington's awkward delivery in his description of the First Inaugural Address: "This great man was agitated and embarrassed more than ever he was by the leveled cannon or pointed musket. He trembled, and several times could scarce make out to read, though it must be supposed he had often read it before." Maclay particularly described the president's gestures as Washington nervously shifted his text from hand to hand and made "a flourish with his right hand, which left rather an ungainly impression. I sincerely, for my part, wished all set ceremony in the hands of the dancing-masters, and that this first of men had read off his address in the plainest manner." Nervously and inappropriately, the president attempted to blend aristocratic forms with republican simplicity. Articulating a republican aesthetic, Maclay expressed his preference for a plain reading of a text, unembellished with gesture. Such a delivery would have corresponded with the plainness of dress that Washington adopted on this occasion, for which he chose a suit made of simple brown American broadcloth adorned with metal buttons stamped with an eagle as a statement of republican simplicity and cultivation of national industry. For Maclay, who wished him to be "first in everything," the president's awkward performance undermined the national pride symbolized by his clothing.[42]

While Maclay lamented the president's imperfect effort to blend the genteel with the republican, other observers interpreted the ungainliness of his performance as evidence of sincerity. Fisher Ames described the moment as "a very touching scene, and quite of the solemn kind." For Ames, the president's delivery revealed, not ineptitude, but his awareness of the moment's significance: "His aspect grave, almost to sadness; his modesty, actually shaking; his voice deep, a little tremulous, and so low as to call for close attention." The absorbing quality of Washington's serious, hesitant, quiet delivery had a powerful impact, "overwhelming" the mind to produce "emotions of the most affecting kind upon the members." Ames saw in the performance "an allegory in which virtue was personified, and addressing those whom she would make her votaries. Her power over the heart was never greater, and the illustration of her doctrine by her own example was never more perfect."[43]

Imagining Washington as a feminine figure of virtue, Ames captured the relationship between Washington's words and his delivery. Ames understood the

---

discloses some defective teeth" (William Alfred Bryan, *George Washington in American Literature, 1775–1865* [New York, 1952], 21). For Adams's calm remark, see Butterfield, ed., *Diary and Autobiography of John Adams,* III, 336.

42. Maclay, *Journal of William Maclay,* 9.

43. Letter to George Minot, May 3, 1789, in W. B. Allen, ed., *Works of Fisher Ames* (Indianapolis, Ind., 1983), I, 568.

delivery as an amplification and enactment of Washington's text. Washington opened his speech with an assertion of the unprecedented "anxieties" and "conflict of emotions" that the call to serve as president evoked in him. He expressed his sense of duty to the country "whose voice I can never hear but with veneration and love" while maintaining his Cincinnatean regret for the loss of the retirement he had chosen in his declining years. He insisted on his own sense of inadequacy for the presidency as one "inheriting inferior endowments from nature and unpracticed in the duties of civil administration." Dwelling on his limitations, Washington offered "fervent supplications" to "the Great Author of every public and private good" for continued guidance as he entered this new office. Moseslike, Washington positioned himself at the boundary between the human and the divine. He acted as the nation's priest, speaking to God for the Congress and "my fellow-citizens at large"; at other moments he spoke as a prophet, articulating quasi-divine "reflections, arising out of the present crisis" that "have forced themselves too strongly on my mind to be suppressed." In his role as prophet-priest for the new nation, Washington staged his subordination to powers equally amorphous: the voice of the people and the voice of God.[44] Confidence at such a moment would have suggested a potentially dangerous assertion of personal authority. The very absence of self-possession that Maclay deplored in this performance demonstrated for Ames the virtuous subordination of individual interest to the greater good. The shifting of his text from hand to hand enacted Washington's sense that he did not hold the government in a firm grasp but would subordinate himself to "the Great Constitutional Charter under which you are assembled." In keeping with his emphasis on subordination, Washington refused to propose specific policy measures. Deferring instead to the legislators themselves, he offered "the tribute that is due to the talents, the rectitude, and the patriotism which adorn the characters selected to devise and adopt" the appropriate means of implementing the Constitution. There were many national characters, he suggested, not one.[45]

Washington's habitual grace and masterful physical presence made the new president's discomfort as an orator particularly remarkable. Long known as a powerful athlete, an elegant and enthusiastic dancer, and a "splendid horseman," Washington's unusual height (he was 6′ 2″) and strength enhanced a "demeanor at all times composed and dignified." Possessing "a pleasing, benevolent, though

44. Karlyn Kohrs Campbell and Kathleen Hall Jamieson discuss Washington's importance in the creation of a priestly role for the president in *Deeds Done in Words: Presidential Rhetoric and the Genres of Governance* (Chicago, 1990), 197. Cincinnatus was a Roman general and statesman celebrated for his willingness both to serve the state even at the cost of personal comfort and to yield the reins of power.

45. "The First Inaugural Address," in Washington, *Writings,* ed. Rhodehamel, 730–734.

a commanding countenance," "graceful" movements and gestures, and a "majestic" walk, Washington modeled himself according to the standards of English gentility. One observer commented on the blend of expressiveness and control evident in his face, qualities that his contemporaries recognized as ideal for an orator: "His features are regular and placid, with all the muscles of his face under perfect control, though flexible and expressive of deep feeling when moved by emotions."[46] But although his features, size and grace—and even his unusually large hands effective for gesturing—might have made him a dynamic orator, Washington never aspired to the role that fellow Virginian Patrick Henry embodied. Internalizing the "Rules . . . of Civility and Decent Behavior in Company and Conversation" that he recorded as a boy, he learned to present himself modestly, with respect to all and deference to social superiors. The effects of his training were evident in 1760, when an observer noted that "in conversation he looks you full in the face, is deliberate, deferential and engaging," and they remained characteristic of him in 1775, when a congressman described his acceptance of the army command as "modest and polite." The fact that his voice was "agreeable rather than strong" and that he lacked the classical education that fueled the ambitions of many of the era's great orators, might have produced a sense of inadequacy. Even his adult reading of Chesterfield's *Letters to His Son* (1773), with their emphasis on the aesthetics of public eloquence, did not help him overcome his reticence.[47]

Washington's inability or unwillingness to become a fluent orator points to a central fact of his public career: his self-effacing persona allowed him to resolve the contradictions of republican authority, at least temporarily. In a letter to Congress during the war, he complained, "I have felt myself greatly embarrassed with respect to a vigorous exercise of Military power" in an army fighting for independence.[48] The exercise of power in a republic proved a persistent embarrassment throughout his subsequent political life. As the Constitution was drafted and ratified, Washington's fame as head of the army and his position as a leader of the ex-

46. George Mercer is quoted in Bryan, *George Washington in American Literature*, 24.

47. The "Rules of Civility" are in Washington, *Writings*, ed. Rhodehamel, 3–10. Washington's conversational style, voice, and modesty are described in passages quoted in Bryan, *George Washington in American Literature*, 24–25. Chesterfield recommended both modesty and eloquence, with particular emphasis on the latter's performance dimensions; see David Roberts, ed., *Lord Chesterfield's Letters* (Oxford, 1992), 65, 164. On Washington's familiarity with Chesterfield, see Longmore, *Invention of George Washington*, 6–8. Richard L. Bushman discusses the importance of Chesterfield's emphasis on "the aesthetics of speech" for the creation of a genteel style in eighteenth-century America and describes the importance of the "Rules" for the formation of Washington's genteel persona (though not his oratory) in "American High-Style and Vernacular Cultures," in Jack P. Greene and J. R. Pole, eds., *Colonial British America: Essays in the New History of the Early Modern Era* (Baltimore, 1988), 345–383, esp. 353–357.

48. Schwartz, *George Washington*, 133.

clusive Society of the Cincinnati raised the specter of military usurpation. Washington sought to distance himself from the conventional image of the conquering hero that Julius Caesar and Oliver Cromwell typified for his era. Regional differences in political culture further complicated Washington's uneasy negotiation of republican modes of power within the new national order. Richard Henry Lee's 1784 term as president of the Confederation Congress clarified and highlighted the conflicts between genteel southern modes of republican authority based on a rigidly hierarchical social structure and the differently inflected republicanism of other regions. Along with his established reputation for Chesterfieldian eloquence, Lee acquired a reputation for courtly extravagance and ineffectiveness.

Washington's resistance to the role of the confident orator points to his complex negotiations of power and authority through the symbolism of speech and text. In a crucial elaboration of his self-effacing persona, he used moments of formal eloquence to stage the covert assertion of his presence through his relation to text, a performance strategy that disturbed Maclay and enraptured Ames at his inaugural address. Washington also employed text to evoke sentiment from others in ways that enhanced his authority. One such moment occurred in his famous 1783 address to the officers at Newburgh. There, he challenged their plans for a mutiny over pay, incited by an address that had been circulated by an anonymous dissenter. As was his custom, Washington read from a prepared text, but the speech's most potent effect occurred in an improvised moment. Pausing after his first paragraph, Washington observed as he reached in his pocket, "Gentlemen, you will permit me to put on my spectacles, for I not only have grown gray but almost blind, in the service of my country."[49] The pathos of the gesture reduced the audience of mutinous officers to tears. Displaying feeling as evidence of sincerity, Washington disrupted the delivery of his text in order to mask its function as performance and make the words on the page appear authentically his own. The tearful response of his officers registered his success in using this gesture to transform his words from a performance to a performative utterance, one that produced their patriotic commitment to the new government.

Washington's seemingly spontaneous comment made dramatically manifest the qualities of representative impersonation implicit in his speech, which staged a series of contrasts between the legitimate visible authority of personal suffering— a suffering identified here with the tool of enhanced vision itself—and the illegitimate invisible authority of anonymity. Playing on the Enlightenment trope that identified reason with light and vision, Washington insisted that "the secret mover of this Scheme (whoever he may be) intended to take advantage of the passions"

49. Washington, *Writings*, ed. Rhodehamel, 496 n. 12, 1109.

and deny the officers opportunity for "cool, deliberative thinking" and reflection in "the calm light of reason." In contrast to the illumination that Washington proffered, the author sought to "insinuate the darkest suspicion, to effect the blackest designs."[50]

Despite the general's exhortation to exercise reason over passion, however, the speech established no clear antithesis between thought and feeling. The anonymous address called on the officers to "remove into the unsettled Country" and "leave an ungrateful Country to defend itself" or, in the event of a peace settlement with Britain, to "turn . . . our Arms against" Congress. Washington responded with a series of rhetorical questions designed to challenge the hidden author's patriotism ("Is he not an insidious Foe?") and criticize him for lacking confidence in "our Understandings." These questions did not open discussion — they invited a single response. Rather than develop an argument against the proposals, Washington offered to "drop the curtain" over these matters, adding that "a moment's reflection" would demonstrate "the physical impossibility of carrying either proposal into execution." Self-evident implausibility, in Washington's adaptation of Jefferson's Declaration trope, need only be made manifest for the threat of a military revolt to be laid to rest.[51]

Emotional identification rather than rational argument illuminated the self-evident in Washington's speech. "The author of the piece, is entitled to much credit for the goodness of his Pen," he observed, "and I could wish he had as much credit for the rectitude of his Heart." Setting sourceless text against the orator's power of sympathy, Washington established his own emotional union with the men in his audience, insisting that "my Heart has ever expanded with joy, when I have heard [the army's] praises, and my indignation has arisen, when the mouth of detraction has been opened against it." Such testimonies established the hegemonic order of sentiment on which his authority came increasingly to be founded. Displaying his emotional union with his troops, he undermined dissent, or what he termed "Civil discord." When the anonymous author insisted that the officers should suspect any man recommending "moderate measures and longer forbearance," he set the terms that allowed Washington to present his own perspective as the only legitimate one. Warning that, according to his opponent, "the freedom of Speech may be taken away, and, dumb and silent we may be led, like sheep, to the Slaughter," the general successfully silenced anyone who might have wished to advocate some form of confrontation. While insisting that "Men see thro' different Optics" and their differing perspectives must be respected, Washington estab-

50. Ibid., 496, 497, 499.
51. Ibid., 497–498.

lished his own point of view, enhanced with his spectacles, as the only truly valid perspective.[52]

Rather than provide a well-developed argument against the anonymous proposal or open a broader discussion, Washington transferred contention away from the army to the confined arena of Congress. Congress and not the army was the proper site for open disputation, he implied; indeed, the cultivation of deliberative governance explained that body's slowness to act on the army's behalf, the source of so much discontent. Deflecting criticism and debate, Washington compensatorily transfigured those receptive to his vision into exemplars "of unexampled patriotism and patient virtue, rising superior to the pressure of the most complicated suffering." When they embraced his charismatic authority, their patriotism would become visible for all to see. In his conclusion, Washington imagined his soldiers elevated into the realm of perpetual visibility as he gave voice to the words of "Posterity": "Had this day been wanting, the World had never seen the last stage of perfection to which human nature is capable of attaining." Washington's famous biographer Mason Weems captured the dynamic of representative impersonation enacted in this episode. After resolving to reject the anonymous address, the officers hurry back to their troops and repeat Washington's speech, which in making him the object of their affectionate attention re-creates them in his image. Like Patrick Henry's uncontainable and transformative speech, Washington's address to the officers at Newburgh generated a mimetic dynamic that produced an expansive national identity. More clearly than Henry's oratory, however, Washington's address established his hegemonic authority while casting that authority as the free speech of his audience.[53]

When Washington urged his soldiers to win fame by subordinating themselves to Congress, he anticipated his own most famous role enacted only months later: that of Cincinnatus giving up military power to a civilian authority. As he prepared to resign his command, Washington inquired whether he should tender that resignation "in writing, or at an Audience." Congress requested that he perform this event in person. The ceremony at Annapolis Statehouse was carefully orchestrated to display the conquering hero's deference to Congress. One spectator noted the unprecedented nature of the event: "It was a solemn and affecting spectacle; such an one as history does not present. The spectators all wept," he continued, "and there was hardly a member of Congress who did not drop tears." At Newburgh, Washington precipitated an outpouring of feeling while remaining composed himself; here, however, his own unsuccessful struggle to maintain self-

52. Ibid., 496–498, 500.

53. Ibid., 500; see also Mason Locke Weems, *The Life of Washington*, 9th ed., ed. Peter S. Onuf (Armonk, N.Y., 1996), 94–98.

command proved the most compelling aspect of his performance: "The General's hand which held the address shook as he read it. . . . But when he commended the interests of his dearest country to almighty God, and those who had the superintendence of them to his holy keeping, his voice faultered and sunk, and the whole house felt his agitations." Republican court poet Annis Boudinot Stockton captured Washington's similarly sentimental tone on the occasion of his farewell to his officers:

> But now, alas! his noble spirit bends,
> When he must bid adieu to all his friends, —
> Beloved warriors, who had always fought
> Fast by his side, and posts of danger sought —
> Whose love to him, and strong attachment bore
> No parallel to aught we've seen before.
> The starting tear roll'd down his manly cheek,
> And words were vain, the sad *farewell* to speak;
> But stronger far the silent eloquence
> That shew'd his soul was all benevolence.

Crucial aspects of Washington's post-Revolutionary public identity flowed from his ability to deploy the mimetic and cathartic effects of strong emotion. At the moment of resignation, his reluctant relinquishment of emotional control enacted the transfer of political power to Congress.[54]

Washington's resignation speech staged, without resolving, the difficulty of relocating power in new forms. The problem of executive speech emerged as an especially pressing problem of sovereign authority. Some perceived Washington's decision to address Congress on the state of the Union orally rather than in writing as another "appendage of royalty." John Adams, who perpetuated this practice during his administration, observed caustically in retrospect, "I was a monarchist because I thought a speech more manly, more respectful to Congress and the nation" than the written messages that Jefferson introduced.[55]

54. Wills, *Cincinnatus*, 11; Schwartz, *George Washington*, 142; "Peace, a Pastoral Dialogue: Part the Second," in Carla Mulford, ed., *Only for the Eye of a Friend: The Poems of Annis Boudinot Stockton* (Charlottesville, Va., 1995), 121–130, esp. 127–128.

55. Adams to Benjamin Rush, Dec. 25, 1811, in Schutz and Adair, eds., *The Spur of Fame*, 201–202. Adams characteristically overlooked the truth of the allegation. His reference to Washington's First Inaugural Address as *"His most gracious speech"* drew a strong response from Maclay; see Maclay, *Journal of William Maclay*, 9–10.

Jeffrey K. Tulis observes, "Prior to this century, presidents preferred written communications between the branches of government to oral addresses to 'the people.'" Tulis traces this practice to Jefferson, whose "practice of sending all messages to Congress in writing remained the rule

Washington, of course, delivered his speeches from a prepared text, a strategy that he followed throughout his career, reinforcing his reputation for unity and stability. As a mirror of monarchical precedent, however, this practice took on a potentially sinister appearance once he assumed the presidency. William Maclay warned the Senate against "echoing" the text of Washington's speech as they formulated their response. A copy of meaning rather than its origination, a "servile echo" would suggest passive acceptance of executive intent. Such a reiteration was doubly risky, for it resembled "a stale ministerial trick in Britain" that put words in the king's mouth to win Parliament's acceptance of the ministry's agenda.[56]

Maclay's warning points to one site of anxiety over the origins of meaning in the new government. If the president merely read his speech, he might not be its author. How could anyone know whether his was the controlling agency behind the text?[57] Reiterating the president's speech in its own message, the Senate risked accepting meanings and intentions derived from an unknown source. Rather than create an image of unity, as such a repetition might suggest, they would introduce an indeterminate and potentially volatile element into the government — an element increasingly identified with the monarchically-minded Alexander Hamilton. Some observers interpreted Washington's practice of reading his speeches as the sign of an ever more unified locus of authority.

The interpretive conflicts over Washington's textual performances emerged most forcefully in disputes over his Farewell Address of 1796. Debating the best means to effect a successful retirement at the end of his second administration, Washington decided to circulate the address exclusively as a text rather than resign orally, as he had resigned his army command. In a political culture where gentlemen did not openly seek public office, he feared that he would appear to be soliciting reelection if he announced his intention to retire in a speech before Congress. Leaving Philadelphia hours before the address appeared in print, Washington's abrupt disappearance evoked Moses' death. The published address successfully eased Washington's departure from office and quickly became a central document in the Washington legacy. Subsequently, however, questions arose over

---

until Woodrow Wilson dramatically broke precedent with his appearance before Congress"; see *The Rhetorical Presidency* (Princeton, N.J., 1987), 5, 56.

56. Maclay, *Journal of William Maclay,* 170–171. Democratic political theorist William Manning similarly complained about the custom of opening legislative sessions with "a kingly speech by the presidents and governors" that the legislature "echo[es] back" (Michael Merrill and Sean Wilentz, eds., *The Key of Liberty: The Life and Democratic Writings of William Manning, "A Laborer,"* 1747–1814 [Cambridge, Mass., 1993], 155).

57. Jefferson described the committee process of drafting an inaugural address in *The Anas,* in Lipscomb and Bergh, eds., *The Writings of Thomas Jefferson,* IX, 410–411.

the authorship of a document to which Madison, Jay, and, most critically, Hamilton had all contributed.[58]

The content of Washington's text intensified the concerns over its composition that arose after 1810. Appealing directly to "Friends and Fellow Citizens" over the heads of Congress, the address warned against party spirit, regionalism, and demagoguery, and tied these domestic concerns to the influence of foreign powers. When it was first published, Washington's rhetorical efforts to transcend faction and region only reinforced the partisan ring of his address. Particularly during his second term, contested relations with France and Britain shaped disputes over the legacy of the American Revolution, and nonpartisanship became the party position of the Federalists. During these years, gossip and scandal in the republican court fueled the development of the first party system. Jefferson suggested as much when he grumbled to the president, "My words were caught, multiplied, misconstrued, and even fabricated and spread abroad to my injury."[59]

After Washington's death in 1799, the tensions that surrounded him in his second administration gradually dissipated, and he became the icon of national unity that he remains today. His Farewell Address emerged as a hallmark of his nonpartisan, national stature, his role as a "Continental Character." But when the textual history of the address became public, Washington's well-known habits of consultation and collaboration, which once had defused fears of his personal ambitions, now undermined the unifying power of his text. He had urged autonomy, consistency, and union upon the American people in a document whose own authenticity and unity of intention were being called into question. No longer a symbol of his self-effacement and sincerity, the text of the Farewell Address became a sign of conspiratorial machinations comparable to the anonymous address that Washington attacked at Newburgh.[60]

58. Victor Hugo Paltsits, ed., *Washington's Farewell Address* (New York, 1935), 36–54. See also Wills, *Cincinnatus*, 87–88. The form of the address is drawn from Moses' farewell address to the Israelites, where he reinterprets and reiterates the covenant immediately before his own death on Mount Pisgah and the Israelites' entry into the promised land. Campbell and Jamieson discuss the Deuteronomic roots of the form in *Deeds Done in Words*, 194. On Moses and the performance semiotic of speech and text, see Appendix, below.

59. Jefferson, *The Anas*, in Lipscomb and Bergh, eds., *The Writings of Thomas Jefferson*, IX, 385. Of the Washington administration, Wiebe notes that "rumor and slander were the everyday weapons of political advantage" (*The Opening of American Society*, 44).

60. For a reading of the Farewell Address, see Burgett, *Sentimental Bodies*, chap. 3. Newman discusses Washington as a Federalist cult figure in "Principles or Men?" *Journal of the Early Republic*, XII (1991), 477–507. According to Newman, the reemergence of Washington as a universal rather than partisan figure occurred only after Washington's death in 1799 and the electoral victory of the Republican Party; see 506–507. Paltsits discusses the controversy over the address's authorship in *Washington's Farewell Address*, chap. 5.

More than any other political leader in the early republic, Washington nego-tiated the complexities of verbal form as it mediated political representation and national sovereignty, issues that preoccupied the founding generation and shaped the new institutions of government. The stability of founding documents was both supplemented by and set in competition with the immediacy of inspired oratory as statesmen worked to create representative national institutions. Early in his po-litical life as general and president, Washington embodied the full union of lan-guage and action that the Federalists hoped the constitutional government would create. He enacted that union in his most famous orations through his ability to both employ and exceed a text. At Newburgh, his break from a prepared manu-script displayed authenticity and re-created the audience of mutinous officers in his image; in his First Inaugural Address, his uneasy grasp of the manuscript en-acted his subordination to the Constitution while permitting his covert assertion of presence and power. Both of these orations achieved the performative effect of uncontainable speech that enacts a transformation in the audience. But the con-troversy over the printed Farewell Address opened a space between intention and realization, between its plural authorship and the document attributed to Wash-ington. The shifting public reception of that text signaled that Washington's presi-dential acts could be received, not as performatives, but as performances.

7 Political Speech in the New Republic

I. REPRESENTATIVE SPEECH

In the 1790s, political dispute routinely took the form of linguistic criticism. The pervasive sensitivity to the ways that language structures society made the force of political utterances as both performances and performatives strikingly clear: the speaker both played a social role and sought to create an ideal social order through his linguistic choices. Over the course of the decade, Republicans cultivated a populist idiom and shifted the terms of political address, establishing themselves as the "Friends" rather than the Federalist-style "Fathers" of the people. Even an antipatriarchal father and hesitant orator such as Washington drew criticism as Republicans rejected genteel modes of eloquence that staged hierarchical authority and deference, cultivating instead direct speech to the unrefined majority in its own language.

The Republican rhetorical shift in both idiom and performance style was central to their political project. In the 1796 election, one Republican newspaper captured the performance dimension of the contest with the Federalists when the editor criticized "*the* Great, *the* Wise, *the* Learned" for their "egregious, supercilious, opinionative performances" and their habit of labeling political opponents "*ignorant, insignificant, and ungrammatical.*"[1] Such disputes over language reflected the violence and conflict that characterized the early republic, when public figures used appeals to unity, harmony, selflessness, and feeling to effect rhetorically an elusive social cohesion. Rhetorical performances provided an especially volatile site for the negotiation of power. Reconfiguring domains of public eloquence, Americans transformed the bases of political authority.

Yet despite such heightened attention to the significance of language and performance and the interest in creating more democratic styles of speech, clear alternatives to genteel eloquence were slow to emerge. Public speakers who employed

---

1. Alan Taylor describes the shift from gentility to populism in the political culture of New York State during the 1790s in *William Cooper's Town: Power and Persuasion on the Frontier of the Early American Republic* (New York, 1995), esp. 245.

democratic styles risked being tarred with the brush of demagoguery. The structural and ideological diffuseness of the "people's voice" necessitated the development of alternative public arenas before a democratic transformation of oratorical forms could take place. John Adams's lament in 1806 that great oratory was no longer being performed in the United States registered an important truth: the forms of eloquence that emerged during the Revolution had been broken and were yet to be remade.[2]

As Adams's complaint suggests, the new Constitution did not resolve the contradictions intrinsic to the figure of popular voice, despite its prominent reliance on that figure for legitimacy. Evoking both the authority of the people's voice and the threat of demagoguery, populist rhetoric generated increasing tensions during the Washington and Adams administrations, when war on the Northwest frontier, British depredations on American ships, and events in revolutionary France together caused widespread anxiety over national stability and identity. Fears of popular speech crystallized in two resonant acts: Washington's criticism of Democratic-Republican Societies as "self-created societies" in his Farewell Address, and the passage of the Alien and Sedition Acts under John Adams in 1798. Washington and Adams employed presidential speech to control the proliferation of voices and the multiplication of interests that they believed threatened the nation. But the monarchical residue attending executive speech undermined their efforts and contributed to the stunning defeat of the Federalist Party in the 1800 elections. Jefferson abandoned formal presidential oratory after winning the election, establishing a centurylong convention of written messages to Congress that, with the important exceptions of Andrew Jackson and Abraham Lincoln, made Congress rather than the president the primary constitutional channel for popular voice. In Congress, sovereign speech was dissipated, fragmented, and multiplied.[3]

Congressional oratory first emerged as high drama in the 1790s, when the agon

2. "Whether the age of oratory will ever return I know not," Adams told Benjamin Rush on Sept. 19, 1806. "At present it seems to be of little use, for every man in our public assemblies will vote with his party" (John A. Schutz and Douglass Adair, eds., *The Spur of Fame: Dialogues of John Adams and Benjamin Rush, 1805–1813* [San Marino, Calif., 1966], 64).

3. The Alien and Sedition Acts restricted immigration and naturalization in ways designed to limit republican political activity; they also curtailed the rights of citizens to political expression. Adams gave a series of addresses championing the Sedition Act, which Madison described as containing some of "the most abominable and degrading [language] that could fall from the lips of the first magistrate of an independent people" (James Roger Sharp, *American Politics in the Early Republic: The New Nation in Crisis* [New Haven, Conn., 1993], 179). Gordon S. Wood argues for a more rapid post-Revolutionary transition from elite to popular forms of political expression than I believe the facts warrant in "The Democratization of Mind in the American Revolution," in *Leadership in the American Revolution* (Washington, D.C., 1974), 62–89; Wood, *The Radicalism of the American Revolution* (New York, 1992), esp. 6–8.

of the House and Senate floors became an absorbing spectacle of national significance. Viewing the performances from the House and Senate galleries and reading reports of them in their newspapers, Americans came to imagine congressional debates as the dramatic enactment and negotiation of political differences
that they, through the electoral process, had embodied in their representatives and
placed on the national stage.[4]

The rise of congressional eloquence in the 1790s was tied in important ways
to the political career of one man: Fisher Ames. Ames developed a style of deliberative oratory that transformed central qualities of Washington's presidential address—notably his strategies for asserting an authority masked as self-effacement
—into a form of representative speech intended to clarify and enlarge the popular
voice. This Harvard-educated son of a Massachusetts almanac writer and tavern-
keeper arrived in the House of Representatives already famous for the oratorical talent that he had displayed before the Massachusetts bar and as a champion
of the Constitution in the state ratifying convention. Early in the session, one
member singled out the youthful Ames as the House's best speaker, remarking
that he "delivers his sentiments with the greatest ease and propriety, and in the
most elegant language of any man in the House." At thirty-one, Ames possessed
a physical beauty, grace, and poise that enhanced his appeal for the visitors in the
House gallery. His rhetorical training at Harvard cultivated the "free and easy, as
well as animated way of speaking" characteristic of the elocutionary school that
by then dominated the college's curriculum.[5] He learned his art in part by performing classical and modern orations and dramatically reciting the works of his
favorite poets, Virgil, Shakespeare, and Milton. Arriving in Cambridge in 1770,
he soon came to echo the impassioned patriot rhetoric that surrounded him as
he was exposed to leading whig orators such as James Otis. Ames recited excerpts
from Benjamin Church's 1773 Boston Massacre oration to the Harvard Speaking
Club just months after Church delivered the address. Through these varied influences, he developed a verbal style characterized by abundant imagery, "terseness,
strength, and vivacity" and "antithesis and point." A stint as a "remarker" for the
speaking club required Ames to point out "the propriety or impropriety of the

4. Robert A. Ferguson discusses the rise of eloquence in the post-Revolutionary period, linking it to the prominence of the legal profession in the new government; see *Law and Letters in
American Culture* (Cambridge, Mass., 1984), 77–84.

5. Thomas Lowther to Judge James Iredell, May 9, 1789, in Griffith J. McRee, ed., *Life and
Correspondence of James Iredell, One of the Associate Justices of the Supreme Court of the United
States*, 2 vols. (New York, 1857–1858), II, 258, quoted in Winfred E. A. Bernhard, *Fisher Ames:
Federalist and Statesman, 1758–1808* (Chapel Hill, N.C., 1965), 92. Bernhard discusses the impor-
tance of oratory and elocution at Harvard in *Fisher Ames*, 24–29. The passage quoted is on 27,
from William Tudor, *The Life of James Otis, of Massachusetts* (Boston, 1823), 354.

Pronunciation and Gesture of the Speakers." This post made Ames particularly attentive to the physical dimensions of the spoken word.[6]

By all accounts, Ames's speeches succeeded as performances rather than as texts. Emphasizing immediacy and authentic emotion over compositional balance, Ames's oratory followed the example set by evangelical ministers who celebrated the spirit over the letter and by political orators such as Patrick Henry and James Otis who made untextualized voice a sign of true representativeness. An early biographer described the impassioned inspiration of the moment that propelled Ames's language, expression, and gestures: "In public speaking he trusted much to excitement, and did little more in his closet than draw the outlines of his speech, and reflect on it, till he had received deeply the impressions he intended to make; depending for the turns and figures of language, illustrations, and modes of appeal to the passions, on his imagination and feelings at the time." Yet Ames anchored his improvised speech in a written poetic tradition, developing the extemporaneous style in ways that distinguished his oratory from that of his Revolutionary precursors. His characteristically elaborate figures and heightened tone reflect an influence of classical and English poetry so pervasive that in his conversation no less than in his oratory he spoke in language "full of imagery, drawing similes to illustrate the topics of his discourse from everything about him." His literary imagery made a social point. Like his fellow Federalist John Adams at the Boston Massacre trial, Ames employed a textual reference to distinguish his extempore oratory from the speech of the·"mob."[7]

Ames reflected on the aesthetic and social dimensions of oral performance in his essay "American Literature" (1809). There he laments the fate of modern poetry doomed to "a cold perusal in a closet, or a still colder confinement unread, in a bookseller's shop." The dead letter of modern poetry compares unfavorably with the "vivacity of its impressions, and the significance of the applauses" that poetry received in an age when "all Greece . . . beheld the contests of wit and valor"

---

6. Bernhard, *Fisher Ames*, 33. Ames further encountered the tradition of Massacre oratory when he studied law under Boston Massacre orator William Tudor. Ames was not yet a student at Harvard when James Otis spoke there in June 1769; however, the event drew substantial attention and permeated the college's political climate in ways that had not dissipated when Ames arrived the following August; see 26, 28. The descriptions of Ames's style belong to his early biographer J. T. Kirkland, whose prefatory essay appeared in the first edition of *The Works of Fisher Ames*, which Kirkland edited (Boston, 1809). The essay is reprinted in W. B. Allen, ed., *Works of Fisher Ames* (Indianapolis, 1983), I, xliii–liii, esp. xlvi. On Ames's "remarker" stint, see Speaking Club Records, Orders, I, 54, 59, Harvard Archives, quoted in Bernhard, *Fisher Ames*, 27–28.

7. Kirkland, preface, in Allen, ed., *Works of Ames*, I, xlvii; Josiah Quincy to Charles Lowell, Mar. 30, 1857, in Charles Lowell, "Letters of Hon. John Lowell and Others," in *Historical Magazine*, I (1857), 257, quoted in Bernhard, *Fisher Ames*, 174.

staged between poets.[8] Championing the ancient world's performance of poetry, Ames modeled the response he imagined for his own oratorical performances. He also obliquely drew boundaries around political speech. His essay celebrates a period in ancient history when deliberation over "refined policy, and calculations of remote consequences were not adapted to the taste or capacity of rude warriors, who did not reason at all, or only reasoned from their passions." Signaling the dangers of including those able to reason only from their passions in political debates, a theme he addressed openly and often in his political works, Ames's essay implicitly circumscribes the audience for the subtleties of deliberative rhetoric.[9]

Ames's belief that the ungoverned passions of the masses unfitted them for political deliberation was his most fundamental political tenet, ubiquitous in his political essays. In an 1805 essay entitled *The Mire of Democracy,* Ames warned against the flattery of the demagogue, employing the same terms of critical analysis that his countryman William Manning applied to the American political scene but drawing the opposite conclusion. While Manning warned the Many against the dissimulating flattery of the Few that kept them in subjection, Ames insisted that the many were all too willing to be guided by the flatterer. "Popular vanity comes hungry to an election ground, and claims flattery as its proper food," he observed. "Of all flattery, the grossest (gross indeed to blasphemy) is, that the voice of the people is the voice of God." Challenging a political truism, Ames openly asserted the irredeemably debased nature of participatory politics. He advanced the mediatory role of the representative, a position that he articulated in his analysis of representation at the Massachusetts Ratifying Convention and aggressively sustained in the face of Jeffersonian Republicanism until his death in 1808.[10]

Attentive to the ways that linguistic forms define the modes of mediation intrinsic to representation, Ames eschewed the language of flattery as the tool of the demagogue, celebrating instead poetic language that governs the passions of those ill equipped for full participation in civic debate. Ames's most famous figure neatly reveals the social function that his language served. "A democracy is a volcano, which conceals the fiery material of its own destruction," he told the Massa-

---

8. Ames, "American Literature" (1809), in Allen, ed., *Works of Ames,* I, 22–37, esp. 31–32. Ferguson notes of Ames's essay, "In the bond of performing artist and audience, Ames captured the nature and meaning of early republican literature, but with one difference. In America, lawyers held the forum and their mode was oratory rather than poetry or drama"; see *Law and Letters in American Culture,* 77.

9. Bernhard, *Fisher Ames,* 29.

10. Michael Merrill and Sean Wilentz, eds., *The Key of Liberty: The Life and Democratic Writings of William Manning, "A Laborer," 1747–1814* (Cambridge, Mass., 1993), 152–155; Ames, *The Mire of Democracy,* in Allen, ed., *Works of Ames,* I, 4–5.

chusetts Ratifying Convention in 1788.[11] The volcano image presents "the people" as powerful through unmotivated and thus uncontrollable natural destruction rather than through the positive exercise of sovereignty. Figured as a volcano, popular power disrupts, rather than confirms, popular agency. Rhetorical figures such as this one exist apart from the audience's self-projection and thus introduce stability in precisely the way that Ames's ideal representative does, by distancing "the people" from their momentary impulses. Drawing on a tradition traced to classical antiquity, figural language imbues the representative with a cultural stability that transcends the individual. Rather than simply release emotion, such language is an elite technology for evoking feeling in order to control it.

Ames used rhetorical talent as a tool and a sign of his social elevation, a projection of self that lifted him above his personal background. The fluid political order of the early republic made the choice of a language a particularly self-constituting performance, and poetic language offered Ames a compelling tool for self-fashioning in the new forum of federal politics. The performance of political identity was a distinctively public act in Ames's case. His older brother Dr. Nathaniel Ames adopted the populist idiom of the tavern where they grew up and became one of the Republican "tavern-haunting politicians" and marketplace orators whom Fisher deplored.[12] The contrast with Nathaniel exposed Fisher's elevated language and theatrical style as conspicuous elements of his political persona, achievements as studied and deliberate as the manipulative words of the flatterer. Where the flatterer uses language to project an image of others and thus gain power over them, however, Ames used language to project an image of himself that provided him with power over others. Ames's "wonderful brilliancy of metaphor" and use of hyperbole, like the powder that he sometimes wore in his hair, foregrounded his training in gentility. John Adams captured the linked effects of Ames's language and appearance in a letter to the congressman's law tutor William Tudor: "Your pupil Ames makes a very pretty figure," he wrote, punning on the physical and rhetorical meanings of figure; "let me congratulate you on his fame." The Ciceronian connection between Ames's body and his language was central to the effect of his performances.[13]

11. "Fisher Ames on Biennial Elections and on the Volcano of Democracy," in Bernard Bailyn, ed., *The Debate on the Constitution* (New York, 1993), part 1, 894.

12. For Nathaniel Ames's perspective on their differences, see Charles Warren, *Jacobin and Junto; or, Early American Politics as Viewed in the Diary of Dr. Nathaniel Ames, 1758–1822* (Cambridge, Mass., 1931); the quoted phrase is from Allen, ed., *Works of Ames,* I, 41.

13. Zephaniah Swift to David Dagett, Dec. 13, 1794, in Franklin B. Dexter, ed., "Selections from Letters Received by David Daggett, 1786–1802," in American Antiquarian Society, *Proceedings,* IV (1887), 374, John Adams to William Tudor, June 28, 1789, Adams Papers, mircrofilm, reel 115, Massachusetts Historical Society, both in Bernhard, *Fisher Ames,* 118, 244. Cicero's understanding of the relation between body and language is discussed in Appendix, below.

FIGURE 17. Fisher Ames. *By John Trumbull. 1792. Courtesy, Yale University Art Gallery, Trumbull Collection*

The "very pretty figure" that Ames cut could disgust as well as impress members of his audience. His elaborate rhetoric was less successful with juries than the courtroom eloquence of lawyers who spoke with fewer figures and more directness. Political opponents offered scathing indictments of his speeches. On one occasion when Republican William Maclay went to hear Ames speak to the House, he responded with contempt to what he viewed as Ames's preciousness: "Ames delivered a long string of studied sentences, but he did not use a single argument that seemed to leave an impression. He had 'public faith,' 'public credit,' 'honor,' and above all 'justice' as often over as an Indian would the 'Great Spirit,' and, if possible, with less meaning and to as little purpose." Maclay's hostile response to his Federalist opponent, and particularly his comparison to a native orator's repeated invocation of the "Great Spirit," emphasizes the ritual element in Ames's rhetoric. Characterizing Ames's language as a type of "savage" speech, Maclay portrayed it as meaningless. When Ames sought to mark himself linguistically as a public guardian, he produced what one Republican journalist dismissed as *"pretty sounding Speeches."* The very elements of literary language that Ames's opponents singled out as evidence of his vacuousness were central to Ames's efforts to protect a hierarchical society.[14]

George Washington embodied the cultural order that Ames sought to sustain. Washington exemplified for Ames the power of emotion, publicly manifested and properly controlled, to maintain social hierarchies. This view is evident in Ames's depiction of Washington's self-effacement in his First Inaugural Address, which Ames described as an allegory of feminine virtue speaking to her votaries and producing "emotions of the most affecting kind." More than a decade afterward in his funeral eulogy for the late president, Ames celebrated Washington's ability to govern, rather than provoke, feeling, in a speech that articulated Ames's theory of political hegemony based on emotional control. Echoing his own famous description of volcanolike popular passions, Ames described the French Jacobins, whom Washington opposed, as a female monster, "with eyes that flash wild fire, hands that hurl thunderbolts, a voice that shakes the foundation of the hills[.] She stands, and her ambition measures the earth; she speaks, and an epidemic fury seizes the nations."[15] The shift in feminine imagery from the benign virtue of the inaugural address to the "licentiousness" and vocal power of revolutionary France in the eulogy marks the incommensurable forms of political feeling that Ames sought to distinguish through his figural language. The gentle hesitance of Washington contrasts sharply with the "epidemic fury" that accompanies the speech of the Jacobin "monster."

The disciplinary nature of Ames's eulogy appears in his focus on moral principles. Rather than portray Washington's eventful career in a heroic narrative, Ames analyzed his character to uncover its central moral principle: the control

---

14. Bernhard, *Fisher Ames,* 44; William Maclay, *The Journal of William Maclay, United States Senator from Pennsylvania, 1789–1791* (1890; New York, 1965), 192; *Boston Gazette,* Sept. 22, 1790, quoted in Bernhard, *Fisher Ames,* 160.

15. Letter to George Minot, May 3, 1789, in Allen, ed., *Works of Ames,* I, 547–569, esp. 568. See my discussion of the inaugural speech in Chap. 6, above. Daniel W. Howe discusses the role of faculty psychology in defining hierarchical relations for Federalists in "The Political Psychology of *The Federalist,*" *WMQ,* 3d Ser., XLIV (1987), 485–509. For the monster metaphor, see Fisher Ames, *An Oration on the Sublime Virtues of General George Washington . . .* (Dedham, Mass., 1800), 22.

that Washington learned to exercise over emotions, first his own and later those of others. According to Ames, Washington's early education in emotional self-discipline prepared him for political leadership. In his public addresses, Washington displayed his effort to control powerful feelings, and that personal struggle made him an exemplary republican leader in Ames's eyes, for if he could control his own emotions, he could govern those of others. Post-Revolutionary America needed a leader "who possessed a commanding power over the popular passions, but over whom those passions had no power." Ames concluded: "That man was Washington." Ames described his own feelings upon hearing of Washington's death: "But how shall I express emotions, that are condemned to be mute, because they are unutterable?" he asked his audience. Like the muteness signaled by Washington's firmly closed mouth, the unutterable nature of Ames's grief projects a disciplinary silence that leads to internalization of self-control rather than externalization of feeling in direct action.[16]

For emotion to require control, it must first be felt. Silence has political meaning only because it can be broken. Ames's celebration of wordless restraint in his eulogy for Washington provides a revealing counterpoint to Ames's most famous oration, the 1796 speech to the House of Representatives on Jay's Treaty. There he performed the loosening of restraint and the breaking forth of speech at great personal cost. The most celebrated instance of congressional eloquence in the new republic's first decade, this speech created a sensation at the time of its delivery and was reprinted in several editions.[17] Ames's performance influenced future generations of American orators, including both Daniel Webster, who memorized the oration as a young man and modeled his style upon it, and Abraham Lincoln, who knew and admired the speech. In his address, Ames confronted the efforts of House Republicans to deny funding for the controversial Jay Treaty. Negotiated at a time when tensions over the French Revolution had mounted to a state approaching political frenzy, the treaty provoked an outburst of hostility directed at Washington, who had once been immune from political attack. Issues of national self-definition were at stake. Supporters viewed the treaty as a satisfactory resolution to trade disputes with Great Britain while opponents believed that it surrendered too much to the British and betrayed both the nation's own independence and its Revolutionary allies, the French.

Widely known to support the treaty but already suffering from the illness that

16. Ames, *An Oration*, 4, 13.

17. Ames assisted two colleagues in writing out his speech after he delivered it (Bernhard, *Fisher Ames*, 272). It was printed as *The Speech of Mr. Ames, in the House of Representatives . . .* (Philadelphia, 1796) and appeared in *Debates and Proceedings in the Congress of the United States, 1789–1824 . . .* , V (Washington, D.C., 1849), 1239–1263. I quote from *Speech on the Jay Treaty*, in Allen, ed., *Works of Ames*, II, 1142–1182.

eventually killed him, Ames remained silent until the concluding days of the debate. His peroration sketched the circumstances that led him finally to break that self-imposed silence:

> I rose to speak under impressions that I would have resisted if I could. Those who see me will believe that the reduced state of my health has unfitted me, almost equally, for much exertion of body or mind. Unprepared for debate, by careful reflection in my retirement, or by long attention here, I thought the resolution I had taken to sit silent, was imposed by necessity, and would cost me no effort to maintain. With a mind thus vacant of ideas, and sinking, as I really am, under a sense of weakness, I imagined the very desire of speaking was extinguished by the persuasion that I had nothing to say.

Ames developed the trope of extempore performance in a distinctive fashion, using his bodily debility to register the urgency of his claims ("I would have resisted if I could") and insisting that those claims arose despite the apparent elimination of "the very desire to speak." Ames's reference to "a mind . . . vacant of ideas" rhetorically expunged all traces of the self, a claim that he made directly when he insisted, "I have, perhaps, as little personal interest in the event as any one here." At the same time, he claimed that he was "led by my feelings" to express his beliefs, filling the emotional void of self-interest and personal desire with pure concern for the public good. Like Washington at Newburgh, Ames insisted upon his effacement of self only to stage the covert assertion of his presence through his relation to text. The texts that Ames referenced included the Jay Treaty and the Constitution that he believed mandated the treaty's passage.[18]

Ames presented his sickly body as an effigy, or surrogate object of social violence, to protect both the Constitution and the treaty. He had been described in the weeks and months before this performance as "a mere ghost" and "a troubled ghost of a politician," and his spectral appearance carried the impact of an effort made on the verge of the grave. Indeed, a friend observed that he missed an opportunity for an even more dramatic conclusion, suggesting, "He ought to have died in the fifth act."[19] Throughout his speech, Ames used his body, visibly weak-

18. Allen, ed., *Works of Ames*, II, 1181–1182.

19. Ames's friend Thomas Dwight and Ames himself penned the descriptions of the ghostly Ames in 1795 and 1796 (quoted in Bernhard, *Fisher Ames*, 252, 264). For Jeremiah Smith's letter of 1796, see 272. Kirkland repeated remarks linking Ames's death to his political engagement, noting that Ames's emotional investment in political issues consumed him: "His health, and perhaps his life, were the costly oblations which he laid on the altar of patriotism. The fine machinery of his system could ill withstand the excitement produced by public speaking, and his keen interest in public affairs" (Kirkland, in Allen, ed., *Works of Ames*, I, 1). Less sympathetic observers attributed his unusually emotional eloquence on the occasion of the Jay Treaty to a

ened and attenuated, as a material form incarnating the condition of the nation. His first words expressed the hope "that my strength will hold me out to speak a few minutes," and, as those minutes extended to an hour and more, he observed that his "momentary strength . . . is lent to me by the zeal of the occasion." A subsequent reference to his "little breath" marked the spectacle of a man consuming his life in the public interest. His concluding words pointedly articulated the relationship between his body and his nation. If the House voted to refuse treaty funding, he warned, "even I, slender and almost broken as my hold upon life is, may outlive the government and Constitution of my country."[20]

Ames achieved tremendous affective power when he visibly expended his strength on behalf of his cause, placing himself within the Pauline tradition that accumulates rhetorical authority from displays of weakness. His dramatic performance also drew directly on the political tradition of the Boston Massacre orations as well as on John Hancock's performance at the Massachusetts Ratifying Convention in 1788. There Hancock, then governor of the state, remained conspicuously silent on the proposed Constitution, attributing his disengagement to illness. At a decisive moment in the convention's proceedings, Hancock had himself carried into the convention to present a speech that offered a successful compromise measure. Ames's oration eight years later recalled the major elements of Hancock's speech, which itself carried references to the Boston Massacre orations and Perez Morton's eulogy for Joseph Warren. Repeating these earlier efforts, Ames acted in a performed effigy; that is, he occupied the already existing role of an orator who perpetuated national identity through his display of self-sacrifice. Oratorical moments such as this dramatized the set of tropes linking the bodily vulnerability of political leaders to the health of the state that characterized the republican rearticulation of the king's two bodies. Consuming himself, Ames offered his life to sustain the federal government founded on the Constitution. His self-consuming, nation-preserving speech stood in contrast to the volcanic, nation-destroying speech of the "mob" of treaty opponents.[21]

---

mind "enfeebled by disease" (Bernhard, *Fisher Ames,* 273). John Quincy Adams extended this evaluation to Ames's whole career, writing that his "best political writing was saturated with the despair of the tomb to which his wasting body was condemned" (Allen, ed., *Works of Ames,* I, vii).

20. *Speech on the Jay Treaty,* in Allen, ed., *Works of Ames,* II, 1143, 1154, 1158, 1182.

21. Joseph Roach develops the idea of the performed effigy in *Cities of the Dead: Circum-Atlantic Performance* (New York, 1996). There he observes that performed effigies "consist of a set of actions that hold open a place in memory into which many different people may step according to circumstances and occasions." Such effigies "provide communities with a method of perpetuating themselves through specially nominated mediums or surrogates" (36). Roach singles out the funerals of English monarchs, where the dead king was represented by a wooden

244 : Political Speech in the New Republic

The emotional manipulation intrinsic to his endeavor was neither subtle nor disguised. Ames frankly performed the operations of emotional stimulation and control on his audience. His opening words sketched a psychology of persuasion that placed nonrational aspects of political decision making uppermost. "Let us not affect to deny the existence and the intrusion of some portion of prejudice and feeling into the debate, when, from the very structure of our nature, we ought to anticipate the circumstance as a probability, and when we are admonished by the evidence of our senses that it is a fact," he urged. "The only constant agents in political affairs are the passions of men—shall we complain of our nature?" Ames labeled such complaints as impious, for "He, from whom we derive our nature, ordained it so; and because thus made, and thus acting, the cause of truth and the public good is the more surely promoted." Acknowledging that "the warmth of such feelings may becloud the judgment, and, for a time, pervert the understanding," he nevertheless insisted that the intensely emotional response to the treaty had "sharpened the spirit of inquiry, and given an animation to the debate." The result of such heated debate, he concluded, was "solid and enlightened" public judgment; "the voice of the people is raised against the measure of refusing the appropriations." Repeating the words of "merchants and traders" whose "sense is not so liable to be mistaken as that of the nation," Ames sought to establish the authenticity of the public voice favoring funding despite opposition claims that the "sound of alarm is a counterfeit expression of the sense of the people." [22]

Ames located the most authentic sources of popular voice on the frontier. Without the Jay Treaty, the British would refuse to hand over their frontier posts, he warned, and without American possession of those posts, renewed Indian warfare was inevitable. With such conflict "the price of the Western lands will fall"; indeed, a "vast . . . tract of wild land will almost cease to be property." In the most melodramatic passages of his speech, Ames dramatized this blunt financial fact and its effect on the national debt, using the familiar imagery of the Indian captivity narrative:

> By rejecting the posts, we light the savage fires—we bind the victims. This day we undertake to render account to the widows and orphans whom our decision will make; to the wretches that will be roasted at the stake; to our country; and I do not deem it too serious to say, to conscience, and to God—we are

effigy to instantiate the concept of the king's two bodies, as a central instance of the performed effigy.

Joseph Warren's union of eloquence and martyrdom created a republican version of the king's two bodies when his actions as Boston Massacre orator and victim of British violence at Bunker Hill were transformed into an oratorical role; see Chap. 5, above.

22. Allen, ed., *Works of Ames*, II, 1144, 1145, 1156.

answerable. . . . I can fancy that I listen to the yells of savage vengeance, and the shrieks of torture. Already they seem to sigh in the West wind; already they mingle with every echo from the mountains.

Here Ames portrayed the imagined consequences of failing to fund the treaty as direct acts of Congress. Earlier, Ames had imposed severe restrictions on House agency, insisting that the representatives were "under coercion" to provide treaty funding. Now he dramatically expanded their agency to make House decisions responsible for anticipated native atrocities, identifying the speech of his opponents with the yells of murderous savages. Treaty opponents became savage speakers who massacred their fellow citizens.[23]

Ames located the most effective response to his opponents on the frontier. "The Western inhabitants are not a silent and uncomplaining sacrifice," he insisted. "The voice of humanity issues from the shade of their wilderness." Imagining that "the cries of our future victims have already reached us," Ames gave his own "unutterable" emotions voice in the most famous passage of his speech, rich with echoes from the Boston Massacre orations that he knew so well:

If I could find words for them — if my powers bore any proportion to my zeal — I would swell my voice to such a note of remonstrance it should reach every log-house beyond the mountains. I would say to the inhabitants, Wake from your false security! Your cruel dangers — your more cruel apprehensions — are soon to be renewed; the wounds, yet unhealed, are to be torn open again. In the day time, your path through the woods will be ambushed; the darkness of midnight will glitter with the blaze of your dwellings. You are a father: the blood of your sons shall fatten your corn-field! You are a mother: the war-whoop shall wake the sleep of the cradle!

Such a description, Ames instructed his audience, produces "a spectacle of horror" that should elicit a unified response: "If you have nature in your hearts, it will speak a language compared with which all I have said or can say will be poor and frigid." Ames evoked the voice of nature and humanity from his immediate audience and from the white residents of the frontier. The image transforms his language of nurturance at the Massachusetts Ratifying Convention, where Ames portrayed the federal government as a source of physical and spiritual sustenance for a swelling national body. In that speech, Ames identified congressional debate with national expansion figured as pregnancy and parturition. Here Ames warned fathers that their sons, rather than being fed themselves, would become food for their cornfields; mothers, that their infants would not be nurtured by the nation

23. Ibid., 1148, 1173, 1176.

but destroyed by it. National reproduction and expansion would be brought to an abrupt and horrifying halt if Congress did not fund the treaty.[24]

Insisting on the sacrificial consequences of the failure to fund the treaty, Ames imagined that his swelling voice called forth the voice of humanity to resist that sacrifice, both within his immediate audience, located at the very center of national power, and from the borders of the nation. Visibly expending his energy in the act of speaking, Ames offered himself as a substitute sacrifice, an effigy representing the settlers on the frontier who themselves stood for the future of the nation. Purging himself of materiality, he presented himself as the pure voice of nature and nation, projected only to echo back to him in a perfect reciprocity. The Republicans tried to forestall the consequences of Ames's rhetorical coup, refusing to hold the vote immediately after he concluded his speech. They succumbed two days later, when that imagined reciprocity between Ames and the nation produced the vote in favor of treaty funding.

Like George Washington's address at Newburgh, Ames's performance on this occasion redefined uncontainable speech, making it resound from the top of the social hierarchy rather than from the margins of society. And like Washington in his first inaugural address, Ames derived the authority of his speech from the Constitution. In the Jay Treaty speech, Ames imagined that the text of the Constitution provided the founding legitimacy for an exercise of voice that could break through geographic barriers and individual resistance, converting his auditors to his perspective. Such developments of the symbolism of voice indicate the readiness with which the radical elements of this central figure for Revolutionary transformation could be suppressed and its affective potency directed toward the preservation of existing power relations.

II. FIGURES OF DIFFERENCE

Among those who experienced the transformative energy of the Revolution only to have their horizons rebounded and their energies recontained in the early national period, perhaps none responded more unconventionally and ambiguously than Deborah Sampson Gannett. Gannett was an impoverished female veteran of the Revolution who conducted a lecture tour of the Northeast in 1802, seeking the pension that had been denied her. Like her earlier military service, her speaking tour was an extraordinary act in the new republic where women's public engagement in civic discourse most often took a written form. Abigail Adams wrote letters to her husband urging him to "Remember the Ladies" while Esther

24. Ibid., 1174–1176.

DeBerdt Reed led prominent Philadelphia women in collecting money for the Continental army and penned the widely reprinted *Sentiments of an American Woman* as part of that patriot effort. Mercy Otis Warren wrote patriotic dramas, Phillis Wheatley and Annis Boudinot Stockton celebrated the achievements of George Washington in published poetry, and after the war Judith Sargent Murray offered the first formal expression of an emerging feminist political stance.

The absence of women's public speech on political issues stands in striking contrast to such prominent written efforts, a contrast made still more striking in light of the long, if often controversial, tradition of women's religious speech. The women who spoke most comfortably and eloquently in public before the Revolution were Quaker women who found themselves largely excluded from the patriot political domain by their loyalist leanings.[25] In the post-Revolutionary period, the importance of oratory in a republic shaped the curricula at the new female seminaries, where young women were given rhetorical training modeled on that of young men. Their graduation speeches sometimes drew illustrious audiences, for instance in 1794 when Martha Washington and members of the House attended the graduation ceremony for the Young Ladies Academy of Philadelphia. The eight young women awarded diplomas on this occasion did not follow their brothers into the political arena, however. Outside the seminaries, women filled the rhetorical roles that Fisher Ames identified with them: as figures for political virtue and vice and, increasingly after Ames intervened to admit women to the gallery in the House of Representatives, as audiences for male eloquence.[26]

The first American woman to orate on secular themes in a broader public arena had little in common with the young women trained in public speaking at elite academies. In May 1782, Gannett disguised herself as Robert Shurtliff and enlisted in the Continental army, where she served undetected for over a year. Economic hardship lent urgency to her postwar attempts to receive the same compensation as male veterans, which included a successful petition for back pay approved in 1792 and an unsuccessful 1797 petition for a military pension. Her lecture tour formed part of her renewed effort to win a pension by publicly establishing the

25. Linda K. Kerber, " 'I Have Don . . . Much to Carrey on the Warr': Women and the Shaping of Republican Ideology after the American Revolution," in Kerber, *Toward an Intellectual History of Women* (Chapel Hill, N.C., 1997), 100–130, esp. 130.

26. On Ames's role in opening the House gallery to women, see Bernhard, *Fisher Ames*, 131–132. For women's roles in post-Revolutionary America, see Nancy F. Cott, *The Bonds of Womanhood: "Woman's Sphere" in New England, 1780–1835* (New Haven, Conn., 1977); Linda K. Kerber, *Women of the Republic: Intellect and Ideology in Revolutionary America* (Chapel Hill, N.C., 1980); Kerber, *Toward an Intellectual History of Women;* Mary Beth Norton, *Liberty's Daughters: The Revolutionary Experience of American Women, 1750–1800* (Boston, 1980); Christine Stansell, *City of Women: Sex and Class in New York, 1789–1860* (Urbana, Ill., 1987); Mary P. Ryan, *Women in Public: Between Banners and Ballots, 1825–1880* (Baltimore, 1990).

legitimacy of her claim. Gannett performed her oration and display of arms before audiences in northeastern towns including Boston, Providence, Springfield, Northampton, Albany, and New York. While making her tour, she paid visits to her former commanding officers to renew their friendships and elicit their support. She sought out men of letters who could publicize her adventures and make her a public figure, including Herman Mann, a Dedham, Massachusetts writer, editor, and printer who assisted her first effort by publishing her biography, *The Female Review* (1797) and who later aided her in preparing her speech and arms drill; and Philip Freneau, who published an ode in 1797 calling on Congress to grant her a pension. Her attempt to win legitimacy in the eyes of the national government, and consequently a permanent income, concluded successfully in 1805 when she was awarded the pension.[27]

Gannett's example countered the emergent ideology of gendered spheres that separated society into masculine public and feminine private domains, even as her words reinforced it. Mandating a domestic arena for women, separate spheres ideology made universal claims but had limited power. Gannett's performances oscillated between aggressive challenges to social conventions and self-conscious submission to them. The final words of her address articulated the ideology of separate spheres with special clarity, when she observed, "The *field* and the *cabinet* are the proper spheres assigned to our MASTERS and our LORDS" and prayed that the women in her audience would share her ambition to "deserve the dignified title and encomium of MISTRESS and LADY, in our *kitchens* and in our *parlours*." Speaking to "my own SEX," she offered instruction in Republican Motherhood: "Let us rear an offspring in every respect worthy to fill the most illustrious stations of their predecessors."[28] Yet she followed these words with a display of the manual

27. Gannett kept a journal of her tour, "Diary of Deborah Sampson Gannett in 1802" (MS), Sharon Public Library, Sharon, Mass. Gannett does not mention New York City performances in her diary, but see George C. D. Odell, *Annals of the New York Stage*, II (New York, 1927), 176. On her helpful connections, see [Herman Mann], *The Female Review: Life of Deborah Sampson* (1797; New York, 1972) (orig. publ. as *The Female Review; or, Memoirs of an American Young Lady* . . . [Dedham, Mass., 1797]). For Mann's background, see Randall Craig, "Herman Mann (1771–1833)," in James A. Levernier and Douglas R. Wilmes, eds., *American Writers before 1800: A Biographical and Critical Dictionary* (Westport, Conn., 1983), 939–940. For Mann's role in composing Gannett's biography and speech, see Judith Hiltner, " 'She Bled in Secret': Deborah Sampson, Herman Mann, and *The Female Review*," *Early American Literature*, XXXIV (1999), 190–220. The Freneau poem is entitled "Ode XIII: A Soldier Should Be Made of Sterner Stuff . . ." (orig. publ. in the *Time-Piece*, Dec. 4, 1797), in Fred Lewis Pattee, ed., *The Poems of Philip Freneau: Poet of the American Revolution*, III (Princeton, N.J., 1907), 182–184.

28. Quotations from Gannett's address are from the reprinted version, entitled "An Address on Life as a Female Revolutionary Soldier," in Judith Anderson, ed., *Outspoken Women: Speeches by American Women Reformers, 1635–1935* (Dubuque, Iowa, 1984), 135–141, esp. 141. Mann origi-

exercise she had learned as a soldier, a complex series of vigorous maneuvers with a large, heavy gun, undermining the very commitment to domesticity that she had just expressed. Throughout her speech, Gannett staged similarly abrupt oscillations between the rhetorics of domesticity and antidomesticity, self-promotion and self-incrimination. The unsettled quality of her rhetoric reflected her multiple projects: her need to authenticate and justify her military experience and patriot commitments while simultaneously attesting to her chastity, the feminine form of self-effacement. Through acts of rhetorical and performative instability, Gannett presented her life story as the site of an ongoing battle over gender and status identities in the early republic.

The opening words of Gannett's oration repeated a commonplace of neoclassical rhetoric when she identified herself with the Cincinnatean hero who reluctantly leaves his rural retirement to serve his nation:

> Not unlike the example of the patriot and philanthropist, though perhaps perfectly so in effect, do I awake from the tranquil slumbers of retirement, to active, public scenes of life, like those which now surround me. That genius which is the prompter of *curiosity,* and that spirit which is the support of *enterprize,* early drove, or, rather illured me, from the corner of humble obscurity — their cheering aspect has again prevented a torpid rest.

George Washington self-consciously modeled his public persona on the farmer-patriot-warrior Cincinnatus, providing the most famous instance of the masculine rhetorical convention that Gannett invoked. Called to serve as the republic's first president, Washington claimed that it was his "sole desire to live and die, in peace and retirement on my own farm." Gannett's wartime experience and subsequent life provided the basis for her claims to Cincinnatean rhetoric, but her financial need as well as her gender disturbed her identification with the gentleman-farmer.[29]

Although one central irony of Gannett's first words to her audience lay in the discrepancy between her neoclassical language of rural repose and her actual life as a hardscrabble farmer, the more obvious irony lay in her linguistic cross-

---

nally published the text as *An Addrss Delivered with Applause, at the* Federal-Street Theatre, *Boston . . . by Mrs. Deborah Gannet, the American Heroine . . .* (Dedham, Mass., 1802).

29. Gannett, "An Address," in Anderson, ed., *Outspoken Women,* 135; Kenneth Silverman, *A Cultural History of the American Revolution . . .* (New York, 1987), 603. On Washington's self-conscious adaptation of Whig literary ideals of the heroic leader, see 430–431. For a thorough discussion of the iconography of Washington as Cincinnatus, see Garry Wills, *Cincinnatus. George Washington and the Enlightenment* (Garden City, N.Y., 1984). Ernest W. Peterkin describes the arms drill in *The Exercise of Arms in the Continental Infantry . . .* (Alexandria Bay, N.Y., 1975).

FIGURE 18. Portrait of Deborah Sampson. *By Joseph Stone Framingham. 1797. Courtesy,* Rhode Island Historical Society

dressing, the verbal counterpart to the Continental army uniform that she wore. Employing a vocabulary of masculine patriotism, she exposed the inadequacy of the distinct gendered languages of nationalism that emerged in the post-Revolutionary period, revealing their inability to account for her wartime experiences. Her appearance heightened her audience's sense of incongruity. At 5′ 7″, she made a convincing enough man in uniform that, as she noted with delight in her tour diary, one audience was "full of unbelieff," claiming "that I was a lad of not more than Eighteen years of age." Gannett's performances revealed her to be a woman who eluded conventional categories by masquerading as a man on the battlefield and on the stage. Her address captured the disequilibrium and instability of the transvestite as she alternated between the representation and the erasure of fixed gender distinctions.[30] Her opening claim to be "not unlike" the male "patriot and philanthropist," which measured her distance from the male ideal, gave way to an asserted perfect identity "in effect." But her second sentence reasserts difference, disrupting her opening effort to acknowledge and then erase gender categories. Initially, she claimed that curiosity and enterprise "drove" her "from the corner of humble obscurity," an assertion resonant with the newly legitimated masculine ambitions of liberalism. But she immediately qualified the masculine language of drive with the feminine language of seduction, describing herself alternatively as "illured" into public activity. Unlike "drive," seduction implies uncontrolled, socially disruptive passions identified with its feminine objects.

The convoluted syntax and multiple, contradictory rhetorics represented in Gannett's opening words anticipated the complexities of the performance that followed. The conflicts intrinsic to Gannett's role are nowhere more obvious than in her repeated insistence on the violence-laden potential of her speech. She explicitly linked her language to the socially disruptive nature of her experiences, claiming to present "a narration of facts in a mode as uncouth as they are unnatural." Although she "bow[ed] submissive to an audience," her submissiveness could not control the potentially destructive effects of her speech, which she claimed might be "wounding to the ear of more refined delicacy and taste" and "ring discord in the ear, and disgust to the bosom of sensibility and refinement." Like Fisher Ames's feminine figure of the French Jacobins, Gannett identified revolution with the violence of female speech. The power she attributed to her wounding words echoed her description of the effects of Revolutionary violence on Bostonians, whose "ears are yet wounded by the shrieks of [Charlestown's] mangled and her distressed." In a similar figural linking of her actions with Revolutionary upheaval, she compared the effects of the war to "the terrific glare of the comet . . . in its excentric orbit," a realm that she herself occupied as she traveled "like a bewildered star traversing out of its accustomed orbit" through the masculine domain of the battlefield. Such astronomical references echoed the ubiqui-

---

30. "Diary of Deborah Sampson Gannett in 1802" (MS), Sharon Public Library, Sharon, Mass., 11. In *Vested Interests: Cross-Dressing and Cultural Anxiety* (New York, 1992), Marjorie Garber observes that, by throwing binary models of social identity into disequilibrium, the transvestite woman exposes uncharted social terrain. She functions as the cultural "third term" that is "*not a term*" but rather "a space of possibility" (11). Judith Butler discusses the performativity of gender in *Gender Trouble: Feminism and the Subversion of Identity* (New York, 1990).

tous cosmic imagery in the eulogies delivered for George Washington in 1800. But Gannett portrayed herself as violating the celestial order that the eulogists credited Washington with creating.[31]

Rhetorically joining her transvestite disguise with the violence and disruption of war itself, Gannett related her performance to the familiar popular culture icon of female disorderliness, the woman-on-top. The cross-dressing woman of the early modern period offered a potent figure that could be used to restructure social relations. The woman-on-top provided Gannett with a broadly familiar figural means of linking her personal experiences to Revolutionary motifs of the world-turned-upside-down, and the related popular tradition of the woman warrior offered a set of narrative traditions that contributed to the shape of Gannett's oration.[32] In the transformative moment of the American Revolution, when patriots drew on popular ritual to reimagine political structure, the figure of the Amazonian woman suggested both a general rebelliousness against established authority and the overthrow of accepted gender roles. Philadelphia women defended their unaccustomed public efforts to collect funds for Washington's troops in a broadside of 1780 that offered historical women warriors as precedents for their actions. These included the biblical Deborah, the Israelite judge and military leader whose name Gannett bore, and Joan of Arc, "the Maid of Orleans who drove from the kingdom of France the ancestors of those same British, whose odious yoke we have just shaken off; and whom it is necessary that we drive from this Continent." Ann Harker repeated this feminized civic rhetoric in her 1794 salutatory oration before the Young Ladies Academy of Philadelphia when she

31. Gannett, "An Address," in Anderson, ed., *Outspoken Women,* 135, 136, 138, 140. Charles Pinckney Sumner offered an extended simile comparing Washington to the sun in a eulogy that Gannett's collaborater Herman Mann printed; see Charles Pinckney Sumner, *Eulogy on the Illustrious George Washington, Pronounced at Milton, Twenty-Second February, 1800* (Dedham, Mass., 1800), 21–23.

32. Her transgressive force was twofold: the unruly woman could operate "first, to widen behavioral options for women within and even outside marriage, and, second, to sanction riot and political disobedience for both men and women in a society that allowed the lower orders few formal means of protest"; see Natalie Zemon Davis, "Women on Top," in *Society and Culture in Early Modern France: Eight Essays* (Stanford, Calif., 1975), 124–151, esp. 131. See also Rudolf M. Dekker and Lotte C. van de Pol, *The Tradition of Female Transvestism in Early Modern Europe* (New York, 1989); Lynne Friedli, " 'Passing Women' — A Study of Gender Boundaries in the Eighteenth Century," in G. S. Rousseau and Roy Porter, eds., *Sexual Underworlds of the Enlightenment* (Chapel Hill, N.C., 1988), 234–260. In *Warrior Women and Popular Balladry 1650–1850* (Cambridge, 1989), Dianne Dugaw traces the wide dissemination of the woman warrior ballad. Many of those printed in England appeared in America, including the story of Hannah Snell. Jay Fliegelman discusses the version of the Snell story printed in *Thomas's New-England Almanack* in *Declaring Independence: Jefferson, Natural Language, and the Culture of Performance* (Stanford, Calif., 1993), 155–160. For the original Snell narrative, see Snell, *The Female Soldier; or, The Surprising Life and Adventures of Hannah Snell* (1750; Los Angeles, 1989).

alluded to "the count d'Eon and the maid of Orleans" who "shall defend our honour with amazonian courage."[33]

Gannett made the Amazonian woman central to the Revolutionary myth when she conflated her convention-breaking acts of personal heroism with nation formation. "I burst the tyrant bands, which *held my sex in awe*," she announced, identifying her personal liberation from gender constraints with the liberation of the American colonies from British rule. The mythmaking imagination at work in her address accounts for her false assertion that she entered the army at a time of severe military crisis when the patriot cause was in danger of collapsing: "Whilst poverty, hunger, nakedness, cold and disease had dwindled the *American Armies* to a handful—whilst universal terror and dismay ran through our camps, ran through our country—while even WASHINGTON himself, at their head, though like a god, stood, as it were, on a pinacle tottering over the abyss of destruction," at that moment, she continued, "did I throw off the soft habiliments of *my sex,* and assume those of the *warrior,* already prepared for battle." Her language implied that by reversing gender order she reversed American military fortunes. As if this claim were not extraordinary enough, Gannett asserted that her actions staged yet another, related cultural reversal. Distinguishing herself from her "reputed Predecessor," Eve, Gannett suggested that her mythic revolution in gender superseded the biblical basis of gender differentiation. Identifying her own person and actions with the war for political independence, Gannett portrayed the Revolution as the source of a new social myth of female heroism that displaced the central biblical myth justifying female subordination.[34]

Gannett was not alone in her revisionary mythography. The woman warrior

---

33. On elements of popular ritual and theater in Revolutionary politics, see Peter Shaw, *American Patriots and the Rituals of Revolution* (Cambridge, Mass., 1981), chaps. 9, 10. Esther DeBerdt Reed authored the petition *The Sentiments of an American Woman,* which is reprinted in Sharon M. Harris, ed., *American Women Writers to 1800* (New York, 1996), 255–259, esp. 257. Thomas Paine also invoked the unifying power of Joan of Arc in a fight against British tyranny; see Thomas Paine, "The American Crisis, Number 1, December 19, 1776," in Paine, *Collected Writings* (New York, 1995), 91–99, esp. 92. For Harker's comments, see J. A. Neal, *An Essay on the Education and Genius of the Female Sex* (Philadelphia, 1795), 15–20, esp. 17. On Eon, see Gary Kates, *Monsieur d'Eon Is a Woman: A Tale of Political Intrigue and Sexual Masquerade* (New York, 1995).

34. Gannett, "An Address," in Anderson, ed., *Outspoken Women,* 137. This passage echoes Sumner's eulogy on Washington, suggesting its influence on the address; see Sumner, *Eulogy on Washington,* 9. One of the central controversies in the historical literature on Gannett focuses on whether she joined the army in time to fight at Yorktown, as both her biography and her address claim. The most reliable documents suggest that she did not enlist until the spring of 1782, when the war was winding down.

Jan Lewis discusses revisions of Eve that took a more domestic direction in "The Republican Wife: Virtue and Seduction in the Early Republic," *WMQ,* 3d Ser., XLIV (1987), 689–721.

figure reached the zenith of her popularity in both England and America in the 1790s, when stage extravaganzas and ballads made her a pervasive feature of popular culture. The imagery of the woman warrior during this decade reflected the prominent role of French women in crowd actions and formal battles, intellectual debates, and revolutionary iconography. The exclusion of American women from the constitutionally established government converged with the French Revolution and the publication of Wollstonecraft's *Vindication of the Rights of Woman* (1792) to make the relationship between gender and citizenship in a republic a central cultural preoccupation in its own right as well as a general figure for the problem of social order. American writers evolved their own symbolic vesture for the cross-dressing female soldier, woven of the disputed issues of political, economic, and gender identity. Gannett offered an example of a woman warrior in whom destabilized gender identity intersected with conflicting definitions of republicanism.[35]

The ideological elements that Gannett's performances share with the woman warrior literature of the 1790s converge on the issues of violence and sentiment as they mutually construct gender and national identities during the period. Describing "the tear of repentance . . . which many times involuntarily stole into my eye, and fell unheeded to the ground: And that too before I had reached the embattled field," Gannett concentrated attention away from her personal battlefield experience and toward her own violation of gender roles. Earlier woman warrior narratives such as those of Christian Davies (1740) and Hannah Snell (1750) have little or nothing to say about the virago's psychological experience upon donning male garb.[36] In contrast, the act of cross-dressing preoccupied Gannett in her 1802 address. Though she offered patriotic celebrations of liberty's virtues and Columbia's economic future, these nationalist and republican themes quickly gave way to the urgent query, *"What particular inducement could she have thus to elope from the soft sphere of her own sex?"* Gannett offered explanations that framed her experience in masculine terms that echo her introduction ("And dost thou ask what fairy hand inspired / A *Nymph* to be with martial glory fired? . . . Then ask— why *Cincinnatus* left his farm?"). Alternatively, she placed herself in the ballad tradition of the woman warrior who follows a man into battle, asking, "Was some

35. See Linda Kerber, "Separate Spheres, Female Worlds, Woman's Place: The Rhetoric of Women's History," in Kerber, *Toward an Intellectual History of Women,* 159–199, esp. 174–175. On the American woman warrior in the 1790s, see Sandra M. Gustafson, "The Genders of Nationalism: Patriotic Violence, Patriotic Sentiment in the Performances of Deborah Sampson Gannett," in Robert Blair St. George, ed., *Possible Pasts* (Ithaca, N.Y., forthcoming).

36. Gannett, "An Address," in Anderson, ed., *Outspoken Women,* 137. See also Snell, *The Female Soldier,* and the anonymous narrative, sometimes attributed to Daniel Defoe, *Life and Adventures of Mrs. Christian Davies . . .* (London, 1740).

hapless *lover* from her torn?" Finally, however, she could provide no adequate explanation for her motivations, for she was fully identifiable with neither Cincinnatus nor the conventional woman warrior. Gannett fell outside the available languages of female subjectivity. Her failed efforts to define herself highlighted the boundary-bursting, uncontainable nature of her speech.[37]

Yet Gannett immediately expressed an acceptance of limitations in a confession designed to contain her potent voice. Rejecting the possibility of adequate explanation for her actions, she turned instead to a testimony of "error and presumption."[38] Her promise of *"repentance"* and "atonement to the Supreme JUDGE of our offenses" paralleled the conversion narrative, a form that may have been familiar to her from her brief experience as a Baptist convert prior to entering the army. Gannett turned to conversion rhetoric, not to justify her unconventional actions through assertions of divinely inspired uncontainability, but to plead for social acceptance.[39] Once again employing the language of seduction, she acknowledged that she walked upon the "precipice of feminine perdition" and "in the precipitancy of passion" readied "a moment for repentance at leisure." She titillated her auditors with a catalog of dissipated characters, including the prodigal, the libertine, the bacchanalian, the debauchee, and the *"baggage* in the streets," then testified, "I cannot, indeed bring the adventures, even of the worst part of my own life, as parallels with this black catalogue of crimes." Appealing to the women in the audience, she solicited their judgment in the language of conversion: "In whatever I may be thought to have been unnatural, unwise and indelicate, it is now my most fervent desire it may have a suitable impression on you—and on me, a penitent for every wrong thought and step." Her linguistic contortions revealed her ambiguously subordinate position before her audience, particularly its female members. She was an object for their judgment as well as a moral monitor, and she hoped to garner support through her humble appeal to the women whose standards she had supposedly violated even as she imposed those standards upon them.[40]

Her conversion rhetoric staged her submission to an audience representing the nation: if her auditors, particularly her female auditors, would accept her repentance, she could be sure to have won God's blessing and, presumably, the money

37. Gannett, "An Address," in Anderson, ed., *Outspoken Women,* 139, 140.

38. Ibid., 140.

39. In *Disorderly Women: Sexual Politics and Evangelicalism in Revolutionary New England* (Ithaca, N.Y., 1994), chap. 4, Susan Juster argues that Protestant sects such as the Baptists which had once held relatively egalitarian attitudes toward women became increasingly conservative at the time of the Revolution.

40. Gannett, "An Address," in Anderson, ed., *Outspoken Women,* 140, 141. On the persistent role of women as confessors, see Cornelia Hughes Dayton, *Women before the Bar: Gender, Law, and Society in Connecticut, 1639–1789* (Chapel Hill, N.C., 1995), 198–199, incl. n. 87.

that she needed to raise her family, perhaps even the pension that she sought. Despite her wandering from the path of convention, she stated, "I still hope for some claim on the indulgence and patronage of the public; as in such case I might be conscious of the approbation of my GOD." Fusing God and nation with "the public," Gannett submitted the disruptive energies of the woman warrior to the control of "this respectable circle."[41]

Gannett's strategy reflected the status dynamics of her situation. One Boston advertisement highlights the "respectable" sponsors of her performance, and her diary reflects her concern to have "respectable" people in the audience and to win the approval of "the Ladies." The "ladies" to whom she addressed her remarks represented a model of femininity that was not fully available to Gannett and her peers, but it was the approbation of the "ladies" that she sought to win through the language of patriotic motherhood and gendered domains. Yet her concluding celebration of republican womanhood and separate spheres undermined itself in its public articulation: her very act of giving such a performance stressed her distance from this mode of femininity, particularly when, "equipt in complete uniform," she concluded her speech with the arms drill display.[42] The performance dimension of her tour—the costume, the arms drill, Gannett's substantial physical presence—both aestheticized her own role and invited members of her audience to recognize the republican woman as a figure requiring a similar, if less dramatic, kind of role-playing. Throughout the address and the military drill, the pervasive texture of ambiguity characteristic of Gannett's opening words heightened attention to linguistic mediation and the theatrical dimension of everyday life, working simultaneously to reinforce and to challenge the audience's understanding of conventional modes of experience.

Gannett's performances exposed the absence of a coherent ideology of nonelite women's experience in particular and the problematic relationship of all American women to patriot identity in general. Rather than offer her example as a viable mode of female patriotism, however, she presented herself as an anomaly and a curiosity and cast the woman warrior in the role of the penitent submitting to the social authority of the ladies in her audience. A figure for forms of Revolutionary transformation that were both celebrated and feared, this woman warrior strate-

41. Gannett, "An Address," in Anderson, ed., *Outspoken Women,* 141.

42. On Gannett's sponsors, see May 5, 1802, in "Diary of Deborah Sampson Gannett in 1802" (MS), Sharon Public Library, Sharon, Mass. The Boston broadside quoted here is reproduced in Elizabeth Evans, *Weathering the Storm: Women of the American Revolution* (New York, 1975), 319.

Jane Elmes-Crahall emphasizes Sampson Gannett's sentimentalism and her investment in the ideology of Republican Motherhood in "Deborah Sampson Gannett," in Karlyn Kohrs Campbell, ed., *Women Public Speakers in the United States, 1800–1925: A Bio-Critical Sourcebook* (Westport, Conn., 1993), 380–392.

gically developed that ambiguity to create an effective voice for herself despite the widespread exclusion of women's public speech from the civic arena. Violating cultural boundaries in the very act of submitting to them, she revealed through her alternating demonstrations of uncontainability and assertions of containment the symbolic ambiguity of women's public speech in the new republic.

The efforts of cultural outsiders such as Gannett to remake forms of eloquence met with real but sharply limited success in the public domains of the early republic. Revolutionary war veteran and Mahican Indian Hendrick Aupaumut confronted similar obstacles as he sought to define a novel speakerly role that would create a place for native Americans in the political forums of the new nation. Drawing on a long tradition of Mahican diplomatic eloquence, Aupaumut sought a position of authority for himself as an ambassador in the Washington administration. Addressing white Americans in a written narrative of his mission, he presented traditions of native oratory and challenged stereotypes of savage speech, much as Canassatego had at Lancaster fifty years earlier. Despite some minor successes, Aupaumut's efforts ultimately failed to win him a position of long-term influence, to protect the Mahicans from exploitation, or to prevent the emergence of increasingly hostile imagery of native Americans as savages.

Aupaumut was born into the Christian Stockbridge community that Jonathan Edwards briefly served in the 1750s. While most native Americans sided with the British or remained neutral during the Revolutionary war, Aupaumut held the rank of captain in the Continental army. In the 1790s, Aupaumut served as ambassador for the United States government on two negotiating missions to establish peace with the northwest Indian nations that for over a decade had engaged in conflict with frontier whites and the United States Army.[43] Like Samson Occom, with whom he collaborated to remove the Stockbridge community west, away from the influence of whites, Aupaumut based the authority of his performances on his dual cultural identity. And like Occom, he sought to use that dual identity both to assert his own authority and to imagine a potent native speaker whose words could overcome cultural differences.

---

43. On Aupaumut and the Stockbridge Indians during the Revolution, see Colin G. Calloway, *The American Revolution in Indian Country: Crisis and Diversity in Native American Communities* (Cambridge, 1995), chap. 3. After the Treaty of Paris, the American government claimed right of conquest to the disputed Great Lakes territory of the *pays d'en haut*, but the nations of the region refused to accept their conquered status. White settlers who resisted the land controls of the federal government contributed to the tense and often violent situation on the frontier, according to Richard White in *The Middle Ground: Indians, Empires, and Republics in the Great Lakes Region, 1650–1815* (New York, 1991), 420. It was this situation that led Washington to take a new approach through peace negotiations and to employ Aupaumut as his ambassador.

In his search for political power within the new republic, Aupaumut identified his role as emissary to the western tribes as a traditional aspect of Mahican culture based on the Mahicans' historical relationships with these nations. "When I come to reflect in the path of my ancestors, the friendship and connections they have had with these western tribes, and my own feelings towards them," he wrote, "I conclude that I could acquaint them my best knowledge with regard of the disposition, desires, and might of the United States, without partiality." [44] Mahicans had employed long-standing diplomatic channels with the western nations on behalf of the Americans during the Revolution, and Aupaumut sought to establish his authority as a cultural mediator for the new government headed by George Washington. If granted a position of power, he hoped to establish a just and peaceable relationship between the American government and the nations on its western borders. This favorable outcome would also create an influential role for eastern Indians such as himself who were both allied with and yet culturally distinct from the America of the whites.

A committed patriot and Christian who believed that accommodation to European religion, education, and agriculture was the only avenue for native American survival, Aupaumut was also a student and preserver of Mahican traditions. His "History of the Muh-he-con-nuk Indians" (written in the early 1790s) sketches his people's precontact habitation and modes of life, outlines their social and governmental structure, and describes their relationships with other nations, including their role as mediators among the natives of the North and Northwest.[45] Aupaumut emphasized certain points of cultural parallelism between the Mahicans and white Americans, for instance when he observed that "before they ever enjoyed Gospel revelation" the Mahicans "acknowledged one Supreme Being" as well as "an evil one, called Mton-toow or Wicked Spirit that loves altogether to do mischief"; or when he noted, "Our ancestors' Government was a Democratical" government (though his explanation of democratic government emphasizes the hereditary nature of the chief sachem's office). But he also insisted on a distinctive and coherent Mahican cultural tradition, particularly when he reproduced

44. Hendrick Aupaumut, *A Narrative of an Embassy to the Western Indians,* in Historical Society of Pennsylvania, *Memoirs* (hereafter cited as HSP, *Memoirs),* II (Philadelphia, 1827), 61–131, esp. 76.

45. Hendrick Aupaumut, "History of the Muh-he-con-nuk Indians," in Bernd Peyer, ed., *The Elders Wrote: An Anthology of Early Prose by North American Indians, 1768–1931* (Berlin, 1982), 25–33. Jeanne P. Ronda and James Ronda discuss Aupaumut's accommodationism and contrast it to the Pan-Indian resistance of Tecumseh, whom Aupaumut actively opposed, in "'As They Were Faithful': Chief Hendrick Aupaumut and the Struggle for Stockbridge Survival, 1757–1830," *American Indian Culture and Research Journal,* III, no. 3 (1979), 43–55. For a similar perspective, see Bernd C. Peyer, *The Tutor'd Mind: Indian Missionary-Writers in Antebellum America* (Amherst, Mass., 1997), 111–116.

the customs "handed down from generation to another" in the form of a speech that the head of each family delivered to her or his children each morning. The speech emphasizes the values of generosity to the elderly and the needy, honesty, industriousness, and obedience to parents, sachems, and chiefs. Such traditions were worth preserving, Aupaumut believed.[46]

The dual nature of Aupaumut's identity manifests itself particularly in his use of linguistic forms. In the "History" he employed distinctive spellings of native words, offering them as more authentic textualizations of Mahican speech than the Anglicized terms. He advocated literacy as "the foundation of learning" and a warrant that "our white brothers . . . cannot so easily cheat us now with regard to land affairs as they have done our forefathers."[47] During his mission, he employed writing and speech with equal authority, and he performed from a manuscript or from wampum as the situation demanded. For Aupaumut, literacy did not preclude the survival of oral tradition, and the power and effects of the spoken word hold a place of prominence in his cultural history. Mahican parents warn against hasty or evil speech, particularly speech directed against the sachem or chiefs, urge against speaking "any harsh word to strangers," and insist that "you must always speak nothing but the truth wherever you are."[48] The importance of oral forms in the constitution of Mahican political life is evident in his description of the chief sachem, who with the advice of his counselors "contemplate[s] the welfare of his people day and night—how to promote their peace and happiness" and seeks "to maintain the belt of friendship with their allies." The orders of the sachem are proclaimed to the nation by the man who holds the office of the Owl, who "must have strong memory, and must be good speaker, and have strong voice." The sachem and counselors periodically go through the community exhorting "people to live in unity and peace" and urging "young people to every good work." Aupaumut emphasizes the spoken word's role in maintaining authority, reproducing the social order, and ensuring peace, productivity, and happiness in Mahican society. Speech also serves to sustain the individual's reputation. Speaking kindly to strangers will ensure that "they will love you and will speak well of you wherever they be; and if you ever come into a strange country you will meet with such kindness." But lying "will bring a bad name to yourself . . . and even when you should bring tidings of importance with the truth," you will not be regarded.[49]

46. Aupaumut, "History," in Peyer, ed., *The Elders Wrote*, 28, 30.

47. Aupaumut made these remarks in an 1803 speech to the Delawares urging them to adopt the Stockbridge accommodationist approach to white society. The speech is available in John Sergeant, "Extracts from the Journal of John Sergeant," *Missionary Herald*, I (1805), 271–272.

48. Aupaumut, "History," in Peyer, ed., *The Elders Wrote*, 29.

49. Ibid., 29, 31–32.

Aupaumut's *Narrative of an Embassy to the Western Indians* (1792), written to defend himself against accusations that he had lied to the northwest nations or "proved unfaithful" to the United States government by failing to attend the council, features a similar preoccupation with the negotiation of power and the manifestation of authenticity through the spoken word. The *Narrative* includes detailed accounts of the speeches that Aupaumut delivered during his mission. Aupaumut's knowledge of treaty council protocol and the similarity of the Mahican language to that of the western nations as well as his Mahican background set him apart from other American negotiators, who frequently lacked the education in native protocols that more often characterized their British counterparts.[50] He began his mission in Philadelphia and traveled to the Iroquois at Canandaigua to solicit their cooperation before heading west to the Maumee Rapids where the Delaware, Shawnee, Miami, and other nations were assembled. He carried his "bag of peace, in which there is ancient wampom" signifying the "friendship and connections, our forefathers, and we, have had with the western tribes." During his journey, Aupaumut repeatedly performed the Condolence rituals based on Iroquois precedent. Responding to "the Chief of the Shawanese," leader of the nation least inclined to a peaceful settlement with the United States, Aupaumut invested the ritual formulas with a particular emphasis on the problems of establishing understanding and shared concern for native welfare. "I, the Muhheuconneew . . . have found you in a gloomy state, now for the reason of many misfortunes and dark clouds I see your tears flowing down, so that you could see but duskily," he began. "But according to our friendship, I now wipe away your tears, and open your eyes that you may see clear and discern what is good." Casting away "all these evil and heavy things" that blocked understanding, "I set your heart aright as it was fixed by our good forefathers in ancient days, that you may now understand both what is good and bad — and that you may contemplate the welfare of our own colar [color] — that our mornings may be lengthened." Invoking their common "colar," Aupaumut repeatedly urged the western nations to "maintain a Union" among native peoples, which he insisted was established by "our good Ancestors," and which he felt was threatened by the war in the Northwest.

50. Joseph Brant accused Aupaumut before the northwest nations of lying, as discussed below. Secretary of War Henry Knox forwarded a report to Washington that Aupaumut "had proved unfaithful" and failed to attend the council (Walter Lowrie and Matthew St. Clair Clarke, eds., *American State Papers: Documents, Legislative and Executive, of the Congress of the United States . . .* , Class II, *Indian Affairs,* IV [Washington, D.C., 1832], 322). Aupaumut indicated that "his language and the language of the Chippawas and others of the western tribes, were so similar, that he could converse with them" (*A Narrative,* in HSP, *Memoirs,* II, 69). On American ignorance of treaty protocol, see White, *Middle Ground,* chaps. 9, 10.

He believed that such a union could be best sustained by attaching native interests to the interests of the United States.[51]

Washington chose Aupaumut as an ambassador for the United States because of the weight that his native background would bring to the government's suit for peace. Aupaumut's words to the western nations as he presented them in his narrative recall the official Indian policy of the Washington administration. The president articulated his paternalistic program in a speech to the Iroquois delegation that Aupaumut accompanied to Philadelphia in March 1792. There Washington promised peace "between the United States and all the natives of this land . . . founded upon the principles of justice and humanity" and expressed the hope that those natives would partake of "civilized life."[52] Aupaumut claimed that he accepted the mission "to convince [the western nations] of the moderation, justice, and desire of the United States for peace" because he believed in the sincerity of the new government's commitments to "the wellfare of all nations." His attested faith in the new federal government of the United States appears in his report describing his efforts to persuade the western nations that sincere American intentions backed his peace proposal. According to his account, he distinguished the government headed by Washington from both the predatory frontiersmen, or "Big Knifes," and the British traders and army officers with whom the western nations had long-standing ties. He went on to inform the western Indians, "Especially since they have their Liberty," the Americans "begin with new things." Aupaumut urged that "now they have new Laws [of] their own, and by these Laws Indians cannot be deceived as usual." "The United Sachems will not speak wrong," he reported telling them. "Whatever they promise to Indians they will perform." Aupaumut described the structure of the constitutional government as proof of American sincerity and reliability. He told the assembled chiefs, "Out of 30,000 men, they chuse one men to attend their great Council Fire — and such men must be very honest and wise, and they will do Justice to all people."[53]

51. Aupaumut, *A Narrative,* in HSP, *Memoirs,* II, 76, 78, 91, 101.

52. Lowrie and Clarke, eds., *American State Papers,* Class II, *Indian Affairs,* IV, 229. Washington feared that America would be classed with Spain in the international court of public opinion unless the nation established a more benign relationship with the continent's native peoples. The administration also felt pressure closer to home, as antiwar and antifrontier sentiment rose in Philadelphia, according to Isabel Thompson Kelsay, *Joseph Brant, 1743-1807: Man of Two Worlds* (Syracuse, N.Y., 1984), 468-469; Francis Paul Prucha, *American Indian Policy in the Formative Years: The Indian Trade and Intercourse Acts, 1790-1834* (Cambridge, Mass., 1962), chaps. 2, 3. More cynical readings of Washington's motives than those offered by Kelsay and Prucha are possible. Jefferson later claimed that the negotiations were window dressing as the army struggled to recover from the defeat of Arthur St. Clair's forces (Ronda and Ronda, " 'As They Were Faithful,' " *American Indian Culture and Research Journal,* III, no. 3 [1979], 49).

53. "Instructions to Captain Hendrick Aupaumut, Chief of the Stockbridge Indians," in Low-

The central act of Aupaumut's mission was his delivery of the message from the federal government of the United States to the sachems of the assembled nations. Taking up a wampum belt, he began: "We the 15 sachems of the United States will now in one voice speak to you—we speak from our hearts—where there is a burden of sorrow" over the war. The federal union, presented as the "15 sachems," further manifested its sincerity by sending "our message of peace, by your own colar, and friend of Muhheaconnuk who we trust will faithfully [deliver] to you, and will impartially acquaint you, according to his best knowledge with regard to the dispositions of the United States." Aupaumut ventriloquized the Americans, evoking a sympathetic bond with the western nations based on a shared care for family. "We have tender effections for our Children, women, young men and old parents," he repeated, and continued, "You likewise brothers, have great regard for your children, women, young men and old parents." The parallel phrasing ended with a direct statement of identity: "In this we are alike." Aupaumut issued an invitation to a treaty conference at Fort Jefferson "where we may use our utmost endeavours to establish happiness for our Children" by settling territorial disputes. To that end, the government promised to control the Big Knives. Both sides were constrained by public opinion to resolve their differences: "Had we not used means to remove all difficulties so as to put an end to the war, the great Nations over the great waters would find fault with us. You likewise, brothers, if you do not regard or comply with what we now offer to you, the great Nations, who resides behind you, will afterwards blame you." The speech figured the western nations and the United States in a reciprocal relationship similar to the one that Canassatego imagined fifty years earlier, with both parties equally bound by concerns for family and equally constrained by the "great Nations" of Europe or the western regions of North America. Concluding that "I have delivered you a great Message in your hands," Aupaumut presented a wampum belt with fifteen rows and fifteen square marks in the middle denoting the fifteen states.[54]

Initially received as "pure good Message" and "the Life of all our Nations," Aupaumut's words were called into question when a messenger from Mohawk sachem Joseph Brant arrived. "I have myself seen Washington, and see his heart

---

rie and Clarke, eds., *American State Papers*, Class II, *Indian Affairs*, IV, 233; Aupaumut, *A Narrative*, in HSP, *Memoirs*, II, 92, 126, 127. White observes that the core of the negotiations as reflected in Aupaumut's *Narrative* was the image of the Americans. Aupaumut sought to create the Americans in the image of Washington while the leaders hostile to the negotiations portrayed the Americans as the Big Knives (*Middle Ground*, 458–459). Aupaumut reflected the Washington administration, which instructed Brigadier General Rufus Putnam to emphasize the significance of the new government, and particularly the fact of union, in his negotiations; see Lowrie and Clarke, eds., *American State Papers*, Class II, *Indian Affairs*, IV, 234.

54. Aupaumut, *A Narrative*, in HSP, *Memoirs*, 93–95.

and bowels," Brant's message stated, and "he did take up dust, and did declare that he would not restore so much dust to the Indians." Aupaumut testified to the virtue and sincerity of the "United Sachems" and insisted that the frontiersmen were renegades beyond the reach of the laws that would control their aggression. Thwarted by "the voice of flying birds" such as Brant, Aupaumut unsuccessfully sought to counter Shawnee arguments that the Americans must pull back over the Ohio River before negotiations could begin.[55]

Aupaumut felt keenly that his own reputation was at stake, with his native negotiating partners as with his white employers, particularly after Brant accused him of counting warriors for the Americans and being "a deceiver or roag." Attacked for misrepresenting Washington's intentions to the northwest nations and for lying about his presence at the negotiations to the Americans, Aupaumut used his *Narrative* to present himself, not as a duplicitous, savage speaker, but as both an authentic Indian and a committed patriot who believed in the justice and sincerity of the United States government's intentions toward the northwest nations. Concluding his self-defense, Aupaumut invoked ancestral authority, offering his Mahican background as proof of his authenticity and promising to respond to accusations against him. He vindicated himself sufficiently to the American government to be included in the diplomatic mission to the northwest nations the following year.[56]

Aupaumut celebrated Mahican oral traditions, manifested his familiarity with spoken forms of native diplomacy, and demonstrated his presence and sincerity at the treaty site of Auglaize, all in writing. Like Canassatego and Samson Occom, he manipulated the performance semiotic of speech and text with confidence. Such manipulation was common practice on the frontier by the 1790s and could take surprising turns. In the negotiations of 1793, the leaders of the northwest nations insisted upon negotiating with Washington's white commissioners through an exchange of written documents. Refusing to let the commissioners join the assembled chiefs at the Maumee Rapids, Wyandot chief Sawaghdawunk informed them, "We have thought it best, that what we had to say should be put into writing, and here (presenting a paper to the commissioners) is the meaning of our hearts." The paper he handed them asked for "an explicit answer in writing." The choice of medium reflected the content of their demand that the United States "firmly fix on the Ohio River, as the boundary line, between your

55. Ibid., 93, 96, 113. Gregory Evans Dowd discusses the significance of rumor on the frontier and notes the frequency of images of both "groundless and flight" and "speed and power" (547) when rumor is described in "The Panic of 1751: The Significance of Rumors on the South Carolina–Cherokee Frontier," *WMQ*, 3d Ser., LIII (1996), 527–560.

56. Aupaumut, *A Narrative*, in HSP, *Memoirs*, 129.

people and ours." In a striking reversal of roles, the Indians sought to create distance through text. Text similarly allowed them to create unity among themselves: if all negotiations were conducted through authorized documents, then individuals could not be intimidated or beguiled into selling off chunks of territory, as in the past. While Aupaumut conferred with the native leaders at the Rapids directly, the commissioners themselves were not permitted to advance. They quickly tired of negotiating in writing and wished for the greater immediacy of speech. "The mode in which the negotiations have hitherto been conducted is new, and as improper as it is new," they complained. "All the questions which have been stated, might have been proposed to our faces, and have received prompt answers." In the end, the negotiations failed, and they returned to Philadelphia without ever meeting their negotiating partners.[57]

Aupaumut knew well the manipulations of text that the native leaders both resented and sought to mimic. In his *Narrative,* he reflected on the knowledge that he had withheld from the western nations as he tried to persuade them to make peace. "I have as it were oblige to say nothing with regard to the conduct of Yorkers, how they cheat my fathers, how they taken our lands Unjustly" despite his ancestors' being "faithful friends to the Whites." Even the rule of law in which Aupaumut sometimes placed tremendous confidence could be abused, as he remarked when he described "how the white people artfully got their Deeds confirm in their Laws." Confessing to his white readers the limits of his honesty during his diplomatic mission, Aupaumut repeated a complaint that had become a familiar feature of native American uses of the performance semiotic: the duplicity of white uses of text. Aupaumut and his people were victims of textual dissimulation, but they could also turn written forms to their own advantage. Like Deborah Sampson Gannett, Aupaumut and his fellow Stockbridges found themselves forced to petition for compensation for their services in the Revolution. The successful petition, which Aupaumut submitted in 1792, also solicited payment for his services as ambassador to the western Indians. In both instances, the favorable government response to petitions registers an official sanction with sharply drawn limits.[58]

The increasing rigidity of the boundaries between whites and natives manifested itself in the rhetoric of Fisher Ames's speech on the Jay Treaty four years after

57. Lowrie and Clarke, eds., *American State Papers,* Class II, *Indian Affairs,* IV, 352, 355. The documents in this exchange are set in a more narrative form in Benjamin Lincoln, "Journal of a Treaty Held in 1793 . . . ," in Massachusetts Historical Society, *Collections,* 3d Ser., V (Boston, 1836), 109–176, esp. 142–143, 158.

58. Aupaumut, *A Narrative,* 128; Calloway, *American Revolution in Indian Country,* 104–105.

Aupaumut's initial mission. The bonds of identification that Ames drew between eastern and frontier whites when he described a deadly Indian attack on a frontier family cut across the bonds of sympathy that Aupaumut's speech sought to create between George Washington's America and the western nations through the parallel images of family affection. Even native patriots such as Aupaumut who shared the tools of literacy, the faith of Christianity, and the language of republicanism were excluded from Ames's vision. Images of difference dominated images of reciprocity and resemblance between whites and Indians as native Americans were increasingly cast in a Romantic tableau as noble savages—or as mere savages. The post-Revolutionary refiguration of the native diplomat appears in the changing images of Aupaumut's ancestor King Hendrick, who in several early eighteenth-century portraits appeared in European coat and hat but in later depictions was stripped of his European garb and his diplomat's identity. King Hendrick's role as diplomat and cultural broker kept him facing east toward England, which he visited on several occasions, including his initial trip to Queen Anne's court in 1710. His descendant Aupaumut found himself and his people pushed off the remainder of their land and migrating westward to a reservation in Wisconsin, where he died in 1830 in the midst of Indian Removal.[59]

Aupaumut's quite literal marginalization within the United States lends a particularly dramatic point and poignancy to the limits of political speech in the early republic. Despite his heritage of diplomatic eloquence, his political ambition, and his ability to stage a dual identity for himself through both oral and textual media, Aupaumut remained excluded from national power. Even as the styles of oratory multiplied in the halls of Congress and new rhetorics of fraternity gradually emerged in the press, the speakers and speech traditions recognized in the civic arena remained circumscribed. Not only native American oratory but also African American and women's speech were largely denied even the provisional and tentative acceptance accorded the emerging forms of democratic speech—while the enlarging and clarifying form of representative speech that Fisher Ames defined remained the dominant rhetorical style in the early republic.

59. See also Timothy J. Shannon, "Dressing for Success on the Mohawk Frontier: Hendrick, William Johnson, and the Indian Fashion," *WMQ*, 3d Ser., LIII (1996), 13–42, esp. 32. Ronda and Ronda describe the shabby governmental treatment of the Stockbridge Indians, who were repeatedly forced off land they occupied or denied land grants that had been promised them. Ultimately, the Rondas celebrate the continued existence of the Stockbridge community, ascribing its longevity in large part to Aupaumut's legacy of accommodationism. They note the persistence of Mahican traditions into the 1960s, when a "modern tribal council president, a descendant of Hendrick's [Aupaumut's] in-laws, revived the ancient intertribal arbiter role by assuming leadership positions in several Pan-Indian organizations" (" 'As They Were Faithful,' " *American Indian Culture and Research Journal*, III, no. 3 [1979], 54).

CONCLUSION

"Founding documents"; "one voice, one vote"; "sign your John Hancock"; "vox populi, vox dei": American identity derives important features from the symbolism of spoken and written language. Lacking the common ethnicity, often marked by a distinctive language, that provided each European state with a sense of nationhood, Americans made the forms of language carry much of the burden of national union. Numerous studies have examined the meanings attached to one form or the other, linking civic life in the United States either to textual media — especially print — or to oral practices and figures of voice. But the full significance of linguistic form for civic self-understanding in the United States emerges only through study of the relationships between speech and writing.

Printers in the new republic published accounts of political events and the orations that accompanied them; later, famed orators of pulpit and platform such as Daniel Webster offered collections of speeches that presented the great address as a major ingredient of civil society. Print amplified the range of an oration, and orators provided the expanding print media with material of civic import. Rather than supplant this oral genre, the growth of print was fueled by audience interest in oratory as a vehicle of national embodiment. At the symbolic level, too, the figural meanings of voice and text evolved in dynamic interaction. A range of orators demonstrated a sophisticated grasp of verbal form, not only in their use of print to extend the range of their speeches but also in their development of the performance semiotic of speech and text to address new political concerns. In the antebellum period, when the inner voice of conscience provided a higher law with which to challenge the written Constitution that permitted slavery, the symbolic meanings of speech and text acquired particular salience. Abolitionist orator Frederick Douglass created a performance style that dramatized the voice transcending the written word. He began his addresses reading from a manuscript but set aside his text to speak extempore, thrilling his audiences. Douglass used the performance semiotic to negotiate political agency for himself as an African American, relating his attack on the written Constitution that legitimated slavery to his improvisational style partly rooted in African orature.[1]

The symbolism of verbal form that Douglass employed also had roots in the ancient worlds of Greece, Rome, and Israel, where speech and writing variously figured immediacy and stability, volatility and inauthenticity. When Europeans

---

1. Sandra Marie Gustafson, "Performing the Word: American Oratory, 1630–1860" (Ph.D. diss., University of California at Berkeley, 1993), 467–468.

brought this dual system of symbols to the Western Hemisphere, one aspect of these paired terms initially predominated: elite purveyors of a textual discipline used literacy technologies to limit challenges to social hierarchy. The witchcraft crisis in Salem signaled both the stringency of these procedures, as female voice was once more the object of discipline, and the undermining of the old order when the prosecutions were revealed as botched, even fraudulent. With the rise of evangelicalism in the 1730s and 1740s, proponents of extempore preaching such as George Whitefield and Gilbert Tennent championed spontaneity, inwardness, and authenticity against the rigidity of the text-based establishment. They attacked ministers who preached from manuscripts for being dead to true spirituality. Even as print became a more familiar aspect of the cultural landscape, then, the symbolic value of speech was on the rise and sacred oratory acquired new interest and significance.

Political speech, too, attracted increasing attention on both sides of the Atlantic as classical republican thought elevated the civic oration to a position of distinction. Oratory became a medium of national emergence in the performances and representational theories of James Otis and Patrick Henry. Verbal form provided a symbolic tool for negotiating political hegemony in such Revolutionary events as the Boston Massacre and the tradition of commemorative oratory that grew up in response to it. In the debates over independence and the Constitution, speech and text were the media for a competition of forms that was simultaneously a competition over representational legitimacy. And in the 1790s, as national identity took shape, social unity and the violence that undermined it were presented through the symbolism of speech and text in the words of George Washington and Fisher Ames.

The revaluation of the spoken arts that accompanied the revivals of the Great Awakening and the activism of the Revolution created opportunities for women, blacks, native Americans, and the lower orders of white men to elude textual discipline. Yet that liberation remained temporary and incomplete. The eighteenth-century revivals stimulated a variety of speech that emphasized spontaneity and emotional honesty over learning. Numerous women who exhorted or preached in the new style found that, despite the novel legitimacy of "uneducated" speech, their sacred eloquence continued to be muffled or silenced, notably in the work of Jonathan Edwards. Later, women who endeavored to join in the political forums of the new republic had few models for political eloquence. In her address, woman warrior Deborah Sampson Gannett emphasized the association of female speech with violence and underscored the absence of coherent civic roles for women. The opportunities for native American and African American orators were more numerous, though ultimately not more satisfactory. Celebrating extemporaneous oratory, evangelicals such as George Whitefield and David Brainerd fostered religious eloquence that blended European, native American, and African American traditions; at the same time, transatlantic fascination with native American diplomatic oratory made treaty proceedings and "savage" speech into objects of intense interest. Yet even relatively assimilated Indians and blacks such as Samson Occom, Hendrick Aupaumut, and John Marrant found that their attempts to revise the image of the savage speaker met with limited success. Contemporary native American and especially African American orators such as Malcolm X demonstrate the continued potency of the savage speaker as a role to be both occupied and critiqued while white reactions manifest the persistence of hostile stereotypes focused on modes of speech. Cultural critic Tom Shachtman has argued that political life in the United States has suffered from a decrease in literacy rates and literary sophistication since the nineteenth century. When Shachtman singles out black English and rap as instances of debased civic discourse, he exploits the persistent figure of the savage speaker as a racialized threat to public life.[2]

Negotiating social hierarchies through the symbolic properties of verbal form, Americans have either celebrated the authentic expression of improvised performance or used textual knowledge to control the potentially transformative impact of such performances. In other circumstances, they have advanced written communication as a democratic mode in contests with those who use formal speech to dominate social inferiors. These practices developed in the eighteenth century and continue today.[3] Particularly since television has replaced the oration, lecture, and sermon as a major source of instruction and entertainment, the operations of the performance semiotic are most visible in art forms other than public eloquence, notably poetry and music. Poetry is a genre with deep ties to the spoken arts, and in recent decades poets have created the poetry slam to strengthen those ties. Participants in the slams insist on the freshness and authenticity of their art, but their critics emphasize the ephemerality and lack of literary polish that they claim characterizes performance poetry.

Similar conflicts mark the musical world even more deeply. For much of the twentieth century, composed (written) forms such as classical music represented a high art set against "low," spontaneous forms like jazz. The controversy over the Pulitzer committee's 1997 decision to award a prize to jazz trumpeter and composer Wynton Marsalis for *Blood on the Fields,* an oratorio on slavery that incorporates improvisation, betrays the persistence of hierarchical meanings attached to written and improvised (or "oral") forms. More than thirty years after

2. Tom Shachtman, *The Inarticulate Society: Eloquence and Culture in America* (New York, 1995), chap. 2, esp. 53–63.

3. In his article on the 2000 presidential campaign, Joe Klein complains of overly scripted election speeches and longs for more spontaneity in candidate performances; see "Where's the Music?" in *The New Yorker,* LXXV (Sept. 27, 1999), 36–42.

the Pulitzer board refused to grant Duke Ellington a special award that the music jury had voted him, Marsalis was the first jazz artist to be granted a Pulitzer prize. The complexities of the performance semiotic are suggested by the fact that some of the criticism directed at Marsalis involved, not his reliance on improvisation, but his alleged lack of authenticity, his co-optation by the mainstream musical world as reflected in the classically based forms in which he chose to work. Here again, authenticity and cultural power emerge as derivatives of "oral" and "written" modes of performance.[4]

The continued use of oral and written genres to privilege cultural products and social identities that is visible in the controversy over Marsalis's award can be traced to the era of exploration and colonization. Then, Europeans "discovered" ancient civilizations with rich oral traditions but no alphabetic writing just as the printing press began to make texts more available and literacy more widely practiced in Europe. The dynamics of cultural encounter produced key elements in the symbolization of speech and writing. In the eighteenth century, the civic dimensions of the performance semiotic emerged as the forms of language provided the media that shaped American national identity. The symbolic meanings of speech and writing persist today not only in the arts of oratory, poetry, and music but in political debates over the significance of rap, the role of Ebonics (as black English has been renamed) in the curriculum, and the meaning of literacy in an electronic culture. Such debates reflect the ways that verbal form continues to structure modes of social power and cultural authenticity in the United States.

4. Greg Sandow, "Improvised Rules," in *Wall Street Journal*, Sept. 17, 1997 (internet).

APPENDIX: TRADITIONS OF THE ANCIENTS

Colonists in British North America drew on classical and biblical traditions to elaborate the symbolism of verbal form in oratorical performance. Studying the Bible and the major texts in classical rhetoric, Euro-Americans encountered a complex set of relationships between linguistic forms, the body of the individual, and the social body. The preoccupations with verbal and physical mediation evident in ancient rhetorical texts helped to shape important features of colonial America's performance semiotic of speech and text. This influence was particularly significant as the symbolism of the spoken and written words bore on unity of intention and expression, of meaning and its articulation. Drawing on ancient symbolic practices, the orator presented his or her ability to convey a higher truth — God's voice or the voice of the people — through the use of central texts such as the Bible or the Constitution or alternatively through the refusal to rely on such texts and the assertion of a higher authority. The meanings of speech, text, and body in classic texts animated the colonists' expectations about oratorical performance. Through the cultural conditions occasioned by colonization and slavery, those meanings also came to determine important aspects of native American and African American oratory.[1]

The four books of the Bible that describe Moses' life (Exodus through Deuteronomy) articulate the problems endemic to the human relationship to a deity who defines himself primarily in linguistic rather than material terms. Language has its own physical forms, a fact that these texts never obscure. The Hebrew Bible situates both the written and the spoken Word on the cusp between the immaterial and the material, between divine intent and the forms it must bear to be humanly comprehended. Neither writing nor speech escapes the contaminations of matter when humans attempt to express divine will. The Law is written on stone tablets whose materiality is fully evidenced when Moses smashes them after discovering the golden calf. Even text written by the finger of God is subject to physical laws. Divine speech, too, requires a medium invisible yet inescapably material: sound, emitted from an interior, borne forth on the air. When God relies on prophets and priests to speak for him, his human agents magnify the already-mediated quality of his words. But speech and writing present different problems as forms for conveying the Lord's intention. The written Law is Moses' most lasting and influen-

---

1. As mentioned in Introduction, above, John Quincy Adams noted the influence of the biblical and classical traditions in *Lectures on Rhetoric and Oratory, Delivered to the Classes of Senior and Junior Sophisters in Harvard University,* I (Cambridge, Mass., 1810), esp. 13–17.

tial expression of the divine will. No challenger offers an alternative set of tablets. The golden calf, a mute animal deity, is the Law's greatest rival. But Moses' oral authority is burdensome and contested. Many make false claims to speak for the Lord. An agonistic element characterizes public speech and repeatedly threatens to disrupt divine order.

The problems of internal and social division that attend prophetic speech arise in its earliest descriptions. When Moses initially refuses to lead the Israelites out of bondage because of a speech defect, the Lord elects Aaron to be Moses' spokesman. In so doing, he literalizes the self-division inherent in human speech, splitting the inspiration granted Moses from the articulation that Aaron will provide. This lack of integrity in the spoken word quickly produces conflict at Mount Sinai when Aaron forges the golden calf. Pure voice, detached from divine meaning and identified with the popular will, swerves into the demagogic and idolatrous worship of pure matter. Moses' self-division, externalized first into the linguistic sphere through his stutter, then represented by the hierarchical relationship between himself and Aaron, is here violently deflected once more into the broader social and political realms as fratricide ensues. Civil strife embodies the same divisive dynamic of meaning and form that Moses articulated when he resisted the Lord's plea to speak for him.

A similar punitive consequence ensues in Numbers 12 when Aaron and his sister Miriam, an important Israelite leader in her own right, set themselves against their brother Moses. God intervenes in the conflict among prophetic authorities on Moses' behalf by distinguishing between mundane prophecy, a product of dreams and visions, and Moses' more immediate knowledge of the divine will: "With him will I speak mouth to mouth, even apparently, and not in dark speeches" (Num. 12:8). Because God uses dark speeches to communicate with his less privileged prophets, they are in greater danger of misinterpreting his will. They must acquire a proper respect for the material element in language, its resistance to interpretation.

God impresses an awareness of linguistic materiality on Moses' siblings when he temporarily afflicts Miriam with leprosy.[2] Miriam's diseased flesh turns livid white and decays, rendering visible the corruption of God's Word. The Lord compares her resulting seven-day expulsion from camp and exclusion from the community to the shame a daughter would feel if her father spit in her face. Spit, like other bodily secretions that traverse the space between the body and the envi-

---

2. Rather than identify a specific illness, biblical leprosy describes diseases of surface. Garments and houses as well as human skin contract leprosy; priests diagnose and treat it according to laws described in Lev. 13–14. The disease's broad definition indicates the potential for disordered mediation between interior and exterior spaces.

ronment, contaminates those who touch it.[3] Analogizing Miriam's leprosy to contamination by paternal spit, God identifies the disease as a defiling externalization of his invisible interiority. Miriam's punishment, then, condenses two problems of the material Word in one powerful image and marks them as feminine. Moving from the invisible interiors of the deity, through the forms of human language and into the world, divine meaning both suffers the contaminating mediation of matter and threatens those material shapes with violence.[4]

Aaron escapes Miriam's suffering because God has chosen him to father a line of priests. Priestly rituals institutionalize modes of mediation and contain threatening contacts with the divine within ordained forms. Aaron's role as spokesman is now limited to teaching "the children of Israel all the statutes which the Lord hath spoken unto them by the hand of Moses" (Lev. 10:11). His mouth is filled with divine text, his body encased in it. The priest's costume incorporates a striking amount of inscription, including the breastplate bearing the names of the sons of Israel and the headpiece engraved with "Holiness to the Lord." Hedged about by prescriptions, the Aaronic priest follows textual tradition to avoid blasphemy. Prophets transcend such limitations. They claim a spiritual proximity to God that permits them freedom from social constraints. The prophet stands at the intersection of the spiritual and material realms, talking with God. After their conference on Mount Sinai, Moses speaks to the people only through the veil that shades his shining face (Exod. 34:29–35). The pure expression of divine meaning symbolized by his glowing countenance represents the conceptual opposite of Miriam's leprous skin. The veil restructures the distinction between inspiration and articulation, originally projected onto the relationship between Moses and Aaron. Moses now speaks down to the people out of his intimacy with God through the veil's material form while Aaron speaks up to God in his role as the people's mediator through the material forms of ritual and the textual forms of his priestly attire.

The Gospels present a scene of performance that differs fundamentally from Hebrew Scripture, for they depict the Deity incarnate speaking directly if somewhat obliquely to the people. Jesus' divine pronouncements are untroubled by human deviance like that of Aaron and Miriam. The evangelists portray Jesus as an uneducated but eloquent teacher preaching in the temple or the fields. The history of early Christian texts reflects the privileging of speech in Jesus' ministry: he left no written works, his sayings were transmitted orally for several decades

3. The Jewish laws on menstrual blood are perhaps the best known rules governing excretions. On the Levitical rules, see Mary Douglas, *Purity and Danger: An Analysis of the Concepts of Pollution and Taboo* (London, 1966), chap. 3. Douglas discusses the body as a boundary and the violation of bodily margins on 145.

4. The encounter with the Deity that risks self-contamination is also evident in Christian beliefs about receiving communion and listening to sermons; see 1 Cor. 11:27–30.

before they began to be recorded, and oral tradition carried special authority into the second century.[5] Apostolic speech imitated Jesus' extempore eloquence, emphasizing the spiritual authenticity of spontaneous utterance. Jesus urges his followers to speak to the moment when they are persecuted: "Settle *it* therefore in your hearts, not to meditate before what ye shall answer. For I will give you a mouth and wisdom, which all your adversaries shall not be able to gainsay nor resist" (Luke 21:14-15). At Pentecost, the assembled apostles "were all filled with the Holy Ghost, and began to speak with other tongues, as the Spirit gave them utterance" (Acts 2:4). The authenticity and power of apostolic speech flows from its spontaneity.

Renouncing the Roman world's "wisdom of words, lest the cross of Christ should be made of none effect" (1 Cor. 1:17), Paul articulates a similar model of uninstructed speech when he insists on his own rhetorical inadequacy as proof of his spiritual authenticity. "And my speech and my preaching *was* not with enticing words of man's wisdom, but in demonstration of the Spirit, and of power: that your faith should not stand in the wisdom of men, but in the power of God" (1 Cor. 2:4-5), he wrote to the Corinthians. Paul's rhetorical self-effacement transforms Moses' stammering speech into the stumbling hesitation of an inarticulate orator who speaks divine "foolishness" (1 Cor. 1:18). He imagines that his lack of fluency testifies to the higher truth of his message.

Paul's characterization of sacred speech resonated with the universalist impulse in Christianity, to which Paul gave a series of influential articulations, most famously in Galatians 3:28: "There is neither Jew nor Greek, there is neither bond nor free, there is neither male nor female: for ye are all one in Christ Jesus."[6] Despite the universalist tendencies evident here, Paul's epistles identify both problematic speakers and problematic forms of speech. He presents the female body in particular as a source of corruption, distancing women from God and imposing restraints on their public expression. Seeking to limit women's speech, Paul insisted that to avoid disgrace they must prophesy only while veiled, signifying their subordination to men. Later he instructs, "Let your women keep silence in the churches" and ask questions of their husbands at home (1 Cor. 14:34). Such passages, in apparent contradiction both to other passages expressing a universalist vision and to the prominent role that women played in the early church, ripened into centuries of conflict over women's sacred speech. Like the leprous Miriam,

5. See Robin Lane Fox, "Literacy and Power in Early Christianity," in Alan K. Bowman and Greg Woolf, eds., *Literacy and Power in the Ancient World* (Cambridge, 1994), 126–148. In the same volume, M. D. Goodman speculates on the role of the scribe in "Texts, Scribes, and Power in Roman Judaea," 99–108.

6. See 1 Cor. 12:13 for a passage that suggests more clearly the role of the body in the universalist impulse; see also Col. 3:11.

women remained excluded from the highest forms of prophetic and priestly authority through the symbolic accentuation of the female body.[7]

Transforming and disciplining the forms of speech, Paul simultaneously redefined the meaning of text. He identified the Corinthians themselves as a text, "written in our hearts . . . not with ink, but with the Spirit of the living God; not in tables of stone, but in fleshy tables of the heart" (2 Cor. 3:2–3). Such living texts became possible only through "ministers of the new testament; not of the letter, but of the spirit: for the letter killeth, but the spirit giveth life" (2 Cor. 3:6). Paul conceives of the New Testament as a new kind of writing that will displace not only the content of Hebrew Scripture but the very conception of the written medium central to those texts. Paul's image of figural writing in the heart and his opposition between the letter that kills and the spirit that gives life planted the seeds of a radical disruption in the authority of sacred text.

Writing both constitutes and scandalizes the oral arts in classical Greece and Rome, as it does the Pauline letters. Reliance on written speeches produced in classical thought both a heightened attentiveness to the forms and techniques of oratory and a disdain for the artifice that writing permits. Teaching others to speak and composing speeches for them, ancient rhetoricians recognized formal linguistic patterns and relationships and developed new argumentative strategies, which they then codified in their manuals.[8] In societies where the ability to speak effectively defined the citizen, the courtroom delivery of speeches written by professional rhetoricians raised fundamental questions of authenticity and intention. In fourth-century Greece, rhetoricians debated the relative merits of skillfully improvised and composed speeches. Long after the great orator Pericles became the first to employ a written speech in a law court in 425 B.C.E., writing retained associations with fraud and deception. The written word appeared to clothe, and thus threatened to disguise and distort, the speaker's meaning that in the tradition of Athenian democracy should remain naked.[9]

---

7. Ben Witherington III, *Women and the Genesis of Christianity,* ed. Ann Witherington (Cambridge, 1990), part 3. On the contradictions between Paul's universalism and the restrictions he places on women, see Daniel Boyarin, *A Radical Jew: Paul and the Politics of Identity* (Berkeley, Calif., 1994), chap. 8. Boyarin's discussion of Moses' veil in chap. 4 is also relevant.

8. In an important sense, classical rhetoric evolved textually, and its historic and geographic dissemination took place through the persistence of key texts by Aristotle, Cicero, and Quintilian; see George A. Kennedy, *Classical Rhetoric and Its Christian and Secular Tradition from Ancient to Modern Times* (Chapel Hill, N.C., 1980), chap. 1; Renato Barilli, *Rhetoric* (Minneapolis, 1989), chap. 1; Thomas Cole, *The Origins of Rhetoric in Ancient Greece* (Baltimore, 1991). Westerners have not always recognized non-Western rhetorical traditions, particularly those that are not textually based, as having distinct forms and rules (introduction to Maurice Bloch, ed., *Political Language and Oratory in Traditional Society* [New York, 1975]).

9. On the meaning of nakedness in democratic Athens, Richard Sennett writes, "To the an-

Romans were more comfortable employing text to prepare a speech than their Greek predecessors. In *De oratore* (55 B.C.E.) Cicero imagines writing as an essential form of discipline for the orator. "The generality of students exercise only their voice (and not even that skillfully)," he warns, "and try their strength of lungs, and volubility of tongue, and please themselves with a torrent of their own words." Purely extemporaneous speech risks being sound without sense, a vocal exercise uninformed by a controlling intelligence. Writing helps control these excesses. Rather than treat text as something imposed from without, he urges the student of oratory to employ an internal textual discipline as he develops the content of his speeches. *"Writing* is said to be *the best and most excellent modeler and teacher of oratory,"* he insists, and sustained attention to the textual forms of language improves oral delivery. A thoughtfully prepared speech surpasses one that is "sudden and extemporary," and "a constant and diligent habit of writing will surely be of more effect than meditation and consideration itself." [10]

Cicero claims that writing has a twofold influence on speech: deepening the reflectiveness involved in the composition process, it links speech more perfectly to intellect; teaching an ordered, rhythmical mode of expression, it gives shape to the verbal product. The written word's influence extends beyond the composed oration, for even when the orator leaves his prepared text or speaks without one, these beneficial effects carry over into his presentation. Quintilian echoes Cicero's emphasis on the importance of composition training for speech preparation in the *Institutio oratoria* (92–95 C.E.), a founding text for rhetorical instruction. He warns that the teacher of oratory who allows students "to prattle extempore nonsense, to speak before they think, to blab out things indiscreetly" courts disaster. Only a constant practice of composition will prepare an orator to deliver eloquent impromptu speeches. "Our manner of speaking must be so formed by much and accurate composition," he insists, "that what we even give utterance to suddenly, might appear as if it was written." Cicero and Quintilian codified a tradition of rhetorical education in which writing supplements speech, completing and transforming oral performance. [11]

In both biblical and classical traditions, the speaker's body provides the prob-

---

cient Athenian, displaying oneself affirmed one's dignity as a citizen. Athenian democracy placed great emphasis on its citizens exposing their thoughts to others, just as men exposed their bodies" *(Flesh and Stone: The Body and the City in Western Civilization* [New York, 1994], 33); William V. Harris, *Ancient Literacy* (Cambridge, Mass., 1989), 92, 206.

10. Henri-Jean Martin, *The History and Power of Writing*, trans. Lydia G. Cochrane (Chicago, 1994), 71; Maud W. Gleason, *Making Men: Sophists and Self-Presentation in Ancient Rome* (Princeton, N.J., 1995), esp. 105–108; J. S. Watson, trans. or ed., *Cicero on Oratory and Orators* (1878; Carbondale, Ill., 1970), 42.

11. Quintilian, *Quintilian's Institutes of the Orator*, trans. J. Patsall, 2 vols. (London, 1774), esp. I, book 2, 85, II, book 10, 251.

lematic nexus between the informing mind or spirit and the audience. Anxiety over the speaker's physical opacity and the implications of that opacity for the social order mark both conceptions of oratorical performance. For Cicero and Quintilian, the expressive male body, with its complex natural language of the emotions, promises elaborate semiotic possibilities. The highly visual world of ancient Rome developed a refined set of gestural regimens with variants appropriate to the theater, the pantomime, and the forum. In *De oratore*, Cicero both acknowledges the affinities of his art with the theater and insists on theoretical and practical differences. The countenance, represented by masks in the theater but left exposed in the forum, has a persuasive "force bestowed by Nature herself" that is particularly effective when speaking to "the illiterate, the vulgar, and even barbarians." More, the full body possesses a universal language of feeling that transcends verbal limitations: "For words move none but those who are associated in a participation of the same language; and sensible thoughts often escape the understandings of senseless men; but action, which by its own powers displays the movements of the soul, affects all mankind; for the minds of all men are excited by the same emotions which they recognize in others, and indicate in themselves by the same token." Ideal oratorical delivery derives from the natural expression of feeling, for "every emotion of the mind has from nature its own peculiar look, tone, and gesture; and the whole frame of a man, and his whole countenance, and the variations of his voice, sound like strings in a musical instrument, just as they are moved by the affections of the mind." Here it would seem is perfect communication: the orator's body expresses his emotions, eliciting from the audience those same feelings in a mimesis of performance. Delivery, rhetoric's most theatrical component, seems its most truthful.[12]

Yet true feeling can be displayed only with the aid of art, for "that emotion of mind, which ought to be chiefly expressed or imitated in delivery, is often so confused as to be obscured and almost overwhelmed." Emotion is complex, even ambivalent. If "the peculiarities which throw that veil over" the desired emotion are to be overcome, its fundamental expressive traits must be identified and portrayed. The orator must transform feeling to reveal its truth. Moses' veil allowed him to communicate divine truth to the Hebrew nation. Undistracted by his radiant face, they listened to his inspired voice. For Cicero, natural feeling itself is like a veil that must be stripped away, revealing a countenance transfigured by

---

12. Watson, trans. or ed., *Cicero on Oratory and Orators*, 256, 259; Sennett, *Flesh and Stone*, 90-101. Book 10 of Quintilian's *Institutio oratoria* contains the only extended surviving account of Roman oratorical gestures. Quintilian addresses the problem of gesture as partly natural, partly mimetic, and partly conventional (Fritz Graf, "Gestures and Conventions: The Gestures of Roman Actors and Orators," in Jan Bremmer and Herman Roodenburg, eds., *A Cultural History of Gesture* [Ithaca, N.Y., 1991], 36–58).

art into the material representation of an "emotion of mind." But in dissociating feeling from its expression, Cicero introduces the possibility of counterfeit passion. And since emotional appeal is the speaker's most powerful tool, rhetorical manipulation emerges at the very heart of Ciceronian oratory. What appears most like joy or fear or sorrow is a representation of emotion and not emotion itself. Cicero's orator must negotiate this fundamental paradox and hazard its main consequence: republican order both requires moving speech and risks contamination from it. Essentially the same dynamic informs the Ciceronian orator's efforts to speak for the common good and the Israelite leaders' attempts to assert divine authority: persuasive speech is both necessary and potentially contaminating. Socially destructive violence results alike from its rejection and its misuse.[13]

13. Watson, trans. or ed., *Cicero on Oratory and Orators*, 256. Thomas Gustafson characterizes such linguistic doubleness as the Thucydidean moment in *Representative Words: Politics, Literature, and the American Language, 1776–1865* (Cambridge, 1992), 13–14; see also Rene Girard, *Violence and the Sacred*, trans. Patrick Gregory (Baltimore, 1977), 58.

INDEX